Studies in the History of Medieval Religion
VOLUME LVII

The Reception of Papal Legates in England, 1170–1250

Studies in the History of Medieval Religion
ISSN 0955-2480

Founding Editor
Christopher Harper-Bill

Series Editor
Frances Andrews

Previously published titles in the series are listed at the back of this volume

THE RECEPTION OF PAPAL LEGATES IN ENGLAND, 1170–1250

NARRATING THE *ADVENTUS* CEREMONY

EMIL LAUGE CHRISTENSEN

THE BOYDELL PRESS

© Emil Lauge Christensen 2025

All Rights Reserved. Except as permitted under current legislation
no part of this work may be photocopied, stored in a retrieval system,
published, performed in public, adapted, broadcast,
transmitted, recorded or reproduced in any form or by any means,
without the prior permission of the copyright owner

The right of Emil Lauge Christensen to be identified as
the author of this work has been asserted in accordance with
sections 77 and 78 of the Copyright, Designs and Patents Act 1988

First published 2025
The Boydell Press, Woodbridge

ISBN 978 1 83765 057 6

The Boydell Press is an imprint of Boydell & Brewer Ltd
PO Box 9, Woodbridge, Suffolk IP12 3DF, UK
and of Boydell & Brewer Inc.
668 Mt Hope Avenue, Rochester, NY 14620-2731, USA
website: www.boydellandbrewer.com

Our Authorised Representative for product safety in the EU is Easy Access System
Europe – Mustamäe tee 50, 10621 Tallinn, Estonia, gpsr.requests@easproject.com

A CIP catalogue record for this book is available
from the British Library

The publisher has no responsibility for the continued existence or accuracy of URLs for external or third-party internet websites referred to in this book, and does not guarantee that any content on such websites is, or will remain, accurate or appropriate

Contents

Acknowledgements	vi
List of Abbreviations	viii
Introduction	1
Part I: Communicating and Perceiving Legatine Expressions	
1. The Papal *Legatus a Latere*: An Everchanging, Contradictory Figure	17
2. Expressing Papal and Legatine Authority: Insignia and *Adventus*	38
3. Instructing a Proper Welcome: Normative Guides to the *Adventus*	72
Part II: Narrating Legatine *Adventus* Ceremonies	
4. Dependent on the King: Roger of Howden and the Legatine *Adventus*	107
5. The Road of St Thomas: Gervase of Canterbury and Local Adaptation	132
6. Treason and Slavery: Roger of Wendover and the Plight of England	162
7. Choosing Submission: Matthew Paris and the Foolishness of the English	187
Conclusion	215
Appendix 1	225
Appendix 2	228
Bibliography	231
Index	259

Acknowledgements

In 1159, John of Salisbury (c. 1120–80) completed his *Metalogicon*: a treatise delving into various subjects, with a primary focus on the role of logic in the education system. He asserted:

> Bernard of Chartres [d. after 1124] used to say that we are like dwarfs sitting on the shoulders of giants so that we are able to see more and further than they, not indeed by reason of the sharpness of our vision or the height of our bodies, but because we are lifted up on high and raised aloft by the greatness of giants.[1]

I like this aphorism because it not only underscores the virtue of humility but it encourages us to recognise our dependence on those who came before us – to recognise the importance of our history – while also acknowledging that we, collectively and individually, can enhance our knowledge and understanding. This aphorism offers a profoundly positive view of humanity.

Reflecting on how we reached the shoulders of the giants is important. I personally received support and encouragement from many individuals. I must first express my gratitude to the Independent Research Fund Denmark, without whose funding this study would not have come to fruition. Special thanks are due to Iben Fonnesberg-Schmidt, Kim Esmark, and Frances Andrews. I am also grateful to Chen Yarong, Étienne Doublier, Stephanie Erlenbach, Michael H. Gelting, Jochen Johrendt, Martin Ottovay Jørgensen, Lars Kjær, William Kynan-Wilson, Maren Lytje, Danielle Magnusson, Torben K. Nielsen, Gesine Oppitz-Trotman, Marianne Sletten Paasch, Per Methner Rasmussen, Michael Staunton, August

---

[1] John of Salisbury, *Metalogicon*, trans. J. B. Hall, Corpus Christianorum in Translation 12 (Turnhout: Brepols, 2013), bk. 3, ch. 4, p. 257; John of Salisbury [Ioannes Saresberiensis], *Metalogicon*, ed. J. B. Hall and Katharine S. B. Keats-Rohan, CCCM 98 (Turnhout: Brepols, 1991), bk. 3, ch. 4, p. 116: 'Dicebat Bernardus Carnotensis nos esse quasi nanos gigantum umeris insidentes, ut possimus plura eis et remotiora uidere, non utique proprii uisus acumine, aut eminentia corporis, sed quia in altum subuehimur et extollimur magnitudine gigantea'. On the history of the use of this famous aphorism, see Robert K. Merton, *On the Shoulders of Giants: A Shandean Postscript* (New York: Free Press, 1965).

Thomsen, Björn Weiler, and Patrick Zutshi. I extend my gratitude to the anonymous reviewer, whose comments significantly improved this study. Any remaining insufficiencies and errors are my own. Whether this study indeed sees further than the giants, I leave to your assessment as you read these pages.

Finally, I want to express my deepest gratitude to my wife, Signe Frederiksen, for her patience during my prolonged physical and mental absences. And to Laurits, our son, for reminding me of what truly matters.

Abbreviations

AM	*Annales Monastici*
Ancient Usages	Martinus Cawley, trans. *The Ancient Usages of the Cistercian Order*. Lafayette, OR: Guadalupe Translations, 1998
The Annals	Roger of Howden. *The Annals of Roger de Hoveden. Comprising the History of England and of Other Countries of Europe from A.D. 732 to A.D. 1201*, translated by Henry T. Riley. 2 vols. London: H. G. Bohn, 1853
ANS	*Anglo-Norman Studies*
CCCM	Corpus Christianorum, Continuatio Mediaeualis
CCR	*Calendar of the Close Rolls*
Chronica	Roger of Howden. *Chronica magistri Rogeri de Houedene*, edited by William Stubbs. 4 vols. RS. London: Longmans, 1868–71
CPR	*Calendar of the Patent Rolls*
Ecclesiastica Officia	Danièle Choisselet and Placide Vernet, eds. *Les 'Ecclesiastica Officia' cisterciens du XIIème siècle*. Reiningue: Documentation Cistercienne, 1989
EHR	*English Historical Review*
Flores Historiarum	Roger of Wendover. *Rogeri de Wendover liber qui dicitur Flores Historiarum ab anno Domini MCLIV. Annoque Henrici anglorum regis secundi primo*, edited by Henry G. Hewlett. 3 vols. RS. London: Longman, 1886–89
Flowers of History	Roger of Wendover. *Roger of Wendover's Flowers of History*, translated by J. A. Giles. 2 vols. London: Henry G. Bohn, 1849
Gervase	Gervase of Canterbury. *The Historical Works of Gervase of Canterbury*, edited by William Stubbs. 2 vols. RS. London: Longman, 1879–80

Gesta	[Roger of Howden]. *Gesta Regis Henrici Secundi Benedicti Abbatis*, edited by William Stubbs. 2 vols. RS. London: Longmans, 1867
JEH	*Journal of Ecclesiastical History*
JMH	*Journal of Medieval History*
Liber Pontificalis	Duchesne, L., ed. *Le Liber Pontificalis: texte, introduction et commentaire*. 2 vols. Paris: Thorin, 1892
Matthew Paris, *CM*	Matthew Paris. *Matthaei Parisiensis, monachi Sancti Albani, Chronica Majora*, edited by Henry Richards Luard. 7 vols. RS. London: Longman, 1872–83
Matthew Paris, *EH*	Matthew Paris. *Matthew Paris's English History: From the Year 1235 to 1273*, translated by J. A. Giles. 3 vols. London: George Bell & Sons, 1889
MGH	Monumenta Germaniae Historica
The Monastic Constitutions	Lanfranc. *The Monastic Constitutions of Lanfranc*, edited by David Knowles and Christopher Nugent Lawrence Brooke. OMT. Oxford: Clarendon Press, 2002
OMT	Oxford Medieval Texts
PL	*Patrologia Latina*, ed. Jacques-Paul Migne
PR	Pipe Rolls
RS	Rolls Series
Rule of Benedict	Saint Benedict. *The Rule of Benedict: An Invitation to the Christian Life*, edited by Georg Holzherr, translated by Mark Thamert. Cistercian Publications. Collegeville, MN: Liturgical Press, 2016
TCE	*Thirteenth Century England*

Introduction

From the middle of the eleventh century, the papacy embarked on a series of ecclesiastical reforms aimed at improving religious observance, repositioning the Church relative to the secular powers, championing papal independence, and asserting papal primacy and authority. These reforms profoundly impacted the relationship between the papacy and the rulers of Latin Christendom. Frictions and disputes erupted, particularly between the popes and the German emperors, but, oftentimes, popes also managed to cooperate peacefully with the emperors and other rulers.[1]

One of the papacy's most important tools of reform was its legates. Legates were the pope's most elevated representatives, acting as his deputies and implementing (sometimes sweeping) changes to local churches while engaging in high-level diplomacy. The most powerful were the *legati a latere*, who ranked above all other prelates. The popes almost exclusively selected these individuals from the cardinalate – the group of men comprising the liturgical, advisory, and jurisdictional body surrounding the pope – hence the denomination *a latere*, meaning from 'the side' of the pope. Cardinal-legate and legate *a latere* were largely synonymous terms.[2]

---

[1] See esp. Kathleen G. Cushing, *Reform and the Papacy in the Eleventh Century* (Manchester: Manchester University Press, 2005); Ian S. Robinson, *The Papacy 1073–1198: Continuity and Innovation* (Cambridge: Cambridge University Press, 1990); J. A. Watt, 'The Papacy', in *The New Cambridge Medieval History: V, c.1198–c.1300*, ed. David Abulafia (Cambridge: Cambridge University Press, 1999), pp. 107–63; Colin Morris, *The Papal Monarchy: The Western Church from 1050 to 1250* (Oxford: Clarendon Press, 1989); Maureen C. Miller, 'The Crisis in the Investiture Crisis Narrative', *History Compass* 7, no. 6 (2009): 1570–80; James K. Otte, 'Church Reform in the Holy Roman Empire and Reform of the Papacy: Cluny or Henry III?', in *Medieval Germany: Associations and Delineations*, ed. Nancy van Deusen (Ottawa: Institute of Mediaeval Music, 2000), pp. 63–69; R. I. Moore, *The First European Revolution, c. 970–1215* (Oxford: Blackwell, 2000); Brenda M. Bolton, *The Medieval Reformation* (London: Edward Arnold, 1983); Walter Ullmann, *A Short History of the Papacy in the Middle Ages*, 2nd edn (London: Routledge, 1974); and the contributions in *Innocent III: Vicar of Christ or Lord of the World?*, ed. James M. Powell, 2nd edn (Washington, D.C.: The Catholic University of America Press, 1994).

[2] See pp. 24–28.

During the era of the reform papacy, these legates travelled extensively across Europe on a variety of missions, including Church reform, crusade preaching, peace making, and tax collection. Legates frequently engaged in direct negotiations and policy making on behalf of the pope, and, significantly, such legates embodied the pope himself. For example, in 1237, Pope Gregory IX (r. 1227–41) directed the English to receive Cardinal-Legate Otto 'just as if our person' ('tanquam personam nostram').[3]

The reception of such individuals, consequently, held great significance. The papacy expected its legates to be welcomed with the ceremonial splendour befitting the station of its foremost representatives, and only an *adventus* ceremony would suffice. The *adventus* ('arrival') was an ancient ceremonial welcome, encompassing social, political, and religious dimensions, centred on the reception of a ruler by his or her subjects. Subjects would form a procession to meet the ruler outside their home territory, whether it was a city, an abbey, a cathedral, or something else. After the initial meeting, the subjects would accompany the ruler back to their own territory.[4]

By the twelfth century, the *adventus* had become an integral part of every ruler's public display of authority. Julie Kerr refers to it as 'a symbolic recognition of ... position and authority'.[5] Susan Twyman describes it as 'the ritual expression *par excellence* of triumphant rulership'.[6] As the first official meeting between two parties (or the initial meeting following an extended absence), it was a defining moment in

---

[3] Lucien Auvray, ed., *Les registres de Grégoire IX: recueil des bulles de ce pape*, 4 vols (Paris: Albert Fontemoing, 1896–1955), vol. 2, no. 3509, col. 563. Concerning legatine history and the legatine offices, see, especially, Claudia Zey, 'Stand und Perspektiven der Erforschung des päpstlichen Legatenwesens im Hochmittelalter', in *Rom und die Regionen: Studien zur Homogenisierung der lateinischen Kirche im Hochmittelalter*, ed. Jochen Johrendt and Harald Müller (Göttingen: De Gruyter, 2012), pp. 157–66; Robinson, *The Papacy 1073–1198*, pp. 146–78; and Robert Charles Joseph Figueira, 'The Canon Law of Medieval Papal Legation' (unpublished PhD dissertation, Cornell University, Ithaca, NY, 1980). Chapter 1 in this book also covers these matters extensively.

[4] See, especially, Margot E. Fassler, '*Adventus* at Chartres: Ritual Models for Major Processions', in *Ceremonial Culture in Pre-Modern Europe*, ed. Nicholas Howe (Notre Dame, IN: University of Notre Dame Press, 2007), pp. 13–62; Michael McCormick, *Eternal Victory: Triumphal Rulership in Late Antiquity, Byzantium, and the Early Medieval West* (Cambridge: Cambridge University Press, 1986); and Ernst Hartwig Kantorowicz, 'The "King's Advent" and the Enigmatic Panels in the Doors of Santa Sabina', *The Art Bulletin* 26, no. 4 (1944): 207–31. This book also examines the *adventus* in chapter 2; see especially pp. 49–55.

[5] Julie Kerr, *Monastic Hospitality: The Benedictines in England, c.1070–c.1250* (Woodbridge: Boydell Press, 2007), p. 115.

[6] Susan E. Twyman, *Papal Ceremonial at Rome in the Twelfth Century* (London: Boydell Press for the Henry Bradshaw Society, 2002), p. 2.

their relationship. It afforded, as Philippe Buc has argued, 'medieval political culture with a recognized way to gauge – qualitatively and quantitatively – the relationship between two parties, qualitatively by detailing the nature of the train and its trappings, quantitatively by evaluating the length an *occursus* [the coming out] traveled to meet its recipient'.[7]

This study is dedicated to the exploration of the receptions of papal legates *a latere*, with a focus on the meanings and perceptions linked to these receptions. The place of investigation is England, from around 1170 to approximately 1250, a significant period in the development of Anglo-Papal relations. The primary (but not the only) sources employed for this inquiry consist of the writings of chroniclers and historians from the pertinent period, as they were the commentators of the time. This study's objective is to explore how these commentators portrayed the receptions of papal legates *a latere* in England and how they depicted Anglo-Papal relations through accounts of legatine reception ceremonies.

The scholarship on the medieval *adventus* is extensive and diverse, with individual studies often concentrating on a distinct type of *adventus*: whether royal, episcopal, papal, or liturgical.[8] These studies create opportunities for comparison and offer insights into the workings of the medieval *adventus*. One particularly valuable study for comparative purposes is Susan E. Twyman's exploration of the papal *adventus* in twelfth-century Rome.[9] According to her research, there was

---

[7] Philippe Buc, *The Dangers of Ritual: Between Early Medieval Texts and Social Scientific Theory* (Princeton: Princeton University Press, 2001), p. 76.

[8] On episcopal *adventus* ceremonies, see, e.g., Katherine Harvey, 'The First Entry of the Bishop: Episcopal *Adventus* in Fourteenth-Century England', in *Fourteenth Century England VIII*, ed. J. S. Hamilton (Woodbridge: Boydell Press, 2014), pp. 43–58; and Maureen C. Miller, 'The Florentine Bishop's Ritual Entry and the Origins of the Medieval Episcopal *Adventus*', *Revue d'histoire ecclésiastique* 98 (2003): 5–28. On royal or princely *adventus* ceremonies, see, e.g., Angelika Lampen, 'Der Einzug des Herrschers in seine Stadt – der *Adventus Domini* als Bühne bürgerlicher und städtischer Repräsentation', in *Europäische Städte im Mittelalter*, ed. Ferdinand Opll and Christoph Sonnlechner (Innsbruck: Studien Verlag, 2010), pp. 267–80; Winfried Dotzauer, 'Die Ankunft des Herrshers: Der fürstliche "Einzug" in die Stadt (bis zum Ende des Alten Reichs)', *Archiv für Kulturgeschichte* 55, no. 2 (1973): 245–88; and Robert Withington, 'The Early "Royal-Entry"', *Publications of the Modern Language Association* 32, no. 4 (1917): 616–23. On liturgical *adventus* ceremonies, see, e.g., Nikolaus Gussone, '*Adventus*-Zeremoniell und Translation von Reliquien. Victricius von Rouen, De laude sanctorum', *Frühmittelalterliche Studien* 10 (1976): 125–33; Iris Shagrir, '*Adventus* in Jerusalem: The Palm Sunday Celebration in Latin Jerusalem', *JMH* 41, no. 1 (2015): 1–20; and Nicholas Vincent, *The Holy Blood: King Henry III and the Westminster Blood Relic* (Cambridge: Cambridge University Press, 2001), esp. pp. 1–4, 7–19. See also Klaus Tenfelde, '*Adventus*. Zur historischen Ikonologie des Festzugs', *Historische Zeitschrift* 235, no. 1 (1982): 45–84.

[9] Twyman, *Papal Ceremonial at Rome*. Other studies of papal *adventus* ceremonies include

an intimate connection between the recording of papal *adventus* ceremonies and the rise of the papacy as an independent, universal power. Historically, the people of Rome had had a say in the election of the pope, but Pope Nicholas II's election decree of 1059 officially stripped that privilege from them. Simultaneously, Twyman argues, the curia reinterpreted the newly elected pope's customary *adventus* into Rome as 'acquiescence in the divine will'. In response, the Romans declined to grant such an *adventus* prior to the customary acclamations. For the Romans, agreeing to provide an *adventus* 'came to mean a right of acceptance or veto by the people'. Hence, according to Twyman, a series of *ordines* and papal biographies debated and redefined the meaning of the papal *adventus* during the twelfth century.[10]

It is from these developments that questions arise regarding the legatine *adventus*. What was the relationship between the papal and the legatine *adventus*? How did the curia perceive the meaning of legatine receptions? How were the receptions of papal legates perceived beyond Rome?

Franz Wasner is one of the first scholars to study the legatine *adventus*. He argues that the legate *a latere* was not merely a representative, but that in 'the *legatus a latere* the pope is made present' and 'that is why he wears the papal mantle, why the ceremonial of the pope surrounds him'.[11] According to Wasner, the legate's *adventus* was a function of his embodiment of the pope. However, Wasner relies on certain fifteenth-century *ordines* to reach these conclusions, and though these texts likely drew inspiration from earlier customary practices, their creation was a product of the prevailing political situation. It is important to exercise caution when using later sources such as these.[12]

Hermann Jakobs, 'Rom und Trier 1147: Der *adventus papae* als Ursprungszeugnis der rheinischen Stadtsiegel', in *Stadt und Bistum in Kirche und Reich des Mittelalters: Festschrift für Odilo Engels zum 65. Geburtstag*, ed. Hanna Vollrath and Stefan Weinfurter (Cologne: Böhlau Verlag, 1993), pp. 349–65; and Anne J. Duggan, 'The Benefits of Exile', in *Pope Eugenius III (1145–1153): The First Cistercian Pope*, ed. Iben Fonnesberg-Schmidt and Andrew Jotischky (Amsterdam: Amsterdam University Press, 2018), pp. 171–95. See also Twyman's 'preliminary study' of the papal *adventus*: Susan E. Twyman, 'Papal *Adventus* at Rome in the Twelfth Century', *Historical Research* 69, no. 170 (1996): 233–53.

[10] Twyman, *Papal Ceremonial at Rome*, quotes at p. 219.

[11] Franz Wasner, 'Fifteenth-Century Texts on the Ceremonial of the Papal "Legatus a Latere"', *Traditio* 14 (1958): 295–358, p. 300. See also Franz Wasner, '"Legatus a Latere": Addenda Varia', *Traditio* 16 (1960): 405–16.

[12] Scholarship on the late medieval and early modern legatine *adventus* includes Richard Cooper, 'Legate's Luxury: The Entries of Cardinal Allesandro Farnese to Avignon and Carpentras, 1553', in *French Ceremonial Entries in the Sixteenth Century: Event, Image, Text*, ed. Nicolas Russel and Hélène Visentin (Toronto: Centre for Reformation and Renaissance Studies, 2007), pp. 133–61; Charles Keenan, 'The Limits of Diplomatic Ritual: The Polish Embassy of Giovanni Francesco Commendone (1572–1573) and Criticism of

The curia produced no *ordines* or instructions concerning the legatine *adventus*, or even much regarding legatine ceremonial prior to the fifteenth century. Scholars exploring the medieval legatine *adventus* during the twelfth and thirteenth centuries must rely instead on a diverse and often random array of sources. Only a few have made the *adventus* their primary focus, with Kriston Rennie being a notable exception. Rennie has produced an important study on the ceremonial reception of medieval papal legates, in which he utilises a varied range of sources, including chronicles, letters, and canon law, to explore the role of legatine receptions in medieval Europe.[13] He argues that a legate's ceremonial entry into his province (the area where he represented the pope) and his dress and insignia were 'characteristics of his authority to govern, rule and administer in the name of St Peter'.[14] The legate's ceremonial reception served as a vital step towards engaging in 'political communications', and it furthermore 'transposed local politics by implying a tacit social and political consensus'.[15] Conversely, declining to welcome a legate 'presented a direct challenge to Rome's authority'.[16]

While Rennie's investigation provides an excellent framework, it nonetheless remains slightly cursory. Rennie suggests the existence of a shared understanding of the legatine ceremony, a 'social and political consensus',[17] but although the papacy might have sought to establish such a consensus, opinions on the legatine *adventus* changed over time and varied from one place to another. This study aims to capture the diversity of voices discussing the legatine *adventus* – to convey the extent of dispute, adaptation, enthusiasm, indifference, and even horror that the legatine *adventus* incited.

The dispatch of a legate was a rare occurrence, especially beyond Italy and the German Empire. The arrival of a legate inevitably disrupted the established social order, if only temporarily. However, legates were most often invited into

---

Papal Legates in Early Modern Europe', *Royal Studies Journal* 3, no. 2 (2016): 90–111; and Antonín Kalous, 'Through the Gates and the Streets of the City: Cardinals and Their Processions in Rome in the Late Fifteenth and Early Sixteenth Centuries', in *Ritualizing the City: Collective Performances as Aspects of Urban Construction from Constantine to Mao*, ed. Ivan Foletti and Adrien Palaldino (Rome: Viella, 2017), pp. 29–44. See also Antonín Kalous, *Late Medieval Papal Legation: Between the Councils and the Reformation* (Rome: Viella, 2017), esp. pp. 112–24.

[13] Kriston Robert Rennie, 'The Ceremonial Reception of Medieval Papal Legates', *JEH* 69, no. 2 (2018): 1–20. Joseph Figueira also briefly discusses legatine receptions in his monumental thesis on the canon law on medieval papal legation; see Figueira, 'The Canon Law', pp. 380–89.

[14] Rennie, 'The Ceremonial Reception', p. 4.

[15] Ibid., p. 6.

[16] Ibid., p. 14.

[17] Ibid., p. 6.

legatine provinces, meaning that legations were permitted to intrude on the established social and political order of European polities. Even when popes dispatched legates under their own initiative, they did so with specific objectives in mind, such as crusade preaching, Church reform, or conducting diplomacy with secular rulers. These objectives directly influenced how the legate was viewed within his province by different commentators, whether they approved of the legatine mission or not. The perspectives of those inhabiting the province shaped how they received the legate, what meaning they attributed to his reception, and how they depicted him in narrative sources. In their accounts of legatine *adventus* ceremonies, commentators chose to highlight, downplay, or challenge certain aspects of the ceremony. This study focuses on these interactions with the ceremony.

Approach and Sources

This focus raises questions about what chroniclers actually recorded when composing accounts of legatine *adventus* ceremonies. Were they documenting the performance itself, the underlying meanings, or the interpretations that the rituals evoked? Historians have long been aware that medieval chroniclers were not impartial observers, providing objective 'anthropological' accounts of rituals. The implications of this have been subject to debate between those who have sought 'general cultural truths' within ritual reporting, to quote Lars Kjær, and those who have dismissed such endeavours as futile.[18]

Philippe Buc is the latter's most ardent advocate. He cautions that 'access to ritual as historical fact is impossible, if by "fact" one understands "event"'.[19] Buc observes that 'medieval political rituals, once performed (or even already at the moment of their performance), were subjected actively to interpretations', and that 'observer, participant, and audience of oral or written reports searched

---

[18] Lars Kjær, *The Medieval Gift and the Classical Tradition: Ideals and the Performance of Generosity in Medieval England, 1100–1300* (Cambridge: Cambridge University Press, 2019), p. 7. See also Timothy Reuter, 'Pre-Gregorian Mentalities', in *Medieval Polities and Modern Mentalities*, ed. Janet L. Nelson (Cambridge: Cambridge University Press, 2006), pp. 89–99, esp. p. 97.

[19] Buc, *The Dangers of Ritual*, p. 248. *The Dangers of Ritual* has provoked controversy; see, e.g., Geoffrey Koziol, 'Review Article: The Dangers of Polemic: Is Ritual Still an Interesting Topic of Historical Study?', *Early Medieval Europe* 11 (2002): 367–88; Philippe Buc, 'The Monster and the Critics: A Ritual Reply', *Early Medieval Europe* 15, no. 4 (2007): 441–52; and Kim Esmark, 'Farlige ritualer – Middelalderens politiske kultur mellem antropologiske og tekstlige vendinger', *Passepartout* 13, no. 25 (2005): 56–67.

behind appearances, asking what kind of spirit had animated the event'.[20] Buc argues that the 'time has come to forget this dangerous word [ritual]'.[21]

Few have gone to the extent of abandoning the term 'ritual', but scholars are attentive to the fact that rituals are subject to interpretation. David Warner, who has studied the *adventus* in Ottonian Germany (919–1024), argues that 'the most useful question to ask may not be whether an informant's account of a ritual corresponds with reality but rather how the informant has manipulated that account to express a different reality of deeper and, from his or her perspective, greater significance'.[22] Twyman notes that 'when a ritual is recorded in detail it is often because the circumstances were unusual or the event had a special significance'.[23]

I concur that it is particularly challenging to study an account of a ritual, including a legatine *adventus*, as an 'objective' report on an event occurring at a specific time and place.[24] At the same time, however, chroniclers provided commentary on the socio-political reality of which they were a part. *Adventus* ceremonies existed beyond the realm of ink and parchment. It is difficult to imagine all medieval rituals as literary tropes with no basis in experiential reality, even if individual accounts are rarely reliable. The question is: if interpretation was all that held importance, why engage in the organisation of – and participation in – rituals?

Christina Pössel has put forward a straightforward yet compelling explanation for the persistence of rituals. She asserts that the strength of ritual communication is its ability to 'communicate fundamental information about the power relations between those acting on the ritual stage'.[25] At the same time, the ritual's 'solemn frame would have made it very hard to disagree'.[26] Hence, 'the ritualized frame

---

[20] Philippe Buc, 'Ritual and Interpretation: The Early Medieval Case', *Early Medieval Europe* 9, no. 2 (2000): 183–210, p. 186.

[21] Buc, *The Dangers of Ritual*, p. 247.

[22] David A. Warner, 'Ritual and Memory in the Ottonian Reich: The Ceremony of Adventus', *Speculum* 76, no. 2 (2001): 255–83, pp. 256–57. See also Kim Esmark, 'Just Rituals: Masquerade, Manipulation, and Officialising Strategies in Saxo's Gesta Danorum', in *Rituals, Performatives, and Political Order in Northern Europe, c. 650–1350*, ed. Wojtek Jerzierski et al. (Turnhout: Brepols, 2015), pp. 237–67; and Hermann Kamp, 'Tugend, Macht, und Ritual: Politisches Verhalten beim Saxo Grammaticus', in *Zeichen – Rituale – Werte*, ed. Gerd Althoff (Münster: Rhema, 2004), pp. 179–200.

[23] Twyman, *Papal Ceremonial at Rome*, p. 45.

[24] Note that Kjær and Benjamin Wild each show that it is possible to study actual rituals in some instances; see Lars Kjær, 'Food, Drink and Ritualised Communication in the Household of Eleanor de Montfort, February to August 1265', *JMH* 37, no. 1 (2011): 75–89; Kjær, *The Medieval Gift*, pp. 160–83; and Benjamin Linley Wild, 'A Gift Inventory from the Reign of Henry III', *EHR* 125, no. 514 (2010): 529–69.

[25] Christina Pössel, 'The Magic of Early Medieval Ritual', *Early Medieval Europe* 17, no. 2 (2009): 111–25, p. 122.

[26] Ibid., p. 122.

can create the illusion of consensus and harmony, and make disagreement and subversion costly'.[27] A ritual served as a mechanism of power, ensnaring participants and observers within a particular interpretation of the ritual, and silence could be interpreted as consent. This consensus might not have been deeply felt or unchallenged; it depended on the circumstances and the perceived trade-offs between the risks and benefits of dissent. Individuals attending a ritual might come away from the occasion assuming that all others present subscribed to the ritual's message merely by virtue of their attendance. Nevertheless, at times, the dissent of a single well-placed individual might have been enough to shatter the illusion of agreement at a ritual; in other instances, this may have proved far more difficult, due to genuine agreement with the message, the vested interests of powerful players, or other factors.

Not all reports on legatine receptions offer only literary tropes, even if some certainly contained specific tropes. However, regardless of the presence of such tropes in the reports of medieval commentators, they still contain interpretations and viewpoints regarding a significant socio-religious and political ritual, which conveyed a distinct relationship between those taking part in the welcome of the legate and the legate's lord, the pope. While the commentators seldom documented what happened at the events themselves, their reports were in nearly all instances based on real events taking place. It was the facts of the events (as the commentators perceived them) which the commentators reacted to and interpreted, and it was their interpretations that they put into writing in the form of reports on legatine receptions. Such reports furnish insights into how information about specific events was received and appropriated. Each individual account conveys a message about a particular reception, often absorbing and reflecting on the broader context of that reception.

In order to explore the implications of reports on legatine receptions, a comprehensive approach involves viewing each account as an intricate fusion of literary and socio-political motives. Each report offers a glimpse into an individual's perceptions and opinions regarding the relationship between England and the papacy. However, the viewpoints of these writers are deeply rooted within a communal, socio-political, religious, and historical backdrop. For modern historians, addressing this requires contextualisation on three separate levels.

Firstly, the context of each author must be established, encompassing their physical and mental positions within the historical framework that moulded their worldviews. Secondly, it is necessary to place each commentator's report on a legatine reception within the broader context of that author's work. Analysing

---

[27] Ibid., p. 123. For a comparable but more theoretical view, see Catherine Bell, *Ritual Theory – Ritual Practice* (Oxford: Oxford University Press, 1992).

each report within such a framework entails examining how each account fits within the structural composition and thematic fabric of the respective chronicle. Thirdly, it is necessary to take into account the circumstances surrounding each reception and each legation.

For these reasons, I have found it necessary to be selective. I have chosen to focus here on the writings of four Anglo-Norman authors: Roger of Howden (d. 1201), Gervase of Canterbury (c. 1145–c. 1210), Roger of Wendover (d. 1236), and Matthew Paris (c. 1200–59). These authors represent the diverse landscape of chronicle writing in England during an era when many chroniclers were monastic. Gervase of Canterbury, Roger of Wendover, and Matthew Paris all hailed from monastic backgrounds. Roger of Howden, distinguished as a royal clerk and parson, offers another voice. Howden originated from Yorkshire, while the remaining three monks all came from southern England. Although Roger of Wendover and Matthew Paris were monks at the same abbey, St Albans, their voices are necessary for bringing the investigation well into the first half of the thirteenth century, since other English writers do not provide similarly comprehensive accounts of the period.

I have allocated each author his own chapter. Each offers a unique narrative, shedding light on legatine receptions from different angles and from within distinct contexts. Such narratives unveil the various ways in which the papacy was viewed through the receptions of its legates, providing further insights into the dynamics at play within England.

The manner in which commentators approached legatine *adventus* ceremonies is put into perspective by another type of source: monastic customaries.[28] Monastic customaries are a very diverse group of sources, but at their core, they all share a focus on proper monastic conduct. Some of the customaries contain what I have termed, for simplicity, '*adventus* instructions', or simply 'instructions'. These offer remarkably detailed guidance regarding how a monastic community should receive high-ranking dignitaries, including papal legates.

Three customaries stand out for their highly detailed and useful instructions: Lanfranc's Monastic Constitutions (c. 1077), the Cistercian *Ecclesiastica Officia* (1184 × 1186), and the rule of the Gilbertine Order (1220 × 1223). Together these offer some of the most detailed normative guidance available on the ritualised receptions of dignitaries during the High Middle Ages. No medieval English chronicler or historian can match the detail found in these comprehensive depictions of the *adventus*. These instructions underscore how much monastic

---

[28] The English royal records – Pipe Rolls, Close Rolls, etc. – as well as charters and various correspondence occasionally mention or provide circumstantial evidence for a reception of a legate *a latere*. I will use these various records whenever they contain useful information.

authors thought about performance. Most notably, they provide an interpretive framework, revealing the concerns and considerations of host communities, and unveiling the significance tied to the ritual reception of a powerful lord, including one of the most powerful lords in Europe – a papal legate.

England and the Papacy

The receptions of papal legates took place against a backdrop of shifting dynamics in the relationship between England and the papacy. The catalysts for these changes were diverse, but three key factors can be discerned. These factors include shifts occurring within the papacy, alterations within the European communication networks, and, finally, an unforeseen and sudden political transformation when King John (r. 1199–1216) pledged England as a fief to the papacy.

Changes within the papacy were tied to the expansion of papal power. This era marked the ascendancy of papal monarchy, when both ecclesiastical and secular leaders sought the papacy's intervention in European and local affairs.[29] The curia evolved into the de facto Supreme Court for the Latin Church. The extent to which litigants and petitioners drove this development in relation to the papacy's assertion of ultimate jurisdiction is unclear. Regardless, everyone from parsons to princes – clergy and laypeople – recognised the advantages of utilising the pope as a supreme judge in ecclesiastical cases.[30] Many Englishmen journeyed to the curia, resulting in a heightened interconnectedness between England and Rome.[31]

---

[29] See esp. Robinson, *The Papacy 1073–1198*, pp. ix–x; Morris, *The Papal Monarchy*, pp. 1–2, 568–70; J. A. Watt, 'The Theory of Papal Monarchy in the Thirteenth Century: The Contribution of the Canonists', *Traditio* 20 (1964): 179–317; and Watt, 'The Papacy', pp. 107–8.

[30] See Patrick Zutshi, 'The Roman Curia and Papal Jurisdiction in the Twelfth and Thirteenth Centuries', in *Die Ordnung der Kommunikation und die Kommunikation der Ordnungen. Band 2: Zentralität: Papsttum und Orden im Europa des 12. Und 13. Jahrhunderts*, ed. Christina Andenna, Klaus Herbers, and Gert Melville, Schriften der Villa Vigoni (Stuttgart: Franz Steiner Verlag, 2013), pp. 213–27; and Patrick Zutshi, 'Petitioners, Popes, Proctors: The Development of Curial Institutions c.1150–1250', in *Pensiero e Sperimentazioni Istituzionali Nella 'Societas Christiana' (1046–1250): Atti Della Sedicesima Settimana Internazionale di Studio Mendola, 21–31 Agosto 2004*, ed. Giancarlo Andenna (Milan: Storia Ricerche, 2007), pp. 265–93.

[31] George B. Parks, *The English Traveler to Italy: The Middle Ages (to 1525)* (Rome: Edizioni di Storia e Letteratura, 1954), pp. 101–41; Jane E. Sayers, *Papal Judges Delegate in the Province of Canterbury, 1198–1254: A Study in Ecclesiastical Jurisdiction and Administration* (Oxford: Oxford University Press, 1971), esp. pp. 118–62; Jane E. Sayers, 'English Benedictine Monks at the Papal Court in the Thirteenth Century: The Experience of Thomas of Marlborough in a Wider Context', *Journal of Medieval Monastic Studies* 2 (2013): 109–29; Iben Fonnesberg-Schmidt and William Kynan-

None of this would have been possible without an increase in the ease of travel. As Europe became more urbanised, lines of communication became stronger, and goods and people were able to move faster and in greater numbers.[32] This, again, raises questions of causality; did better lines of communication spur travel activities, or did the demands of travellers for better infrastructure stimulate developments? Regardless of the answer, papal authority became sought after and seen as a useful tool of legitimisation.

In England, archbishops of Canterbury began to covet legatine appointments, often placing a higher value on such positions than their claims to primacy over the English Church.[33] Kings, too, came to recognise the utility of papal and legatine authority. King Henry II (r. 1154–89) petitioned Pope Urban III (r. 1185–87) for legates to crown his son, John, as king of Ireland.[34] King Richard (r. 1189–99), on the verge of embarking on the Third Crusade, persuaded the papacy to bestow the legatine office upon the regent, William Longchamp, bishop of Ely (r. 1189–97), in order to empower him to rule the English Church during Richard's absence.[35]

It was events in 1213 that sparked the swiftest and most striking shift in Anglo-Papal relations, however. The catalyst was the dispute between King John and Pope Innocent III (r. 1198–1216) concerning Innocent's role in the election of Cardinal Stephen Langton as archbishop of Canterbury (r. 1207–28). Innocent proved to be stronger. Mounting pressure forced John's hand, as rebellion, an interdict, and an imminent French invasion threatened to depose him. In the face of such dire circumstances, John extended an offer to the papacy, pledging England as a fief to the pope in order to obtain Innocent's favour. John's scheme worked. When civil war erupted a few years later, largely driven by issues of taxation and military failures, Innocent extended support to King John. Pope Honorius III (r. 1216–27) continued papal support, backing John's underage son, Henry, and providing crucial

---

Wilson, 'Smiling, Laughing and Joking in Papal Rome: Thomas of Marlborough and Gerald of Wales at the Court of Innocent III (1198–1216)', *Papers of the British School at Rome* 86 (2018): 1–29.

[32] Derek Keene, 'Towns and the Growth of Trade', in *The New Cambridge Medieval History, IV c. 1024–c. 1198, Part I* (Cambridge: Cambridge University Press, 2004), pp. 47–85; Kathryn L. Reyerson, 'Commerce and Communications', in *The New Cambridge Medieval History, V c. 1198–1300*, ed. David Abulafia (Cambridge: Cambridge University Press, 1999), pp. 50–70. England participated in this development; see Eljas Oksanen, 'Trade and Travel in England during the Long Twelfth Century', in *ANS XXXVII*, ed. Elisabeth van Houts (Woodbridge: Boydell Press, 2015), pp. 181–204.

[33] Ilicia Jo Sprey, 'Papal Legates in English Politics, 1100–1272' (unpublished PhD dissertation, University of Virginia, Charlottesville, 1998), pp. 212–20.

[34] Helene Tillmann, *Die päpstlichen Legaten in England bis zur Beendigung der Legation Gualas, 1218* (Bonn: Hch. Ludwig, 1926), pp. 80–81; *Gesta*, vol. 2, pp. 3–4.

[35] Tillmann, *Die päpstlichen Legaten*, pp. 85–87; Sprey, 'Papal Legates', pp. 221–38.

assistance through his legate, Cardinal Guala (d. 1227). Eventually, the royal party emerged victorious.[36] Until an act of parliament in 1366 invalidated the fiefdom status, the vassal relationship with the papacy influenced English attitudes to the papacy and informed English constitutional thought.[37]

This book explores the attitudes to the legatine *adventus* in England both before and after the enfeoffment. However, the time frame of this book was chosen not only to include the enfeoffment, but also because this period represents the height of the legate *a latere*. It was only around 1170 that the legate *a latere* emerged as a distinct and relatively well-defined office – a development largely fostered by initiatives undertaken during the pontificate of Alexander III (r. 1159–81). Alexander's innovations significantly amplified both the reach and numbers of legates *a latere*. However, changes during and following the pontificate of Alexander IV (r. 1254–61) gradually diminished the prominence of the legates *a latere*, as popes increasingly substituted them with other representatives.[38] The period under investigation thus represents the zenith of the papacy, the pinnacle of the legate *a latere*, and a time of great change.

The book is divided into two parts, which are further subdivided into three and four chapters, respectively. The first chapter is dedicated to the papal legate *a latere*. It provides a close examination of the legatine office, its history, its powers, and its conceptual framework. The objective is to offer an elucidation of what a legate, particularly a legate *a latere*, represented in Europe. What and who did popes dispatch from Rome to the provinces? The second chapter investigates legatine insignia and legatine receptions. It explores the types of insignia utilised by legates *a latere* and the purposes behind displaying them. The chapter also scrutinises how legatine insignia were interpreted beyond Rome. Additionally, this chapter studies the *adventus*, investigating how the curia viewed the meaning and purpose of the legatine *adventus*. Finally, the discussion probes how the papal perception of the legatine *adventus* was received. The third chapter delves into the

---

[36] Christopher Harper-Bill, 'John and the Church of Rome', in *King John: New Interpretations*, ed. Stephen D. Church (Woodbridge: Boydell Press, 1999), 289–315; David A. Carpenter, *The Minority of Henry III* (Berkeley: University of California Press, 1990), pp. 5–262; Christopher R. Cheney, 'King John and the Papal Interdict' and 'King John's Reaction to the Interdict on England', in *The Papacy and England 12th–14th Centuries: Historical and Legal Studies* (London: Variorum Reprints, 1982), IX: 295–317, X: 129–50; Fred A. Cazel, Jr., 'The Legates Guala and Pandulf', in *TCE II*, ed. P. R. Coss and S. D. Lloyd (Woodbridge: Boydell Press, 1988), pp. 15–21. For further information, see pp. 168–72.

[37] Rose Catherine Clifford, 'England as a Papal Fief: The Role of the Papal Legate in the Early Period, 1216–1241' (unpublished PhD dissertation, University of California, Los Angeles, 1978), p. 352.

[38] See pp. 24–26, 34–36.

monastic *adventus* instructions. The purpose of this chapter is to contextualise the accounts of commentators, exploring the relationship between written guidelines and practical application, as well as the numerous themes woven into the *adventus*, such as hierarchy, familiarisation, communality, inclusion, and more. This chapter is pivotal, as monastic instructions offer important interpretative keys for unlocking the writings of medieval commentators.

In part two, chapters 4 to 7 explore the accounts of legatine *adventus* ceremonies as presented by each of the four commentators, in chronological order. Chapter 4 is dedicated to Roger of Howden. Roger's works are interesting for various reasons: he encountered several papal legates and directly witnessed their receptions. His interpretations of several legatine *adventus* ceremonies were influenced by his dual service to the king and to several bishops. Nonetheless, Roger maintained a prevailing perception of legatine authority as contingent upon the English king, which in turn influenced the portrayal of the legatine *adventus* in his accounts. Roger's revision of his first work, the *Gesta Regis Henrici Secundi*, into the *Chronica* also underscores how the passage of time and shifting political contexts left their mark on memories and narratives of the legatine *adventus*.

Chapter 5 centres on the writings of Gervase of Canterbury. Gervase's distinctive interpretation of the reception of two papal legates at Canterbury during Christmas 1186 stands out. Gervase and his monastic chapter at Canterbury Cathedral were embroiled in a fervent dispute with Archbishop Baldwin of Forde (r. 1184–90), during which the papacy became a symbol of hope for the chapter. In his account of this particular legatine *adventus*, Gervase transformed the *adventus* into a symbol of papal might and justice, artfully interweaving attributes associated with the recently canonised St Thomas of Canterbury into the imagery of the *adventus*. This adaptation imbued the legatine *adventus* with a highly personalised and localised meaning.

Chapter 6 studies Roger of Wendover's perception of the legatine *adventus*. Roger commenced writing at least a decade after England's enfeoffment to the papacy, a shift that is reflected in his views on the papacy, papal legates, and the legatine *adventus*. He was hostile towards the enfeoffment, viewing it as tantamount to enslavement. Roger's portrayal of the reception of Cardinal Nicholas in 1214, the first legate *a latere* to enter England following the enfeoffment, is a poignant illustration of this stance. Roger inflated the *adventus* of the legate in order to exaggerate its significance and thus drive home his opinion of the enfeoffment. According to Roger, the *adventus* of Cardinal-Legate Nicholas marked the beginning of a dark age, in which the papacy took possession of England.

If Roger witnessed the dawn of a dark age, then Matthew Paris spent his entire life living in that darkness. Chapter 7 centres on his writings. As Roger's inheritor,

Matthew shared and expanded upon Roger's interpretations and viewpoints, taking them a step further. While Roger believed that the English clergy had been deceived, portraying them as victims of collusion between the pope and the king, Matthew did not share this perspective. In Matthew's view, the clergy were guilty of sycophantic collaboration. Matthew used the reception of Cardinal Otto de Tonenga in 1237 as a vehicle to criticise everyone involved: the pope, the legate, the clergy, and, most pointedly, King Henry III (r. 1216–72). Matthew exaggerated, compressed timelines, ridiculed, and more. In his view, the arrival and reception of Legate Otto was a catastrophe for England.

The legatine *adventus* was an important tool in the papacy's arsenal of authority, which likely explains why it elicited such strong feelings from commentators. The *adventus* was about power, the silencing of dissenting voices, and the promotion of a specific interpretation of the ritual. When the king or another prince, whether secular or ecclesiastical, extended an invitation for a legate to visit, they therein signified acceptance of the papal governance of the Church: the legatine *adventus* was the necessary precondition and expression of this acceptance. English monarchs and members of the English Church (sometimes in opposition to each other) invited the legate into national politics and domestic matters, allowing legates to involve themselves with local hierarchies, and to reform and pass sentences. The history of the legatine *adventus* in England in the decades around 1200 is a story of how papal authority became integrated into the web of English politics and society, and how various commentators perceived and responded to this.

PART I

Communicating and Perceiving Legatine Expressions

1

The Papal *Legatus a Latere*: An Everchanging, Contradictory Figure

In 1077, Pope Gregory VII (r. 1073–85) composed a letter addressed to the Christian communities of Narbonne, Gascony, and Spain. In this letter, he recommended his legate, Bishop Amatus of Oléron, to the addressees:

> We charge you [recipients of the letter] by apostolic authority to receive him [Legate Amatus] as though we, or rather St Peter, were present; out of reverence for the Apostolic See whose messenger he is, we charge you to obey and heed him in all things as though you saw our own face or actually heard us speaking. For it is written: 'He who hears you hears me' [Luke 10:16].[1]

In this directive, Pope Gregory VII not only stressed Bishop Amatus' role as a representative of the papacy but also urged the recipients to offer him the same reverence and obedience as if they were interacting directly with the pope, and with St Peter no less. According to Kriston Rennie's extensive research, this was an important conceptual underpinning of papal legation. Rennie argues that legates did not merely represent the pope; they embodied the pre-eminence of the Roman Church. Legates personified the Petrine doctrine that Christ had entrusted the keys of heaven to St Peter, who passed them on to his successors in perpetuity: the popes.[2]

While this conceptual understanding is significant, papal legates, including *legati a latere*, were at the same time complex, multifaceted, and contradictory

---

[1] H. E. J. Cowdrey, ed. and trans., *The Epistolae Vagantes of Pope Gregory VII* (Oxford: Clarendon Press, 1972), ep. 21, pp. 56–9: 'Quem sicut nostram immo beati Petri Presentiam uos suscipere apostolica auctoritate iubemus; ac sic pro reuerentia apostolicae sedis cuius nuncius est, uos in omnibus sibi obedire atque eum audire mandamus ut propriam faciem nostram seu nostrae uiuae uocis oracula. Scriptum est enim: "Qui uos audit, me audit".'

[2] Kriston Robert Rennie, *The Foundations of Medieval Papal Legation* (New York: Palgrave Macmillan, 2013), pp. 23–26.

entities. Delving into the history of the *legati a latere*, their classification and powers, and the underlying framework governing their presence across Christendom will highlight such nuances, shedding light on what was at stake when commentators observed and reacted to the presence of papal legates.

The Concept of Papal Legation

Returning to Pope Gregory VII's letter of recommendation, it is evident that Gregory envisioned the legate as a (temporary) carrier of the pontifical office: the legate brought St Peter with him. The legate was, as the pope explicitly mentioned, his messenger ('nuncius') – but he was also clearly much more. The concept of a wider, divine form of representation is not only evident in the writings of Gregory VII. In a letter to the clerics and citizens of Milan, Pope Innocent III also offered his reasons for dispatching papal legates:

> Since our daily practice according to the obligation of apostolic service should be the continuous solicitude of all churches, whenever we cannot personally attend to the promotion of their various items of business, we are compelled to expedite these matters through our brothers [cardinals] whom we dispatch from our own side (*a nostro latere*); we follow here the example of Him who, his disciples sent out throughout the world, personally worked for salvation in the midst of the world.[3]

Innocent's legates acted in his stead. However, there was also something deeper at stake: the pope compared himself to Him, who had also sent out apostles (Christ). In short, the pope likened his legates to the apostles. Innocent was (the Vicar of) Christ; his legates were the (vicars of the) apostles, representing a truth higher than 'mere' representation. Papal legation was greater than ordinary princely legation. Whereas the legate of a prince or anyone else had no authority outside the principal's territory – making such legates more akin to ambassadors – the

---

[3] *Liber Extravagantium Decretalium*, ed. Emil Friedberg, 2 vols, Corpus Iuris Canonici 2 (reprint, Leipzig; Graz: Bernhard Tauchnitz; Akademische Druck u. Verlagsanstalt, 1959), vol. 2, X 3.39.17; available at www.hs-augsburg.de/~harsch/Chronologia/Lspost13/GregoriusIX/gre_0000.html (accessed 15 April 2024): 'Quum instantia nostra quotidiana sit secundum debitum apostolicae servitutis omnium ecclesiarum sollicitudo continua, quoties ipsarum negotiis promovendis non possumus personaliter imminere, per fratres nostros ea expedire compellimur, quos a nostro latere destinamus, illius exemplum in hac parte secuti, qui, discipulis suis in mundum universum transmissis, ipse in medio terrae salutem fuit personaliter operatus.' Translated by Rennie, *The Foundations*, p. 174.

Church knew no regional bonds.[4] Papal legates represented 'the obligation of apostolic service', which equalled 'the continuous solicitude of all churches'.

According to Rennie, papal legates were the 'connecting links', the 'vessels' of sacred institutionalised charisma, capable of 'saturating' Christendom with papal power.[5] Rennie argues that the *papal* legate stood apart relative to other types of legates because he represented the Universal Church. Rennie calls it the 'right of legation', that is, the notion that the troubles of Christendom were the pope's responsibility and that his legates shared in that responsibility. Other legates lost their jurisdiction when they left their master's territory. Papal legates, on the other hand, represented the omnipresence of papal authority: the Church was catholic, that is, universal.[6]

Papal authority was also Roman authority, and, accordingly, legates needed to be seen as 'Roman'.[7] The pope was, after all, the bishop of Rome, and Rome was pervasive: throughout the early Middle Ages, 'Roman' liturgy, 'Roman' architecture, and more had spread throughout Europe.[8] With the rise of the reform papacy, legates of the Roman bishop began advancing along the old Roman roads. When twelfth- and especially thirteenth-century canonists thought about legatine powers, they looked to Roman imperial offices such as proconsul, senator, and praetorian prefect, explaining the transference of power from the pope to his legates using Roman legal concepts.[9] This approach seemingly served the purpose

---

[4] See also Robert Charles Joseph Figueira, 'The Canon Law of Medieval Papal Legation' (unpublished PhD dissertation, Cornell University, Ithaca, NY, 1980), pp. 229–53.

[5] Rennie, *The Foundations*, p. 27.

[6] Rennie, *The Foundations*, pp. 21–29. Gino Paro first coined the concept of 'right of legation'; see Gino Paro, *The Right of Papal Legation* (Washington, D.C.: The Catholic University of America Press, 1947). Sabine MacCormack notes that the late Roman emperors developed a doctrine of universal presence. It is conceivable that popes took notice of this concept; see Sabine G. MacCormack, 'Change and Continuity in Late Antiquity: The Ceremony of "Adventus"', *Historia: Zeitschrift für Alte Geschichte* 21, no. 4 (1972): 721–52, pp. 722, 741–42.

[7] Rennie, *The Foundations*, p. 26.

[8] See, e.g., the contributions in *Rome Across Time and Space: Cultural Transmission and the Exchange of Ideas c.500–1400*, ed. Claudia Bolgia, Rosamond McKitterick, and John Osborne (Cambridge: Cambridge University Press, 2011), especially, Éamonn Ó Carragain, 'The Periphery Rethinks the Centre: Inculturation, "Roman" Liturgy and the Ruthwell Cross', pp. 63–83; Jesse D. Billett, 'The Liturgy of the "Roman" Office in England from the Conversion to the Conquest', pp. 84–110; Yitzhak Hen, 'The Romanization of the Frankish Liturgy: Ideal, Reality and the Rhetoric of Reform', pp. 111–23; and Judson J. Emerick, 'Building *More Romano* in Francia during the Third Quarter of the Eighth Century: The Abbey Church of Saint-Denis and Its Model', pp. 127–50.

[9] Figueira, 'The Canon Law', pp. 135–56, 409.

of enabling canonists to describe the legatine office within a well-defined legal framework, simultaneously using this basis to 'Romanise' the pope and his legates.

English chroniclers were aware of these textual manoeuvres. William Kynan-Wilson notes how the appointment of Henry of Blois, bishop of Winchester (r. 1129–71), as a papal legate had immediate consequences for how the chronicler William of Malmesbury (c. 1090–c. 1143) described him.[10] According to William of Malmesbury, Henry immediately gave a speech *latialiter* upon appointment.[11] *Latialiter* is a rare term, meaning 'in Roman manner' or 'according to Roman custom'. According to Kynan-Wilson, William of Malmesbury used *latialiter* to enhance Henry's 'Romanness'.[12] When Henry, immediately upon appointment to the legatine office, delivered a speech 'in Roman manner', it showed his Romanisation as a papal legate.

The interconnectedness between 'Rome' and 'papacy' meant that criticism of the papacy could be couched as criticism of Rome and Romanness. It was an established tradition to liken Rome to Babylon, the city of harlots. Scripture provided models for this juxtaposition (1 Peter 5:13; Revelation 17:5).[13] 'Roman greed' became a staple in the arsenal of criticism against the papacy, especially amongst Anglo-Norman writers.[14] For these writers, Rome was an ambiguous symbol and an ambiguous place. Kynan-Wilson has studied the representation of Rome in Anglo-Norman authorship, c. 1100–1250. He concludes that 'the textual evidence … presents no single, homogenous vision of Rome and Roman culture':[15]

---

[10] On William of Malmesbury, see Rodney M. Thomson, *William of Malmesbury*, 2nd edn (Woodbridge: Boydell Press, 2003), and Rodney M. Thomson, Emily Dolmans, and Emily A. Winkler, eds, *Discovering William of Malmesbury* (Woodbridge: Boydell Press, 2017). On Henry of Blois, see William Kynan-Wilson and John Munns, eds, *Henry of Blois: New Interpretations* (Woodbridge: Boydell Press, 2021).

[11] William of Malmesbury, *Historia Novella: The Contemporary History*, ed. Edmund King, trans. K. R. Potter, OMT (Oxford: Clarendon Press, 1998), bk. 2, ch. 25, pp. 50–53.

[12] William Kynan-Wilson, 'Roman Identity in William of Malmesbury's Historical Writings', in *Discovering William of Malmesbury*, ed. Rodney M. Thomson, Emily Dolmans, and Emily A. Winkler (Woodbridge: Boydell Press, 2017), pp. 81–91, at pp. 85–86.

[13] Sylvia Schein, *Gateway to the Heavenly City: Crusader Jerusalem and the Catholic West (1099–1187)* (London and New York: Routledge, 2016), pp. 58–59; Josef Benzinger, *Invectiva in Romam: Romkritik im Mittelalter vom 9. bis zum 12. Jahrhundert* (Lübeck and Hamburg: Matthiesen Verlag, 1968), pp. 1–74.

[14] See, e.g., Iben Fonnesberg-Schmidt and William Kynan-Wilson, 'Smiling, Laughing and Joking in Papal Rome: Thomas of Marlborough and Gerald of Wales at the Court of Innocent III (1198–1216)', *Papers of the British School at Rome* 86 (2018): 1–29, p. 9.

[15] William Kynan-Wilson, 'Rome and Romanitas in Anglo-Norman Text and Image (c.1100–c.1250)' (unpublished PhD dissertation, University of Cambridge, 2012), p. 232.

On the one hand, Rome boasted a rich cultural legacy and its grandeur remained apparent through the city's great buildings, statues, images, and relics, but on the other hand, the corruption of the papal curia and the physical decline of the city formed a stark contrast to these great expectations.[16]

To complicate matters, John Doran has shown how the English monk and writer, Lucian of St Werburgh's Abbey, Chester, took the opposite approach. Writing around 1195, Lucian praised contemporary, Christian, Rome, which St Peter and his successors (the popes) had rescued from the death of paganism. According to Doran, Lucian argued that 'Romulus raised Rome up to great dignity … built great palaces and erected monuments … [but] he was outdone by [St] Peter, who constructed morals and piety'.[17]

While Rome and the papacy became increasingly entwined – eliciting both positive and negative responses – the curia instituted changes in papal self-perception. Especially from the time of Pope Innocent III, the association of the pope with Christ was stressed over that of St Peter, as mentioned above. Key to this change was Innocent's revival of the title *Vicarius Christi* (Vicar of Christ), usage of which can be traced back to Pope Nicholas II (r. 1058–61),[18] but whose full implications Innocent was the first to utilise.[19] As Vicar of Christ, the pope in principle possessed unlimited authority over the Church. Katarína Štulrajterová has noted that the Arab geographer Yāqūt, an outside observer, around 1220 reported that the Christians regarded the pope as the 'vicar of the Messiah'.[20]

Innocent extended this perception to his legates. In a letter from 1198 to the prelates of France, Innocent asserted that one of his legates, tasked with securing peace between France and England, was 'legate of the Apostolic See, nay more of

---

[16] Kynan-Wilson, 'Rome and Romanitas', p. 232.
[17] John Doran, 'Authority and Care: The Significance of Rome in Twelfth-Century Chester', in *Roma Felix: Formation and Reflections of Medieval Rome*, ed. Éamonn Ó Carragain and Carol Neuman de Vegvar (Aldershot: Ashgate, 2007), pp. 307–32, at p. 322.
[18] Michele Maccarrone, *Vicarius Christi: storia del titolo papale* (Rome: Facultas Theologica Pontificii Athenaei Lateranensis, 1952), p. 86; Walter Ullmann, 'The Pontificate of Adrian IV', *The Cambridge Historical Journal* 11, no. 3 (1955): 233–52, pp. 238–39.
[19] Agostino Paravicini-Bagliani, *The Pope's Body*, trans. David S. Peterson (Chicago and London: University of Chicago Press, 2000), pp. 58–59, 71–73, 82–83. Note the 'transitional' character of Cardinal Boso's description of Alexander III (penned shortly after 1178), when 'Lord Pope Alexander was sitting as Christ's Vicar in the Chair of Blessed Peter' ('domnus Alexander papa in beati Petri cathedra tamquam Christi vicarius resideret'); see Cardinal Boso, *Boso's Life of Alexander III*, trans. G. M. Ellis, (Oxford: Basil Blackwell, 1973), p. 67; *Liber Pontificalis*, vol. 2, p. 413.
[20] Katarína Štulrajterová, 'Convivenza, Convenienza and Conversion: Islam in Medieval Hungary (1000–1400 CE)', *Journal of Islamic Studies* 24, no. 2 (2013): 175–98, p. 188.

Christ' ('legatum sedis apostolicae imo Christi').[21] In a letter from 1204, Innocent was even more poignant, claiming that his legates could trace a line to Christ through the pope. In 1204, Cardinal Leo Brancaleoni was on his way to Bulgaria as a legate *a latere* when King Imre of Hungary (r. 1196–1204) detained him.[22] Innocent wrote to Imre:

> … and we advise you [King Imre] to make satisfaction so as to abolish the injury to the cardinal, indeed, actually more to us than to him, but rather directed against the Lord Jesus Christ in us, so that we can experience your devotion in this and are not forced on this account to do anything that can be injurious to you.[23]

The injury to the cardinal was an injury to the pope, which again was an injury to Christ, as Christ was in the pope: 'the Lord Jesus Christ in us' ('domino Iesu Christo in nobis').[24]

The Origins and Development of the Legate a latere

The history of the office of legate *a latere* is long and erratic, and it began in the halls of the Roman bureaucracy. *Legatus*, a Roman term, referred to anyone commissioned or dispatched (from the verb *lego*), which included army commanders, provincial governors, and ambassadors. Medieval usage retained the Roman meaning: *legatus* denoted anybody representing or exercising jurisdiction on behalf of someone else;[25] hence, the important conceptual difference between

---

[21] *Innocentii III Romani Pontificis Opera Omnia*, PL (Paris, 1855), vol. 214, no. 345, col. 320.

[22] On Cardinal Leo Brancaleoni, see Werner Maleczek, *Papst und Kardinalskolleg von 1191 bis 1216. Die Kardinäle unter Coelestin und Innocenz III.* (Vienna: Verlag der Österreichischen Akademie der Wissenschaften, 1984), pp. 137–39. On the legatine mission, see James Ross Sweeney, 'Innocent III, Hungary and the Bulgarian Coronation: A Study in Medieval Papal Diplomacy', *Church History* 42 (1973): 320–34.

[23] James M. Powell, trans., *The Deeds of Pope Innocent III by an Anonymous Author* (Washington, D.C.: The Catholic University of America Press, 2004), ch. lxxviii, p. 121; David Richard Gress-Wright, 'The "Gesta Innocentii III": Text, Introduction and Commentary' (unpublished PhD dissertation, Bryn Mawr College, 1981), p. 148: '… et monemus, in remissionem tibi peccaminum iniungentes, quatenus iniuriam cardinali predicto, immo verius nobis in ipso, quinpotius illatam domino Iesu Christo in nobis, ita satagas abolere …'.

[24] For Innocent's approximation to Christ, see Agostino Paravicini-Bagliani, 'Innocent III and the World of Symbols of the Papacy', trans. Gesine Elisabeth Oppitz-Trotman, in *The Papacy and Communication in the Central Middle Ages*, ed. Iben Fonnesberg-Schmidt et al., *JMH* 44, no. 3 (2018): 261–79.

[25] Figueira, 'The Canon Law', pp. 10–14, 259–60. See also John W. Perrin, '"Legatus" in Medieval Roman Law', *Traditio* 29 (1973): 357–78.

papal legation and other types of legations. Gratian's *Decretum* from the middle of the twelfth century stated that priests and bishops served in Christ's legation ('Iesum Christum, cuius legatione funguntur').[26]

The collocation *a latere* (sometimes *de*, *e*, or *ex latere*) was added in Late Antiquity as a papal qualifying denomination (it is first attested in the conciliar decrees from 343 AD from Sardica).[27] *A latere* translates as 'from the side', implying that the legate was dispatched from the pope's inner circle.

With the fall of the western Roman Empire, papal legation became an erratic occurrence, conceptually imprecise, but used with some vigour in the ninth century by what is sometimes known as the early or the first reform papacy. Nevertheless, legates did not abound in the historical records in the centuries prior to the (second) reform papacy.[28] Between 786 and the rise of the reform papacy in the middle of the eleventh century, evidence of only three legatine missions to England have survived.[29] More legates went to France and Germany, but comparisons with, say, the pontificate of Honorius III (r. 1216–27), reveal stark differences. Honorius III was responsible for sixty-two legations,[30] while France received sixteen legations between 870 and 1049,[31] and Germany around ninety between 739 and 1044.[32] It was the reform popes, particularly Pope Gregory VII,

---

[26] *Decretum magistri Gratiani*, ed. Emil Friedberg, Corpus Iuris Canonici, I (Leipzig: Tauchnitz, 1879), C.7 q.1 c.36; available at https://geschichte.digitale-sammlungen.de/decretum-gratiani/online/angebot (accessed 15 April 2024). For an exposition of the Romano-canonical citation system see James A. Brundage, *Medieval Canon Law* (London: Longman, 1995), pp. 190–205. On the *Decretum*, see Anders Winroth, *The Making of Gratian's Decretum* (Cambridge: Cambridge University Press, 2000); and Melodie Harris Eichbauer, 'Gratian's Decretum and the Changing Historiographical Landscape', *History Compass* 11, no. 12 (2013): 1111–25.

[27] Hamilton Hess, *The Early Development of Canon Law and the Council of Serdica*, 2nd edn (Oxford: Oxford University Press, 2002), c. 7, pp. 214–17. The council of Carthage (419) affirmed the usage of *a latere*; see Charles Munier, ed., *Concilia Africae, A. 345–A.525*, Corpus Christianorum, Series Latina 149 (Turnhout: Brepols, 1974), p. 91.

[28] Rennie, *The Foundations*, esp. pp. 133–35, 137–38, 162–69. See also Kriston Robert Rennie, 'The "Injunction of Jeremiah": Papal Politicking and Power in the Middle Ages', *JMH* 40, no. 1 (2014): 108–22, pp. 113–17.

[29] Helene Tillmann, *Die päpstlichen Legaten in England bis zur Beendigung der Legation Gualas, 1218* (Bonn: Hch. Ludwig, 1926), pp. 7–11.

[30] Heinrich Zimmermann, *Die päpstliche Legation in der ersten Hälfte des 13. Jahrhunderts: Vom Regierungsantritt Innocenz' III. bis zum Tode Gregors IX. (1198–1241)* (Paderborn: Ferdinand Schöningh, 1913), pp. 72–103, 305–9.

[31] Theodor Schieffer, *Die päpstlichen Legaten in Frankreich vom Vertrage von Meersen, 870, bis zum Schisma von 1130* (Berlin: Verlag Dr. Emil Ebering, 1935), pp. 11–48.

[32] Otto Engelmann, *Die päpstlichen Legaten in Deutschland bis zur Mitte des 11. Jahrhunderts*. (Marburg: Chr. Schaaf, Spezialdruckerei für Dissertationen, 1913), pp. 1–108.

who reinvented the legatine institution as part of their reform programme.[33] It is this fact more than anything else that explains the nature of the legatine institution in the High Middle Ages.

In the beginning of the era of the reform papacy, the popes mainly relied on local churchmen to be their legates. Gregory VII's two most famous and effective legates were Bishop Hugh of Die (r. 1073–82) and Bishop Amatus of Oléron (r. 1073–89), later archbishop of Bourdeaux. Gregory, especially, appointed local prelates as legates for extended periods to assert his authority throughout Christendom. For that reason, Gregory took an interest in their powers, but he never bothered to distinguish between various kinds of legates.[34]

Gregory's pontificate ended in a schism that lasted into the reigns of three of his successors. Schism was a recurrent phenomenon during much of the twelfth century (1080–1102, 1105–11, 1118–21, 1130–38, and 1159–77), mainly due to papal–imperial conflicts. These schisms made communication between regional legates and the curia difficult, and it was because of this issue that popes began to rely more on curial legates, especially cardinals, rather than regional prelate-legates.[35]

Popes also revived the *a latere* terminology which, by then, had nearly disappeared. Popes favoured such legates over other types of legates.[36] During his pontificate, Pope Adrian IV (r. 1154–59), for instance, exempted the abbey of St Gilles from the legatine authority of the archbishop of Narbonne but not from the authority of legates *a latere*.[37]

Arguably, the watershed moment was represented by Alexander III's pontificate. Popes had appointed a third of the cardinalate as legates between 1099 and 1159; in contrast, Alexander appointed more than half of his cardinals as legates.

---

[33] Richard Antone Schmutz, 'Medieval Papal Representatives: Legates, Nuncios and Judges-Delegate', *Studia Gratiana* 15 (1972): 441–63, p. 447; Rennie, *The Foundations*, pp. 170–71. See also Kriston Robert Rennie, '*Imbutus divinis dogmatibus*: Some Remarks on the Legal Training of Gregorian Legates', *Revue historique de droit français et étranger* 85, no. 2 (2007): 301–13.

[34] Rennie, *The Foundations*, pp. 118–19, 168–69; Claudia Zey, 'Die Augen des Papstes. Zu eigenschaften und Vollmachten päpstlicher Legaten', in *Römisches Zentrum und Kirchliche Peripherie. Das Universale Papsstum als Bezugspunkt der Kirchen von den Reformpapsten bis zu Innozenz III*, ed. Jochen Johrendt and Harald Müller (Berlin: Walter de Gruyter, 2008), pp. 99–103, at p. 86; Richard Antone Schmutz, 'The Foundations of Medieval Papal Representation' (unpublished PhD dissertation, University of Southern California, Los Angeles, 1966), p. 16.

[35] Zey, 'Die Augen des Papstes', pp. 98–103.

[36] Schmutz, 'The Foundations', p. 16.

[37] Étienne Goiffon, ed., *Bullaire de l'abbaye de Saint-Gilles* (Nîmes: P. Jouve, 1882), pp. 77–78.

He used them to combat the schism facing him in the years between 1159 and 1177.[38] In his biography of Alexander III, Cardinal Boso (d. after 1178) wrote:

> Since, moreover, the very schismatics [Antipope Victor IV (r. 1159–64) and his supporters], lacking faith in either justice or truth, had ensnared the prelates of the churches and the princes of the world with cunning contrivances of lies and had tried to make them side with their error, it seemed a useful counsel to the pope that he should send some of his brothers [cardinals] from his own side (*ex latere suo*) to the various regions of the world. Only by their zeal and labours would enlightenment come about the facts of the election to the Apostolic See, and the whole body of the faithful, once the truth was known, be made united and firm in their trust in Catholic unity.[39]

The cardinals assumed a key role in Alexander's fight for his pontificate; they carried his version of events to Christendom.[40] Cardinals were even noted appearing in the Holy Land. In his *Chronicon*, Archbishop William of Tyre (r. 1175–84/5) reported that much consternation arose at the court of the king of Jerusalem when Cardinal John arrived in 1161, since the manner of his reception would signal whose side King Baldwin III (r. 1143–63) took.[41]

---

[38] Zey, 'Die Augen des Papstes', pp. 95–108. See also Schmutz, 'The Foundations', p. 16; Karl Rueß, *Die rechtliche Stellung der päpstlichen Legaten bis Bonifaz VIII.* (Paderborn: Ferdinand Schöningh., 1912), p. 110; and Barbara Zenker, 'Die Mitglieder des Kardinalkollegiums von 1130 bis 1159' (unpublished PhD dissertation, Julius-Maximilians-Universität zu Würzburg, 1964), p. 229.

[39] Cardinal Boso, *Boso's Life of Alexander III*, pp. 51–52 (translation adjusted); *Liber Pontificalis*, vol. 2, p. 403: 'Et quoniam ipsi scismatici de iustitia et veritate diffidentes, prelatos ecclesiarum et principes orbis exquisitis mendaciorum figmentis circumvenerant et in partem sui erroris inducere temptaverant, utile consilium domno pape visum est ut aliquos de fratribus suis ad diversas mundi provincias ex latere suo destinare deberet, per quorum siquidem studium et laborem super facto electionionis apostolice declaratio fieret, et universitas fidelium in fide unitatis catholice cognita veritate solidaretur.'

[40] Ian S. Robinson, *The Papacy 1073–1198: Continuity and Innovation* (Cambridge: Cambridge University Press, 1990), pp. 146–49, 166–69; Myriam Soria, 'Alexander III and France: Exile, Diplomacy and the New Order', in *Pope Alexander III (1159–81): The Art of Survival*, ed. Peter D. Clarke and Anne J. Duggan (Farnham: Ashgate, 2012), pp. 181–201, at pp. 181–82. See also Cletus Chidozie Nwabuzo, 'Ambassadors of Reform: Legates and Legatine Authority in the Pontificate of Alexander III (1159–1181)' (unpublished PhD dissertation, Saint Louis University, 2001).

[41] William of Tyre, *A History of Deeds Done Beyond the Sea*, trans. Emily Atwater Babcock and A. C. Krey, 2 vols (New York: Columbia University Press, 1943), vol. 2, bk. 18, ch. 29, p. 286; William of Tyre [Willelmvs Tyrensis], *Chronicon*, ed. R. B. C. Huygens, H. E. Mayer, and G. Rösch, 2 vols, CCCM 63 (Turnhout: Brepols, 1986), vol. 2, bk. 18, ch. 29,

It was the role of the cardinals in the schism more than anything else that catapulted the cardinal-legates to the fore. Claudia Zey argues that when 'Alexander III finally triumphed over Frederick Barbarossa, the cardinals triumphed with him'.[42] The cardinals 'stepped forth as the alter ego of the bishop of Rome', as Harald Müller asserts, 'and thereby became almost one with the pope himself'.[43] The pre-eminence of the cardinal-legates *a latere* was to a great extent a product of the pontificate of Alexander III, during which time the cardinals appropriated the highest legatine office. It is telling that the Third Lateran Council (1179) restricted the size of the entourages of cardinals, not of legates as such.[44] The canonist Johannes Teutonicus, writing in 1215/18, simply assumed that cardinals were legates whenever encountered outside the pope's entourage.[45]

This confidence should not obscure the fact that the development of the legatine office was erratic and, to some degree, random. When thirteenth-century canonists undertook the daunting task of defining the legatine office, they were confronted with a plethora of decretals, some of which contradicted each other. More often than not, each decretal directed a legate to address a specific issue rather than making general rulings on the office or its powers.[46] It was from this

---

p. 853. See also Cardinal Boso, *Boso's Life of Alexander III*, pp. 51–52; *Liber Pontificalis*, vol. 2, p. 403.

[42] 'Alexander III. schließlich über Friedrich Barbarossa triumphierte, triumphierten die Kardinäle mit ihm': Zey, 'Die Augen des Papstes', p. 107.

[43] Harald Müller, 'The Omnipresent Pope: Legates and Judges Delegate', in *A Companion to the Medieval Papacy: Growth of an Ideology and Institution*, ed. Keith Sisson and Atria A. Larson (Leiden: Brill, 2016), pp. 199–219, at p. 205.

[44] Norman P. Tanner, ed., *Decrees of the Ecumenical Councils, Vol. 1: Nicaea I to Lateran V*, 2 vols (London: Sheed & Ward, 1990), c. 4, p. 213: 'cardinals should not exceed twenty or twenty-five [horses]' ('cardinales vero viginti vel viginti quinque non excedant').

[45] Figueira, 'The Canon Law', p. 109. For the dating of Johannes Teutonicus' writings, see Kenneth Pennington and Wolfgang P. Müller, 'The Decretists: The Italian School', in *The History of Medieval Canon Law in the Classical Period, 1140–1234: From Gratian to the Decretals of Pope Gregory IX*, ed. Kenneth Pennington and Wilfried Hartmann (Washington, D.C.: The Catholic University of America Press, 2008), pp. 121–73, at p. 148.

[46] Sources illuminating the procedure for appointing legates are very sparse before the late Middle Ages; see Franz Wasner, 'Fifteenth-Century Texts on the Ceremonial of the Papal "Legatus a Latere"', *Traditio* 14 (1958): 295–358, pp. 302–4; Charles Keenan, 'The Limits of Diplomatic Ritual: The Polish Embassy of Giovanni Francesco Commendone (1572–1573) and Criticism of Papal Legates in Early Modern Europe', *Royal Studies Journal* 3, no. 2 (2016): 90–111, pp. 92–96; Zimmermann, *Die päpstliche Legation*, pp. 243–44; J. B. Sägmüller, *Die Thätigkeit und Stellung der Cardinale bis Papst Bonifaz VIII. Historisch-canonistisch untersucht und dargestellt* (Freiburg im Breisgau: Herdersche Verlagshandlung, 1896), p. 60; and Ina Feinberg Friedländer, *Die päpstlichen Legaten in Deutschland und Italien am Ende des XII Jahrhunderts (1181–1198)* (Berlin: Matthiesen Verlag, 1928), p. 135.

state of affairs that the canonists strove to extract some form of consistency and general applicability. That the canonists managed to do so with some success is a testimony to their abilities.

The Classification of the Legate a latere

The usual approach to classifying the legate *a latere* both in modern scholarship and in medieval writings is by contrasting various types of legates. Apart from the *legatus a latere*, the traditional classification of papal legates recognises two other types: the *legatus natus* and the *legatus missus* (or *nuncius apostolicus*). The *legatus natus* is classified as a resident legate (often a bishop or an archbishop) with a wide array of powers over a province (often a kingdom or a number of dioceses), and the *legatus missus* as a sort of messenger-legate with limited powers.[47] However, Joseph Figueira has pointed out that these designations rarely appear in the medieval records; they were products of the reforms during and after the Council of Trent, held between 1545 and 1563. Medieval canonists and other ecclesiastical writers used a variety of designations. Only legates *a latere* are (somewhat) consistently labelled in the medieval records, but sometimes also appear as cardinal-legates (*cardinalis legati*).[48] I will use these designations interchangeably, unless circumstances warrant otherwise.

The most important definition can be uncovered in one of Pope Gregory IX's decretals, located within his important collection of decretals, the *Liber Extra* (1234). The decretal defines the legate *a latere* as the only legate with the power to absolve excommunicates everywhere for violent crimes against the clergy.[49]

---

[47] A series of early twentieth-century German studies initiated modern scholarship on papal legates and introduced the now traditional classifications. Illicia Sprey provides a succinct overview of the scholarship; see Ilicia Jo Sprey, 'Papal Legates in English Politics, 1100–1272' (unpublished PhD dissertation, University of Virginia, Charlottesville, 1998), pp. 13–26; but see, e.g., Rueß, *Die rechtliche Stellung*; Otto Schumann, *Die päpstlichen Legaten in Deutschland zur Zeit Heinrichs IV. und Heinrichs V. (1056–1125)* (Marburg: Universitäts-Buchdruckerei von Joh. Aug. Koch, 1912); Zimmermann, *Die päpstliche Legation*; Johannes Bachmann, *Die päpstlichen Legaten in Deutschland und Skandinavien (1125–1159)* (Berlin: Matthiesen Verlag, 1913); Engelmann, *Die päpstlichen Legaten in Deutschland*; Friedländer, *Die päpstlichen Legaten*; and Werner Ohnsorge, *Päpstliche und gegenpäpstliche Legaten in Deutschland und Skandinavien 1159–1181* (Berlin: E. Ebering, 1928). See also Claudia Zey, 'Stand und Perspektiven der Erforschung des päpstlichen Legatenwesens im Hochmittelalter', in *Rom und die Regionen: Studien zur Homogenisierung der lateinischen Kirche im Hochmittelalter*, ed. Jochen Johrendt and Harald Müller (Göttingen: De Gruyter, 2012), pp. 157–66.

[48] Figueira, 'The Canon Law', pp. 254–64, 272, 283–84.

[49] Friedberg, *Liber Extra*, X 1.30.9; Figueira, 'The Canon Law', pp. 260–61, 264.

According to Figueira, subsequent typology hinged on this criterion: the differing abilities of legates to absolve violent crimes.[50]

Succeeding canonists and popes expanded upon Pope Gregory's earlier definition. These include Cardinal Geoffrey of Trani (d. 1245), Cardinal Hostiensis/Henry of Segusio (d. 1271), Pope Innocent IV (r. 1243–54), Bernard of Parma (d. 1266), and Bernard of Montmirat/Abbas Antiquus (d. 1296). Innocent IV's assertion that only cardinals could be legates *a latere* is particularly noteworthy.[51] Also of significance is one of Pope Clement III's decretals, which equates cardinal-legates with legates *a latere*, although, as Figueira notes, the decretal 'does not assert that the latter group [legates *a latere*] consists exclusively of members of the former [cardinal-legates]'.[52] Nevertheless, according to Figueira, thirteenth-century canonists consistently assumed that cardinal-legates were legates *a latere* and only rarely discussed the possibility that someone other than a cardinal could be a legate *a latere* – and in those instances usually dismissed the notion outright.[53]

This leaves the question of what characterised cardinal-legates *a latere*. Figueira has meticulously studied all of the writings of the canonists until *c.* 1300, arriving at some general attributes. According to him, legates *a latere* were defined relative to other types of legates by:[54]

1. Their ability to absolve individuals excommunicated for violent crimes against clerics everywhere, and at all times.
2. Their right to larger procurations (*procuratio*) even outside their legatine area of operation.[55]
3. Their pre-eminent jurisdiction in the presence of other legates.
4. Their right to confer vacant benefices in their legatine area.
5. Their right to use legatine insignia in the presence of other legates.
6. Their privileged recruitment, with membership being almost exclusively drawn from the cardinalate.

---

[50] Figueira, 'The Canon Law', p. 260.
[51] Ibid., pp. 265–66.
[52] Ibid., p 267; Friedberg, *Liber Extra*, X 5.39.20
[53] Figueira, 'The Canon Law', pp. 264–75.
[54] See ibid., esp. pp. 254–95. See also Paul Hinschius, *System des Katholischen Kirchenrechts: Mit besonderer Rücksicht auf Deutschland*, 6 vols (Berlin: Verlag von I. Guttentag, 1869), vol. 1, pp. 511–22; and Rueß, *Die rechtliche Stellung*, pp. 103–15.
[55] Procurations were the duty of ecclesiastical institutions to supply food and lodging to superiors; see Carlrichard Brühl, 'Zur Geschichte der procuratio canonica vornehmlich im 11. und 12. Jahrhundert', in *Le istituzioni ecclesiastiche della 'societas christiana' dei secoli XI–XII* (Milan: Vita e pensiero, 1974), pp. 419–31. For procurations in England, see William E. Lunt, *Financial Relations of the Papacy with England to 1327* (Cambridge, MA: The Mediaeval Academy of America, 1939), pp. 532–70.

Cardinal-legates *a latere* were closer to the pope, possessing greater authority and more rights than other legates. Popes often permitted cardinals to demand procurations despite exemptions.[56] Nevertheless, this list remains incomplete, failing to outline what legates *a latere* truly could do or what the popes expected them to do, and even legates themselves might have had some doubts. In 1213, Pope Innocent III dispatched Cardinal-Legate Nicholas to England to facilitate reconciliation between King John and the prelates of the English Church following years of conflict. Shortly after his arrival, Nicholas wrote to the pope:

> I beg your Holiness, for the avoidance of every kind of ambiguity, to let me know your will by letter, clearly and distinctly, and give me power to act notwithstanding earlier letters obtained from the Apostolic See.[57]

Cardinal Nicholas faced an extraordinarily complex situation,[58] but his desperate plea for clarity and sufficient authority speaks volumes about the limitations of his office, underscoring contrasts between the conceptual grandeur of the legatine office and the realities on the ground. Did Nicholas not bring Christ with him? Did he not saturate his surroundings with Petrine power? According to the canonist Bernard of Pavia (d. 1213), writing sometime in the 1190s, 'a legate is said to be someone to whom the rule over a country or province is committed'.[59] Figueira observes that Bernard's dictum became a canonistic commonplace, with numerous writers repeating it almost verbatim,[60] but the extent to which a legate truly ruled his province was obviously unclear.

Nicholas Vincent argues that 'there was no such thing as a typical legation'.[61] Vincent is to some extent correct. Nearly all legations were responses to breakdowns in normalcy, with legates only appearing when an issue could not be

[56] Rueß, *Die rechtliche Stellung*, p. 189.
[57] Angelo Mercati, 'La Prima Relazione del Cardinale Nicolò de Romanis sulla sua legazione in Inghilterra', in *Essays in History Presented to Reginald Lane Poole*, ed. H. W. C. Davis (Oxford: Clarendon Press, 1927), pp. 274–89, at p. 285: 'quare uestre obnixe supplico sanctitati quatinus ad amouendam ambiguitatem omnimodam clare distincte et aperte per uestras litteras uestram mihi aperiatis de omnibus uoluntatem, mandantes ut non obstantibus litteris hactenus a sede apostolica impetratis rite procedere ualeam in predictis.' Translated by Christopher R. Cheney, *Pope Innocent III and England* (Stuttgart: Hiersemann, 1976), p. 350.
[58] See pp. 162–63, 172–74 for further details.
[59] Bernard of Pavia, *Summa Decretalium*, ed. Bernard Ernst Adolph Laspeyres (Regensburg: G. Iosephum Manz, 1860), p. 18: 'legatus dicitur, cui aliqua patria vel provincia regenda committitur.' Translated by Figueira, 'The Canon Law', pp. 420–21.
[60] Figueira, 'The Canon Law', pp. 420–21.
[61] Nicholas Vincent, ed., *The Letters and Charters of Cardinal Guala Bicchieri, Papal Legate in England, 1216–1218* (Woodbridge: Boydell Press, 1996), p. xlvi.

resolved through existing local power structures or by direct referral to Rome. The pope dispatched legates when he was unable to resolve the matter himself. Pope Innocent III, as cited above, told the clerics and citizens of Milan that he was 'compelled' to act 'through our brothers [cardinals]' whenever 'we cannot personally attend'.[62] These instances varied considerably, and popes almost always issued legatine mandates tailored to specific instances.

Legatine Powers

The varying circumstances of each legation are likely responsible for the ambiguities surrounding the powers of the legate *a latere*. Nevertheless, it would be misleading to claim that it is impossible to make any general assessments. Figueira, whose impressive thesis is the leading work on the canon law of papal legation, has made some important observations.[63]

According to Figueira, the powers of papal legates centred on the *provincia* (the province), denoting the geographical region in which a legate operated. Although canonists only coined the term *provincia* in the thirteenth century, a similar notion seems to have guided earlier practice. The extent to which a legate could exercise his array of powers depended on his presence within his province. All legates, including legates *a latere*, could only employ a limited set of their powers outside their province, usually procuration, which enabled them to travel and reach their province. The province was usually equated to a well-defined ecclesiastical structure (such as a metropolitan area) or a secular division (often a kingdom), but the popes occasionally employed imprecise terms such as 'German parts' or 'Gallican parts' to delineate a province.[64]

The legate's entry into his own province revolved around the recognition, identification, and acceptance of legatine authority, making it a crucial step in the overall mission. The canonists agreed that the letter of credence was the crucial instrument of legatine authentication (even if they disagreed about the implications of damaged or missing letters).[65] Some canonists argued that cardinals did not need to show letters of credence, including the aforementioned Johannes Teutonicus (writing 1215/18) and Cardinal Hostiensis (writing c. 1250–71).[66]

---

[62] Friedberg, *Liber Extra*, X 3.39.17.
[63] Other studies include Rueß, *Die rechtliche Stellung*; Perrin, '"Legatus" in Medieval Roman Law'; and Zey, 'Stand und Perspektiven', p. 164, n. 21.
[64] Figueira, 'The Canon Law', pp. 415–61.
[65] Ibid., pp. 96–105, 109.
[66] Ibid., pp. 109, 398–404. Figueira dates Hostiensis' writings on p. 127. On Hostiensis, see, e.g., Kenneth Pennington, 'Henricus de Segusio (Hostiensis)', in *Popes, Canonists, and Texts, 1150–1550* (Aldershot: Variorum, 1993), XVI: 1–12.

However, neither Johannes nor Hostiensis explained how papal subjects were to identify cardinals, leaving one to assume that identification depended on such things as appearance and ceremony. The next chapter will revisit this issue.

When a legate entered his province, his full range of powers became available to him. Canonists of both the twelfth and thirteenth centuries assumed that the pope retained some powers, which he needed to delegate expressly.[67] By the middle of the thirteenth century, canonists had settled on calling them 'papal reserved powers', although it is clear that canonists of the twelfth century took the existence of such powers for granted. Thirteenth-century canonists distinguished between the 'general mandate', which contained legatine powers *ex officio*, and the 'special mandate', which contained those powers specifically delegated.[68]

The fiercest debate among canonists was about the extent of the general mandate. Huguccio, a canon lawyer writing in the late 1180s, argued that legatine powers encompassed both the spiritual and the temporal, enabling legates to suspend, depose, institute, and demote clerics as well as grant prebends and decide criminal and civil cases, and even minor cases pertaining to the faith. He also asserted that legates could administer papal property.[69] Huguccio was supported by the so-called *Summa 'Animal est substantia'/Summa Bambergensis* (written 1206 × 1210). Most canonists were much more restrictive, particularly (though not exclusively) when it came to legatine authority over bishops. Suggestions for constraints on legatine powers over bishops included compulsory cooperation with the episcopate (Benencasa, writing in the 1190s); possession of a special mandate (Johannes Teutonicus, 1215/18; Bartholomeus Brixiensis, *c.* 1236); or sufficient sacramental rank (Johannes Faventinus, 1170s; Simon of Bisignano, 1177 × 1179; Sicardus of Cremona, *c.* 1180). Most twelfth-century canonists also considered the ability of legates to depose and excommunicate to be limited in cases involving other prelates and lower ranks of clergy.[70] However, during the first half of the thirteenth century, most canonists did away with the restrictions on legatine disciplinary powers over non-bishops, arguing that legates could excommunicate, demote, and depose. Most, however, retained the view that legatine authority was

---

[67] Figueira, 'The Canon Law', pp. 49–56.
[68] Ibid., pp. 298–330.
[69] Figueira, 'The Canon Law', pp. 58–61. For the dating, see Pennington and Müller, 'The Decretists', p. 148.
[70] Figueira, 'The Canon Law', pp. 58–70. For introductions to these canonists, see Pennington and Müller, 'The Decretists'; and Rudolf Weigand, 'The Transmontane Decretists', in *The History of Medieval Canon Law in the Classical Period, 1140–1234: From Gratian to the Decretals of Pope Gregory IX*, ed. Kenneth Pennington and Wilfried Hartmann (Washington, D.C.: The Catholic University of America Press, 2008), pp. 174–210.

restricted on major episcopal matters, such as deposition, transfer, and restoration. Similarly, legatine sentences on the faith necessitated a special mandate.[71]

Most canonists accepted the legate as a judge-ordinary, that is, a judge with powers to hear cases not specifically delegated to him. Local prelates (and a few canonists) argued against the right of legates to interfere in episcopal and abbatial courts, even though popes insisted that legates had such powers. It was thus possible to appeal to the legate in place of the pope.[72] However, unless the pope forbade it, an aggrieved party could also appeal to the pope from the legatine court.[73]

The majority of canonists argued that legates could not convene councils *ex officio*. This is surprising, considering that archbishops were permitted to do so.[74] It was precisely this point that made Hostiensis express the minority opinion that legates *a latere* had the authority to convene councils in their provinces without a special mandate.[75]

As this overview of the powers of papal legates illustrates, legates were powerful forces within the Church, even if it remains unclear precisely how powerful they were. Canon law on papal legation was no different from other types of canon law insofar as the impetus (at least in part) for its development was to strengthen papal authority.[76] Canon law on papal legates aimed to assert the papal right of legation – the right to govern the Church. To that effect, legatine jurisdiction surpassed other ordinary jurisdiction, temporarily creating a supreme governing body with executive and judicial powers in the legatine province. Legates might intervene in local ecclesiastical affairs to rectify abuses or reform recalcitrant clergy, demoting and deposing as well as granting prebends. The purpose was to bring papal authority and papal reform to the provinces.

Nonetheless, legatine powers and their delimitation often remained vague and contested. This is not merely due to some modern inability to fully comprehend the past; Cardinal Nicholas' desperate plea to Pope Innocent III demonstrates that even legates could find it difficult to interpret their own powers and their authority to act independently. Waiting for Innocent's response might have delayed

---

[71] Figueira, 'The Canon Law', pp. 303–20, 493–503.
[72] Ibid., pp. 75–99, 404–7. See also Kenneth Pennington, 'Johannes Teutonicus and Papal Legates', *Archivum Historiae Pontificiae* 21 (1983): 183–94.
[73] Figueira, 'The Canon Law', pp. 342–45.
[74] Ibid., pp. 23–43, 308, 498.
[75] Robert Charles Joseph Figueira, 'Papal Reserved Powers and the Limitations on Legatine Authority', in *Popes, Teachers and Canon Law in the Middle Ages*, ed. James Ross Sweeney and Stanley Chodorow (Ithaca, NY: Cornell University Press, 1989), pp. 191–211, at pp. 197–98.
[76] See, e.g., Robinson, *The Papacy 1073–1198*, pp. 179–208. For an overview of the development of canon law in the twelfth and thirteenth centuries, see, e.g., Brundage, *Medieval Canon Law*.

Nicholas' mission by several weeks if not months. Furthermore, such ambiguities highlight how the purpose of dispatching legates was never to create a permanent class of powerful prelates situated between the pope and the rest of the Church. Popes created legates to enhance their own authority and to expand their sphere of influence. They usually maintained tight control over their legates and occasionally reversed their decisions.[77] Popes had no problem dispensing with their legates once they were no longer needed.

Restricting Legatine Powers and Autonomy

The reform papacy needed its legates. The popes of that time, especially Gregory VII, believed they were facing massive, urgent problems requiring immediate correction. Consequently, they equipped regional prelate-legates with considerable autonomy and extensive powers.[78] Bishop Hugh of Die, one of Gregory VII's most renowned legates, convened councils and deposed bishops on his own initiative.[79] Gregory did the same as a legate before becoming pope.[80]

Eleventh-century legates were not exempt from oversight – Gregory VII demanded reports and reserved the ultimate right of appeal – but their freedom of movement was substantial.[81] However, from the beginning of the twelfth century, popes slowly, yet progressively, curtailed legatine autonomy. According to Ian Robinson, Amadeus of Lyon was the last to wield 'Gregorian' legatine powers when he deposed Archbishop Stephen of Vienne in 1143.[82] Henceforth, popes made such decisions themselves. Pope Innocent III reprimanded one of his cardinal-legates, Cinthius of S. Lorenzo in Lucina, for translating the bishop of Troia to Palermo, and forbade legates from making translations in the future.[83] Cardinal-

---

[77] Figueira, 'The Canon Law', pp. 250–53.
[78] Robinson, *The Papacy 1073–1198*, pp. 149–57; Wilhelm Janssen, *Die päpstlichen Legaten in Frankreich von Schisma Anaklets II. bis zum Tode Coelestins III. (1130–1198)* (Cologne: Böhlau, 1961), pp. 170–73.
[79] Kriston Robert Rennie, '"Uproot and Destroy, Build and Plant": Legatine Authority under Pope Gregory VII', *JMH* 33, no. 2 (2007): 166–80; Kriston Robert Rennie, 'Hugh of Die and the Legatine Office under Gregory VII: On the Effects of a Waning Administration', *Revue d'histoire ecclésiastique* 103, no. 1 (2008): 27–49.
[80] H. E. J. Cowdrey, *Pope Gregory VII, 1073–1085* (Oxford: Clarendon Press, 1998), p. 32.
[81] See, e.g., H. E. J. Cowdrey, ed. and trans., *The Register of Pope Gregory VII: An English Translation* (Oxford: Oxford University Press, 2002), bk. 1, no. 16, pp. 17–18 and bk. 6, no. 16, pp. 297–98; Caspar Erich, ed., *Das Register Gregors VII. (Gregorii VII Registrum)*, 2 vols, MGH: Epp. sel. 2 (Berlin: Weidmannsche Buchhandlung, 1920–23), vol. 1, bk. 1, no. 16, pp. 25–26; vol. 2, bk. 6, no. 16, pp. 421–23.
[82] Robinson, *The Papacy 1073–1198*, p. 177. See also Janssen, *Die päpstlichen Legaten in Frankreich*, p. 161.
[83] Figueira, 'Papal Reserved Powers', pp. 192–93. The ruling was included in the *Liber*

Legate Otto spent several years (1237–41) advising King Henry III of England and enacting reforming measures. Julian Gardner observes that the chronicler Matthew Paris 'disapprovingly described the legate Otto as "… alter Papa in Anglia"'. Gardner argues that this was perhaps 'a juridical truism'.[84] However, Otto took no independent action regarding episcopal or royal cases brought before him; he always referred such cases back to Rome for instructions or judgement.[85] Otto was no 'alter Papa in Anglia', despite Matthew's hostile assertion.

During the thirteenth century, the number of reserved papal powers grew steadily, if erratically. Around 1216, Johannes Teutonicus listed sixteen reserved papal powers.[86] On the other hand, Cardinal Geoffrey of Trani only mentioned six reserved powers in the 1240s, and Pope Innocent IV, in his capacity as a canonist, only listed three. However, Geoffrey's and Innocent's lists were in all likelihood samples rather than exhaustive catalogues.[87] In his *Summa* (completed around 1253), Hostiensis listed sixty-three reserved powers. In 1279, William Durand (the famous canonist and later bishop of Mende) listed eighty-nine reserved powers.

The significance of the papal reserved powers is underscored by a noteworthy poem first recorded by Hostiensis. The poem lists the reserved powers, and although the origins of the poem are unclear, Figueira argues that the canonist Raymond of Peñafort probably composed the poem around 1220.[88] Figueira emphasises the poem's mnemonic character, arguing that it was designed to assist individuals in remembering each of the reserved powers.[89] Successive canonists added new verses to the poem, demonstrating its continued relevance.[90]

Concurrently with the development of reserved powers, a change in papal representation took place. Examining the frequency of legatine missions, Clifford Kyer has identified an uneven but undeniable decline in the frequency of such missions from the latter half of the thirteenth century. Meanwhile, the frequency of papal nuncios (messengers) substantially increased, more than compensating

---

    Extra; see Friedberg, *Liber Extra*, X I.30.3–4. On episcopal translations, see Mary Ellen Sommar, 'The Changing Role of the Bishop in Society: Episcopal Translation in the Middle Ages' (unpublished PhD dissertation, Syracuse University, New York, 1998).

[84] Julian Gardner, 'Legates, Cardinals, and Kings: England and Italy in the Thirteenth Century', in *L'Europa e l'arte italiana*, ed. Max Seidel (Venice: Marsilio, 2000), pp. 75–94, at p. 76. Gardner referred to Matthew Paris, *CM*, vol. 5, p. 414. See pp. 200–13 for more information on Cardinal Otto and Matthew Paris.

[85] See Dorothy M. Williamson, 'Some Aspects of the Legation of Cardinal Otto in England, 1237–41', *EHR* 64, no. 251 (1949): 145–73.

[86] Figueira, 'Papal Reserved Powers', pp. 196–97.

[87] Ibid., p. 197.

[88] Ibid., pp. 200–1.

[89] Ibid., p. 201. The poem is quoted in full ibid., pp. 199–200.

[90] Ibid., pp. 198–201.

for the decrease in legatine missions. Popes also equipped these nuncios with highly specific powers tailored to each individual mission (Kyer suggests calling them 'solemn nuncios'). The outcome was a limitation on comprehensive, semi-independent legatine power and presence in Europe, while simultaneously maintaining tight control over those who represented papal authority in the provinces. Popes did not entirely do away with legates, but their apex was over as the thirteenth century drew to a close.[91]

These changes likely resulted from interrelated developments within the Church and in society at large. As mentioned previously, during the twelfth and thirteenth centuries, travel activity and urbanisation increased, while communication networks became stronger and more reliable, facilitating faster and easier transfer of decision-making to Rome.[92] By the Late Middle Ages, popes expected legates to dispatch reports weekly.[93]

Simultaneously, in Rome (and wherever the pope resided), the bureaucratic, administrative, and legal structures improved substantially. Initially, when the curia assumed the role as the Church's Supreme Court, it was understaffed and ill-equipped for the task.[94] One way for the popes to ease the workload was to appoint legates, particularly regional archbishops, to filter and judge local cases. Robinson has labelled these legates 'archbishop-legates' in order to distinguish them from their predecessors of the reform papacy. These figures relieved the curia of much work, until the judges-delegate gradually appropriated their usefulness to the

---

[91] See Clifford Ian Kyer, 'The Papal Legate and the "Solemn" Papal Nuncio 1243–1378: The Changing Pattern of Papal Representation' (unpublished PhD dissertation, University of Toronto, 1979), esp. pp. 26–36.

[92] See, e.g., Derek Keene, 'Towns and the Growth of Trade', in *The New Cambridge Medieval History, IV c. 1024–c. 1198, Part I*, ed. David Luscombe and Jonathan Riley-Smith (Cambridge: Cambridge University Press, 2004), pp. 47–85; and Kathryn L. Reyerson, 'Commerce and Communications', in *The New Cambridge Medieval History, V, c. 1198–1300*, ed. David Abulafia (Cambridge: Cambridge University Press, 1999), pp. 50–70.

[93] Vincent, *The Letters and Charters*, p. xlvi.

[94] See Patrick Zutshi, 'The Roman Curia and Papal Jurisdiction in the Twelfth and Thirteenth Centuries', in *Die Ordnung der Kommunikation und die Kommunikation der Ordnungen. Band 2: Zentralität: Papsttum und Orden im Europa des 12. und 13. Jahrhunderts*, ed. Christina Andenna, Klaus Herbers, and Gert Melville, Schriften der Villa Vigoni (Stuttgart: Franz Steiner Verlag, 2013), pp. 213–27; and Patrick Zutshi, 'Petitioners, Popes, Proctors: The Development of Curial Institutions c.1150–1250', in *Pensiero e Sperimentazioni Istituzionali Nella 'Societas Christiana' (1046–1250): Atti della Sedicesima Settimana Internazionale di Studio Mendola, 21–31 agosto 2004*, ed. Giancarlo Andenna (Milan: Storia Ricerche, 2007), pp. 265–93. See also Benedict Wiedemann, 'Doorkeepers, the Chamberlain and Petitioning at the Papal Court, c.1150–1200', *Historical Research* 91, no. 253 (2018): 409–25.

papacy in the decades around 1200.[95] The judges-delegate were papally appointed local judges, whom popes tasked with delivering judgements in specific cases. A litigant would initially present a case in Rome. The pope would refer the case to a group of local ecclesiastics, appointing them as judges on an *ad hoc* basis. Having the court operate locally was much easier than transferring the whole process to Rome, but the pope simultaneously retained centralised control.[96] One might view the judges-delegate in the same way as the 'solemn nuncios', as a transition from broader legatine powers to routine, *ad hoc* commissions aimed at resolving specific issues.

In the last decades of the twelfth century, the scope of legatine activity simultaneously broadened (somewhat paradoxically) to encompass aspects of the secular sphere. The shift is attributable to Alexander III's pontificate. According to Robinson, 'legates were compelled to be diplomats and statesmen not only by the needs of the Alexandrine cause but also by the serious conflict which coincided with the schism, the Becket dispute in England'.[97] Legates went from being only reformers and chairs of councils to acting as diplomats in secular matters as well. In 1181, Henry of Marcy, cardinal-bishop of Albano, became the first papal legate to personally direct an army (he directed it against heretics in Languedoc).[98] In northern Italy, cardinals began to hold long-term legations to cement alliances with the Lombard cities against the Empire even after the conclusion of the Alexandrine schism.[99] Popes also used legates to compel kings to participate in crusades. Legates, moreover, worked hard to obtain peace between the kings of England and France.[100]

---

[95] Robinson, *The Papacy 1073–1198*, pp. 170–76; Müller, 'The Omnipresent Pope', pp. 215–19.

[96] See Jane E. Sayers, *Papal Judges Delegate in the Province of Canterbury, 1198–1254: A Study in Ecclesiastical Jurisdiction and Administration* (Oxford: Oxford University Press, 1971), esp. pp. 1–41; and Harald Müller, 'Generalisierung, dichte Beschreibung, kontrastierende Einzelstudien? Stand und Perspektiven der Erforschung delegierter Gerichtsbarkeit des Papstes im Hochmittelalter', in *Rom und die Regionen: Studien zur Homogenisierung der lateinischen Kirche im Hochmittelalter*, ed. Jochen Johrendt and Harald Müller (Göttingen: De Gruyter, 2012), pp. 145–56.

[97] Robinson, *The Papacy 1073–1198*, p. 167. On the Becket dispute, see Anne J. Duggan, *Thomas Becket* (London: Arnold, 2004).

[98] Robinson, *The Papacy 1073–1198*, p. 169. For another conspicuous example, see Joseph P. Donovan, *Pelagius and the Fifth Crusade* (Philadelphia: University of Pennsylvania Press, 1950).

[99] Robinson, *The Papacy 1073–1198*, pp. 168–69. One may note the interest of Pope Innocent III's biography, the *Gesta Innocentii III*, in legatine military and diplomatic action in Italy; see Powell, *The Deeds*, esp. ch. ix–xl, pp. 9–55; Gress-Wright, 'Gesta Innocentii', esp. pp. 6–60.

[100] Robinson, *The Papacy 1073–1198*, p. 169.

Conclusion

Legates were grand and contradictory figures. On the one hand, the cardinalate absorbed the highest legatine powers and honours during the latter part of the twelfth century. The cardinalate became almost one with the pope, embodying both him and the papal doctrine of the Universal Church. Legates dispensed papal reform and governed the churches of Europe, and over time their influence extended beyond ecclesiastical matters, encompassing diplomacy and secular affairs. On the other hand, as Latin Christendom recognised papal and legatine pre-eminence, popes gradually reined in legatine autonomy. The codification of legal principles only occurred simultaneously with the reduction of legatine independence. As canonists asserted that legates ruled provinces, popes limited their ability to rule independently. As cardinals increasingly travelled the European roads, reforming and passing sentences, recourse and appeal to the pope himself became more prevalent and feasible. Legates were not powerless figures, but the popes subjected their pre-eminence and authority to increased oversight. However, none of this mattered if they could not effectively argue and assert their legatine offices beyond Rome.

2

Expressing Papal and Legatine Authority: Insignia and *Adventus*

As an extension of papal authority, it was crucial for a papal legate to be easily recognisable. At the core of a legate's authority lay his ability to associate himself with all things papal, including Rome, St Peter, and, ultimately, Christ. Invoking one aspect automatically invoked the others through association: to invoke 'Rome' was automatically to invoke 'pope', 'St Peter', and, eventually, 'Christ' (or *Vicarius Christi*). The *a latere* designation facilitated these associations because it highlighted the legate's close proximity to the pope. Entering his province, the legate had to display his connection to the pope, thereby reinforcing the concept of the universal Roman Church and compelling people to believe that he ultimately brought the presence of St Peter and Christ with him.

To achieve this objective, the curia employed a strategy centred around insignia and ceremony. This was (and still is) one of the most potent languages of power. The pope acted, in this way, no differently from other medieval lords, operating largely within an existing framework of lordship.

Both apostolic insignia and apostolic ritual evolved significantly during the age of the reform papacy. This was part of a broader development within Christendom among the clergy. During the early Middle Ages, according to Maureen Miller, ecclesiastics had adhered to 'the exhortation of Jesus not to worry about clothes'.[1] However, during the eleventh century, clerics moved to embrace 'the gold-embellished finery of the Old Testament priesthood'.[2] The papacy's influence on these changes was undoubtedly complex, but whatever the causal factors, papal insignia and clothing evolved significantly during the age of the reform papacy,

---

[1] Maureen C. Miller, *Clothing the Clergy: Virtue and Power in Medieval Europe, c. 800–1200* (Ithaca, NY: Cornell University Press, 2014), p. 2. This choice not to worry about clothes was a deliberate inversion of the language of power and, hence, recognisable as such. In effect, the Church sought to remove the prestige associated with conspicuous consumption, instead arguing that poor clothing and inattention to display were signs of true spirituality and, hence, prestigious.

[2] Ibid., p. 2. These changes in clerical dress sparked fierce debate; see ibid., esp. pp. 177–237.

even if apostolic appearance had always been – and continued to be – subject to continuous reconfiguration and reinterpretation.[3]

The papal *adventus*, too, underwent significant development during this period. As previously mentioned, Twyman has unveiled the link between the rise of the reform papacy and the battles for the meaning of the papal *adventus*.[4] Often absent from Rome, papal ceremonial activities also had to adapt to various locations.[5] In other instances, the papal *adventus* influenced *adventus* ceremonies elsewhere. For instance, according to Miller, the Florentine bishop's inauguration *adventus* was modified to incorporate certain elements of the papal *adventus*.[6]

And what of the papal legates? Rennie suggests that the origins of legatine clothing and ceremony date back to the early Middle Ages.[7] The Annals of St-Bertin recorded that the papal legates at the synod of Ponthion in 876 were 'clad in the Roman fashion' ('more Romano vestitis').[8] The terseness of the description implies that 'Roman fashion' was self-evident. In Thangmar of Hildesheim's *Vita Bernwardi*, composed shortly after the turn of the millennium, Thangmar seems to have assumed that his audience were able to visualise the appearance of Cardinal-Legate Frithericus: 'he was clothed with the complete apostolic insignia as the pope himself would go forth'.[9]

---

[3] See esp. Agostino Paravicini-Bagliani, *The Pope's Body*, trans. David S. Peterson (Chicago and London: University of Chicago Press, 2000); but also Agostino Paravicini-Bagliani, 'Innocent III and the World of Symbols of the Papacy', trans. Gesine Elisabeth Oppitz-Trotman, in *The Papacy and Communication in the Central Middle Ages*, ed. Iben Fonnesberg-Schmidt et al., *JMH* 44, no. 3 (2018): 261–79; and Maureen C. Miller, 'Clothing as Communication? Vestments and Views of the Papacy c.1300', in ibid., 280–93.

[4] See Susan E. Twyman, *Papal Ceremonial at Rome in the Twelfth Century* (London: Boydell Press, 2002).

[5] See Anne J. Duggan, 'The Benefits of Exile', in *Pope Eugenius III (1145–1153): The First Cistercian Pope*, ed. Iben Fonnesberg-Schmidt and Andrew Jotischky (Amsterdam: Amsterdam University Press, 2018), pp. 171–95; and esp. Pascal Montaubin, 'Qu'advient-il du cérémonial papal hors de Rome (milieu XIe–milieu XVe siècles)?', in *Rituels et transgressions de l'antiquité à nos jours*, ed. Geneviève Hoffmann and Antoine Gaillot (Amiens: Encrage, 2009), pp. 109–19.

[6] Maureen C. Miller, 'The Florentine Bishop's Ritual Entry and the Origins of the Medieval Episcopal *Adventus*', *Revue d'histoire ecclésiastique* 98 (2003): 5–28.

[7] Kriston Robert Rennie, *The Foundations of Medieval Papal Legation* (New York: Palgrave Macmillan, 2013), pp. 167–68; Kriston Robert Rennie, 'The Ceremonial Reception of Medieval Papal Legates', *JEH* 69, no. 2 (2018): 1–20, pp. 1–2.

[8] Janet L. Nelson, trans., *The Annals of St-Bertin* (Manchester: Manchester University Press, 1991), p. 194; G. Waitz, ed., *Annales Bertiniani*, MGH: SS rer. Germ. 5 (Hannover: Hahn, 1883), p. 131.

[9] Thangmar of Hildesheim, 'Vita Bernwardi episcopi Hildesheimensis', in *Annales, chronica et historiae aevi Carolini et Saxonici*, ed. Georg Heinrich Pertz, MGH: SS 4

Papal legates drew inspiration from the pope, both in terms of their insignia and their ceremonial practices. This is the focus of the present chapter, which will commence with an exploration of legatine insignia, before moving on and devoting considerable attention to the ceremony of the *adventus*.

Legatine Insignia

For all the importance of legatine insignia – and the evidence bears out that it was important – our knowledge of the evolution and even composition of legatine insignia is scanty. Not until the later Middle Ages did members of the curia produce extensive tracts on legatine insignia. Other sources, mainly narrative, only reported on legatine insignia when something unusual warranted it. For instance, in the *Vita Gunneri*, a biography of Bishop Gunner of Viborg (r. 1222–51), the biographer never mentioned the insignia of Cardinal Gregory, who was in Denmark in 1222, despite the cardinal-legate's prominent and, according to the *Vita*, laudable part in the election of Gunner as bishop of Viborg.[10] The cardinal's insignia was not relevant to the biographer's story, even if the actions of the legate were.

What remains are only a handful of reports on legatine insignia. Other researchers have examined these (I have only identified a couple of hitherto unknown reports), including Karl Rueß, Wasner, Figueira, Tapio Salminen, and Kriston Rennie.[11] There are no major disagreements, nor do I challenge the general con-

---

(Hannover: Hahn, 1841), pp. 754–82, at p. 771: 'omnibus insigniis apostolicis acsi papa procedat infulatus'; translated by Rennie, 'The Ceremonial Reception', p. 7.

[10] M. Cl. Gertz, ed., 'Vita Gvnneri episcopi Vibergensis', in *Scriptores Minores Historiæ Danicæ Medii Ævi* (Copenhagen: Selskabet for udgivelse af kilder til dansk historie, 1970), vol. 2, pp. 265–78, at pp. 265–67; Jesper Hjermind and Kristian Melgaard, eds, 'Vita Gunneri episcopi Vibergensis', in *Gunner: Bisp i Viborg 1222–1251*, trans. Johannes Thomsen (Løgstrup: Forlaget Viborg, 2010), pp. 10–27, at pp. 10–12. On Cardinal Gregory's mission, see Michael H. Gelting, 'Skånske Lov og Jyske Lov: Danmarks første kommisionsbetænkning og Danmarks første retsplejelov', in *Jura & Historie: Festskrift til Inger Dübeck som forsker*, ed. Finn Taksøe-Jensen (Copenhagen: Jurist- og Økonomforbundets Forlag, 2003), pp. 43–80, at pp. 73–76.

[11] Karl Rueß, *Die rechtliche Stellung der päpstlichen Legaten bis Bonifaz VIII.* (Paderborn: Ferdinand Schöningh., 1912), pp. 185–210, esp. pp. 204–10; Franz Wasner, 'Fifteenth-Century Texts on the Ceremonial of the Papal "Legatus a Latere"', *Traditio* 14 (1958): 295–358; Franz Wasner, '"Legatus a Latere": Addenda Varia', *Traditio* 16 (1960): 405–16; Robert Charles Joseph Figueira, 'The Canon Law of Medieval Papal Legation' (unpublished PhD dissertation, Cornell University, Ithaca, NY, 1980), pp. 380–89; Tapio Salminen, 'In the Pope's Clothes: Legatine Representation and Apostolic Insignia in High Medieval Europe', in *Roma, magistra mundi. Itineraria culturae medievalis: mélanges offerts au Père L. E. Boyle à l'occasion de son 75e anniversaire*, ed. Jacqueline

sensus. The sources include: the *Chronica* of Gervase of Canterbury, the *Gesta Regis Henrici Secundi* of Roger of Howden, the *Chronica Majora* of Matthew Paris, and the *Annals* of George Acropolita (mid thirteenth century). Statutes from the Fourth Lateran Council supply additional information, as do glosses from Bernard of Montmirat, writing *c.* 1259–66, and Hostiensis, completing his *Commentaria/Lectura* just before 1271.[12] A few genuine and forged papal letters also mention legatine insignia. By combining these disparate sources, it is possible to outline a plausible and distinct stereotypical image of the insignia of a papal legate *a latere*. The image produced shows the legate wearing red clothes, using a mitre, riding a white horse, having a processional cross borne before him, and perhaps being shaded by a baldachin. The legate, in many respects, looked like the pope from afar.

Several sources strongly suggest that red was the most important and conspicuous outward signifier for the legate. This is unsurprising given that the colour red was one of the most important apostolic signifiers. The pope was vested in a red mantle upon his election, making a direct link between the colour and the office. Red's symbolism was multifaceted, alluding to the Roman Empire, the high priests of the Old Testament, and the passion of Christ (the blood).[13]

Roger of Howden noted that the two legates (one a cardinal) visiting England at the turn of 1186 were 'clothed in red garments' ('rubeis indumentis induti').[14] In their commentaries on canon law, Bernard of Montmirat and Hostiensis asserted that legatine insignia included 'red garments' ('vestes rubeas' and 'vestibus rubeis', respectively).[15] George Acropolita stressed Cardinal Pelagius' red dress when he visited Constantinople.[16] In a letter from 1248 to the patriarch of Jerusalem, Pope

---

Hamesse (Louvain-la-Neuve: Brepols, 1998), pp. 349–54; and Rennie, 'The Ceremonial Reception', pp. 7–12. See also Pascal Montaubin, 'De Petits papes en voyage: les légats en France et en Angleterre au XIIIe siècle', in *Se déplacer du moyen âge à nos jours: actes du 6e colloque européen de Calais, 2006–2007*, ed. Stéphane Curveiller and Laurent Buchard (Calais: Les amis du Vieux Calais, 2009), pp. 58–70, esp. pp. 66–68.

[12] For the dating of Bernard of Montmirat, see Figueira, 'The Canon Law', pp. 126–27. For the dating of Hostiensis, see Brian Tierney, *Foundations of the Conciliar Theory: The Contribution of the Medieval Canonists from Gratian to the Great Schism* (Cambridge: Cambridge University Press, 1955), p. 259.

[13] Francesca Pomarici, 'Papal Imagery and Propaganda: Art, Architecture, and Liturgy', in *A Companion to the Medieval Papacy: Growth of an Ideology and Institution*, ed. Keith Sisson and Atria A. Larson (Leiden: Brill, 2016), pp. 85–120, at pp. 92, 104–5; Paravicini-Bagliani, *The Pope's Body*, pp. 83–87.

[14] *Gesta*, vol. 2, pp. 3–4. For further information about Roger of Howden and this passage, see pp. 116–18.

[15] Figueira, 'The Canon Law', p. 340 and p. 380, respectively.

[16] Petrus de Marca, *Dissertationum de Concordia Sacerdotii et Imperii, seu de Libertatibus Ecclesiae Gallicanae, Libri Octo: Quibus accesserunt eiusdem auctoris Dissertationes*

Innocent IV mentioned that only his 'legates *a latere*' ('legato a latere') were allowed 'to walk in red garments' ('incedere cum rubeis').[17] In one of Matthew Paris' drawings in the *Chronica Majora*, Cardinal-Legate Otto is depicted draped in red at the council of London in 1237. Otto is not the only figure draped in red in this illustration, but red dominates his figure.[18]

In 1215, the Fourth Lateran Council prohibited clerics from wearing red outside the church.[19] Thirteenth-century councils occasionally reiterated the prohibition, showing that the ban continued to matter.[20] The prohibition was not only about papal and legatine exclusivity; the Fourth Lateran also banned green clothing and gilded spurs, taking pains to argue against extravagance, while subsequent local councils also banned other colours, such as yellow.[21] Yet, the fact that among the clergy only the pope, his legates, and his cardinals were allowed to wear red outside the church undoubtedly set them apart. The cardinals acquired the right to wear red as part of their everyday trappings sometime around the middle of the thirteenth century. Wasner assumes that Pope Boniface VIII (r. 1294–1303) granted this right,[22] but when the Perugians in protest burned effigies of Pope Martin IV (r. 1281–85) and his cardinals, the chronicler Salimbene de Adam (c.

Ecclesiasticae Varii Argumenti, ed. Stephanus Baluzius (Roboreti [Rovereto, Italy]: Societatis, 1742), bk. 5, ch. 52, 9, p. 302. See also Rueß, *Die rechtliche Stellung*, p. 204; Wasner, 'Fifteenth-Century Texts', p. 301; Richard Antone Schmutz, 'The Foundations of Medieval Papal Representation' (unpublished PhD dissertation, University of Southern California, Los Angeles, 1966), pp. 79–80; Figueira, 'The Canon Law', p. 384; and Rennie, 'The Ceremonial Reception', pp. 8–9.

[17] Élie Berger, ed., *Les registres d'Innocent IV: Recueil des bulles de ce pape*, vol. 2 (Paris: Ernest Thorin, 1887), no. 4225, p. 21.

[18] See Suzanne Lewis, *The Art of Matthew Paris in the Chronica Majora* (Berkely and Los Angeles: University of California Press, 1987), plate IX, between pp. 290 and 291 (Corpus Christi College, Cambridge, MS 16, fo. 107). Cardinal Otto is also depicted in Matthew's *Historia Anglorum*; see Lewis, fig. 158, p. 250 (British Library, London, MS Royal 14, C.VII, fo. 126).

[19] 'Let them [clerics] not enjoy cloth of red or green nor long sleeves or shoes with embroidery or peaked toes, saddles, harness, breastplates and gilded spurs, or wearing another superfluity' ('pannis rubeis aut viridibus, necnon manicis aut sobtularibus consutitiis seu rostratis, sellis, frenis, pectoralibus et calcaribus deauratis aut aliam superfluitatem gerentibus non utantur'); see Antonio García y García, ed., *Constitutiones Concilii quarti Lateranensis una cum commentariis glossatorum*, Monumenta iuris canonici, A: Corpus glossatorum 2 (Vatican City: Biblioteca Apostolica Vaticana, 1981), c. 16, pp. 64–65.

[20] Thomas M. Izbicki, 'Forbidden Colors in the Regulation of Clerical Dress from the Fourth Lateran Council (1215) to the Time of Nicholas of Cusa (d. 1464)', *Rutgers University Community Repository* (2005): 105–14, pp. 106, 108–9.

[21] Izbicki, 'Forbidden Colors', pp. 108–14; Miller, *Clothing the Clergy*, pp. 11–50, esp. pp. 35–50.

[22] Wasner, 'Fifteenth-Century Texts', p. 315.

1221–90) reported that they dressed the effigies in red.[23] The use of red clothing was clearly a well-established practice at the time.

Legates also wore mitres. The mitre is a sort of white bicorn hat. The pope initially reserved its use for himself, but the cardinals and later the bishops slowly appropriated its use – the cardinals probably during the eleventh century and the bishops during the twelfth.[24] The pope also sometimes granted the use of the mitre as a special privilege to certain abbots.[25] Nevertheless, when cardinal-legates ordained as priests or deacons used mitres, the mitre became a legatine symbol. Gervase of Canterbury reported that the two legates (one a cardinal) visiting England at the turn of 1186 were 'both advancing mitred' ('ambo mitrati incedentes'), although the cardinal was 'but a deacon' ('sed diaconus'), and the other legate merely the 'elect of the church of Coventry' ('Coventrensis ecclesiæ electus').[26] Roger of Howden, reporting on the same legates as Gervase, simply noted that they used 'mitres' ('mitrati').[27] Matthew Paris also depicted Cardinal-*Deacon* Otto with a mitre.[28] It is likewise noteworthy that Pope Leo IX (r. 1049–54) granted the use of the mitre as a papal insignia to Bishop Eberhard of Trier (r. 1047–66) and Archbishop Adalbert of Bremen (r. 1043–72).[29] Later in the eleventh and twelfth centuries, the archbishops of Hamburg-Bremen found themselves in a precarious situation. They sought to protect themselves by fabricating a series of papal grants, in which they insisted on the grant of the mitre as a papal insignia.[30]

Sometimes the legate rode a white horse. Hostiensis claimed that the use of a 'white palfrey' ('palefredo albo') was a legatine prerogative.[31] Helene Tillmann and Ilicia Sprey both note that King Henry II supplied Cardinal Vivian with a white horse.[32] The Pipe Rolls note in 1176 the payment of 'ten [probably marks or

---

[23] Salimbene de Adam, *Chronica*, ed. Giuseppe Scalia, 2 vols, CCCM 125 (Turnhout: Brepols, 1998–99), vol. 2, pp. 773–74.

[24] Miller, *Clothing the Clergy*, pp. 201–6; Joseph S. J. Braun, *Die liturgische Gewandung im Occident und Orient: Nach Ursprung und Entwicklung, Verwendung und Symbolik* (Freiburg im Breisgau: Herdersche Verlagshandlung, 1907), pp. 447–53; Joseph S. J. Braun, 'Mitre', in *The Catholic Encyclopedia* (New York: Robert Appleton, 1911); available at www.newadvent.org/cathen/10404a.htm (accessed 15 April 2024).

[25] Braun, *Die liturgische Gewandung*, pp. 452–57.

[26] Gervase, vol. 1, p. 346. For further information on Gervase and this passage, see pp. 143–44.

[27] Gervase, vol. 2, pp. 3–4

[28] Lewis, *The Art of Matthew Paris*, plate IX, between pp. 290 and 291.

[29] Braun, 'Mitre'; Wolfgang Seegrün and Theodor Schieffer, eds, *Provincia Hammaburgo-Bremensis*, Regesta Pontificum Romanorum: Germania Pontifica 6 (Göttingen: Vandenhoeck & Ruprecht, 1981), no. 81, pp. 56–57.

[30] Seegrün and Schieffer, *Provincia Hammaburgo-Bremensis*, nos. 15, 16, 27, 43, 45, pp. 28–29, 35–36, 43–45.

[31] Cited in Figueira, 'The Canon Law', p. 380.

[32] Helene Tillmann, *Die päpstlichen Legaten in England bis zur Beendigung der Legation*

pounds] for a white palfrey for the use of the legate Vivian' ('pro .j. palefrido albo ad opus Viuiani legati').[33] It is noteworthy that both Hostiensis and the Pipe Rolls refer to a palfrey. The palfrey was a high-status horse, valued for its smooth gait and used for riding long distances.[34] The origins of the white horse as a legatine insignia probably lay with the pope, who rode a white horse from the early twelfth century or even earlier.[35] At the end of the thirteenth century, the pope might drape the horse in red, playing on a red-white contrast which symbolised Christ-like and imperial virtues.[36]

Legates, too, used certain paraphernalia for themselves or for their mounts while travelling on horseback. A couple of papal grants to Archbishop Adalbert of Bremen refer to a *naccus* as some form of horsecloth.[37] Hostiensis mentioned the use of gilded spurs ('calcaribus deauratis') by papal legates.[38] Since the Fourth Lateran prohibited the clergy from using gilded spurs, the legatine use of such spurs supports the notion of their exclusivity.[39]

A cross-bearer might head a legatine procession. Processional crosses had been in regular use since the early Middle Ages and were not reserved for legates. The pope at some point acquired his own special processional cross, but other prelates,

---

Gualas, 1218 (Bonn: Hch. Ludwig, 1926), p. 77; Ilicia Jo Sprey, 'Papal Legates in English Politics, 1100–1272' (Unpublished PhD Dissertation, University of Virginia, Charlottesville, 1998), pp. 216–18.

[33] PR, vol. 26, Henry II (1176–77), p. 47.

[34] R.H.C. Davis, *The Medieval Warhorse: Origin, Development and Redevelopment* (London: Thames and Hudson, 1989), p. 67.

[35] See Miller, 'The Florentine Bishop's Ritual Entry', p. 21. Concerning the importance of the horse to the pope, see Jörg Traeger, *Der reitende Papst: Ein Beitrag zur Ikonographie des Papsttums* (Munich: Verlag Schnell & Steiner, 1970), esp. pp. 71–104; but note the corrections to the study in Elisabeth Garms-Cornides, 'Review of *Der Reitende Papst*', *The Art Bulletin* 55, no. 3 (1973): 451–56.

[36] See Paravicini-Bagliani, *The Pope's Body*, pp. 83–92.

[37] Seegrün and Schieffer, *Provincia Hammaburgo-Bremensis*, nos. 78, 81, pp. 55–57. Baldric of Florennes (d. 1157/58), in his *Gesta Alberonis*, inserted an account of the Christmas procession at Trier at the end of 1147, in which Baldric noted how Pope Eugenius III (r. 1145–53) used a *naccus* on his horse; see Baldric of Florennes [Baldericus], 'Gesta Alberonis Archiepiscopi', in *Chronica et gesta aevi Salici*, ed. Georg Heinrich Pertz, MGH: SS 8 (Hannover: Hahn, 1848), pp. 243–60, at ch. 23, p. 255: 'when the lord pope, riding with a horsecloth' ('cum dominus papa, cum nacco equitans'). The Roman clergy used white saddlecloths from time immemorial; see L. Duchesne, *Christian Worship: Its Origin and Evolution: A Study of the Latin Liturgy up to the Time of Charlemagne*, trans. M. L. McLure, 4th edn (London: Society for Promoting Christian Knowledge, 1912), pp. 396–97. See also Duggan, 'The Benefits of Exile', pp. 182–87.

[38] See Appendix 1.

[39] García y García, *Constitutiones Concilii quarti Lateranensis*, c. 16, pp. 64–65. See also Appendix 1.

including archbishops and bishops, also used processional crosses.[40] The use of the cross as a legatine insignia was therefore a matter of legates taking precedence over other clergy. Gervase of Canterbury reported that the two legates entering England around Christmas 1186, apparently to the chagrin of Archbishop Baldwin, 'had mitres and crosses in the presence of the archbishop of Canterbury' ('præsentia Cantuariensis archiepiscopi … mitras habuerunt et cruces').[41] Roger of Howden mentioned how the same two legates always used their crosses wherever they went ('cruces ante se portari fecerunt ubicunque ambulabant').[42] Roger also quoted a letter from Bishop Hugh de Nonant (r. 1185–98) which detailed how Bishop William Longchamp, King Richard's chancellor and papal legate, 'hurried to Canterbury, in order that he there might receive the cross of the pilgrim as he seemly should, and lay aside the cross of legation'.[43] In his *Chronica Majora*, Matthew Paris provided an account of Cardinal Otto's use of a cross at the council in 1237. He reported how Otto, legate and cardinal – but also 'just' deacon – went in procession into the church of St Paul with the two English archbishops (York and Canterbury) following him, but only the legate had a cross with him.[44]

Two other groups of sources provide further evidence. First, some of the aforementioned genuine and forged papal grants to Archbishop Adalbert of Bremen insist on the cross as a legatine insignia.[45] Second, canon five of the Fourth Lateran forbade the patriarch of Constantinople from using the cross banner/flag ('crucis uexillum') in the presence of the pope and his legates.[46] It was not a cross per se, but it seems likely that there was some sort of connection.

---

[40] Herbert Thurstan, 'The Cross and Crucifix in Liturgy', in *The Catholic Encyclopedia* (New York: Robert Appleton, 1908); available at www.newadvent.org/cathen/04533a.htm (accessed 15 April 2024). See also pp. 144–45.

[41] Gervase, vol. 1, p. 346.

[42] *Gesta*, vol. 2, pp. 3–4.

[43] Ibid., p. 218: 'Cantuariam properavit, ut ibi sicut decebat crucem acciperet peregrinationis, et deponeret crucem legationis.'

[44] 'And with the Archbishops of Canterbury and York preceding him, with a solemn procession, with the cross and lit candles, and with a litany, he ascended his throne' ('Et præcedentibus archiepiscopis Cantuariensi et Eboracensi eum, cum processione sollenni, cum cruce et cereis accensis, et cum letania, sedem suam ascendit'); see Matthew Paris, *CM*, vol. 3, p. 416.

[45] See Seegrün and Schieffer, *Provincia Hammaburgo-Bremensis*, nos. 15, 16, 27, 81, pp. 28–29, 35–36, 56–57.

[46] 'Indeed, let them have before themselves the banner of the Lord's cross carried everywhere, except in the city of Rome and anywhere the supreme pontiff is present or his legate using the insignia of apostolic dignity' ('Dominice uero crucis uexillum ante se faciant ubique deferri, nisi in urbe Romana et ubicumque summus pontifex presens extiterit aut eius legatus utens insigniis apostolice dignitatis'); see García y García, *Constitutiones Concilii quarti Lateranensis*, c. 5, p. 52. See also Figueira, 'The Canon Law', p. 340.

Lastly, Bernard of Montmirat mentioned the baldachin ('tentorium') as a legatine insignia.[47] Although he is the only one to mention a baldachin, there is no inherent reason to distrust his information. Perhaps the reason only Bernard of Montmirat mentions the baldachin was that it was not a very important legatine insignia?

MEANING AND SIGNIFICANCE

The status of the baldachin as a legatine insignia aside, Cardinal-Legate John of SS. Giovani e Paolo presumably would have liked a baldachin to shade him from the sun when he visited the Holy Land in 1161. His mission, as Pope Alexander III's legate *a latere*, was to enlist the support of King Baldwin III against Antipope Victor IV.[48]

The chronicler Archbishop William of Tyre reported on the legate's visit.[49] He described how King Baldwin initially denied the legate entry, because, as William claimed, Baldwin feared taking sides in the schism. The king argued that they should bar the legate entry. However, according to William, the king also said that 'if the legate, laying aside his legatine insignia, desired to go as a pilgrim to the holy places for the sake of prayer, permission should be given'.[50] William never mentioned the composition of the insignia, ostensibly presuming his audience's familiarity with the items. Still, it is obvious that the legatine insignia had prominent symbolic significance in his account. If the legate displayed his insignia openly, it would signal the king's acceptance of the legate's papal authority; hence, it would show the king's acceptance of Alexander as pope. Conversely, transforming the legate into a pilgrim and removing his insignia would eliminate his symbolic significance: he would no longer carry the pope's authority. In the end, 'however, the opinion of those, who asserted that the legate should be received, prevailed' ('tamen prevaluit sententia eorum, qui legatum esse recipiendum asserebant'). Archbishop William quipped that, upon entry, the legate proved

---

[47] Figueira, 'The Canon Law', p. 340.
[48] Cardinal Boso, *Boso's Life of Alexander III*, trans. G. M. Ellis (Oxford: Basil Blackwell, 1973), pp. 51–52; *Liber Pontificalis*, vol. 2, p. 403.
[49] On William of Tyre, see Peter W. Edbury and John Gordon Rowe, *William of Tyre: Historian of the Latin East* (Cambridge: Cambridge University Press, 1988).
[50] William of Tyre, *A History of Deeds Done Beyond the Sea*, trans. Emily Atwater Babcock and A. C. Krey, 2 vols (New York: Columbia University Press, 1943), vol. 2, bk. 18, ch. 29, p. 286 (translation adjusted); William of Tyre [Willelmvs Tyrensis], *Chronicon*, ed. R. B. C. Huygens, H. E. Mayer, and G. Rösch, 2 vols, CCCM 63 (Turnhout: Brepols, 1986), vol. 2, bk. 18, ch. 29, p. 853: 'legato vero, si tanquam peregrinus orationis gratia, absque insignibus legationis, ad loca sancta vellet accedere, dandam esse licentiam … faciendi.' See also Ian S. Robinson, *The Papacy 1073–1198: Continuity and Innovation* (Cambridge: Cambridge University Press, 1990), pp. 162, 363.

'burdensome' ('onerosus') to 'many, who had approved of his arrival' ('multis, quibus eius adventus placuerat').[51]

Cardinal-Legate John's visit to the Holy Land during a schism was unusual, but it was under such conditions that commentators began to take an interest in the meaning of the legatine insignia. It seems commentators only showed interest in insignia when their use was part of something unusual or had some special significance. This is analogous to the commentators' reporting on rituals. It is probably the case that any type of symbolic communication had to have some special significance to arouse the interest of commentators.

Matthew Paris also noted the importance of legatine insignia. In 1247, Pope Innocent IV and Frederick II (king 1198–1250, emperor 1220–50) were locked in conflict, causing the pope to dispatch legates across Europe in order to propagandise against the emperor (at least according to Matthew). The problem was – again according to Matthew – that English kings could legally deny admittance to papal legates.[52] However:

> He [Pope Innocent IV] therefore dispatched one legate into Germany, another into Italy, another into Spain, another indeed into Norway; besides certain (sophistic) legates with great power, whom he commanded should be sent into England (deceitfully) without insignia, lest he should appear to violate the manifest privilege of the lord king [Henry III].[53]

'Sophistocos' (sophistic) and 'subdole' (deceitfully) are written under erasures. This was clearly part of an attempt to make the text less offensive.[54] Possible offences aside, Matthew's assertion here is plain: the deliberate removal of legatine display on these figures exercising legatine powers constituted a scandalous subversion of the established order. In Matthew's eyes, the pope tampered with the symbolic meaning of legatine insignia in a most irregular and problematic fashion.

---

[51] William of Tyre, *A History of Deeds*, vol. 2, bk. 18, ch. 29, p. 286 (translation adjusted); William of Tyre, *Chronicon*, vol. 2, bk. 18, ch. 29, p. 854.
[52] See p. 211.
[53] Matthew Paris, *EH*, vol. 2, p. 218 (translation adjusted); Matthew Paris, *CM*, vol. 4, p. 612: 'Unum igitur legatum in Alemanniam, alium in Ytalium, alium in Hispaniam, alium vero in Norwegiam destinavit, præter quosdam legatos (sophisticos) cum magna potestate, quos in Angliam (subdole) sine insignibus, ne videretur manifeste privilegium domini regis infringere, duxit transmittendos.'
[54] See Richard Vaughan, *Matthew Paris* (Cambridge: Cambridge University Press, 1958), pp. 117–20; and David A. Carpenter, 'Chronology and Truth: Matthew Paris and the *Chronica Majora*', in *Matthew Paris Essays*, ed. James Clark (forthcoming); available at https://finerollshenry3.org.uk/redist/pdf/Chronologyandtruth3.pdf (accessed 15 August 2023).

Notions about the intimate connection between insignia and legatine identity and authority likely had their roots in ideas about the nature of communities and representation. Scholars have pointed out that medieval representational thinking saw communities as single beings, and in keeping with the scriptural model, casting them in bodily terms.[55] Romans 12:4–5 states:

> For as in one body we have many members, but all the members have not the same office [or function] / So we, being many, are one body in Christ; and every one members one of another.[56]

Commentators such as Abbot Bernard of Clairvaux (r. 1115–53), John of Salisbury (c. 1120–80), and Bishop Otto of Freising (r. 1138–58) applied ideas about bodily unity to the pope and his cardinals, referring to cardinals as 'part of the pope's body' (*pars corporis pape*).[57] The curia held similar ideas, as evidenced in the writings of Cardinal Boso:

> His brothers [Pope Alexander's cardinal-bishops] who had remained in the City [Rome] after his departure followed in his footsteps and remained attached to their head like limbs to their body.[58]

Figueira argues that once the cardinalate absorbed the highest legatine honours, an intermingling of beliefs surrounding cardinals and legates took place, particularly in thirteenth-century decretalist thinking.[59] Hostiensis, for example, argued that only cardinals could be legates *a latere*.[60] In his *Summa*, Hostiensis asserted that 'these legates, who emanate from the side of the lord pope … and these are

---

[55] See, e.g., Jeannine Quillet, 'I – Community, Counsel and Representation', in *The Cambridge History of Medieval Political Thought c.350–c.1450*, ed. James Henderson Burns (Cambridge: Cambridge University Press, 1988), pp. 520–72. See also Salminen, 'In the Pope's Clothes', pp. 343–49.

[56] *The Holy Bible, Douay-Rheims Version: Translated from the Latin Vulgate*, revised by Richard Challoner (1752), Romans 12:4–5; Robert Weber and Bonifatius Fischer, eds, *Biblia Sacra: iuxta vulgatem versionem*, 3rd edn (Stuttgart: Deutsche Bibelgesellschaft, 1983), Romans 12:4–5: 'sicut enim in uno corpore multa membra habemus omnia autem membra non eundem actum habent / ita multi unum corpus sumus in Christo singuli autem alter alterius membra.'

[57] Paravicini-Bagliani, *The Pope's Body*, pp. 63–64.

[58] Cardinal Boso, *Boso's Life of Alexander III*, p. 73; *Liber Pontificalis*, vol. 2, p. 417: 'Fratres vero qui post eum in Urbe remanserant secuti sunt eius vestigia et suo capiti tamquam menbra sui corporis adheserunt'.

[59] Figueira, 'The Canon Law', pp. 143–44. See also Paravicini-Bagliani, *The Pope's Body*, pp. 64–65.

[60] Figueira, 'The Canon Law', p. 144.

[have] the greatest of authority … they are understood [to be] part of the body of the lord pope'.[61]

The *Gesta Innocentii III* (The Deeds of Innocent III), composed around 1210 by an anonymous member of the papal curia, expresses ideas about the presence of the pope in his legates.[62] The author at one point noted that Byzantine messengers had approached Innocent III, 'asking that he himself would visit his [Emperor Alexios III's] empire through his legates' ('rogans ut ipse per legatos suos eius imperium visitaret').[63] Note the use of 'ipse', which denotes the presence of the pope. Clear evidence for such beliefs led Franz Wasner to argue that:

> In the *legatus a latere* the pope is made present, and the papal *auctoritas* causes the human, in fact even the ecclesiastical, person of the envoy to be forgotten. That is why he wears the papal mantle, why the ceremonial of the pope surrounds him.[64]

Essentially, legates *a latere* wore papal attire and used papal ceremony to communicate and insist on their papal affiliation. The legate *a latere* looked and behaved like the pope to convey the presence of papal authority.

The Legatine Ceremonial Welcome: The Adventus

One important way for the legate to convey papal authority was through the *adventus*: the ceremonial welcome bestowed on all great dignitaries upon their initial entry. This was a pivotal moment, providing the framework for the immediate relationship between the dignitary and the hosts.

As cited previously, the basic meaning of the ceremony was, in the words of Julie Kerr, 'a symbolic recognition of … position and authority'.[65] It is also worth citing Margot Fassler's description of the *adventus* as 'the fundamental ritual structure underlying the great majority of liturgical processions and public

---

[61] Cited in Figueira, n. 43, pp. 143–44: 'Quidam legati qui emanent ex latere domini Papae … et hi maximae authoritatis sunt … intelliguntur pars corporis domini Papae.'

[62] On the *Gesta Innocentii*, see, e.g., Brenda M. Bolton, 'Too Important to Neglect: The Gesta Innocentii PP III', in *Church and Chronicle in the Middle Ages: Essays Presented to John Tayler*, ed. Ian Wood and G. A. Loud (London: The Hambledon Press, 1991), pp. 87–99.

[63] James M. Powell, trans., *The Deeds of Pope Innocent III by an Anonymous Author* (Washington, D.C.: The Catholic University of America Press, 2004), p. 77 (translation adjusted); David Richard Gress-Wright, 'The "Gesta Innocentii III": Text, Introduction and Commentary' (unpublished PhD dissertation, Bryn Mawr College, 1981), p. 85.

[64] Wasner, 'Fifteenth-Century Texts', p. 300.

[65] Julie Kerr, *Monastic Hospitality: The Benedictines in England, c.1070–c.1250* (Woodbridge: Boydell Press, 2007), p. 115.

ceremonies of the antique and the medieval Christian worlds'.[66] The *adventus* ceremony functioned as a template that could be used in multiple ways and for a range of purposes. In other words, this was a malleable ceremony, adaptable to varying circumstances. For this reason, it can sometimes be difficult to distinguish the *adventus* from other related ceremonies, or it might be unclear if a reception qualified as an *adventus*. Medieval authors seldom used a strict technical vocabulary in describing examples of the *adventus*. Kerr points out that the most common label was 'honourably received' (*honorifice receptus/susceptus est*) or something similar, such as 'fittingly' or 'aptly' received.[67] Modern historians have followed suit, seldom using a technical vocabulary, and often content to use 'entry ceremony', 'procession', and '*adventus*' interchangeably.[68] A template, of course, has a basic form. Fassler argues that an *adventus* was made up of three components:

> (1) a gathering and arranging of those who will receive the person or persons coming; (2) the coming in itself, which commonly features some sort of procession; and (3) a ceremony of reception by prominent persons, who will then escort the one received to a destination for vows or other regalia.[69]

Martin Heinzelmann also identifies three steps, finding grounds in the sources, after all, for the existence of a technical vocabulary. The first step was the *occursus*, the 'coming out' of the ruler's subjects to greet the ruler; the second was the meeting between the ruler and the subjects in procession outside the subjects' home area (the *susceptio*); and the third step was the *ingressus*, when the subjects would conduct the ruler back into their home.[70]

Although both Fassler and Heinzelmann have identified three steps, their steps do not correspond precisely to each other. Both scholars are unquestionably describing the same ceremony, but the slight discrepancies that appear in

---

[66] Margot E. Fassler, '*Adventus* at Chartres: Ritual Models for Major Processions', in *Ceremonial Culture in Pre-Modern Europe*, ed. Nicholas Howe (Notre Dame, IN: University of Notre Dame Press, 2007), pp. 13–62, at p. 13.

[67] See Kerr, *Monastic Hospitality*, p. 114.

[68] For the entry-ceremony, see, e.g., L. M. Bryant, 'The Medieval Entry Ceremony at Paris', in *Coronations: Medieval and Early Modern Monarchic Ritual*, ed. János M. Bak (Berkeley, Los Angeles, and Oxford: University of California Press, 1990), pp. 88–118, and Gordon Kipling, *Enter the King: Theatre, Liturgy, and Ritual in the Medieval Civic Triumph* (Oxford: Clarendon Press, 1998). For a variant of the procession, see, e.g., Helen Gittos, *Liturgy, Architecture, and Sacred Places in Anglo-Saxon England* (Oxford: Oxford University Press, 2013), pp. 103–45; and Kerr, *Monastic Hospitality*, p. 112.

[69] Fassler, '*Adventus* at Chartres', pp. 13–14.

[70] Martin Heinzelmann, *Translationsberichte und andere Quellen des Reliquienkultes* (Turnhout: Brepols, 1979), pp. 72–74.

their scholarship serve to further highlight the indistinctness of the template overall. The ceremony had a recognisable structure and order, but one that could be stretched, compressed, and moulded to emphasise or deemphasise certain aspects. In his monastic constitutions (composed around 1077), Lanfranc of Canterbury, for instance, emphasised the preparations for receiving a dignitary.[71] In his account of the arrival in 1213 of Cardinal-Legate Nicholas, Roger of Wendover, on the other hand, made no mention of such preparations.[72] Here, I take a pragmatic approach, combining Fassler's first step with Heinzelmann's three steps, therein relying on a four-step template, while recognising its malleability and adaptability. To illustrate how an *adventus* might proceed, I have found Sabine MacCormack's summary of the *adventus* particularly instructive. Although MacCormack describes the entry of a late imperial ruler into a city, one might just as easily substitute the Roman gods for the Christian God or imagine a different location, such as an abbey, a cathedral, or a manor.[73] The *adventus* template may, in fact, be incredibly old. Some Babylonian rituals probably shared many similarities with the *adventus*.[74] Broadly speaking, it seems likely that ritualised public acclamations at the arrival of a ruler are as old as civilisation itself. I have inserted the four steps into MacCormack's text:

> [1: preparations] when the arrival of a ruler in a city was announced ahead of time, the citizens would decorate their city, [2: *occursus*] and on the appointed day, a procession of citizens, headed by their dignitaries, would go out to a certain point outside the city walls, where they would meet the ruler. ... Those in the procession would carry flowers, olive or palm-branches, lights and incense, and there could be the signs of the various guilds and corporations of the town, and more important, the statues of the gods. Singing and acclamations are also regularly mentioned. The ruler did not, of course, appear alone, but had a splendid retinue of his own. [3: *susceptio*] After greetings were exchanged, [4: *ingressus*] the citizens accompanied their ruler into the city, where there could be further ceremonies of welcome.[75]

---

[71] *The Monastic Constitutions*, pp. 104–9. See also p. 80.
[72] *Flowers of History*, vol. 2, p. 289; *Flores Historiarum*, vol. 2, pp. 93–94.
[73] See, e.g., Ernst Hartwig Kantorowicz, 'The "King's Advent" and the Enigmatic Panels in the Doors of Santa Sabina', *The Art Bulletin* 26, no. 4 (1944): 207–31, pp. 211–13.
[74] Amélie Kuhrt, 'Usurpation, Conquest and Ceremonial: From Babylon to Persia', in *Rituals of Royalty: Power and Ceremonial in Traditional Societies*, ed. David Cannadine and Simon Price (Cambridge: Cambridge University Press, 1987), pp. 20–55.
[75] Sabine G. MacCormack, 'Change and Continuity in Late Antiquity: The Ceremony of "Adventus"', *Historia: Zeitschrift für Alte Geschichte* 21, no. 4 (1972): 721–52, p. 723. The fundamental study on the ritual reception of Hellenistic kings is E. Peterson, 'Die Einholung des Kyrios', *Zeitschift für systematische Theologie* 7 (1930): 682–702.

Christendom inherited the ceremony from the Roman Empire, which in turn acquired it from the Greeks. In Hellenistic Greece, subject populaces received Hellenistic kings as representatives of the gods, and their reception was called *hypantesis* or *apantesis*. When the Romans conquered Greece (second century BC), they adopted the ceremony, calling it *adventus* ('arrival').[76]

The Romans already had a reception ceremony: the *triumphus*. The *triumphus* focused on military triumph and was only awarded occasionally as a special accolade. The *triumphus* concluded with a sacrifice to Jupiter Optimus Maximus on the Capitoline Hill. However, when the emperors became Christians, this ceremonial feature became an issue. In contrast, the *adventus* was considered less controversial and had a broader applicability, ensuring the absorption of the *triumphus* into the *adventus*. The *adventus* incorporated the *triumphus*' emphasis on triumph but eschewed the sacrifice to Jupiter.[77] Accordingly, triumph became an innate part of the Roman imperial *adventus*, regardless of any actual military victory having taken place.[78]

Despite its pagan and imperial origins, the *adventus* became deeply ingrained within the Christian imagination. The Gospels modelled their accounts of Christ's entry into Jerusalem on the *adventus*. The Gospel of John states:

> And on the next day, a great multitude that had come to the festival day, when they had heard that Jesus was coming to Jerusalem, / Took branches of palm trees and went forth to meet him and cried Hosanna. Blessed is he that cometh in the name of the Lord, the king of Israel. / And Jesus found a young ass and sat upon it, as it is written: / Fear not, daughter of Sion: behold thy king cometh, sitting on an ass's colt. / ... / The multitude therefore gave testimony, which was with him when he called Lazarus out of the grave and raised him from the dead. / For which reason also the people came to meet him, because they heard that he had done this miracle.[79]

---

[76] Kantorowicz, 'The "King's Advent"', pp. 211–13.

[77] Twyman, *Papal Ceremonial at Rome*, pp. 7–8; Sabine G. MacCormack, *Art and Ceremony in Late Antiquity* (Berkeley: University of California Press, 1981), pp. 33–41.

[78] Twyman, *Papal Ceremonial at Rome*, p. 8; MacCormack, 'Change and Continuity', pp. 722, 725–26; MacCormack, *Art and Ceremony*, pp. 33–34. See also Peter Franz Mittag, 'Processus Consularis, Adventus und Herrschaftsjubiläum. Zur Verwendung von Triumphsymbolik in der mittleren Kaiserzeit', *Hermes* 137, no. 4 (2009): 447–62.

[79] *The Holy Bible, Douay-Rheims Version*, revised by Challoner, John 12:12–15, 17–18; Weber and Fischer, *Biblia Sacra*, John 12:12–15, 17–18: 'in crastinum autem turba multa quae venerat ad diem festum cum audissent quia venit Iesus Hierosolyma / acceperunt ramos palmarum et processerunt obviam ei et clamabant osanna benedictus qui venit in nomine Domini rex Israhel / Et invenit Iesus assellum et sedit super eum / noli timere filia Sion ecce rex tuus venit sedens super pullum asinae / ... / testimonium ergo perhi-

Annual recreations of Christ's processional entry into Jerusalem on Palm Sunday were common throughout medieval Christendom.[80] In the words of Iris Shagrir, it 'exerted a great influence on the Christian collective memory'.[81]

Scriptural accounts of Christ's entry into Jerusalem had important conceptual ramifications. Being received with an *adventus* could be a form of *imitatio Christi* (imitation of Christ). Gregory Nazianzen's description of the return of the exiled Bishop Athanasius of Alexandria (r. 328–73) is a case in point:

> He [Athanasius] rode upon a colt, almost blame me not for folly, as my Jesus did upon that other colt ... He was welcomed with branches of trees, and garments with many flowers and of varied hue were torn off and strewn before him and under his feet.[82]

Pope Alexander III's return to Rome in 1178 is another example. According to Cardinal Boso, the Romans met Alexander with olive branches ('ramis olivarum')

---

bebat turba quae erat cum eo quando Lazarum vocavit de monumento et suscitavit eum a mortuis / propterea et obviam venit ei turba quia audierunt eum fecisse hoc signum.'

[80] Craig Wright, 'The Palm Sunday Procession in Medieval Chartres', in *The Divine Office in the Latin Middle Ages: Methodology and Source Studies, Regional Developments, Hagiography: Written in Honor of Professor Ruth Steiner*, ed. Margot E. Fassler and Rebecca A. Baltzer (Oxford: Oxford University Press, 2000), pp. 344–71; Fassler, 'Adventus at Chartres', p. 14. The Carolingian renaissance probably exported processional activity from Rome to the rest of Christendom; see Roger E. Reynolds, 'The Drama of Medieval Liturgical Processions', *Revue de musicologie* 86, no. 1 (2000): 127–42, p. 128.

[81] Iris Shagrir, '*Adventus* in Jerusalem: The Palm Sunday Celebration in Latin Jerusalem', *JMH* 41, no. 1 (2015): 1–20, p. 13. See also Twyman, *Papal Ceremonial at Rome*, pp. 10–11; MacCormack, *Art and Ceremony*, pp. 64–65; and MacCormack, 'Change and Continuity', pp. 747–48. It is possible that bishops imitated the consulate, who received such *adventus*-like ceremonies; see Michael McCormick, *Eternal Victory: Triumphal Rulership in Late Antiquity, Byzantium, and the Early Medieval West* (Cambridge: Cambridge University Press, 1986), pp. 330–31.

[82] Gregory Nazianzen, 'Select Orations', in *A Select Library of the Nicene and Post-Nicene Fathers of the Christian Church*, ed. and trans. Charles Gordon Browne and James Edward Swallow. Second Series, series eds Philip Schaff and Henry Wace (New York: The Christian Literature Co., 1894; repr. Edinburgh: T & T Clark, 1996), vol. 7, pp. 185–498, at p. 278; Gregory Nazianzen [S. P. N. Gregorii Theologi Archiepiscopi Constantinopolitani], 'In laudem magni Athanasii episcopi Alexandrini', in *Patrologia Graeca*, ed. Jacques-Paul Migne, vol. 1, 35 (Paris: Imprimerie Catholique, 1857), cols. 1081–1128, at cols. 1115–18: 'Pullus ipsum vehebat (ac peto a vobis, ne me amentiæ accusetis), non secus fere, ac Jesum meum pullus ille ... Illum etiam rami, et varia variis picta coloribus indumenta ante eum projecta et substra excipiunt.'

and the pope saw 'all eyes staring at his face just as at the face of Jesus Christ' ('oculos omnium vultum eius intuentes tamquam vultum Iesu Christi').[83]

Another conceptual consequence was the fusion of 'kingship' or 'empire' with Christian ideas.[84] St John described Christ's arrival as *hypantesis*; St Paul used *apantesis* to describe the second coming of Christ. Both were Hellenistic terms denoting the entry of a ruler.[85] Shagrir argues that the king of Jerusalem utilised 'the processional qualities of the Palm Sunday ritual' when he entered Jerusalem on Palm Sunday, fusing the regal and the divine:

> In the specific fusion of Palm Sunday ritual and the *adventus*, the ritual space was experienced by the participants as both a religious space and a political one, an *adventus Christi* and an *adventus regis*, in the spirit of the biblical verse, 'behold, your king is coming to you'.[86]

The king of Jerusalem's moulding of the *adventus* to suit his own needs highlights the adaptability of the ceremony: it could be modified to serve specific local needs while retaining enough of its universal features to render it recognisable to outsiders. Miller demonstrates how the newly appointed bishop of Florence undertook an intricate inauguration *adventus* in three stages. These stages aligned with the Florentine marriage tradition, which consisted of, firstly, a meeting between two families to plan a wedding; secondly, the ring-day, where the groom placed a ring on the finger of the betrothed; and, thirdly, the consummation of the marriage in the house of the bride's father in a bed prepared for the occasion. The bishop-elect's inauguration *adventus* followed these stages (interspersed with 'regular' *adventus* features). The elect first met with the leaders of Florence outside the city to plan the *adventus*, before he proceeded to the abbey of San Pier Maggiore, where he presented the abbess with a ring and slept in a bed prepared by the abbess. The abbess of San Pier Maggiore always hailed from one of the leading families of the city. The bishop's symbolic marriage to the abbess symbolised his marriage not just to his church (which became canon law doctrine at the time of

---

[83] *Liber Pontificalis*, vol. 2, p. 446. See also Cardinal Boso, *Boso's Life of Alexander III*, p. 2.
[84] On the intertwining of empire, kingship, and Christ, see, e.g., Per Beskow, *Rex Gloriae: The Kingship of Christ in the Early Church*, trans. Eric J. Sharpe (Eugene, OR: Wipf & Stock, 1962).
[85] MacCormack, 'Change and Continuity', pp. 723–25; Kantorowicz, 'The "King's Advent"', p. 211.
[86] Shagrir, '*Adventus* in Jerusalem', p. 14. Matthew 21:5; Zechariah 9:9. See also Bernard Hamilton, 'The Impact of Crusader Jerusalem on Western Christendom', *The Catholic Historical Review* 80, no. 4 (1994): 695–713.

Pope Innocent III),[87] but also his marriage to Florence.[88] Not every contemporary might have grasped the intricate symbolism, but the processional activities and other festivities still made the bishop's entry into Florence recognisable to outsiders as an *adventus*.

In this way, the medieval *adventus* was, to quote Fassler again, a 'fundamental ritual structure'.[89] It contained some regularities and customary vocabulary, but the details of the ceremony were subject to malleability and creativity. Many local variations doubtless existed across Europe, with each designed to convey a specific message within the greater significance of the ritual as a recognition of authority, rank, and power. The legatine *adventus* was one such variation of the ceremony, with its own particular message.

THE CURIAL PERSPECTIVE

Popes expected to be received with an *adventus*. The curia, accordingly, produced *ordines* intending to satisfy papal expectations and composed (idealised) papal receptions in the *Liber Pontificalis*, the book of papal biographies.[90] Nothing comparable exists for legates until the fifteenth century,[91] except for a few tantalising glimpses from the late thirteenth century. The great canonist William Durand (1232 × 1233–96) mentioned the legatine *adventus* in passing in his *Speculum iuris/iudiciale* (first edition 1270s, second edition 1291).[92] As the bishop of Mende (r.

---

[87] See Mary Ellen Sommar, 'The Changing Role of the Bishop in Society: Episcopal Translation in the Middle Ages' (unpublished PhD dissertation, Syracuse University, New York, 1998), pp. 297–361.

[88] Maureen C. Miller, 'Why the Bishop of Florence Had to Get Married', *Speculum* 81, no. 4 (2006): 1055–91, esp. pp. 1077–84.

[89] Fassler, '*Adventus* at Chartres', p. 13.

[90] See Twyman, *Papal Ceremonial at Rome*, esp. pp. 23–40.

[91] See Wasner, 'Fifteenth-Century Texts'.

[92] William Durand, *Speculum iuris Gulielmi Durandi, episcopi Mimatensis, I.V.D. cum Io. And. Baldi de Vbaldis, aliorumque aliquot praestantiss. iurisc. theorematibus. Nunc denuo ab innumeris, quibus antea scatebat, erroribus atque mendis summa industria, & labore repurgatum. Pars prima quarta* (Venice, 1602), § 7, p. 53: 'A legate will indeed act rightly if, before he enters the province decreed [assigned] to him, he despatches in advance a proclamation about his arrival (*adventu*), indicating when he will enter' ('Recte autem faciet legatus, si, priusquam sibi decretam ingrediatur provinciam, edictum de suo adventu premittat, significans quando ingressuris sit)'. On William Durand and the *Speculum iuris/iudiciale*, see Timothy M. Thibodeau, trans., *The Rationale Divinorum Officiorum of William Durand of Mende: A New Translation of the Prologue and Book One* (New York: Columbia University Press, 2007), pp. xvii–xviii; and Beatrice Pasciuta, 'Speculum Iudiciale (A Mirror of Procedure): 1271–1276/1296, Ed. Pr. 1474. Guilelmus Durantis (Guillaume Durand/Durant; William Durand, the Elder) (1240/1232–1296)', in *The Formation and Transmission of Western Legal Culture: 150 Books that Made the Law in the Age of Printing*, ed. Serge Dauchy et al. (Cham: Springer, 2016), pp. 37–40.

1285–96), Durand composed a pontifical (*c.* 1295), a book on episcopal ceremony and affairs, in which he included an 'ordo about the reception in procession of a prelate or a legate' ('ordo ad recipiendum processionaliter prelatum vel legatum').[93] The *ordo* describes an *adventus* in some detail, but it contains nothing more than contemporary or earlier monastic customaries, which sometimes mention papal legates as well.[94] Durand's ordo is significant in that it demonstrates the importance of legates, but it offers no distinct legatine *adventus* nor a curial perspective on such an *adventus*.[95]

Legates were usually content to provide very brief reports. In 1169, Master Vivian, a juriconsult at the curia and member of the third legatine mission to address the Becket dispute, wrote a report to Alexander III about the negotiations.[96] Vivian noted that 'we were received sufficiently honourably by him [King Henry II] and his nobles' ('a quo et principibus suis satis honeste recepti fuimus').[97] In 1172, the cardinals Albert and Theodwin wrote to the archbishops of Sens and Ravenna to tell them about proceedings at Avranches, reporting that 'we proceeded in procession to the aforementioned city [Avranches], at which place … we met with a great many people and they met with us' ('ad præedictam processimus civitatem, ad quam … convenimus cum personis plurimis et ipse nobiscum').[98] The report from Cardinal-Bishop Nicholas of Tusculum is unusually informative (he was the legate imploring Pope Innocent III for clarity). Nicholas came to England in 1213 in order to negotiate a settlement in the wake of the dispute between King John and Pope Innocent III over the election of Archbishop Stephen Langton in 1207.[99] Nicholas reported home about his reception:

> Let it therefore be known, your holiness [Pope Innocent III], that on the vigil of the holy Matthew [20 September], by God's grace, I crossed successfully with the ships, which the venerable father S[tephen], archbishop of Canterbury, had sent to me; he, coming to the port of Dover with the necessary horses and great devotion to me, received me honourably and explaining liberally about the services of the churches themselves and their possessions,

[93] See Wasner, '"Legatus a Latere"', p. 411.
[94] Chapter 3 studies these monastic customaries.
[95] See also Montaubin, 'De Petits papes en voyage', p. 67.
[96] Anne J. Duggan, *Thomas Becket* (London: Arnold, 2004), p. 163.
[97] James Craigie Robertson and J. Brigstocke Sheppard, eds, *Materials for the History of Thomas Becket, Archbishop of Canterbury*, 7 vols, RS (London: Longmans, 1875–85), vol. 7, no. 562, pp. 78–82, quote at p. 78.
[98] Ibid., nos. 774–775, pp. 520–23, quote no. 774, pp. 520–21. On the compromise of Avranches, see Anne J. Duggan, '*Ne in dubium*: The Official Record of Henry's Reconciliation at Avranches, 21 May 1172', *EHR* 115, no. 462 (2000): 643–58.
[99] For further details, see pp. 162–63, 169–74.

he came all the way to London with me. Moreover, at the entry into London, the illustrious king of England went to meet me sufficiently (*satis*) honourably outside the city and kindly and devotedly received me for your sake.[100]

The existence of the report merits comment. Nicholas likely went into some detail because relations between the pope and the king had been tense for years. The king had scorned papal authority throughout the dispute, but the honourable reception of the cardinal-legate signalled his recognition of papal authority and, accordingly, the reestablishment of amicable relations. Both the pope and the legate probably deemed the *adventus* a precondition for negotiations. Nicholas was personally close to the pope, so he likely knew what the pope would find relevant.[101] Furthermore, the reception signified the papal presence within the legate. Nicholas told Innocent that he was received honourably 'for your sake' ('uestri gratia'). Of course, actions directed at the legate were truly directed at the pope.

The report's brevity, nevertheless, is striking. It implies that such receptions were the norm. Nicholas 'ticked off' the most important components, using two of Heinzelmann's terms. He mentioned the arrival, the coming out to meet him (using 'occurrens'), the meeting, and him being accompanied into his province (using 'ingressu'). However, the majority of details concerning the ritual were hidden within the adverbs 'honorifice', 'benigne', and 'deuote'. Evidence from contemporary monastic customaries shows that such ritual details might include festive clothing, incense, bell-ringing, holy water, Bible presentation, kissing, singing, and prayer.[102]

Nicholas assessed how Archbishop Stephen and King John received him. This reception was important, as it signalled their respective acknowledgement of his – and by extension the pope's – authority. Nicholas was apparently pleased with Archbishop Stephen, who received him 'honourably' ('honorifice') and with 'great devotion to me' ('magna mihi de[uot]ione'). They probably knew each

---

[100] Angelo Mercati, 'La Prima Relazione del Cardinale Nicolò de Romanis sulla sua legazione in Inghilterra', in *Essays in History Presented to Reginald Lane Poole*, ed. H. W. C. Davis (Oxford: Clarendon Press, 1927), pp. 274–89, at pp. 277–8: 'Nouerit itaque uestra sanctitas quod in uigilia beati Mathei per Dei gratiam prospere transfretaui cum nauibus quas mihi miserat venerabilis frater S. Cantuariensis archiepiscopus, qui in portu Douarie cum equis necessariis et magna mihi de[uot]ione occurrens, honorifice me recepit et exponens ad ecclesie obsequia liberaliter se et sua, usque Londonias mecum uenit. In ingressu autem Londonie illustris rex Anglie mihi satis honorifice extra ciuitatem occurrit et benigne ac deuote uestri gratia me recepit.'

[101] See Werner Maleczek, *Papst und Kardinalskolleg von 1191 bis 1216. Die Kardinäle unter Coelestin und Innocenz III.* (Vienna: Verlag der Österreichischen Akademie der Wissenschaften, 1984), pp. 147–48.

[102] See chapter 3.

other personally from Stephen's time as a cardinal. Innocent made Nicholas a cardinal-bishop in 1204 and Stephen a cardinal-priest in 1206.[103] The archbishop also took care of the legate's transport, sending ships and horses for the cardinal's use. This was perhaps not unusual, as cardinal-legates expected papal subjects to provide for them on their travels. However, Nicholas probably mentioned it to indicate that the archbishop – not the king – was the most welcoming. One might have expected a humble, converted sinner (as King John was supposed to be) to have made some provisions for the cardinal. As mentioned previously, King Henry II had bestowed a white horse upon Cardinal Vivian for his journey through England in 1176, even though Henry had not wanted Cardinal Vivian to enter his kingdom.[104] King John, having spent years defying the pope, did not provide anything for the cardinal, even if John did nothing wrong as such. Nicholas described the king's reception with the words 'honorifice' (honourably), 'benigne' (kindly), and 'deuote' (devotedly), but added the word 'satis'. 'Satis' has a range of meanings between 'sufficiently', 'fairly', 'adequately', 'quite', etc. Within this context, it appears likely that the king's reception was merely adequate, not elevated. The cardinal subtly pointed out that he considered the archbishop to have shown himself the better servant of the pope.

Nicholas' account is interesting in that it provides sufficient information to indicate that he received an *adventus*, while also implying that he expected the pope and the cardinals back home to be immediately aware of the meaning of his reception. Thus, Nicholas offered only little information about the meaning of his reception that modern historians can access today; instead, papal propaganda offers a way to access these beliefs for further study. Cardinal Boso's biography of Pope Alexander III is particularly useful for these purposes because he wrote it in the wake of a schism, which forced the curia to rearticulate papal identity and purpose.

Cardinal Boso and His Papal Biographies

Boso was a cardinal during the time of popes Adrian IV and Alexander III. Hadrian made him cardinal-deacon of SS. Cosma e Damiano in 1157, and Alexander elevated him to cardinal-priest of S. Pudenziana in 1165/6.[105] Boso was an important supporter of Pope Alexander during the schism. He was part of the pope's inner circle, 'clearly involved in the formulation of policy at the highest level', as John Doran puts it.[106] Boso also composed several papal biographies during the 1160s and 1170s. The biographies were a part of the ideological positioning of the papacy,

---

[103] Maleczek, *Papst und Kardinalskolleg*, pp. 147–48, 164–66.
[104] See pp. 123–25 for more details.
[105] John Doran, 'Remembering Pope Gregory VII: Cardinal Boso and Alexander III', *Studies in Church History* 49 (2013): 87–98.
[106] Ibid., p. 89.

and can cautiously be interpreted as the official voice of the papacy, close to Alexander's own words. The most important of Boso's biographies centred on Alexander III. In it, Boso penned an account of the travels of three cardinal-legates, which provides a window into curial perceptions of the legatine *adventus*.

The travels took place on the background of the siege of Alessandria in 1175. During the schism, most of the papacy's fighting against Emperor Frederick I was done by the North Italian Lombard cities, whose own objective was to gain independence from the Empire. They had recently re-founded and renamed the city of Alessandria, choosing the name Alessandria in honour of Pope Alexander and as a deliberate insult to the emperor.[107] Frederick decided to make his way to Alessandria and lay siege to it.[108]

Boso's account of the siege is very interesting as he wrote with the knowledge of hindsight, knowing that the Lombard victory at Alessandria was a key step towards winning the war.[109] Boso explained that 'the Lombards had recently built it [Alessandria] in honour of St Peter' ('quam noviter Lombardi construxerant ad honorem beati Petri').[110] Preparing to defend their home, the citizens, according to Boso, did so 'trusting in the intercession of the blessed apostles Peter and Paul' ('de beatorum Petri et Pauli apostolorum suffragio confidens').[111] Peter and Paul were the most important papal saints, and in response to these events, God helped the defenders by causing a downpour, which made life miserable for the besieging army.[112] Frederick, in contrast to the citizenry's pious behaviour, behaved like a villain, attacking the city on Good Friday, and breaking the traditionally accepted truce associated with that day. However, the citizens, 'with the aid of St Peter, whom they saw at their head mounted on a white charger and clad in flashing armour, brought their enemies to the ground' ('cum beato Petro, quem ante se in albo equo et corruscantibus armis preire cernebant, prostraverunt in terram').[113] In Boso's eyes, the victory thus belonged to St Peter and to St Peter's successor,

---

[107] John Freed, *Frederick Barbarossa: The Prince and the Myth* (New Haven: Yale University Press, 2016), pp. 379–81.

[108] See Edward Coleman, '"A City to Be Built for the Glory of God, St Peter, and the Whole of Lombardy": Alexander III, Alessandria and the Lombard League in Contemporary Sources', in *Pope Alexander III (1159–81): The Art of Survival*, ed. Anne J. Duggan and Peter D. Clarke (Farnham: Ashgate, 2012), pp. 127–52, at pp. 145–50.

[109] Coleman, 'A City to Be Built', pp. 132–34. Cardinal Boso, *Boso's Life of Alexander III*, pp. 88–92; *Liber Pontificalis*, vol. 2, pp. 427–30.

[110] Cardinal Boso, *Boso's Life of Alexander III*, p. 88; *Liber Pontificalis*, vol. 2, p. 427.

[111] Cardinal Boso, *Boso's Life of Alexander III*, p. 88 (translation adjusted); *Liber Pontificalis*, vol. 2, p. 427.

[112] Cardinal Boso, *Boso's Life of Alexander III*, p. 88; *Liber Pontificalis*, vol. 2, p. 427.

[113] Cardinal Boso, *Boso's Life of Alexander III*, p. 90 (translation adjusted); *Liber Pontificalis*, vol. 2, p. 428.

Pope Alexander. After Alessandria, the emperor and the pope commenced negotiations. Alexander dispatched three cardinal-legates to the talks. They set out:

> Accordingly, they [the legates] went their separate ways through various regions, and all the people rejoiced in the Lord at the happy sight and when they beheld their credentials, they presented to them a large number of infant children to be blessed. The [Cardinal-]Bishop of Porto and the Cardinal of St Peter-ad-Vincula journeyed through Spoleto, Imola, and Bologna. They reached Piacenza and there awaited for some days the arrival of the [Cardinal-]Bishop of Ostia who, with pomp and ceremony, had travelled through Pisa and Lucca ... Then the legates left Piacenza with a great assembly of clerics and soldiers, went in procession to the bank of the Po and, crossing in boats which had been made ready, entered Pavia [Frederick's residence], where they were received honourably and lodged.[114]

This is not a clear-cut entry into a clearly defined physical space, such as a city or a cathedral, but the account clearly rests on the *adventus* as a fundamental ritual structure (to paraphrase Fassler).[115] The passage mentions a number of significant ritual features and ideas, such as the joyous nature of the reception, travel through the relevant area, the pomp and ceremony of the event, the attraction of followers, and the procession. The account, incidentally, reveals the flexibility of the *adventus*, with Boso moulding the ceremony to fit his own agenda.

Boso's plan was to show that papal authority was recognised everywhere (specifically in Italy). Papal authority was not a given, having been under threat. Boso asserted that the recipients were 'all the people' ('plebs universa'), and that their home area was 'various regions' ('diversas regiones'). Boso's strategic naming of some of the places that the cardinals travelled through contributed to an impression of comprehensiveness, with Boso casting their travels as a sort of extended *adventus* journey. Boso was telling a propagandistic story about the recognition of

---

[114] Cardinal Boso, *Boso's Life of Alexander III*, p. 93; *Liber Pontificalis*, p. 430: 'Eis igitur segregatim per diversas regiones proficiscentibus, plebs universa in iocunda eorum inspectione letabatur in Domino et ad consignationem puerorum ipsis copiosam multitudinem infantium presentabat. Episcopus namque Portuensis et cardinalis sancti Petri ad Vincula per Spoletum et Imolam atque Bononiam honorifice transeuntes usque Placentiam processerunt, ibique adventum Hostiensis episcopi qui per Pisanam et Lucanam civitates cum gloria et honore transivit, per dies aliquot expectarunt ... Tunc legati de civitate Placentia cum magno clericorum et militum comitatu exeuntes, processerunt ad Padi ripam, et in preparatis navibus transeuntes, venerunt in civitatem Papiam, in qua honorifice recepti fuerunt et hospitati.'

[115] See Fassler, '*Adventus* at Chartres', p. 13.

papal authority in Italy, and his account contains some striking similarities with his earlier description of Pope Alexander III's triumphant entry into Rome in 1178:

> the Pope and his brothers [the cardinals] quickly girded themselves for their return to the City [Rome]. ... he [Alexander] left Tusculum after Mass on his journey to the City, not without much pomp and ceremony. The Roman clergy had gone far out of the City to meet him with banners and crosses ... The Senators and Magistrates went with them with strident trumpets, the nobles with their men-at-arms in fitting livery, and the populace on foot, with olive branches, shouting the accustomed *Laudes* for the Pontiff. When he was seeing all eyes staring at his face just as at the face of Jesus Christ, whose commissions he bore on Earth, his white palfrey could scarcely move forward because of the pressure of the throng, which was applying their lips to its footprints. The right hand of its rider grew heavy with the toil of bestowing blessings.[116]

These similarities are particularly instructive: both the pope and his legates travelled with pomp and ceremony ('gloria et honore'), both the pope and the legates were received triumphantly, and both the pope and his legates were encouraged to bless the people.[117] Alexander's *adventus* was more significant, and his approximation to Christ more pronounced (he was *the* pope). Nevertheless, Boso alluded to the same ideas in his account of the three legates, with their travels aligned with Christ's entry into Jerusalem. The difference between these entries was merely one of degree.

The papal *adventus* signified 'acquiescence in the divine will',[118] that is, acquiescence to papal authority and lordship; the same applied to the legatine *adventus*, only to a lesser degree. The papacy had just won a resounding victory at

---

[116] Cardinal Boso, *Boso's Life of Alexander III*, pp. 117–18 (translation adjusted); *Liber Pontificalis*, vol. 2, p. 446: 'domnus papa et fratres eius ad reditum Urbis festinanter se accinxerunt. ... post missam, exivit de Tusculano proficiscens ad Urbem, non sine gloria et honore multo. Exierant enim obviam sibi extra urbem in longum clerus Romanus cum vexillis et crucibus ... senatores et magistratus populi cum concrepantibus tubis, nobiles cum militia in apparatu decoro, et pedestris populositas cum ramis olivarum, laudes pontifici consuetas vociferans. Tunc videns oculos omnium vultum eius intuentes tamquam vultum Iesu Christi cuius vices in terris gerit, pre nimia veri multitudine ipsius vestigia deosculantium albus palafridus ambulare vix poterat, et sessoris dextera in dandis benedictionibus nimium laborabat.'

[117] Boso mentioned other legatine and papal receptions, but none were as important as these two. For legatine receptions, see Cardinal Boso, *Boso's Life of Alexander III*, pp. 54, 85, 102; *Liber Pontificalis*, vol. 2, pp. 405, 425, 436. For papal receptions, see Cardinal Boso, *Boso's Life of Alexander III*, pp. 45–46, 53–54, 59, 66–67, 73, 82, 102–3, 104, 105, 108; *Liber Pontificalis*, vol. 2, pp. 399, 404, 408, 412–13, 417, 423, 436–37, 437, 438, 440.

[118] Twyman, *Papal Ceremonial at Rome*, p. 219.

Alessandria. According to Boso, God and St Peter had orchestrated the victory, indicating that God favoured Pope Alexander. When the people of Italy received the three cardinal-legates with an *adventus*, they acquiesced to this 'fact', recognising the pope's divine authority through his cardinal-legates. The cardinals were, in Boso's own words, 'limbs' ('membra') of the 'body' ('corporis'), with the pope as the 'head' ('capiti').[119] The cardinals were extensions of the pope and therefore extensions of both St Peter and even of Christ.

The *adventus* travels were also a form of *possessio*: a lord's taking possession of the place he entered during an *adventus*.[120] In this particular instance, the three cardinals took possession of (parts of) Italy on behalf of the pope. Prior to the schism, Boso had spent his career working to reclaim St Peter's patrimony (the Papal States) for the papacy, which suggests that the taking-possession part of the ceremony was important to him.[121] However, this was no mundane possession, with the biography's conclusion revealing ultimately what the greater purpose was: the pope's possession of Rome. The very last sentence, presented immediately after the papal *adventus* into Rome, reads: 'at Easter, he [Pope Alexander III] solemnly assumed the kingdom' ('in Pascha regnum solemniter induit').[122] It is hardly necessary to point out the significance of Easter; nonetheless, the last word in the entire biography, 'induit', is perhaps equally significant. 'Induit' is often used in connection with the Incarnation: God/Christ puts on (another meaning of *induere*) human form.[123] The pope's approximation to Christ is overt as he enters Rome, taking possession of his kingdom. The kingdom may be understood in multiple overlapping ways: as the earthly Rome, as the Roman Church, and as the Kingdom of God. The cardinal-legates were accordingly extensions, radiating out from Rome, the pope, St Peter, and Christ. While lesser than the pope, cardinal-legates remained extensions nonetheless, taking possession of the kingdom on behalf of the pope while the populace joyfully acquiesced.

AMBIGUITY AND RESISTANCE

It is not clear whether recipients of papal legates interpreted the *adventus* in accordance with curial understanding. The ceremony was ambiguous at its

---

[119] Cardinal Boso, *Boso's Life of Alexander III*, p. 73; *Liber Pontificalis*, vol. 2, p. 417.

[120] See esp. Miller, 'The Florentine Bishop's Ritual Entry'; and Katherine Harvey, 'The First Entry of the Bishop: Episcopal *Adventus* in Fourteenth-Century England', in *Fourteenth Century England VIII*, ed. J. S. Hamilton (Woodbridge: Boydell Press, 2014), 43–58.

[121] See Doran, 'Remembering Pope Gregory VII', pp. 87–89; and Robinson, *The Papacy 1073–1198*, pp. 254–55.

[122] Cardinal Boso, *Boso's Life of Alexander III*, p. 118 (translation adjusted); *Liber Pontificalis*, vol. 2, p. 446.

[123] 'Induere', in *Dictionary of Medieval Latin from British Sources*; available at https://logeion.uchicago.edu/induere (accessed 15 August 2023).

core. On the one hand, the ceremony required the (voluntary) presence of large numbers of people without any recognised political voice; on the other hand, a lord expected his subjects to acclaim him. The ceremony contained a tension between the lord demanding an *adventus* from his subjects, and the subjects being required to voluntarily offer an *adventus* of their own accord. Twyman argues that 'it was desirable for the occasion [the *adventus*] to have an air of spontaneity in order that the honours shown to the ruler should appear unsolicited and that he avoid accusations of tyranny'; and: 'it was on this basis of a consensus, freely given and without extortion, that monarchical government rested'.[124] Boso, accordingly, left no doubt that the Italian populace willingly flocked around the three cardinals on their own accord. Conversely, a writer could present a reception as illegitimate or somehow improper if the honours shown were not freely given. Roger of Howden, probably writing around 1194, had nothing but disdain for William Longchamp, bishop of Ely, King Richard's chancellor and papal legate, whom Roger accused of having maltreated Roger's patron, Bishop Hugh de Puiset (r. 1153–95).[125] When enemies of William drove him into exile, Roger was apparently happy to imply that the honours bestowed on William at his reception in Paris were contaminated because he paid for them:

> And proceeding thence, he [William Longchamp] arrived at Paris, and gave to Bishop Maurice [de Sully (r. 1160–96)] sixty marks of silver, for that he himself received him with a solemn procession at that place in the archiepiscopal church.[126]

Commentators could delegitimise the ceremony in other ways. Eadmer of Canterbury's account of Cardinal-Legate Peter Pierleoni's entry into England is an interesting case of active resistance against the meaning of the legatine *adventus*. Eadmer (c. 1060–after 1128) was the biographer of Archbishop Anselm of Canterbury (r. 1093–1109).[127] Eadmer had come to detest what he saw as the

---

[124] Twyman, *Papal Ceremonial at Rome*, p. 16. It is hardly necessary to mention that papal monarchy fell within this purview.

[125] *Chronica*, vol. 3, p. 35. See also *Gesta*, vol. 2, p. 109.

[126] *Gesta*, vol. 2, pp. 220–21: 'Et procedens inde venit Parisius, et dedit Mauricio episcopo sexaginta marcas argenti, pro eo quod ipse eum recepit ibidem in metropolitana ecclesia cum solemni processione.'

[127] On Eadmer, see, e.g., the introduction in Eadmer of Canterbury, *Lives and Miracles of Saints Oda, Dunstan, and Oswald*, ed. Andrew J. Turner and Bernard J. Muir, OMT (Oxford: Clarendon Press, 2006), pp. xiii–xxxv. On Archbishop Anselm, see Richard W. Southern, *Saint Anselm: A Portrait in a Landscape* (Cambridge: Cambridge University Press, 1990) and Sally N. Vaughn, *Archbishop Anselm 1093–1109: Bec Missionary, Canterbury Primate, Patriarch of Another World* (Farnham: Ashgate, 2012).

encroachment of curial legates on the archbishop of Canterbury, who, he believed, customarily held the right to legatine commissions in England. In 1121, Legate Peter came to England.[128] In his *Historia Novorum*,[129] Eadmer described the arrival:

> However, his [Peter Pierleoni's] reputation had exceeded all of those who had been sent to these parts from the Roman See before him; and abbots and others, men evidently respected, were sent ahead by him in order to herald his arrival in England. For he was the son of Peter, the very illustrious and mighty noble of the Romans ... The whole land was, therefore, astonished at the expectation about so great an arrival ... Accordingly, led to the king [Henry I (r. 1100–35)], he was received worthily by him.[130]

The account seemingly praises the legate, especially Peter's heritage. Peter duly impressed the English, who received him 'worthily'. Eadmer, however, was being sarcastic: recording how the king suddenly turned against the legate, Eadmer stated that Henry 'testified that he in no way would surrender his ancestral customs calmly', including 'the freedom of England from any legate's lordship'.[131] According to Eadmer, Cardinal Peter was taken aback by the king's sudden outburst:

> And he [Cardinal Peter], who had come to work as legate in the whole of Britain, was sent out of England by the king the same way he had arrived with such enormous pomp, free from all duties.[132]

---

[128] See M. Brett, *The English Church under Henry I* (Oxford: Oxford University Press, 1975), pp. 34–43, and Tillmann, *Die päpstlichen Legaten*, pp. 26–27.

[129] On the *Historia Novorum*, see, e.g., Charles C. Rozier, 'Between History and Hagiography: Eadmer of Canterbury's Vision of the *Historia novorum in Anglia*', JMH 45, no. 1 (2019): 1–19.

[130] Eadmer of Canterbury, '*Historia Novorum in Anglia*', in *Eadmeri Historia Novorum in Anglia, et Opuscula Duo de Vita Sancti Anselmi et Quibusdam Miraculus Ejus*, ed. Martin Rule, RS (London: Longman, 1884), pp. 1–302, at p. 295: 'Supercreverat autem fama istius famam omnium ante eum in has partes a Romana sede destinatorum; et abbates ac nonnulli alii, viri videlicet honorati ejus adventum Angliæ præconaturi ab eo præmittebantur. Erat enim filius Petri præclarissimi ac potentissimi principis Romanorum ... Attonita igitur tota terra in expectatione quasi tanti adventus .... Perductus igitur ad regem, digne ab eo susceptus est.' I am grateful to Peter Bruun Rasmussen from Det Danske Sprog- og Litteraturselskab (DSL) for discussing the translation of this passage with me.

[131] Ibid., p. 295: 'sibi patrias consuetudines ... nequaquam se æquanimiter amissurum fore testabatur' and 'regnum Angliæ liberum ab omni legati ditione'.

[132] Ibid., p. 296: '... et qui legati officio fungi in tota Britannia venerat, immunis ab omni officio tali cum ingenti pompa via qua venerat extra Angliam a rege missus est'.

The cardinal returned home without achieving anything. He left, so to speak, with his tail between his legs in a mock reversal of his entry.[133] In Eadmer's rendering of the events, the king effectively negated the meaning of the legatine entry. He did not accept the legate's authority.

Katherine Harvey points out that canon law never conferred any legal significance to the *adventus*, presumably due to opportunities for resistance at *adventus* ceremonies.[134] The *adventus* was one of the rare occasions for direct ritual negotiation to take place between rulers and subjects. As Margot Fassler argues: 'the crowd was (and is) almost as important as those feted'.[135] Without participation, an *adventus* would fizzle out in awkward silence and empty streets. Gregory Nazianzen (*c.* 329–90), biographer of Bishop Athanasius of Alexandria, claimed that even more people welcomed Athanasius on his return from exile than those who had welcomed the emperor.[136] The size of the crowd mattered. If being received with an *adventus* was a legal prerequisite for one's office, whether as legate, abbot, bishop, or pope, empty streets and the refusal to welcome a prospective lord could be disastrous.

Empty streets were something the curia had to contend with. During the eleventh century, the curia excluded the Romans from their customary part in the election of the pope, making the cardinalate the sole electoral body. Henceforth, once the cardinals elected a pope, the position of the curia was that the elect was pope, regardless of Roman opinion. As mentioned, the curia simultaneously advanced an interpretation of participation in the papal *adventus* inauguration 'as acquiescence in the divine will',[137] that is, as tacit consent to papal rule. In this way, the curia not only suppressed Roman influence on the election of a new pope but also required the Romans to accept whomever the cardinals elected as pope 'by the grace of God'. This arrangement left the Romans embittered – after all, the pope was the secular lord of Rome.

According to Twyman, the Romans refused to attend the papal *adventus* into Rome if the cardinals physically moved outside of the city, proceeding to elect someone pope outside of the walls,[138] therein withholding recognition of the pope's lordship 'until the people's right of ratification had been expressed'.[139] Boso

---

[133] See also Sprey, 'Papal Legates', pp. 111–16.
[134] Harvey, 'The First Entry', esp. pp. 47–49.
[135] Fassler, '*Adventus* at Chartres', p. 13.
[136] Gregory Nazianzen, 'In laudem Athanasii', cols. 1113–14.
[137] Twyman, *Papal Ceremonial at Rome*, p. 219.
[138] Ibid., esp. pp. 139–164.
[139] Ibid., p. 219. See also Paravicini-Bagliani, *The Pope's Body*, pp. 44–45. For another explanation, see Joëlle Rollo-Koster, *Raiding Saint Peter: Empty Sees, Violence, and the Initiation of the Great Western Schism (1378)* (Leiden: Brill, 2008), p. 68.

stressed the reception of Pope Alexander at Rome because he needed to demonstrate public acquiescence.[140] Nevertheless, the inability to safeguard the *adventus* from Roman public opposition might have dissuaded the curia from inserting the ceremony into canon law. If the ceremony had legal implications, such as pope-making or the acceptance of legatine authority, the recipients could nullify an election or an appointment simply by refusing to grant an *adventus*. It seems likely (even if I cannot prove it definitively) that the ceremony remained out of the legal sphere, not because the ceremony did not matter, but because it *did* matter.

Papal subjects sometimes refused to grant a papal legate an *adventus*. In 1096, the clergy of Tours refused to receive one of Pope Urban II's legates, Amatus of Oléron, with a solemn procession. Amatus was so outraged that he promptly excommunicated the clergy (the pope later rebuked the clergy but relaxed the sentence).[141] In 1192, Pope Celestine III (r. 1191–98) dispatched two legates *a latere* to Normandy, tasking them to mediate between William Longchamp and Walter de Coutances, archbishop of Rouen (r. 1184–1207). However, according to Roger of Howden, William FitzRalph, the seneschal of Normandy, shut the gates of Gisors against the legates. In retaliation, the legates excommunicated William FitzRalph and subjected the whole of Normandy to interdict.[142]

Conversely, those in power might refuse to be received in order to express their disfavour. Roger of Howden reported that King John declined the canons of Beverley's invitation to receive him with a procession:

> When the canons of Beverley wished to receive him [King John] with a procession and the ringing of bells, he refused to be received, nor would he allow them [the bells] to be rung.[143]

The cause of the discord is unknown, but it is possible that the king's dispute with Archbishop Geoffrey of York (r. 1189–1212) played a part. Whatever the case, it probably made the canons nervous.

---

[140] See also Twyman, *Papal Ceremonial at Rome*, pp. 165–67.
[141] See *Urbani II Pontificis Romani Epistolæ, Diplomata, Sermones, PL* (Paris, 1853), vol. 151, no. 177, col. 450.
[142] *Gesta*, vol. 2, pp. 246–47, 249–50. See also Wilhelm Janssen, *Die päpstlichen Legaten in Frankreich von Schisma Anaklets II. bis zum Tode Coelestins III. (1130–1198)* (Cologne: Böhlau, 1961), pp. 130–40.
[143] *The Annals*, vol. 2, p. 517 (translation adjusted); *Chronica*, vol. 4, p. 156: 'cum canonici Beverlacenses vellent eum cum processione et sonitu campanarum recipere, noluit recipi, nec permisit eos sonare'.

LEGATINE VULNERABILITY

A legatine entry was doubtless an impressive sight, aiming to impress on those present that papal lordship had arrived. At the head of the procession would be the cross-bearer, followed closely by the legate, who would be leading the procession of his entourage – with all involved dressed in their finest. The cardinal-legate *a latere* would enter his province surrounded by apostolic insignia and ceremony, making him indistinguishable from the pope at a distance. He would arrive as a lord with considerable power and extensive jurisdiction. Canon law granted legates the right to exercise their powers immediately upon entry into their provinces.[144] Papal subjects could not legally refuse his authority nor deny him help, support, or procurations. Since the pontificate of Gregory VII (and possibly before), the clergy were obliged to take an oath, promising support for papal legates.[145] It is included in Gratian's *Decretum*: 'I will treat honourably a legate of the Apostolic See (whom I will have recognised as a genuine legate) both in his coming and going, and I will aid him in his necessities.'[146]

In reality, papal subjects were not always keen to take on the burden of hosting a legate. Gerhoch of Reichersberg (1093–1169) claimed that legatine retinues swelled to 'forty or more horses, so that the wealthiest monasteries (to say nothing of the poorer or middling houses) and even bishops and princes cannot afford to supply the wants of such a crowd'.[147] Roger of Wendover claimed that 'coming into England [in 1213] with only seven horsemen, he [Cardinal Nicholas] in a short time advanced with fifty [horses/horsemen] and was surrounded closely by an excessively great household'.[148]

The veracity of such claims is difficult to corroborate, but the papacy certainly did legislate against excessive retinues. In 1179, the Third Lateran Council limited

---

[144] Figueira, 'The Canon Law', pp. 415–61.

[145] Ibid., p. 397. See also Rueß, *Die rechtliche Stellung*, p. 187.

[146] *Liber Extravagantium Decretalium*, ed. Emil Friedberg, 2 vols, Corpus Iuris Canonici 2 (reprint, Leipzig; Graz: Bernhard Tauchnitz; Akademische Druck u. Verlagsanstalt, 1959), vol. 2, X 2.24.4; available at www.hs-augsburg.de/~harsch/Chronologia/Lspost13/GregoriusIX/gre_0000.html (accessed 15 April 2024): 'Legatum apostolicae sedis, quem certum legatum esse cognovero, in eundo et redeundo honorifice tractabo, et in suis necessitatibus adiuvabo'. Translated by Figueira, 'The Canon Law', p. 397.

[147] Gerhoch of Reichersberg, 'De Investigatione Antichristi', in *Libelli de lite imperatorum et pontificum*, eds Ernst Dümmler and Ernst Sackur, MGH: Ldl 3 (Hannover: Hahn, 1897), c. 50, pp. 305–95, at p. 357: 'quadraginta aut eo amplius equos se moderans, ut ne dicam pauperiora vel mediocria cenobia, sed ne predivitia quidem, vix autem episcopi et principes eorum multitudini ad voluntatem servire sufficiant'. Translated by Robinson, *The Papacy 1073–1198*, p. 162.

[148] *Flowers of History*, vol. 2, p. 90 (translation adjusted); *Flores Historiarum*, vol. 2, p. 94: 'cum septem tantum equitaturis in Angliam veniens, quinquaginta in brevi et familia multa nimis stipatus incessit'.

the size of the retinues of cardinal-legates to twenty-five horses. The Fourth Lateran reiterated the limit in 1215.[149] Even if it is unclear whether the twenty-five horses equalled the number of people in the entourage, or if cardinals always abided by the restrictions, the popes were at least aware of the optics of putting some restrictions in place. Archbishop Stephen's provision of 'the necessary horses' ('equis necessariis') to Cardinal Nicholas implies that Nicholas arrived with fewer horses than men.[150] Although contemporary evidence regarding the composition of legatine retinues is sparse, later evidence reveals that legates staffed their retinues from their own households (their *familiae*) and that legates organised their staffs in imitation of the papal chancery.[151] A legate might also hire staff from within his own province.[152]

Nevertheless, for all the support, glamour, and power, a cardinal-legate *a latere* was also vulnerable to physical threats. In 1238, scholars from Oxford attacked Cardinal-Legate Otto and his retinue at Oseney Abbey over a perceived slight. At least one of Otto's men was killed. Otto had to flee and seek the help of King Henry III.[153] Under canon law, Otto had diplomatic immunity, rendering the actions of the Oxford scholars punishable as lèse-majesté.[154] Pope Innocent's reaction to the murder in 1208 of one of his legates, Pierre de Castelnau, suggests that he viewed it as an attack upon his own person, launching the Albigensian crusade in response.[155]

Such retaliation cannot disguise the fact that cardinal-legates were largely dependent on the cooperation of their subjects. Unique among contemporary lords, a cardinal-legate was a lord within his legatine province, but his resources

---

[149] Norman P. Tanner, ed., *Decrees of the Ecumenical Councils, Vol. 1: Nicaea I to Lateran V*, 2 vols (London: Sheed & Ward, 1990), c. 4, p. 213: 'cardinals should not exceed twenty or twenty-five [horses]' ('cardinales vero viginti vel viginti quinque non excedant'). García y García, *Constitutiones Concilii quarti Lateranensis*, c. 33, p. 77.

[150] Mercati, 'La prima relazione', p. 277.

[151] See Frances Ann Underhill, 'Papal Legates to England in the Reign of Henry III (1216–1272)' (unpublished PhD dissertation, Indiana University, Bloomington, 1965), pp. 58–60; and B. R. Beattie, *Angelus Pacis: The Legation of Cardinal Giovanni Gaetano Orsino, 1326-1334* (Leiden: Brill, 2007), pp. 157–65. For an introduction to the chancery, see Robinson, *The Papacy 1073-1198*, pp. 93–98.

[152] Ina Feinberg Friedländer, *Die päpstlichen Legaten in Deutschland und Italien am Ende des XII Jahrhunderts (1181–1198)* (Berlin: Matthiesen Verlag, 1928), pp. 137–38. See also Antonín Kalous, *Late Medieval Papal Legation: Between the Councils and the Reformation* (Rome: Viella, 2017), pp. 129–35.

[153] See David L. Sheffler, 'An Early Oxford Riot: Oseney Abbey, 1238', in *History of Universities*, ed. Mordechai Feingold and Jane Finucane, vol. 21 (Oxford: Oxford University Press, 2006), pp. 1–32.

[154] Figueira, 'The Canon Law', pp. 15–23, 389–95; Rueß, *Die rechtliche Stellung*, pp. 185–87.

[155] See, e.g., Elaine Graham-Leigh, *The Southern French Nobility and the Albigensian Crusade* (Woodbridge: Boydell Press, 2005), esp. pp. 46–50.

and networks were usually located in and around Rome. Some of a legate's subjects were great lords themselves, kings even, and not accustomed to being ordered around by any individual. A legate was dependent on such great men, entering their domains and lordships, and requiring their protection and support in order to be able to move around inside the legatine province. While it is impossible to know for certain if King Henry I verbally assaulted Cardinal Peter the way Eadmer claimed, this was apparently conceivable.

Using David Smith's work, Rennie argues that legates may be considered to be 'projected leaders':[156]

> whose 'charismatic' traits are thus a function of public belief and action. That these exalted figures are elevated far above the crowd is a reflection of how they are treated and regarded … Their 'magnetism' is never inherent; it is an emergent result of popular projection.[157]

Such projection never existed in a vacuum, but rather was informed by the circumstances of the legation – was the legate welcome? what was at stake? – and by the doctrine of papal legation.

Communicating the concept of papal legation was crucial for legatine success. Christina Pössel argues that 'whilst gestures can be subtle, they cannot communicate elaborate symbolic meanings involving Christian theology: those require words'.[158] The curial view on legates was and is indiscernible by rituals and insignia alone. We have some knowledge of the curial view because papal letters and propaganda strove to rhetorically foster a sensitivity to and understanding of the curial view on legates. Had Christendom accepted his claims without question, Gregory VII would not have needed to write a letter demanding that papal subjects receive his legate as if St Peter were present himself. Similarly, Innocent alleged that his legate embodied Christ, which would not have been necessary to assert had the claim been popularly accepted.

However, recipients did not need to comprehend everything or accept all claims. Kim Esmark argues that:

---

[156] Rennie, *The Foundations*, esp. pp. 29–30.
[157] David Norman Smith, 'Faith, Reason, and Charisma: Rudolf Sohm, Max Weber, and the Theology of Grace', *Sociological Inquiry* 68, no. 1 (1998): 32–60, p. 52.
[158] Christina Pössel, 'The Magic of Early Medieval Ritual', *Early Medieval Europe* 17, no. 2 (2009): 111–25, p. 122.

Ritual actors and audiences did not need to believe wholeheartedly in the sincerity of everything that went on in a particular ceremony or to share the same perception of deep-lying meaning(s) of the symbols, gestures, and speeches involved: as long as they agreed to, or accepted the need for, participation, it worked.[159]

Of course, the less consensus there was, the higher the risk of dissent. The curia argued that legates were limbs of the pope, capable of saturating their surroundings with Romaness, Petrine power, and Christly presence. Legatine display – with ritual and insignia – was designed to foster such ideas. The curia strove to influence 'popular projection': to make the public adopt specific behaviours towards papal legates. However, neither the curia nor its legates could utterly control this projection. While legates might nurture it, popular projection was ultimately a negotiation between the reception of papal doctrine outside of Rome and the interpretation and assessment of papal claims by the populaces and their leaders.

For all these reasons, the *adventus* probably mattered more to curial legates than to other lords, being a crucial point of contact, of ritual negotiation, and of testing one another. A king who returned home from abroad might decide to exact revenge on a city if he did not feel the citizens offered a proper welcome. The powers of cardinal-legates should not be taken lightly, especially if the pope decided to back his legates, but legates did not wield brute, violent force in the same manner as kings or warrior aristocrats (a few exceptions aside). A legate's ability to get things done centred around diplomacy, optics, and perception. It is reasonable to imagine a cardinal-legate nearing his province with some trepidation. Letters and messengers would have been exchanged prior to his arrival, providing him with some sense of the mood and the attitude in his province, but it was at the entry into his province that the crucial first impressions took place. The perceived success or failure of the *adventus* would have significantly impacted the perception of the legate's authority and the legate's ability to exercise his powers.

Conclusion

The exploration of the legatine insignia and the legatine *adventus* reinforces the image of an elusive figure. The legate's identity, purpose, and power were shaped by various changing ideas and influences. At one end of the spectrum was the papal projection. As an extension of the pope, the legate was granted access to the apostolic language of power: insignia and ritual. The bedrock of legatine authority

---

[159] Kim Esmark, 'Just Rituals: Masquerade, Manipulation, and Officialising Strategies in Saxo's Gesta Danorum', in *Rituals, Performatives, and Political Order in Northern Europe, c. 650–1350*, ed. Wojtek Jerzierski et al. (Turnhout: Brepols, 2015), pp. 237–67, at p. 243.

and achievements was built on the success of the papacy to champion papal pre-eminence. This was the reason the legate mirrored the pope in both appearance and in ceremonial entry, communicating his intimate connection to the pope and to papal concepts: this was a visible claim to authority and jurisdiction.

This very image of authority was put to the test at the point of entry into the province, and the interpretation of the legatine *adventus* could vary. While few questioned the meaning of the *adventus*, granting that it signified acceptance of lordship and authority, the interpretations of its implications might fluctuate. The curia viewed the legatine reception as an acknowledgement of the legate's divinely ordained apostolic authority. Boso argued for this interpretation, while Cardinal Nicholas assumed that the pope and his fellow cardinals required no explanation. Eadmer of Canterbury, on the other hand, pushed back against the curial interpretation in his account of King Henry I's reaction to Legate Peter Pierleoni.

The legate found himself far from home, reliant on kings, bishops, and others to accept the curial perspective. He depended on his subjects' cooperation more than most lords of the period. Hence, the legate's insignia and his ritual entrance carried immense symbolic importance. While it would be misleading to suggest that all (or perhaps even most) legatine *adventus* ceremonies were met with resistance or subjected to subversive interpretations, some were. A legate nearing his province could never be entirely certain about his reception or the mark he left on the pages of the chronicles. The legate, whether overtly or implicitly, argued that he brought with him the presence of St Peter and Christ. Did people accept these assertions? Perhaps this did not (always) matter. Regardless, the legate's office and his abilities were dictated not solely by the papacy but also by those who received him and interpreted the meaning of his reception.

3

Instructing a Proper Welcome: Normative Guides to the *Adventus*

Most cardinals were Italians.[1] They found themselves far from home, far from their networks, and far from their resources, which left them in a vulnerable position. Still, they were considered to be powerful lords, and as such, they wielded significant power. Not only might legates have anticipated the *adventus* with unease, recipients of cardinal-legates might have felt likewise. Recipients, especially if they were minor players, needed to live up to expectations, executing the *adventus* successfully, lest they wanted to risk the ire of one of the most powerful ecclesiastical lords in Europe.

Numerous *adventus* ceremonies have left no written evidence beyond the casual note. Many have undoubtedly been lost to the passage of time, leaving no trace whatsoever. In many instances, the preparations for and the performance of the ceremony likely depended on collective experience and tradition. Medieval authors only showed interest in the specifics of a reception if something particularly significant was at stake or if a reception held a special meaning. In like manner, some authors composed treatises on the appropriate way to welcome a dignitary with an *adventus*, often in response to some form of monastic reassessment or reform. The titles of these treatises vary in the medieval sources – sometimes there are no titles – but I have labelled them collectively as '*adventus* instructions' for the sake of convenience.

The *adventus* instructions are a kind of semiregular subgenre within the broader genre of monastic customary. 'Monastic customary' is also a term of convenience, as medieval authors employed various labels such as *constitutiones* (constitutions), *statuta* (statutes), and *consuetudines* (customs/habits). Monastic authors produced monastic customaries for a range of purposes at various houses throughout their history. The customaries primarily addressed needs not covered

---

[1] Werner Maleczek, 'Die Kardinäle von 1143 bis 1216. Exklusive Papstwähler und erste Agenten der päpstlichen *plenitudo potestatis*', in *Geschichte des Kardinalats im Mittelalter*, ed. Jürgen Dendorfer and Ralf Lützelschwab (Stuttgart: Hiersemann, 2011), pp. 95–154, esp. pp. 106–9.

by the authoritative monastic rules, most notably the Rule of St Benedict.[2] According to Isabelle Cochelin, they varied in nature from the inspirational and aspirational to the normative. Customaries were composed by insiders as deliberations on proper monastic life. During the early Middle Ages, customaries primarily served as sources of inspiration. By the twelfth century, however, authors of customaries often had a more normative agenda, even if the transition from inspirational to normative was neither smooth nor universal.[3] From the eleventh century onward, authors of customaries began to include thoughts on ceremonial receptions (*adventus* instructions).[4]

In this chapter, I will study three *adventus* instructions in detail. The first is a part of Archbishop Lanfranc of Canterbury's Monastic Constitutions, the second is a part of the Cistercian *Ecclesiastica Officia*, and the third is contained within the Rule of St Gilbert. The Rule of St Gilbert was composed at a time when it was evident that it was useful to include the *adventus* instruction in the rule. Additionally, I will discuss other less informative instructions towards the end of the chapter. I have selected instructions that were in usage in twelfth- and thirteenth-century England.

The study of these instructions serves two interrelated purposes. Firstly, the instructions show the significance of ritual practice. As Buc and others note, the nature of the evidence militates against the view that any recorded instance of a ritual is a concrete record of an actual performance. However, the *adventus* instructions reveal that certain monastic authors dedicated substantial thought to the practice of receiving a dignitary with an *adventus*. In this way, the instructions showcase the anxieties of the recipients: their worries and even the potential dangers.

Second, studying the *adventus* instructions reveals that most narrative accounts of receptions provide brief outlines of what likely transpired. The instructions illuminate the extensiveness of the *adventus* and its potential for multiple layers of meaning. Conversely, the narrative accounts often exhibit selectivity, emphasising and singling out certain elements of the ceremony to create the desired impression of the relationship defined or reinforced during the *adventus*.

---

[2] For an introduction to the most important rules and customaries, see the studies in *A Companion to Medieval Rules and Customaries*, ed. Krijn Pansters (Leiden: Brill, 2020).

[3] Isabelle Cochelin, 'Customaries as Inspirational Sources', in *Consuetudines et Regulae: Sources for Monastic Life in the Middle Ages and the Early Modern Period*, ed. Carolyn Marino Malone and Clark Maines (Turnhout: Brepols, 2014), pp. 27–72.

[4] The eleventh-century Cluniac *Consuetudines Farfa* alludes to the existence of tenth-century ordos regulating receptions at monasteries; see Martin Heinzelmann, *Translationsberichte und andere Quellen des Reliquienkultes* (Turnhout: Brepols, 1979), p. 74; and Ernst Hartwig Kantorowicz, 'The "King's Advent" and the Enigmatic Panels in the Doors of Santa Sabina', *The Art Bulletin* 26, no. 4 (1944): 207–31, pp. 208–9.

Producing Adventus *Instructions*

The impetus for producing *adventus* instructions undoubtedly lay in the Rule of St Benedict's two contradictory principles of hospitality and isolation. The Rule of St Benedict was the most important rule in England during the twelfth and thirteenth centuries,[5] not only because England had a large community of ancient Benedictine houses, but because the most important new order emerging out of the 'medieval reformation', the Cistercian order, also relied on the Rule of St Benedict.[6] The Gilbertines, moreover, looked to the Cistercians for guidance.[7]

The duty to provide hospitality was enshrined in chapter 53 of the Rule:

> All guests who present themselves are to be welcomed as Christ, for he himself will say: I was a stranger and you welcomed me [Matthew 25:35].[8]

The chapter further requires that the monks receive guests 'with all the courtesy of love' ('cum omni officio caritatis').[9] This reception would include prayer, the kiss of peace, gestures of humility (bowing or prostration), and washing of feet and hands. Monastic hosts should also provide lodging and food.[10] Julie Kerr characterises these provisions for hospitality as moral and sacred imperatives, given for honour, networking, and gifts.[11] Kerr argues that monks shared a 'culture

---

[5] Concerning the history and importance of the Rule of St Benedict, see *Rule of Benedict*, pp. lvii–lxii; and James G. Clark, 'The Rule of Saint Benedict', in *A Companion to Medieval Rules and Customaries*, ed. Pansters, pp. 37–76, at pp. 37–46. Concerning the Benedictines, see esp. James G. Clark, *The Benedictines in the Middle Ages* (Woodbridge: Boydell Press, 2011).

[6] Brenda M. Bolton, *The Medieval Reformation* (London: Edward Arnold, 1983). See also, e.g., David Knowles, *The Monastic Order in England: A History of Its Development from the Times of St Dunstan to The Fourth Lateran Council, 940–1216*, 2nd edn (Cambridge: Cambridge University Press, 1963).

[7] Brian Golding, *Gilbert of Sempringham and the Gilbertine Order, c.1130–c.1300* (Oxford: Clarendon Press, 1995), esp. pp. 26–33, 78–138.

[8] *Rule of Benedict*, ch. 53, 1, translation at p. 406, Latin at p. 405: 'omnes supervenientes hospites tamquam Christus suscipiantur, quia ipse dicturus est: *Hospes fui et suscepistis me*'.

[9] Ibid., ch. 53, 3, translation at p. 406, Latin at p. 405.

[10] Ibid., ch. 53, translation at pp. 406–7, Latin at pp. 405–6. Some of the detailed prescriptions about lodging and food may be later interpolations; see ibid., p. 414.

[11] Julie Kerr, *Monastic Hospitality: The Benedictines in England, c.1070–c.1250* (Woodbridge: Boydell Press, 2007), pp. 23–49. St Benedict's prescriptions on the reception of non-dignitaries were taken up by later customaries; see, e.g., *The Customary of the Benedictine Abbey of Eynsham in Oxfordshire*, ed. Antonia Gransden (Siegburg: Franciscum Schmitt, 1963), ch. 19, ii, pp. 198–201, esp. 198–99. See also Kerr, *Monastic Hospitality*, pp. 94–110.

of hospitality' with the rest of society.[12] The Augustinian Barnwell Observances maintained that 'by showing cheerful hospitality to guests the reputation of the monastery is increased, friendships are multiplied, animosities are blunted, God is honoured, charity is increased, and a plenteous reward in heaven is promised'.[13] Their rule(s) did not even mention hospitality.[14]

St Benedict, however, was aware that the presence of visitors might be disruptive:[15]

> No one is to speak or associate with guests unless he is bidden [presumably by the abbot]; however, if a brother meets or sees a guest, he is to greet him humbly, as we have said. He asks for a blessing and continues on his way, explaining that he is not allowed to speak with a guest.[16]

The famous Hildegard of Bingen (c. 1098–1179), German abbess and preacher, wrote a commentary on St Benedict's Rule. It is tentatively dated to 1160.[17] She commented on chapter 53:

> At that time [of St Benedict] monks did not yet feel the press of a tumult of strangers crowding upon them. However, those who did come to them were seeking there nothing else but Christ; and they found Him there in the holy works.[18]

---

[12] Julie Kerr, 'The Open Door: Hospitality and Honour in Twelfth/Early Thirteenth-Century England', *History* 87, no. 287 (2002): 322–35.

[13] John Willis Clark, ed., *The Observances in Use at the Augustinian Priory of S. Giles and S. Andrew at Barnwell, Cambridgeshire* (Cambridge: Macmillan and Bowes, 1897), pp. 192–93: 'ex hospitum hyllari suscepcione accrescit honor monasterii, multiplicantur amici, hebetantur inimici, deus honoratur, caritas augetur, et in celis merces copiosa promittitur'.

[14] See Saint Augustine, *The Monastic Rules*, ed. Boniface Ramsey, trans. Agatha Mary and Gerald Bonner (New York: New City Press, 2004).

[15] See also Kerr, *Monastic Hospitality*, pp. 64–75, 162–66; and Clark, *The Benedictines*, pp. 14–15, 130–31, 167–69.

[16] *Rule of Benedict*, ch. 53, 23–24, translation at p. 407, Latin at p. 406: 'Hospitibus autem cui non praecipitur ullatenus societur neque colloquatur; sed si obviaverit aut viderit, salutatis humiliter, ut diximus, et petita benedictione pertranseat, dicens sibi non licere colloqui cum hospite.'

[17] Hildegard of Bingen, *Explanation of the Rule of Benedict*, trans. Hugh Feiss (Eugene, OR: Wipf & Stock, 2000), p. 8.

[18] Hildegard of Bingen, ch. 26, p. 63; Hildegard of Bingen [Hildegardis], 'Regulæ S. Benedicti Explanatio', in *PL*, 2nd edn, 197 (Paris: Garnier Printing, 1882), cols. 1053–66, col. 1061: 'Illo etenim tempore. monachi tumultum supervenientum extraneorum

The world had changed since the time of St Benedict (sixth century). Not only did monasteries experience an increase in numbers of visitors, but, according to Hildegard, the reasons for visiting were not always pious, leaving the orderliness of monastic life open to disruption.

Two developments in the twelfth and thirteenth centuries show that English ecclesiastics shared Hildegard's assessment. The first development took the form of internal disputes over the cost of visitors. Many houses had separate revenues for the head and the convent, resulting in controversies about the distribution and financial burden of guests.[19] The second development was the widespread erection of separate accommodations for visitors. Many also appointed a guestmaster (often a monk with assistants), whose task was to receive and entertain the guests. In this way, a house could retain a sense of isolation whilst showing hospitality.

The great ceremonial receptions – the *adventus* ceremonies – probably proved the most troublesome because they involved the entire community. Some customaries therefore prohibited repetition. The Cistercian *Ecclesiastica Officia* stipulates that 'this procession is never made more than once for one and the same person, the only exception being the lord pope'.[20] The Barnwell Observances state that 'our bishop, on his first visit after his consecration, ought to be received with a solemn procession'.[21] It is evident from the context that they should *only* receive the bishop with a procession on his first visit.

It is in all likelihood the monastic contradictions, hospitality and fear of disruption, which explain (in combination with the existence of experienced monastic scribes) why monasteries were the main producers of *adventus* instructions, even if each instruction was the product of a set of particular circumstances. Papal curialists also produced *adventus* instructions, but they viewed the *adventus* from the point of view of the one being received.[22] The twelfth and thirteenth centuries also saw an increase in works on etiquette and hospitality across Europe.[23]

---

nondum sentiebant; sed qui eos adibant, Christum et non aliud ibi quærebant, quem etiam in sanctis operibus ibi inveniebant.'

[19] Kerr, *Monastic Hospitality*, pp. 50–63. See, e.g., *The Customary of the Benedictine Abbey of Bury St Edmunds in Suffolk (from Harleian MS. 1005 in the British Museum)*, ed. Antonia Gransden (Chichester: Moore and Tillyer, The Regnum Press, 1966), pp. xix–xxi, 5–7, 66, 104; and Barbara F. Harvey, ed., *Documents Illustrating the Rule of Walter de Wenlock, Abbot of Westminster, 1283–1307* (London: Butler & Tanner, 1965), pp. 217–22.

[20] *Ancient Usages*, ch. 86, 11–12 (translation adjusted); *Ecclesiastica Officia*, ch. 86, 12, p. 246: 'nulli horum omnium nisi domno pape plusquam semel hec fit processio'.

[21] Clark, *The Observances*, ch. 30, pp. 150–51: 'in primo aduentu suo post consecracionem debet episcopus noster suscipi cum processione sollempni'.

[22] Susan E. Twyman, *Papal Ceremonial at Rome in the Twelfth Century* (London: Boydell Press, 2002), esp. pp. 23–36.

[23] See, e.g., Jonathan Nicholls, *The Matter of Courtesy: Medieval Courtesy Books and the Gawain-Poet* (Cambridge: D.S. Brewer, 1985); and John Gillingham, 'From Civilitas to

England produced the *Urbanus magnus*. Uncertainty surrounds its authorship and composition, but the most likely scenario is that a certain Daniel of Beccles, probably a secular clerk, began composing the work *c.* 1180, and that it was later expanded and edited in the middle of the thirteenth century. It was written for the head of a wealthy household.[24] It devotes a few lines to receptions, advising that:

> If a cleric or knight comes to stay with you / hurry to greet him and make him feel welcome when he arrives. / If he is dear to you, embrace him and kiss him, / and have all of your comforts laid out to show your affection for him.[25]

The *Urbanus magnus* is interesting in its own right, but it does not contain a detailed *adventus* instruction. Only the monastic communities produced comprehensive instructions, and unsurprisingly this somewhat skews the picture, giving the impression that only monks cared about the reception of powerful dignitaries. While it is true that papal legates were generally more important to the clergy than to the secular nobility, it is not accurate to state that the king cared little about papal-legatine authority. In fact, this authority was very important to the English kings, who often distrusted foreign papal legates, regarding them as challengers to their authority over the English Church. However, English monarchs were also keen on utilising the domestic (arch)bishop-legates to their advantage, even if this was not always executed successfully.[26] Just before departing on the Third Crusade, King Richard effected the appointment of his chancellor and co-justiciar, Bishop William Longchamp of Ely, as papal legate because he needed him to govern England in his absence. Richard would later use Archbishop Hubert Walter of Canterbury (r. 1193–1205) in a similar way.[27] However, when Cardinal-Legate John of Anagni (a curial legate and, hence, not subservient to King Richard) arrived at Dover in late 1189, Richard forbade him from proceeding

---

Civility: Codes of Manners in Medieval and Early Modern England', *Transactions of the Royal Historical Society* 12 (2002): 267–89.

[24] Fiona Whelan, *The Making of Manners and Morals in Twelfth-Century England: The Book of the Civilised Man* (London: Routledge, 2017), pp. 1–19, esp. pp. 18–19.

[25] Daniel of Beccles, *The Book of the Civilised Man: An English Translation of the Urbanus Magnus of Daniel of Beccles*, trans. Fiona Whelan, Olivia Spenser, and Francesca Petrizzo (London: Routledge, 2019), ll. 2343–46, pp. 121–22; Daniel of Beccles, *Urbanus Magnus Danielis Becclesiensis*, ed. J. Gilbert Smyly (Dublin: Dublin University Press, 1939), ll. 2343–46, p. 77: 'Clericus aut miles ad te si uenerit hospes, / Occurrens properes illi mellire salutes. / Si tibi sit carus, amplexus, oscula prestes, / Et tibi que bona sunt mensentur frontis honore.'

[26] Ilicia Jo Sprey, 'Papal Legates in English Politics, 1100–1272' (unpublished PhD dissertation, University of Virginia, Charlottesville, 1998), pp. 92–240.

[27] Ibid., pp. 221–40.

inland. The legate was on a mission to resolve the dispute between the archbishop of Canterbury and the chapter at Canterbury Cathedral. Richard had the cardinal wait at Dover until he had settled the case himself; only then did he allow the cardinal to proceed to Canterbury, receiving him with an *adventus*.[28]

Lanfranc of Canterbury and the Adventus Instruction

Archbishop Lanfranc of Canterbury was born at Pavia in Italy around 1010.[29] For reasons not fully known, he went to Normandy in the early 1030s. There, he had a distinguished career as a teacher, theologian, and prior at Bec Abbey, where he wrote a highly praised commentary on St Paul's epistles.[30] In 1063, Lanfranc became abbot of the important ducal house of St Étienne at Caen. In 1070, papal legates helped William (duke of Normandy 1035–87, king of England 1066–87) to oust Archbishop Stigand from Canterbury, paving the way for Lanfranc's promotion to that see the same year.[31] Lanfranc held this position until his death in 1089.

Lanfranc was an atypical choice for an ambitious duke and eventual king to promote to high office. Lanfranc had no landed wealth or armed retainers to offer; however, as David Bates argues, he could offer William access to the curia. Lanfranc had travelled with Pope Leo IX's entourage in 1050, probably forging ties with the major curial figures who would come to dominate papal policy for the next thirty-five years. William had use for such contacts.[32] It was, as mentioned, papal legates who deposed Archbishop Stigand, paving the way for Lanfranc. Lanfranc later maintained that he owed his archsee to the papacy.[33]

---

[28] William Stubbs, ed., *Epistolæ Cantuarienses, the Letters of the Prior and Convent of Christ Church, Canterbury. From A.D. 1187 to A.D. 1199*, RS (London: Longman, 1865), nos. 325–34, pp. 310–22. See pp. 125–28 for more information on the incident and the dispute.

[29] Biographies of Lanfranc include H. E. J. Cowdrey, *Lanfranc: Scholar, Monk, Archbishop* (Oxford: Oxford University Press, 2003); Margaret Gibson, *Lanfranc of Bec* (Oxford: Clarendon Press, 1978); and Allan John MacDonald, *Lanfranc: A Study of His Life, Work and Writing*, 2nd edn (London: Society for Promoting Christian Knowledge, 1944). David Bates, *William the Conqueror* (New Haven: Yale University Press, 2016) devotes some space to Lanfranc.

[30] Cowdrey, *Lanfranc*, pp. 5–16, 19–20, 46–59.

[31] Helene Tillmann, *Die päpstlichen Legaten in England bis zur Beendigung der Legation Gualas, 1218* (Bonn: Hch. Ludwig, 1926), pp. 13–14; Cowdrey, *Lanfranc*, pp. 79–81. John Godfrey suggests that Pope Alexander II (r. 1061–73) supported the invasion of England to depose Stigand; see John Godfrey, *The Church in Anglo-Saxon England* (New York: Cambridge University Press, 1962), p. 406.

[32] Bates, *William the Conqueror*, p. 101. See also Cowdrey, *Lanfranc*, pp. 38–45.

[33] See Lanfranc, *Beati Lanfranci archiepiscopi Cantuariensis Opera quae supersunt omnia*, ed. J. A. Giles, 2 vols (Oxford: Paul Renouard, 1844), vol. 1, no. 3, pp. 19–20.

Lanfranc composed his Monastic Constitutions c. 1077,[34] with his own two monastic communities in mind: Canterbury Cathedral, where he doubled as abbot, and St Albans, where his nephew was abbot.[35] He sought inspiration in the 'customs of those monasteries, which in our day have the greatest prestige in the monastic order',[36] in particular, the abbeys of Bec and Cluny.[37] He made his Constitutions available to anyone interested,[38] but, as J. Armitage Robinson showed more than a hundred years ago, Lanfranc did not intend to impose his Constitutions on the Anglo-Saxon Church, as was previously believed.[39] Besides Canterbury Cathedral and St Albans, Arnold Klukas has identified at least thirteen houses that used Lanfranc's Constitutions.[40]

It is unclear how long the Constitutions remained in use. Matthew Paris, writing sometime in the 1240s and 1250s, mentioned the existence of a manuscript at St Albans,[41] but not whether its provisions were actually in use. A late twelfth-century Norwegian translation of the Constitutions provides us with better evidence. This translation probably owes its existence to Archbishop Øystein of Nidaros, who was in exile in England between 1180 and 1183.[42] The production of this doc-

---

[34] On the dating of Lanfranc's Monastic Constitutions, see *The Monastic Constitutions*, p. xxviii.

[35] Ibid., pp. xxxiii–xxxv.

[36] Ibid., p. 2: 'consuetudinibus eorum cenobiorum, que nostro tempore maioris auctoritatis sunt in ordine monachorum'.

[37] Ibid., pp. xxxvi–xliii.

[38] Ibid., pp. xxx–xxxi. Seven manuscripts and one fragment of the Constitutions exist today; see ibid., pp. xliii–liv.

[39] J. Armitage Robinson, 'Lanfranc's Monastic Constitutions', *The Journal of Theological Studies* 10, no. 39 (1909): 375–88.

[40] These were Westminster Abbey, Battle Abbey, Durham Cathedral Priory, Evesham Abbey, Eynsham Abbey, Great Malvern Priory, Lindisfarne Priory, St Augustine's Abbey, Rochester Cathedral Priory, St Martin's Priory (Dover), Binham Priory, Tynemouth Priory, Wymondham Priory, and perhaps Thorney Abbey and Croyland Abbey. Worcester and Hereford cathedrals had copies of the Constitutions, but they did not use them; see Arnold William Klukas, 'The Architectural Implications of the Decreta Lanfranci', in *ANS VI*, ed. R. Allen Brown (Woodbridge: Boydell Press, 1984), pp. 136–71, at pp. 140–44. See also *The Monastic Constitutions*, pp. xxx–xxxiii.

[41] Matthew Paris, 'Gesta Abbatum', in *Gesta abbatum monasterii Sancti Albani, a Thoma Walsingham, regnante Ricardo Secundo, ejusdem ecclesiæ præcentore, compilata*, ed. Henry Thomas Riley, 3 vols, RS (London: Longmans, 1867), vol. 1, pp. 3–324, at p. 52.

[42] Lilli Gjerløw, *Adoratio Crucis: The Regularis Concordia and the Decreta Lanfranci: Manuscript Studies in the Early Medieval Church of Norway* (Oslo: Norwegian Universities Press, 1961), pp. 80–97. On Øystein's exile, see Anne J. Duggan, 'The English Exile of Archbishop Øystein of Nidaros (1180–83)', in *Exile in the Middle Ages*, ed. Laura Napran and Elisabeth van Houts (Turnhout: Brepols, 2004), pp. 109–30.

ument strongly suggests that the Constitutions were in use at that time, and that the Norwegian archbishop regarded them as useable and 'modern'.

The Constitutions cover an extensive range of monastic life, including liturgy, administration, discipline, and child oblation, but it is the chapter on the reception of dignitaries, chapter 81, which is of particular interest to this study. The chapter is situated between the sections on the liturgical year and the monastic offices, respectively.

The instruction moves chronologically through each step of the reception of a dignitary. The text is both detailed and coherent. With a bit of imagination, a modern group of people would probably be capable of following the instruction, performing an *adventus* as Lanfranc envisioned it.

The instruction begins with the decision to receive a dignitary 'with a festive procession' ('cum festiua processione'). Bell-ringing then served to signal that it was time to gather and prepare:

> ... one of the greater bells shall be thrice tolled for a short space, that warned by this all the brethren may gather in the church to vest. When all are vested in copes, if there is a sufficiency of these, or otherwise in chasubles and dalmatics if copes are lacking, with the boys wearing tunicles, all shall sit waiting in the choir till the procession begins.[43]

Once all had gathered in the church, the sacristan ('secretarius') should lay a carpet on the top step before the high altar and in front of the central crucifix. Next, two of the great bells should be rung when the dignitary came close. The senior monks ('maioribus') were to pick up processional items (holy water, incense, and the gospel book), before the whole convent moved outside, lining up according to rank, with the abbot and the prior at the head.[44] It is unclear how far the convent was to move, but given the centrality of the bell-ringing, it seems most likely that everything happened within earshot of the house.

All bells should be rung at the arrival of the dignitary, and the processional items put to use at the point of meeting. The abbot should be given the aspergillum to sprinkle the guest, unless the guest was a bishop, in which case the bishop should use it. The abbot was then to offer incense, while the prior presented the gospel book.

---

[43] *The Monastic Constitutions*, pp. 104–7 (translation adjusted): 'tangatur ter breuiter unum de maioribus signis, ut hoc signo conueniant omnes fratres in ecclesiam ad induendum se. Et cum omnes cappis induti fuerint, si tanta capparum copia est, aut casulis et dalmaticis, si cappe desint, et pueri tunicis, expectent sedentes in choro, donec procedant.'

[44] The imprecision of the term 'maiores' was probably mitigated by custom, as processional items were used in all festive processions. The chapter on Palm Sunday states that 'the abbot or prior shall arrange for the procession, as to what each one shall carry and how the brethren shall go and return in due order' ('ordinet abbas uel prior processionem, et quid quisque portare debeat, et qualiter ordinate eant ac redeant fratres'); see ibid., pp. 34–35.

After the meeting, Lanfranc directed that 'the cantor shall then begin a chant that is suitable to the dignitary' ('Cantor uero incipiat cantum, qui conueniat persone'),[45] before returning to the monastic church in procession in inverse order – the abbot and the dignitary returning last. The cantor, however, could hardly intone anything before the bells had fallen silent. One may imagine the bells quieting, their vibrations slowly coming to a halt as the receding echoes of their voices disappear. There is a moment of silence before a single voice rises, and as all return to the church in procession in inverse order, the procession contains a new element: the dignitary.

Inside the church, the monks should first position themselves at the crucifix according to rank. The dignitary was to pray at the crucifix (presumably on the sacristan's carpet) until the chant was done. When the dignitary had risen from prayer, the cantor should intone the antiphon or responsory of the church's patron saint. The bearers of the processional items should return the items to their place at the high altar, which the procession should then approach with the monks lining up in the choir and the presbytery according to seniority. The convent was to chant while the dignitary prayed at the altar (again, supposedly, on the sacristan's carpet). If the dignitary was a bishop, he should bless and kiss the brethren in order of rank. If not, he should simply kiss them. The monks were normally expected to genuflect in front of a dignitary, but because of the liturgical vestments, they instead performed a low bow before the kiss. The abbot could decide to hold chapter together with the dignitary if he was a clergyman. The monks should unvest and sing the *Tu autem Domine* in that case. The dignitary might deliver a sermon. He should stand at the door of the chapter house and kiss the monks as they left if he was an abbot. If the dignitary did not partake in the chapter, he should kiss the monks at some other time in the cloister.

The instruction is only vague on the decision to grant an *adventus* and on the identities of those deserving to be received with an *adventus*. Lanfranc made no mention of how a convent should decide if a dignitary was worthy of a ritual reception. He, similarly, only identified the dignitary as a 'persona', in the first part of the instruction, although he later mentioned that a visitor could be a bishop, an abbot, an ecclesiastic ('spiritualis persona'), and a 'principem terre' – a vague phrase likely referring to a secular lord or even the king. Lanfranc was probably being intentionally vague on this point: no one could know who would visit a certain monastery in the future or the reasons for the visit. Roman visits were rare during Lanfranc's time (although on the rise); hence, Lanfranc neither needed nor anticipated special provisions for legates. Nevertheless, there is no reason to think that Lanfranc's 'persona' or 'spiritualis persona' could not be a papal legate.

---

[45] Ibid., pp. 106–7.

The overarching purpose of the reception was to recognise the position and authority of a given dignitary, and the most important tool was the reception itself. The reception followed the '*adventus* template', by which a dignitary was honoured and recognised. Lanfranc divided the reception into three phases, which roughly correspond to the *occursus* (moving out), the *susceptio* (the meeting), and the *ingressus* (escorting the dignitary into the home area of the recipients).

However, Lanfranc's instruction was also about much more than simply recognising a given dignitary. The instruction is an organised profusion of overlapping meanings and messages. The way Lanfranc structured the reception into different parts was meaningful in and of itself because he used bell-ringing to differentiate between the different parts. Bell-ringing was a Christian signifier. Some liturgical texts equated bells with the silver trumpets of Moses, while others provided instructions for a consecration-like ritual to be performed on bells.[46] The sound of bells (their 'voices') sanctified the surrounding area, creating a notion of a shared churchly community, while also creating an impressive soundscape. Even today church bells cut through the sound of combustion engines and the noise of construction sites; in the Middle Ages, bells must have dominated their surroundings to an even greater degree. At the time of Lanfranc, large sonorous cast bells were common at monasteries.[47] Bell-ringing was typically used to structure the daily life of the monks,[48] but in this instance (the reception of a dignitary), bell-ringing instead interrupted daily life, marking off the occasion as noteworthy. Bell-ringing marked the time to gather, the time to move out, and, most importantly, the point of meeting.

Another key feature of the reception was the ritual inclusion of the dignitary into the family of the monastic community. The purpose was to familiarise the dignitary with the monastery while fostering personal investment in it and its members. This process began even before the physical meeting, as the dignitary entered what Caroline Goodson and John Arnold call the 'sound-field' of a religious community. They argue that a bell 'sits at the epicenter of a potentially circular sound-field, the borders of which might be imagined as roughly corresponding to the social unit to which it belongs'.[49] When a dignitary entered this field, it marked his intrusion into that 'social unit'. It is not clear when exactly

---

[46] Caroline J. Goodson and John Arnold, 'Resounding Community: The History and Meaning of Medieval Church Bells', *Viator* 43, no. 1 (2012): 99–130, pp. 118–19.

[47] Ibid., esp. pp. 102–18.

[48] See, e.g., Julie Kerr, *Life in the Medieval Cloister* (London: Continuum, 2009), pp. 86–87, 154.

[49] Goodson and Arnold, 'Resounding Community', p. 124. See also Lucy Donkin, 'Roman Soil and Roman Sound in Irish Hagiography', in *The Papacy and Communication in the Central Middle Ages*, ed. Iben Fonnesberg-Schmidt et al., *JMH* 44, no. 3 (2018): 365–79, esp. pp. 373–77.

he entered the sound-field; however, it is conceivable that the dignitary would at least have heard the second bell-ringing. The intention was to establish a common 'sound-space': this was both a gesture of welcome and a sign of recognition.

The crucial moment of inclusion was the physical meeting (the *susceptio*), when the dignitary came close enough to be able to touch the abbot and the prior. Bells, again, played a noteworthy part. The monks gathered at the sound of one bell, moved out to the sound of two, and then, at the meeting, 'all the bells are rung' ('pulsentur omnia signa'). The meeting sat at the end of a crescendo – structured as a dramaturgic and ritual climax. The point of meeting also featured a range of important Christian characteristics:

> At the reception the abbot, if a bishop is being received, gives him the aspergillum of holy water into his hand; any other person he sprinkles himself; then incense is proffered by the abbot, and the gospel book by the prior, while this is done all the bells are rung.[50]

The point of meeting mimicked a church service: there was the sound of bells, the sense of (holy) water, the sight of Scripture, and the smell of incense. As Bissera Pentcheva argues: 'Christianity is a religion of the incarnate God: the Logos empties itself into the flesh, sanctifying matter, and exposing the senses as channels for the experience of this divine'.[51] As such, 'sight, hearing, and touch were orchestrated to produce a sense of divine presence'.[52] The instruction's meeting was no quotidian, secular event, but infused with divine presence: a (church) service.

The physical meeting was the pivotal moment of ritual inclusion. It was at that point that the dignitary changed status from outsider to insider. Until the meeting, the monastic community and the dignitary had been two different entities, separated not only by unfamiliarity but by physical space. When the monks had moved out in procession, the dignitary had been absent, but when they returned in procession to the monastic church, the dignitary was included in the procession; he was now a part of the community. The dignitary did not become a monk, of course, but ritual, space, and symbolic gesture expressed broader notions of Christian unity, friendship, and communality. The change of status might last

---

[50] *The Monastic Constitutions*, pp. 106–7 (translation adjusted): 'Que cum suscipitur, det ei abbas aspersorium cum aqua in manum, si episcopus fuerit, aliam personam aspergat ipse; dehinc porrigatur ei incensum similiter ab abbate, textus a priore. Dum hec fiunt, pulsentur omnia signa.'

[51] Bissera V. Pentcheva, *The Sensual Icon: Space, Ritual, and the Senses in Byzantium* (Philadelphia: The Pennsylvania State University Press, 2010), p. 19.

[52] Ibid., p. 20.

no longer than a visit, or, as Osbert of Clare (monk at Westminster Abbey, active 1120s–50s) recounted, it was the welcome he received at Lewes Priory that led to his great friendship with Prior Hugh.[53] Conversely, Peter of Blois (c. 1130–1211) at one point complained about the disrespectful reception at Wallingford Priory.[54]

The process of familiarising the dignitary with the community picked up pace once inside the church. Lanfranc instructed the dignitary to pray at the crucifix and at the high altar. Both were important devotional objects, but they were also significant as objects of identity for a community. The prayer was Christian and monastic. In the chapter on greetings, St Benedict argued that 'prayer must always precede the kiss of peace because of the delusions of the devil' ('pacis osculum non prius offeratur nisi oratione praemissa, propter illusiones diabolicas').[55] Holzherr has commented that 'prayer is a guarantee of an authentic community of faith and also a guarantee of the interpersonal *pax* so strongly emphasized by Benedict'.[56] After the prayer, the cantor was to intone the antiphon or the responsory of the convent's patron saint. It is hardly necessary to point out how much a patron saint mattered to a monastic community.

The dignitary was also expected to kiss the assembled monks. This kiss – doubtless a kiss of peace – was another way to bond and facilitate feelings of affinity, predisposing hosts and guests to show benevolence towards each other.[57] In his treatise *De spirituali amicitia* (On Spiritual Friendship), Abbot Aelred of Rievaulx (r. 1147–67)[58] defined a kiss thus:

> Through our lips, then, for survival we inhale and exhale. What is inhaled or exhaled has received the name spirit. In a kiss, therefore, two spirits meet, blend, and unite. Begotten from these two spirits, a sweetness of mind awakens and engages the affection of those who exchange a kiss.[59]

---

[53] E. W. Williamson, ed., *The Letters of Osbert of Clare, Prior of Westminster* (Oxford: Oxford University Press, 1929), ep. 1, pp. 40–41. For the identification of Prior Hugh, see Brian Briggs, 'The Life and Works of Osbert of Clare' (unpublished PhD dissertation, University of St Andrews, 2004), pp. 8–9.

[54] *Petri Blesensis Bathoniensis Archidiaconi, Opera Omnia*, ed. J. A. Giles, 4 vols, RS (Oxford: I. H. Parker, 1846–47), vol. 1, ep. 29, pp. 102–4. On Peter of Blois, see, e.g., John D. Cotts, *The Clerical Dilemma: Peter of Blois and Literate Culture in the Twelfth Century* (Washington, D.C.: The Catholic University of America Press, 2009).

[55] *Rule of Benedict*, ch. 53, 3–5, translation at p. 406, Latin at p. 405.

[56] Ibid., pp. 410–11.

[57] On the kiss of peace, see Kiril Petkov, *The Kiss of Peace: Ritual, Self and Society in the High and Late Medieval West* (Leiden: Brill, 2003).

[58] For an introduction to Aelred of Rievaulx, see, e.g., the studies in Marsha L. Dutton, ed., *A Companion to Aelred of Rievaulx (1110–1167)* (Leiden: Brill, 2017).

[59] Aelred of Rievaulx, *Spiritual Friendship*, ed. Marsha L. Dutton, trans. Lawrence C.

For Aelred, a kiss engaged spiritual affection, if given for the right reasons. One such was 'as a sign of catholic unity, as is done when a guest is received' ('in signum catholicae unitatis, sicut fit cum hospes suscipitur').[60] The monks should also bow before the kiss as a gesture of humility, showing the right Christian spirit in the welcoming. St Benedict prescribed that 'all humility should be shown in addressing a guest on arrival ... [and] by a bow of the head or by a complete prostration of the body, Christ is to be adored because he is indeed welcomed in them'.[61]

Despite these efforts to welcome the dignitary honourably and win his goodwill, success was not guaranteed. The abbot, especially, had reason to be on guard, as powerful dignitaries (not least papal legates) could pose a threat to his position within the convent.[62] According to Lanfranc, the abbot's position was near absolute. Lanfranc prescribed that 'all the ordering of the monastery shall depend upon his [the abbot's] will' ('omnis totius monasterii ordinatio ex eius arbitrio pendeat').[63] The monks were subjected to the abbot's military-like discipline:

> If a brother go to him [the abbot] without the cloister he shall first say *Benedicite* and then say for what cause he has come. He shall not venture to sit before him nor to depart without his permission. When this is granted, he shall first say *Benedicite* and then depart.[64]

Braceland (Collegeville, MN: Liturgical Press, 2010), bk. 2, 22–23, pp. 75–76 (translation adjusted); Aelred of Rievaulx, *Aelredi Rievallensis Opera omnia*, ed. A. Hoste and C. H. Talbot, 7 vols, CCCM 1 (Turnhout: Brepols, 1971), vol. 1, bk. 2, 22–23, p. 307: 'Itaque ut uiuamus, ore haurimus aerem et remittimus. Et ipsum quidem quod emittitur uel recipitur, spiritus nomen obtinuit. Quocirca in osculo duo sibi spiritus obuiant, et miscentur sibi et uniuntur. Ex quibus quaedam mentis suauitas innascens, osculantium mouet et perstringit affectum.'

[60] Aelred of Rievaulx, *Spiritual Friendship*, bk. 2, 24, p 76; Aelred of Rievaulx, *Aelredi Rievallensis Opera omnia*, vol. 1, bk. 2, 24, p. 307. See also, e.g., Willem Frijhoff, 'The Kiss Sacred and Profane: Reflections on a Cross-Cultural Confrontation', in *A Cultural History of Gesture: From Antiquity to the Present Day*, ed. Jan Bremmer and Herman Roodenburg (Cambridge: Polity Press, 1993), pp. 210–36; and J. A. Burrow, *Gestures and Looks in Medieval Narrative* (Cambridge: Cambridge University Press, 2002), esp. pp. 32–34, 50–57, 150–52.

[61] *Rule of Benedict*, ch. 53, 6–7, translation at p. 406, Latin at p. 405: 'In ipsa autem salutatione omnis exhibeatur humilitas omnibus venientibus ... hospitibus: inclinato capite vel prostrato omni corpore in terra, Christus in eis adoretur qui et suscipitur.'

[62] See also Clark, *The Benedictines*, pp. 122–24.

[63] *The Monastic Constitutions*, ch. 82, pp. 110–11.

[64] Ibid., ch. 82, pp. 110–11: 'Quicunque frater ad eum extra claustrum uenerit, primum dicat *Benedicite*, deinde indicet propter quam causam uenerit. Nec sedere coram eo, nec recedere ab eo audeat sine eius licentia; accepta ab eo recedendi licentia, primum dicat *Benedicite*, deinde recedat.'

And:

> When he [the abbot] is making a stay outside the monastery, and sends the community greeting or asks for prayers, all in chapter shall bow, bending their knees to the footstool. The pope and the king are saluted in this manner also, but for other dignitaries only a profound bow is made.[65]

Monks should show less bodily submission to bishops and archbishops than to their abbot. The abbot held a position equal to the pope and the king, instilling an embodied hierarchy in which only the highest authorities on Earth were to be on parity with – but not above – the abbot.[66]

However, a disgruntled convent could challenge an abbot when a powerful dignitary visited the monastery. Thomas of Marlborough (d. 1236), monk and later abbot at Evesham Abbey, provides an account of such an instance. In 1213, the oft-mentioned Cardinal Nicholas had come to England. The monks of Evesham had long wanted to depose Abbot Roger Norreys, whom King Richard and Archbishop Baldwin had imposed on them in 1190.[67] With Cardinal Nicholas in England, they seized the opportunity. Thomas reported on the disturbance it brought Abbot Roger once he learned about the legate's upcoming visit:

> In fact, as we [Thomas and Abbot Roger Norreys] were leaving the gate of the abbey [of Bruern], a messenger brought the abbot a letter from the lord legate [Cardinal Nicholas] stating that he would be coming to Evesham the next day. As soon as the abbot heard this, his heart sank, and he said, 'What

---

[65] Ibid., ch. 82, pp. 110–11 (translation adjusted): 'Cum alicubi extra monasterium moram faciens mandat conuentui salutes seu orationes, omnes qui in capitulo sunt inclinent, flexis usque ad suppedaneum scabellum genibus. Eodem modo fit pro pape uel regis salutatione. Pro aliarum uero personarum salutationibus, humiliter inclinetur tantum.'

[66] It was the same principle when an absent abbot addressed a monk: 'when he [the abbot] sends a command to any brother, whenever the message reaches him he is straightway to do obeisance kneeling to the ground' ('cum autem alicui fratri mandat huiusmodi aliquid, ubicunque dicatur ei ipsa salutatio, continuo humiliter inclinet, flexis ad terram genibus'); see ibid., ch. 82, pp. 110–11.

[67] The imposition was part of a settlement between Baldwin and the monks of Christ Church, Canterbury. The monks had demanded the demotion of Roger from his priorate at Christ Church; see James Barnaby, *Religious Conflict at Canterbury Cathedral in the Late Twelfth Century: The Dispute between the Monks and the Archbishops, 1184–1200* (Woodbridge: Boydell Press, 2024), pp. 132–34; Knowles, *The Monastic Order*, pp. 331–45; and G. G. Coulton, *Five Centuries of Religion. Volume II: The Friars and the Dead Weight of Tradition, 1200–1400 A.D.* (Cambridge: Cambridge University Press, 1927), pp. 347–78. See also pp. 157, 175–76 in this book.

does he want with so sudden a command when he said nothing of this to us when we left him?'[68]

Abbot Roger suspected that the legatine visit boded ill for him – and he was right: Nicholas deposed Roger on the convent's request.[69] At another instance, Cardinal Nicholas deposed the abbot of Westminster on the request of the Westminster monks.[70] As mentioned, Lanfranc owed his archiepiscopal dignity to papal legates removing his predecessor.

Not all dignitaries posed the same threat, but papal legates – especially cardinal-legates *a latere* – posed considerable risk to an abbot. As Beattie puts it, 'legatine authority was by its very nature disruptive; it intruded into established hierarchies and overrode ordinary ecclesiastical jurisdictions'.[71] Lanfranc's instruction shows awareness of this, not of the legatine threat as such, but of the opportunity for the monks to use a visiting dignitary to challenge the abbot's authority. Lanfranc took steps to preserve the hierarchy of the monastery. His strategy was to provide the abbot (and sometimes the prior) with privileged access to the dignitary. They met him first:

> At the reception the abbot, if a bishop is being received, gives him the aspergillum of holy water into his hand; any other person he sprinkles himself; then incense is proffered by the abbot, and the gospel book by the prior, while this is done all the bells are rung.[72]

The abbot and to a lesser extent the prior shared the outdoor 'service' with the dignitary. The service fulfilled several purposes, but one was to convey a message of

---

[68] Thomas of Marlborough, *History of the Abbey of Evesham*, ed. Jane E. Sayers and Leslie Watkiss, OMT (Oxford: Oxford University Press, 2003), bk. 3, pt. 5, 457, p. 437 (translation adjusted): 'Et ecce nobis egredientibus per portam abbatie, uenit quidam nuncius deferens abbati litteras domini legati continentes quod in crastino ueniret Eueshamiam. Quas cum audisset dominus abbas statim concidit cor eius, et dixit, "Quid sibi uult tam subitum mandatum cum nichil inde dixerit nobis legatus in recessu nostro?"'.

[69] Thomas' description of the legate's *adventus* at Evesham is brief: 'Around nine o'clock the next morning the lord legate arrived, and he was received in solemn procession' ('In crastino uero circa horam terciam uenit dominus legatus, et recepto eo cum sollempni processione'); see Thomas of Marlborough, bk. 3, pt. 5, 459, p. 439 (translation adjusted).

[70] Emma Mason, *Westminster Abbey and Its People, c.1050–c.1216* (Woodbridge: Boydell Press, 1996), pp. 131–32.

[71] B. R. Beattie, *Angelus Pacis: The Legation of Cardinal Giovanni Gaetano Orsino, 1326–1334* (Leiden: Brill, 2007), p. xx.

[72] *The Monastic Constitutions*, pp. 106–7 (translation adjusted): 'Que cum suscipitur, det ei abbas aspersorium cum aqua in manum, si episcopus fuerit, aliam personam aspergat ipse; dehinc porrigatur ei incensum similiter ab abbate, textus a priore.'

solidarity at the top. Only the abbot and the dignitary shared the water's sacredness, only they and the prior could properly witness the magnificence of the gospel book (which was also an item of familiarisation, as its contents could be highly localised). The burning of incense further sharpened a sense of Christian community. Pentcheva observes that incense could have Eucharistic undertones, and as the fragrance encased the participants, they took part in the same 'Eucharistic experience', where matter (incense) transformed into spirit (smoke).[73] Furthermore, the burning of incense was an exclusive experience. While the burning of incense might fill a church with fragrant smoke, this was different in an outside space. Some of the monks might pick up a hint of the incense (depending on the wind), but only the heads of the community and the guest really shared what might be termed a 'fragrant communality'.

Within this exclusive group, the burning of incense simultaneously imposed a gift-giving logic on the dignitary. Incense was a luxury item, which consumed itself through use. Although rites needed to be said over holy water, water is no scarcity in England, and even if Gospel books might be costly, they were reusable for centuries. In that sense, incense was a sacrifice as well as a gift: the host put the guest under obligation to reciprocate the largesse in some way.[74] Although the host, in a wider sense, was the entire monastic community, members of the small 'fragrant community' shared a special reciprocal bond.

The abbot had exclusive access to the dignitary. When the procession returned to the monastic church, only the abbot accompanied the dignitary: 'last of all comes the abbot with the person who has been received' ('extremus ueniat abbas cum suscepta persona').[75] Although the monks subsequently kissed the dignitary, it was hardly an opportune moment for voicing dissent while 'standing at attention'. The abbot also decided on the dignitary's involvement with monastic life, since the

---

[73] Pentcheva, *The Sensual Icon*, p. 17.
[74] The reciprocal nature of gift-giving in medieval times – really throughout all of human history – has been widely documented and studied. Essentially, receiving a gift puts one under obligation to reciprocate, repaying materially or as a form of service or goodwill. Modern scholarship is heavily indebted to the classic study by Marcell Mauss, *Essai sur le don* (1923) (latest reissue: Marcel Mauss, *The Gift*, trans. Jane I. Guyer, expanded edition [Chicago: Hau Books, 2016]). Important modern studies include Stephen D. White, *Custom, Kinship, and Gifts to Saints: The 'Laudatio Parentum' in Western France, 1050–1150* (Chapel Hill: The University of North Carolina Press, 1988); Barbara H. Rosenwein, *To Be the Neighbor of Saint Peter: The Social Meaning of Cluny's Property, 909–1049* (Ithaca, NY: Cornell University Press, 1989); Arnoud-Jan A. Bijsterveld, *Do ut des: Gift-Giving, Memoria, and Conflict Management in the Medieval Low Countries* (Hilversum: Verloren, 2007); and Lars Kjær, *The Medieval Gift and the Classical Tradition: Ideals and the Performance of Generosity in Medieval England, 1100–1300* (Cambridge: Cambridge University Press, 2019).
[75] *The Monastic Constitutions*, pp. 106–7 (translation adjusted).

dignitary might attend chapter 'if the visiting dignitary be an ecclesiastic, and the abbot judge it fitting' ('si spiritualis persona fuerit, et abbas expedire iudicauerit').[76]

Lanfranc also showed consideration for the internal hierarchy of the monastic community. Everyone had to remain in line – literally:

> Then some of the seniors shall take holy water and all else that is usual in festive procession; they shall be followed by the abbot and the rest in order. The boys with their masters shall come last, and when the ranks are formed to receive the dignitary, they shall stand in order between the two choirs of monks.[77]

Everyone – even the boys ('pueri') – were to participate in the welcoming, arranging their bodies hierarchically. This bodily arrangement was one of Lanfranc's favourite techniques. After the abbot and the prior had met the dignitary:

> the procession thereafter returns; the boys and their masters shall be the first to enter the church, followed by the rest in the order in which they were previously standing; last of all comes the abbot with the person who has been received, preceded immediately by the bearers of incense and holy water.[78]

To the modern observer, Lanfranc's directives conjure up images of marching soldiers. Indeed, monks were soldiers of Christ (*milites Christi*).[79] A procession might look like an organism, a *corpus*, in medieval thinking (recall the discussion about representational power in chapter 2), but participants were spaced rigorously inside the procession. Barnwell priory's customary dictated that 'the canons regular ought in every procession to take pains to walk, two and two, in such order that each move straight forward evenly and regularly with respect to the brother opposite to him'.[80] Bodies and space enforced internal hierarchy. In Lanfranc's

---

[76] Ibid, pp. 106–7. Lanfranc also required that any guest wishing to speak with a monk should petition the guestmaster for permission. The guestmaster should pass the request on to the abbot. If the abbot declined, the monk in question was not to be informed about the request; see ibid., ch. 90, pp. 128–33.

[77] Ibid., pp. 106–7 (translation adjusted): 'Tunc aliqui de maioribus accipiant aquam benedictam, et cetera que ad festiuam processionem portari solent, hos precedentes sequantur abbas, et ceteri, ut sunt priores. Pueri cum magistris suis extremi ueniant, et in ordine suo stent inter duos choros, cum facta fuerit statio ad susceptionem persone.'

[78] Ibid., pp. 106–7 (translation adjusted): '… dehinc reuertatur processio; pueri cum magistris suis primi ingrediantur ecclesiam, hos sequantur reliqui sicut in statione fuerunt, extremus ueniat abbas cum suscepta persona, precedentibus eos supradictis portitoribus.'

[79] See esp. Katherine Allen Smith, *War and the Making of Medieval Monastic Culture* (Woodbridge: Boydell Press, 2011), pp. 71–111.

[80] Clark, *The Observances*, pp. 148–49: 'Hanc quidem modestiam debent canonici regu-

instruction, the segregation between ranks was pronounced at the meeting. In the ritualised environment, in which categories were both adaptable and sacralised once fixed,[81] the abbot became 'captain' of the 'regiment', while the prior became his 'adjutant'. Together they wielded the power of the community. The dignitary, if he was a bishop, became an active member as the head of the community. If not, he still became an honorary member.

Once inside the church, Lanfranc linked the worship of the patron saint with the established hierarchy, ensuring the disciplined movement of the convent:

> when they have entered the church, they are to halt at the crucifix, the boys standing as before between the two choirs, while the bearers go forward a little in their midst and stand facing the crucifix. ... [and] when they have entered the choir, they shall stand near the altar in order of seniority on each side of the presbytery.[82]

When the dignitary was to kiss the monks, Lanfranc maintained hierarchical order, stating that the dignitary should kiss 'all the brothers in order' ('omnes fratres per ordinem').[83]

Lanfranc's attention to hierarchy and authority was not unique, given the existing social structures. Medieval England was a hierarchical society. It is nevertheless telling to find the abbot at the forefront of the reception and the monks lined up in procession. It was an expression – as well as a reminder and a reinforcer – of existing wider hierarchical structures. Processions worked as spatial and bodily exercises, instilling embodied subordination in the monks, much like an army drilling ceaselessly on the parade ground.[84] Rank within the monastery mattered at the welcoming of an external figure of authority.

* * *

Altogether, the reception aimed to welcome the dignitary, recognise his authority, impress the community's identity on the dignitary, familiarise the dignitary, and instil and reinforce the hierarchy of the monastic community. The purpose was

---

lares habere in omni processione, vt uidelivet bini et bini incedant, ita ut quilibet directe et equaliter contra fratrem suum ex opposito regulariter incedat.'

[81] See Catherine Bell, *Ritual Theory – Ritual Practice* (Oxford: Oxford University Press, 1992), esp. p. 109.

[82] *The Monastic Constitutions*, pp. 106–7 (translation adjusted): 'Ingressi monasterium faciant stationen ante crucifixum. Pueri uero similiter stent inter utrosque choros. Predicti portitores paulatim progrediantur per medium eorum, et stent ante crucifixum uersis uultibus ad eum. ... Ingressi chorum stent a parte altaris ex utraque parte sicut sunt priores.'

[83] Ibid., pp. 106–7 (translations slightly adjusted).

[84] This was not only a reception issue. Note for instance the detailed description of the Palm Sunday procession; see ibid., ch. 25, pp. 34–41.

to address and alleviate the potential for disruption, while turning the visit into a positive relationship. The ceremony itself was a tool to this effect: it communicated acceptance of the dignitary's status and authority, blunting potential hostility and strengthening feelings of goodwill. Lanfranc moreover strove to facilitate feelings of inclusion and communality between the visitor and the hosts. The convent should introduce the dignitary to its key features: the voice of its bells, the smell of its incense, the visual expression of its Scripture, its patron saint, its crucifix, its high altar, and its members. Familiarisation and inclusion through outdoor churchly performance, prayer in church, procession, and kissing served to make the dignitary adopt or recognise the outlook and cares of the monastic convent, predisposing him towards friendship. Space, gesture, and interaction concurrently combined to set up the abbot as the ruler of the monastery, creating and reinforcing the internal hierarchy, but also communicating it to the dignitary.

Performance mattered to Lanfranc: it produced perceptions, meanings, and relationships. Lanfranc did not write his instruction for a specific occasion, and it is this fact more than anything else that makes his instruction a convincing expression of practice. He did not try to press home the meaning of a specific event. Rather, the instruction guides an abbot to arrange an *adventus* such that he preserves the internal structure of his abbey, simultaneously fostering feelings of communality between the dignitary and the monastic community.

Some caution here is necessary: the extent to which anyone followed Lanfranc's instruction is unknowable. Lanfranc, as an influential archbishop, thought carefully about how to instruct his convents in the proper reception of a dignitary, but whether they and others listened is unknown, even if the text within which Lanfranc included the instruction disseminated to a number of important English houses and even made its way to Norway around a century after its production. The problem remains, however, that legates play no part in Lanfranc's instruction. There are, however, other instructions that mention papal legates, and one such is the Cistercian instruction.

The Cistercians and Their Instruction

The Cistercian order was founded in 1098, expanding rapidly and successfully.[85] The Cistercians established their first house in England in 1132; by 1200, they

---

[85] Constance Berman argues that the Cistercians only truly became an order in the 1160s, at which point they invented the history of their foundation in order to impose uniformity and control; see Constance Hoffman Berman, *The Cistercian Evolution: The Invention of a Religious Order in Twelfth-Century Europe* (Philadelphia and Oxford: University of Pennsylvania Press, 2000), esp. pp. 97–110. Berman's interpretation has provoked debate; see, e.g., Brian Patrick McGuire, 'Bernard's Concept of a Cistercian

had forty-nine houses in England and Wales combined.[86] The Cistercians are sometimes called 'reformed Benedictines' because the aim of the order was strict adherence to the Rule of St Benedict. However, like the 'old' Benedictines, they found that the Rule did not cover all aspects of monastic life; and in response, they produced their own customary, the *Ecclesiastica Officia*.[87] The *Ecclesiastica Officia* includes an *adventus* instruction.

The earliest version of the *Ecclesiastica Officia* dates to around 1135, but a master copy was produced between 1184 and 1186 (Dijon, Bibliothèque municipale MS 114).[88] Henceforth all Cistercian abbeys presumably used the Dijon recension, even if it is possible to find some adaptations and changes, especially in the later Middle Ages.[89] There are a few noteworthy differences between the instruction in earlier manuscripts and that found in the Dijon recension. These differences are marked in the body text and footnotes below in *italics*, indicating the Dijon recension's additions to earlier versions of the instruction.

The *adventus* instruction takes up chapter 86 of the *Ecclesiastica Officia*.[90] It is not as detailed and meticulous as Lanfranc's instruction, but it still provides a decent impression of the Cistercian expectations. This instruction is tailored to the reception of bishops, at every turn describing the dignitary exclusively as a bishop. However, the instruction ends with a clause (having the appearance of an afterthought) which mentions those whom the community should also receive

---

Order: Vocabulary and Context', *Cîteaux: Commentarii Cistercienses* 54, nos. 3–4 (2003): 225–49; and Giles Constable, 'Review of *The Cistercian Evolution: The Invention of a Religious Order in Twelfth-Century Europe* by Constance Hoffman Berman', *EHR* 115, no. 464 (2000): 1267–68. The expansion was, in any case, rapid and successful; see Janet Burton and Julie Kerr, *The Cistercians in the Middle Ages* (Woodbridge: Boydell Press, 2011), pp. 9–55.

[86] Burton and Kerr, *The Cistercians*, p. 38; Knowles, *The Monastic Order*, pp. 707–9. Twelve more were founded during the thirteenth century, one in the fourteenth century, and one again in the fifteenth century.

[87] See also Janet Burton, 'Past Models and Contemporary Concerns: The Foundation and Growth of the Cistercian Order', in *Revival and Resurgence in Christian History*, ed. Kate Cooper and Jeremy Gregory (Woodbridge: Boydell, 2008), pp. 27–45, esp. pp. 41–42.

[88] Martinus Cawley argues that the purpose of the *Ecclesiastica Officia* was to define the role of the cantor, citing as evidence the attention given to the cantorial office in the *Ecclesiastica Officia*. The office of cantor takes up nineteen per cent of the text, the sacristan and the gatekeeper thirteen per cent apiece, the abbot eleven per cent, etc.; see *Ancient Usages*, pp. v, xi. The attention to the cantorial office is noteworthy, but not decisive. The text is clearly 'just' a customary.

[89] See Emilia Jamroziak, 'The Cistercian Customaries', in *A Companion to Medieval Rules and Customaries*, ed. Pansters, pp. 77–102.

[90] The instruction is found in Latin in *Ecclesiastica Officia*, ch. 86, p. 246; and in translation in *Ancient Usages*, ch. 86 (no page number).

with a procession. Among those mentioned were papal legates.[91] Martha G. Newman argues that the Cistercians primarily courted episcopal support during their early period of expansion,[92] which might be the reason for the instruction's focus on bishops.

The instruction begins by setting out guidelines roughly similar to those of Lanfranc. Bells should be used to summon the monks to the choir, and once assembled, the cantor should instruct a person to pick up the holy water. This individual would lead the procession out of the choir, followed by the abbot. The monks were to proceed behind this individual according to rank, lining up outside the monastery in due order:

> For the welcoming of a bishop, the brethren are summoned to choir by a bell. Then, at a nod from the cantor, someone takes up the holy water. It is this one who leads off, followed by the abbot, and then the community *and the novices*, all two-by-two and in the same order as they stand in the choir, with the priests foremost. All come out like this and stand in line in front of the monastery.[93]

The instruction further requires that the porter or someone else should escort the bishop towards the procession. When the bishop approached, the monks should kneel, and the abbot should hand the bishop the aspergillum with holy water, kissing his hand. Although the instruction fails to mention this detail, the bearer of the holy water must have passed it on to the abbot at this point. The instruction does not mention the bishop's retinue, 'his companions' ('comites eius'), at this stage either; the retinue only appears later in the text, although it is logical to assume their presence at the meeting. After the kissing of the bishop's hand, the cantor was to intone one of two responsories, depending on the number of bishops. The monks should then move back through the gate (presumably while responding to the responsory). The monks then returned in reverse order with the abbot at the rear 'holding the bishop by the hand' ('manu tenens episcopum').[94] The collective were then to proceed to the choir, where the bishop should pray on his knees. The abbot was to retire to 'his place' ('locum suum')

---

[91] *Ancient Usages*, ch. 86, 11–12; *Ecclesiastica Officia*, ch. 86, 11–12, p. 246.
[92] Martha G. Newman, *The Boundaries of Charity: Cistercian Culture and Ecclesiastical Reform 1098–1180* (Stanford, CA: Stanford University Press, 1996), pp. 143–48.
[93] *Ancient Usages*, ch. 86, 1–3a (translation adjusted); *Ecclesiastica Officia*, ch. 86, 1–3, p. 246: 'Ad suscipiendum episcopum convocentur fratres in chorum campana. Tunc sumat aliquis aquam benedictam nutu cantoris. quo precedente sequatur abbas. deinde conventus *et novicii* bini et bini. sacerdotibus preeuntibus eo ordine quo in choro stant. Cunctisque egressis et stantibus ordinatim ante fores monasterii.'
[94] *Ancient Usages*, ch. 86, 6b–7 (translation adjusted); *Ecclesiastica Officia*, ch. 86, 6, p. 246.

at the bishop's prayer, and the monks were to line up behind the abbot as for Mass.[95] The abbot should then prompt the bishop to rise after they had finished the responsory. The abbot was further required to escort the bishop to the chapter room, where – 'when all are seated in proper order' ('ubi cunctis ordine residentibus') – the reader of the rule should ask the bishop for a blessing before reading a passage.[96] The abbot should thereupon say the *benedicite*. The bishop might then say something 'for edification' ('pro edificatione'),[97] upon which the abbot was to kiss the bishop and the bishop's companions (the companions are not otherwise mentioned). The abbot should next ask the bishop for a blessing if he had not already blessed the community in the oratory (the instruction only mentions this possibility here). All should rise and bow for the blessing before the convent was to leave the chapter house. The bishop was then to be escorted to the guesthouse.[98]

Like Lanfranc's instruction, the Cistercian instruction echoes the '*adventus* template'. The Cistercians left the decision to receive a dignitary vague, as Lanfranc did, but the instruction mentions the preparations, the moving out, the meeting, and how they should conduct the dignitary back into their home for further ceremonies. Like Lanfranc, the Cistercian instruction addresses and navigates how to cope with the arrival of an external dignitary, even if there are differences. The Cistercian reception is less splendid: there are fewer ceremonial items, no carpet, less prayer, and less kissing. Compared with Lanfranc's instruction, the Cistercians stripped their instruction down to its 'core' message of hierarchy and authority. The instruction primarily addresses the relationship between internal and external hierarchy, ensuring that the abbot retained control of the situation, while acknowledging the position and authority of the dignitary.

The recognition of the dignitary was primarily achieved through the *adventus* ceremony itself, but the Cistercians also emphasised the authority of the dignitary at the point of meeting (the *susceptio*). Their instruction stipulates that 'when the bishop draws near, all go on their knees before him' ('Quo appropinquante flectant omnes genua ante eum').[99] The Cistercian monks, on the other hand, had no outdoor church service nor much of anything else. In this, their instruction differed notably from Lanfranc's.

The Cistercian instruction used bodily movements and space in much the same way as Lanfranc did to instil internal hierarchy. When moving out to greet the dignitary, the bearer of holy water should lead with the abbot behind him. The

---

[95] *Ancient Usages*, ch. 86, 6b–7; *Ecclesiastica Officia*, ch. 86, 7, p. 246.
[96] *Ancient Usages*, ch. 86, 8–9; *Ecclesiastica Officia*, ch. 86, 8, p. 246.
[97] *Ancient Usages*, ch. 86, 8–9; *Ecclesiastica Officia*, ch. 86, 9, p. 246.
[98] *Ancient Usages*, ch. 86, 8–10; *Ecclesiastica Officia*, ch. 86, 9–10, p. 246.
[99] *Ancient Usages*, ch. 86, 3b–6a; *Ecclesiastica Officia*, ch. 86, 4, p. 246.

convent should follow as they stood in the choir two-by-two. The convent should stand 'in order in front of the monastery' ('ordinatim ante fores monasterii').[100] When they returned in procession, the hierarchical ordering of the monastic community remained in place: 'the novices entering first, and then the non-clerical monks and then the rest, in such wise that the abbot comes last, holding the bishop by the hand'.[101] There are other examples: one is in the church, where 'the abbot retires to his own place, while all the rest line up behind him' ('abbas veniat in locum suum. ceteris post eum ... ordinatis').[102] Another example can be found in the chapter room, where the convent should only proceed 'when all are seated in order' ('ubi cunctis ordine residentibus').[103]

The Cistercian instruction also puts emphasis on the abbot's access to the dignitary and his control of the dignitary's whereabouts. The pre-Dijon recension states that 'the porter has meanwhile escorted the bishop along to meet them' ('portaris interim obvium eis adducat episcopum').[104] The abbot appointed the porter,[105] but if the abbot should lose trust in the porter, the Dijon recension interpolated 'or someone else suited to this by order of the abbot' ('vel alius quilibet ad hoc idoneus ab abbate iussus'),[106] ensuring abbatial control. The abbot's privileged access is also visible in a number of other arrangements. The abbot met the bishop at the head of the procession, giving him the aspergillum and kissing his hand. They returned in procession to the monastery with the abbot holding the bishop's hand. It was also the abbot who escorted the bishop into the chapter room, where it seems that only the abbot kissed the bishop and his companions. The instruction allowed the bishop to say something 'for edification' ('pro edificatione'),[107] but this was hardly a moment for conventual rebelliousness; nor would the blessing of each monk be a very opportune moment for dissent.

The Cistercians appear more austere and less extravagant in their receptions than Lanfranc's monks. It is noticeable that there is no gospel book, no incense, and less sophistication in the use of bells. Compared with Lanfranc's *adventus* instruction, the Cistercians downplayed the aspect of familiarisation, even if it

---

[100] *Ancient Usages*, ch. 86, 1–3a (translation adjusted); *Ecclesiastica Officia*, ch. 86, 1–3, p. 246.
[101] *Ancient Usages*, ch. 86, 6b–7 (translation adjusted); *Ecclesiastica Officia*, ch. 86, 6, p. 246: 'introeant primum novicii. deinde ceteri. laicis monachis preeuntibus. ita ut abbas eat posterior. manu tenens episcopum.'
[102] *Ancient Usages*, ch. 86, 6b–7; *Ecclesiastica Officia*, ch. 86, 6, p. 246.
[103] *Ancient Usages*, ch. 86, 8–9 (translation adjusted); *Ecclesiastica Officia*, ch. 86, 8, p. 246.
[104] *Ancient Usages*, ch. 86, 3b–6a (translation adjusted); *Ecclesiastica Officia*, ch. 86, 3, p. 246.
[105] See *Ancient Usages*, ch. 110, 6–11; *Ecclesiastica Officia*, ch. 110, 7 p. 312.
[106] *Ancient Usages*, ch. 86, 3b–6a (translation adjusted); *Ecclesiastica Officia*, ch. 86, 3, p. 246. The sentence reads: 'portaris *vel alius quilibet ad hoc idoneus ab abbate iussus* interim obvium eis adducat episcopum'.
[107] *Ancient Usages*, ch. 86, 8–9; *Ecclesiastica Officia*, ch. 86, 9, p. 246.

is possible to find examples of this theme in their instruction. One instance of familiarisation is the bishop's prayer in the choir (where the high altar would presumably only be paces away). Another instance is the bishop's blessing of each member of the convent (but it is striking that the dignitary should only kiss the abbot). Perhaps the Cistercians downplayed the familiarisation aspect because of the strong uniformity of the order.

However, it is possible that this impression is (in part) misleading, for two reasons. The first reason is the nature of some of the confusions and omissions, burdening the instruction. The second reason is the way the Dijon recension's changes to the subsequent chapter, chapter 87, differ profoundly from the changes to chapter 86. This is all a bit convoluted, but still important to consider.

To begin with the confusions and omissions, the instruction mentions that a monk should pick up the 'holy water' ('aquam benedictam'), before the aspergillum suddenly appears in the hands of the abbot, who passes it on to the bishop, at which point it simply disappears, never to be mentioned again. Lanfranc made sure that the liturgical implements were accounted for. Secondly, in the chapter room, the bishop's companions are said to appear abruptly, mentioned neither before nor again. Thirdly, having placed everyone in the chapter room, the instruction suddenly voices the possibility that the bishop had blessed the monks in the oratory previously, although the oratory had played no part in the ceremony. Fourthly, there are some noticeable discrepancies between the text's ceremonial rights and the dignitaries of the final clause (diocesan, archdiocesan, papal legate, king, pope, and the house's own abbot). Was a king to attend chapter? Should a cardinal-*deacon* use the aspergillum? Lanfranc distinguished between the ceremonial rights of bishops and others.

The shortcomings of chapter 86 were nonetheless unlikely to cause difficulties for a forewarned and well-trained monastic body. When to hand over the aspergillum to the abbot, for instance, was in all likelihood a trivial matter for monks well versed in liturgy and in processional activities. This is a point in and of itself: the instruction might not be as detailed and impressive as Lanfranc's, but it was in all likelihood 'useable' both before and after the Dijon amendments.

The same cannot be said about chapter 87 of the *Ecclesiastica Officia*. Chapter 87 addresses 'mundane' receptions without processions.[108] The pre-Dijon version of chapter 87 is confusing and deficient, but the Dijon recension transformed it into a detailed chapter, more than doubling its length. There are no prescripts in the pre-Dijon version of chapter 87 about how to prepare a reception. In the Dijon version, the gatekeeper was to announce the arrival of guests to the abbot, who should then determine the subsequent course of action. If guests arrived during the

---

[108] *Ancient Usages*, ch. 87; *Ecclesiastica Officia*, ch. 87, pp. 246–48.

Compline reading (the final church service of the day), the gatekeeper should make a sign to two pre-appointed monks, who were to leave the service discreetly to help the gatekeeper receive the guest(s). The abbot was to have prepared a list of several such monks for the gatekeeper to choose from.[109] All this (and more) is lacking in the pre-Dijon version of chapter 87, which begins at the point of meeting, making no provisions for those chosen to receive the guests and on whose authority these monks were chosen. The pre-Dijon version of chapter 87 was inadequate. This is probably the reason why the Dijon editors gave it a thorough overhaul.

In contrast, chapter 86 only received a few updates. These updates are important, particularly the update to the list of dignitaries, worthy of being received with a procession. The pre-Dijon recension included the diocesan, the archdiocesan, papal legates, and the pope; the Dijon recension added kings and the house's own abbot. This shows that chapter 86 was still relevant. But why did they not sort out the other issues? Most likely, they felt no need to do so because they were all minor issues: the instruction was useable and adequate. Why bother? The instruction covered the crucial themes of hierarchy and authority. Omissions, such as the return of the aspergillum after use, were likely sufficiently trivial for each monastery to address. On the other hand, reinforcing and instilling internal and external hierarchy was not trivial. Maybe some of the 'extravagance' of Lanfranc's instruction found its way into local practice, and perhaps some Cistercians used bells more proactively than their instruction invited them to do.

Whatever local adaptations, the Cistercian and Lanfrancian instructions are products of affinity, being part of the same family of rituals, sharing the *adventus* template to a high degree – yet their emphases differ. Lanfranc had the broadest view, being concerned with themes such as familiarisation, communality, hierarchy, and authority, while also taking the dramaturgical part seriously. His meticulousness and attention to detail strongly imply that he took the performance of the ceremony seriously. The Cistercians were, surprisingly, less concerned about micromanaging every detail of the *adventus*. However, they obviously understood the implications of the *adventus*, focusing on those parts that mattered the most: internal and external hierarchy.

The Gilbertines and the Gilbertine Instruction

Out of 'the medieval reformation' (to cite Brenda Bolton), another order arose: the Gilbertines.[110] They were a wholly English order, founded by St Gilbert of Sempringham (*c.* 1100–89). Initially beginning as an order of nuns in 1131,

---

[109] *Ancient Usages*, ch. 87, 1–7; *Ecclesiastica Officia*, ch. 87, 1–7, pp. 246–48.
[110] See Bolton, *The Medieval Reformation*.

they evolved into a dual-order, where the male component eventually came to dominate. By 1200, they had eighteen foundations, and this number grew to twenty-nine by 1300.[111]

Cistercian influence on the Gilbertine order was immense,[112] so much so that the Gilbertine instruction on the ceremonial reception of dignitaries is almost a verbatim reproduction of the Cistercian instruction, although with some significant changes.[113] The Gilbertine *adventus* instruction is part of their rule. Composing a new rule, the Gilbertines had the opportunity to draw on the experience of the Cistercians (and other monastic traditions), accounting for issues in their rule that other traditions, by necessity, had relocated to customaries. The Gilbertine rule addresses many issues reserved for customaries in older monastic traditions. The rule survives in a manuscript dated 1220 × 1223 (Oxford, Bodleian Library, MS Douce 136).[114]

Although the Gilbertines reproduced the Cistercian instruction almost verbatim, it is not the similarities but the differences that are interesting. These offer insight into Gilbertine concerns and priorities. The changes also suggest that 'getting it right' mattered. The Cistercian instruction might be a useable template for an *adventus* ceremony, but it had to be adapted to Gilbertine cares and realities.

One reality was the order itself. The Gilbertines replaced 'fratres' (brothers) with 'omnes' (all), as their order comprised both men and women. They replaced the abbot with a prior, since they were not abbatial communities. They made alterations in the list of responsories, replaced monks with canons, and replaced the abbot of the ending clause with 'the newly appointed master' ('magistrum de novo creatum'). The master was the leader of their order.[115]

They also made alterations to the meeting (the *susceptio*). The Gilbertines reproduced the Cistercian genuflection, the use of the aspergillum, and the kissing of the bishop's hand, adding that 'then the gospel book should be kissed' ('deinde textum ad osculandum').[116] They also used incense, tersely affixing 'quo thurificato', which might be translated as 'after he [the bishop] is incensed'. The Gilbertines apparently wanted an outdoor church service in the spirit of Lanfranc,

---

[111] Golding, *Gilbert of Sempringham*, pp. 16–26, 60–70, 448–49.
[112] Ibid., esp. pp. 26–33, 78–138.
[113] See Appendix 2 for an exhaustive comparison of the two instructions.
[114] Golding, *Gilbert of Sempringham*, pp. 81–82, 455. It is published in William Dugdale, ed., *Monasticon Anglicanum: A History of the Abbies and Other Monasteries, Hospitals, Frieries, and Cathedral and Collegiate Churches, with Their Dependencies in England and Wales; Also of All Such Scotch, Irish, and French Monasteries, as Were in Any Manner Connected with Religious Houses in England*, 2nd edn, 6 volumes in 8 volumes (London: James Bohn, 1846), vol. 6:2, pp. xix–lix.
[115] Dugdale, *Monasticon Anglicanum*, p. xxxvi.
[116] Ibid., p. xxxvi.

even if their respective wordings were so far apart that it is obvious the Gilbertines did not copy anything directly from Lanfranc's instruction.[117] It is still possible, however, that the source of inspiration was Lanfranc's instruction. Alternatively, perhaps these alterations were products of widespread English practice.

Another difference is the way the visiting bishop/dignitary should interact with the community in the church. The Cistercian abbot was supposed to retire to his place while the bishop was praying. The Gilbertine prior, on the other hand, should remain 'standing near him [the bishop/the dignitary]' ('stans juxta eum').[118] The Cistercians proceeded to the chapter room after the bishop's prayer, but the Gilbertines remained in the church, singing psalms. The bishop should also kiss everyone, not just the prior, and only then should the Gilbertines proceed to the chapter room. Here, the bishop was to hold a sermon, if he wished, or be shown to the guesthouse, 'if he did not wish to enter the chapter room' ('si capitulum intrare noluerit').[119]

These alterations are important. Tweaking the Cistercian instruction with a few words, the Gilbertines shifted the emphasis of the instruction. While hierarchy and authority were still very much present, the Gilbertines added some of the same themes Lanfranc emphasised: inclusion and communality, familiarisation and friendship. The Gilbertines did not use bells as effectively as Lanfranc, but they aspired to have an outdoor church service; and their instruction directed the dignitary to exchange kisses with everyone, not just the head of the house. The revisions are best understood as a desire to adjust performance – and in this way to transmit a different message. The Gilbertine editors would have had no reason to revise the instruction if they did not believe the alterations were of importance. Correct performance mattered.

Other Customaries, Instructions, and Accounts

Not all customaries contained detailed instructions; some did not even mention receptions. The Carthusians, for instance, chose to do without the *adventus*. They valued seclusion, swimming 'against the current of contemporary thought', as Kerr puts it,[120] noting that hospitality was considered important at the time.[121] The

---

[117] *The Monastic Constitutions*, p. 106: 'dehinc porrigatur ei incensum similiter ab abbate, textus a priore'; Dugdale, *Monasticon Anglicanum*, p. xxxvi: 'deinde textum ad osculandum. Quo thurificato'.
[118] Dugdale, *Monasticon Anglicanum*, p. xxxvi.
[119] Ibid.
[120] Kerr, *Monastic Hospitality*, p. 41.
[121] Ibid., pp. 23–49.

Carthusian customary had no processions, only a duty for the Carthusian monks to prostrate themselves at the reception of abbots and bishops.[122]

The Benedictine abbey of Bury St Edmunds likewise produced no *adventus* instruction, even if in that case it was not about disapproving of the *adventus*. Jocelin of Brakelond, chronicler at Bury St Edmunds, wrote in detail about the grandeur of Abbot Samson's first entry in 1182.[123] Another Bury chronicler, Master Nicholas of Dunstable, composer of the *Electio Hugonis*, reported on the ceremonial reception of Cardinal Nicholas in 1213.[124] However, the Bury customary contains no instruction on the ceremonial reception of dignitaries. The customary does, on the other hand, discuss the financial burden of guests.[125]

The absence of an instruction probably had to do with the abbey's fight to remain exempt. Bury St Edmunds had, since the late twelfth century, been exempted from ecclesiastical jurisdiction save that of legates *a latere* and the pope.[126] The abbey valued its exemption and was ready to fight for it. Jocelin of Brakelond reported how Archbishop Hubert Walter announced his intention to visit the abbey in late 1198. Hubert was a papal legate, but not *a latere*. Abbot Samson appealed to Pope Innocent III, who ruled that only legates *a latere* were entitled to ceremonial receptions at the abbey and that only they held powers of reform over the abbey.[127] The link between ritual reception and jurisdiction is interesting to consider.

In 1232, Pope Gregory IX nevertheless ordered visitations of exempted monasteries, including Bury St Edmunds. According to Matthew Paris, the abbot of Bury St Edmunds appealed. The pope agreed to appoint other visitors, but was otherwise adamant: Bury St Edmunds was to be visited.[128] The visitors came to Bury in 1234. According to Gransden, the Bury monks composed their customary

---

[122] See Guigo [Guigues], 'Consuetudines', in *PL*, 153 (Paris, 1854), cols. 631–760, ch. 20, 36, cols 673–74, 711–12.

[123] Jocelin of Brakelond, *Cronica Jocelini de Brakelonda de rebus gestis Samsonis, Abbatis Monasterii Sancti Edmundi*, trans. H. E. Butler, Medieval Classics (London: Thomas Nelson and Sons Ltd, 1949), pp. 24–25. The identity of Jocelin of Brakelond is subject to debate. For an overview of the debate, see Kerr, *Monastic Hospitality*, pp. 203–4.

[124] Rodney M. Thomson, ed., *The Chronicle of the Election of Hugh, Abbot of Bury St. Edmunds and Later Bishop of Ely*, OMT (Oxford: Clarendon Press, 1974), pp. 26–27.

[125] *The Customary of the Benedictine Abbey of Bury St Edmunds*, pp. 5–7.

[126] Besides Bury, the abbeys of Westminster, St Albans, Evesham, Malmesbury, and St Augustine at Canterbury enjoyed exemption from episcopal jurisdiction; see Christopher R. Cheney, *Episcopal Visitation of Monasteries in the Thirteenth Century*, 2nd edn (Manchester: Manchester University Press, 1983), p. 39.

[127] Jocelin of Brakelond, *Chronica*, pp. 81–85; Walther Holtzmann, ed., *Papsturkunden in England*, 3 vols (Berlin: various publishers, 1930–52), vol. 3, no. 477, pp. 571–72. See also Vivian H. Galbraith, 'The East Anglian See and the Abbey of Bury St Edmunds', *EHR* 40, no. 158 (1925): 222–28.

[128] Matthew Paris, *CM*, vol. 3, pp. 235–40.

either just before or after the visitation, drafting the customary in response to the visitation and as a defence of the *status quo* at the abbey.[129] The visitors were papal appointees, but not papal legates, much less *a latere*. The abbey's house chronicle, the *Chronica Buriensis*, compiled c. 1265, does not mention the visitation.[130] It is tempting to suggest that this was deliberate. In any case, an unwelcome visitation was probably an inopportune moment to compose an *adventus* instruction, because ritual reception and jurisdiction were interlinked.

The Carthusians and the monks of Bury St Edmunds show that not only institutional attitudes to the *adventus* ceremony but also the circumstances surrounding the production of a given customary affected the making of *adventus* instructions. The instruction included in the customary of St Mary's Abbey at York (from around 1326) presumably remained underdeveloped and taciturn due to issues of a nature similar to those at Bury St Edmunds.[131] St Mary's fought recurrently with the archbishops of York about the archbishop's right of visitation, including how the monks should receive him.[132]

A few other customaries warrant mention. These include the *De Obedientiariis* of Abingdon Abbey, the Observances from the Augustinian Barnwell Priory, and the customary of the priory of Norwich Cathedral. The *De Obedientiariis* of Abingdon (produced 1220s or 1230s) contains a brief note on ceremonial receptions, but otherwise devotes most of its text to the monastic *obedientiarii*, the monastic officials (hence its title).[133] The Observances from the Augustinian Barnwell Priory (late thirteenth century) and the customary of the priory of Norwich Cathedral (around 1260) devote extensive chapters to processions.[134] The monks at these

---

[129] Antonia Gransden, *A History of the Abbey of Bury St Edmunds 1182–1256: Samson of Tottington to Edmund Walpole* (Woodbridge: Boydell Press, 2007), pp. 178–79, 203–9; *The Customary of the Benedictine Abbey of Bury St Edmunds*, pp. xxviii–xxix, xxxiii–xxxvi. See also Rose Graham, 'A Papal Visitation of Bury St. Edmunds and Westminster in 1234', *EHR* 27, no. 108 (1912): 728–39.

[130] See Antonia Gransden, ed. and trans., *The Chronicle of Bury St Edmunds, Chronica Buriensis, 1212–1301* (London: Nelson, 1964), pp. 8–9.

[131] 'When he [the abbot] is outside of the monastery and has stayed away for a year or a half, and he returns, he is received with a procession by all the brothers dressed in white' ('Cum extra monasterium est et per annum uel dimidium moratus, reuersus fuerit, cum processione recipitur ab omnibus fratris [albis] indutis'); see H. H. E. Craster and M. E. Thornton, eds, *The Chronicle of St Mary's Abbey, York: From Bodley MS. 39* (Durham: Andrews & Co., 1934), p. 81.

[132] Ibid., pp. 20, 37, 41, 124, 126–28. For the dating of the customary, see ibid., pp. ix–xiii.

[133] The *De Obedientiariis* are published in Joseph Stevenson, ed., *Chronicon Monasterii de Abingdon*, 2 vols, RS (London: Longman, 1858), vol. 2, Appendix 4, pp. 335–417, the instruction at pp. 338–39. The *De Consuetudinibus Abbendoniæ* (About the Customaries of Abingdon) is chiefly about customary payments and rents; see ibid., Appendix 3, pp. 296–334.

[134] Clark, *The Observances*, pp. 146–53; *The Customary of the Cathedral Priory Church of Norwich*, ed. J. B. L. Tolhurst (London: Harrison and Sons, 1948), pp. 206–12. The extant

places were undoubtedly able to perform elaborate and well-instructed receptions, but in both customaries, the particularities of the instructions' reception rituals drown in a torrent of various feast days. On Ascension Day, the Norwich monks would, for instance, proceed with banners, holy water, crosses, relics, and a bier.[135] How they would receive a visiting dignitary, say a papal legate, is not mentioned.

Conclusion

Monastic customaries present a diverse range of perspectives regarding the appropriate receptions of dignitaries. Some are silent, some are brief, while others offer lengthy guidance on elaborate ceremonies. The need for regulation clearly varied, and these disparities are not coincidental. Lanfranc composed his Monastic Constitutions with the aim of reform, the Cistercian *Ecclesiastica Officia* sought to establish uniformity, and the Gilbertines produced their instruction as part of the foundation of their order. All three arose as part of monastic reassessment. In contrast, well-established houses such as the Benedictine abbey of Bury St Edmunds produced little comparable content, even though the monks composed a detailed customary. Evidently, the monks did not feel compelled to revise established practices or saw little need to put their reflections into written form. People typically write down rules and regulations when they aim to bring about change, reform something, or safeguard against changes.

This is all the more reason to assume that the authors producing these instructions did so with the intention of providing performable ceremonies. If instructions were models and style guides, the fact that they underwent modifications implies that authors considered performance and its significance. It is highly probable that monastic communities indeed employed bells, incense, Scripture, processions, prayer, kissing, sermons, and more, as prescribed by the instructions. In doing so, they emphasised notions of internal and external hierarchy, communality, familiarisation, inclusion, and relationship to varying degrees. The authors aimed to preserve the internal composition of the institution while simultaneously cultivating a friendly relationship with the dignitary. There is an underlying tension, fear of disruption, but also an awareness of the opportunity to foster positive relations with powerful people. Cardinal-legates *a latere* undoubtedly belonged to the realm of high potential equals high risk. Even kings might take a stand on their receptions.

---

recension of the Norwich customary is probably based on earlier recensions dating back to the 1110s; see *The Customary of the Cathedral Priory Church of Norwich*, pp. vi–viii, x–xi, xiii–xix.

[135] *The Customary of the Cathedral Priory Church of Norwich*, p. 211.

The *adventus* instructions also serve as important guides for interpreting narrative accounts. While they cannot shed light on how any actual event played out, nor do they isolate a distinctive papal-legatine reception, the instructions highlight the underlying stakes. A reception was a vital moment for defining the authority of the guest and for establishing his relationship with the recipients. At least three perspectives emerge from the instructions: that of the dignitary, that of the head of the community, and that of the ordinary members of the community. Each of these might have their own agendas, and it is even possible that various subdivisions and rifts existed within the community or were magnified as a result of the reception and presence of a powerful external dignitary. All four commentators within this study positions themselves to view the legatine *adventus* primarily through the lens of one of these distinctive positions.

PART II
Narrating Legatine *Adventus* Ceremonies

4

Dependent on the King: Roger of Howden and the Legatine *Adventus*

The previous chapters have each, in various ways, explored attitudes, expectations, and concepts related to legates, insignia, and the *adventus*. What is uncovered therein is a complicated, contradictory, and everchanging picture. On the one hand, papal legates *a latere* were not merely among the most powerful lords within Latin Christendom; they were extensions of papal authority. Even kings sometimes felt that curial legates were meddling in their affairs. On the other hand, cardinal-legates were usually far away from their primary bases and central networks. They were dependent on their subjects to a greater degree than most other rulers, not being part of the local structures of power. The reception of a papal legate held both opportunities and dangers.

In the ensuing four chapters, I will explore how different authors viewed and represented the *adventus* of cardinal-legates *a latere*. This exploration necessitates a comprehensive study of each author, encompassing their life, experiences, and viewpoints. It is also essential to study the specific circumstances surrounding each legate and his mission, as these influenced the opinions of the commentators. Such an analysis will illustrate the remarkable diversity with which the commentators interpreted and presented the legatine *adventus*. While none of the commentators were immune to the authority radiating out from papal Rome, they reinterpreted the curial image within their own unique frameworks. The result is four different perspectives.

I will initiate this exploration by studying Roger of Howden's interpretation of the legatine *adventus*. His perspective is interesting for two reasons. He mainly viewed the legatine *adventus* through the lens of the king, a vantage point that profoundly influenced his understanding of the meaning of the legatine *adventus*. Moreover, his approach to recording and editing, evident in his two chronicles, reveals how meaning and significance might change with the passage of time.

Roger of Howden and His Authorship

Roger of Howden was presumably born around 1130. His father, Robert, was the parson of the large and wealthy minster church of Howden in Yorkshire.[1] Roger inherited the church, although Pope Alexander III initially opposed it. Alexander's motives are unknown, but Frank Barlow suggests that the pope acted on the urging of some local party. The extant sources do not answer how Roger overcame the opposition, but he succeeded his father in 1173 or 1174.[2]

Roger has left little information about his education. William Stubbs suggests that Roger was educated at Durham Cathedral, and that one *Willelmus de Houeden*, who attested several of the bishop of Durham's charters, was Roger's brother.[3] John Gillingham, on the other hand, argues more convincingly that Roger was educated at the cathedral school at York.[4] He had at least two close friends in those parts, Geoffrey, provost of Beverley, nephew of Roger de Pont L'Évêque, archbishop of York (r. 1154–81), and Robert Magnus, master of the schools of York. Roger wrote with sorrow about their drowning in 1177, temporarily suspending his writings for two years afterwards.[5]

Roger of Howden was, in all likelihood, a servant of Archbishop Roger of York. After the death of the archbishop, he went on to serve Hugh de Puiset (r. 1153–95), bishop of Durham, and probably his successor, Philip of Poitou (r. 1196–1208). He also became a canon of Glasgow in 1195 or earlier.[6] Throughout much of this time, Roger also served the king.

---

[1] John Gillingham, 'Writing the Biography of Roger of Howden, King's Clerk and Chronicler', in *Writing Medieval Biography, 750-1250: Essays in Honour of Professor Frank Barlow*, ed. David Bates, Julia Crick, and Sarah Hamilton (Woodbridge: Boydell Press, 2006), pp. 207–20, at pp. 207–8.

[2] Frank Barlow, 'Roger of Howden', *EHR* 65, no. 256 (1950): 352–60, pp. 355–56; Gillingham, 'Writing the Biography', p. 208; Walther Holtzmann, ed., *Papsturkunden in England*, 3 vols (Berlin: various publishers, 1930–52), vol. 2, no. 148, pp. 338–39.

[3] *Chronica*, vol. 1, p. xiv.

[4] Gillingham, 'Writing the Biography', p. 208; John Gillingham, 'The Travels of Roger of Howden and His Views of the Irish, Scots and Welsh', in *ANS XX*, ed. Christopher Harper-Bill (Woodbridge: Boydell Press, 1998), pp. 151–69, at p. 156. See also David Corner, 'The *Gesta Regis Henrici Secundi* and *Chronica* of Roger, Parson of Howden', *Bulletin of the Institute of Historical Research* 56, no. 134 (1983): 126–44, esp. pp. 126–30.

[5] Gillingham, 'The Travels of Roger', p. 156.

[6] Ibid., pp. 155–57; Gillingham, 'Writing the Biography', pp. 216–18; Archibald A. Duncan, 'Roger of Howden and Scotland, 1187–1201', in *Church, Chronicle and Learning in Medieval and Early Renaissance Scotland: Essays Presented to Donald Watt on the Occasion of the Completion of the Publication of Bower's Scotichronicon*, ed. Barbara E. Crawford (Edinburgh: Mercat Press, 1999), pp. 135–59, at pp. 135–39. See also Corner, 'The *Gesta Regis*', pp. 134–44, esp. p. 139; and David Corner, 'The Earliest Surviving Manuscripts of Roger of Howden's "Chronica"', *EHR* 98, no. 387 (1983): 297–310, p. 309.

Roger probably began his career as a royal clerk in 1170, the year in which one of his works, the *Gesta Regis Henrici Secundi*, begins, although no firm evidence for his service exists until 1174, when he reported on one of his own missions.[7] He was particularly involved in Anglo-Scottish relations, often travelling to Scotland on the king's behalf, but he also visited the papal curia, France, and probably Ireland.[8] Roger was justice of the forest between 1184 and 1190.[9] He followed King Richard on crusade to the Holy Land, but returned home with the French fleet in 1191, ostensibly as a spy for Richard, who (for good reasons) distrusted the intentions of his formal ally, King Philip II Augustus of France (r. 1180–1223).[10] Gillingham, in this vein, argues that the king often used Roger as an escort to foreign dignitaries, including papal legates. Roger likely accompanied Cardinal Vivian in 1176 and 1177, the legate Alexius in 1180, and perhaps the legates Abbot Silvan of Rievaulx and Roland, papal subdeacon and bishop-elect of Dol, in 1182.[11] Roger was superbly positioned to chronicle the missions and receptions of legates, probably being an eyewitness on a number of occasions.

Doris Stenton and David Corner believe that Roger retired to his parsonage to write after his return from the crusade around 1191.[12] Gillingham, on the other hand, notes that Roger still travelled on royal business to Scotland and Rome during the late 1190s.[13] He probably died in 1201, when his *Chronica* ends abruptly and in a confused manner. A scribe presumably entered the late Roger's unfinished notes into the *Chronica*.[14]

Roger wrote two chronicles: the *Gesta Regis Henrici Secundi* and the *Chronica*. Roger likely also produced three guides on navigation.[15] The *Gesta* is Roger's

[7] See *Gesta*, vol. 1, p. 80.
[8] See especially Gillingham, 'The Travels of Roger', but also Duncan, 'Roger of Howden and Scotland'; Sean Duffy, 'Ireland's Hastings: The Anglo-Norman Conquest of Dublin', in *ANS XX*, ed. Christopher Harper-Bill (Woodbridge: Boydell Press, 1997), pp. 69–85, at pp. 81–82; and Jane E. Sayers, *Innocent III, Leader of Europe, 1198–1216* (London: Longman, 1994), pp. 8, 25.
[9] Michael Staunton, *The Historians of Angevin England* (Oxford: Oxford University Press, 2017), p. 54.
[10] Doris M. Stenton, 'Roger of Howden and Benedict', *EHR* 68, no. 269 (1953): 574–82, pp. 576–81; John Gillingham, *Richard I*, revised edition (New Haven: Yale University Press, 1999), p. 165; John Gillingham, 'Roger of Howden on Crusade', in *Richard Coeur de Lion: Kingship, Chivalry and War in the Twelfth Century* (London: The Hambledon Press, 1994, orig. 1982), pp. 141–53, at pp. 147–49.
[11] Gillingham, 'The Travels of Roger', pp. 159–62; Paul Craig Ferguson, *Medieval Papal Representatives in Scotland: Legates, Nuncios, and Judges-Delegate, 1125–1286* (Edinburgh: The Stair Society, 1997), pp. 53–63.
[12] Stenton, 'Roger of Howden', pp. 581–82; Corner, 'The *Gesta Regis*', pp. 130–44.
[13] Gillingham, 'The Travels of Roger'; Gillingham, 'Writing the Biography'.
[14] Stenton, 'Roger of Howden', p. 582.
[15] See Patrick G. Dalché, *Du Yorkshire à l'Inde: une 'geographie' urbaine et maritime de la*

first chronicle. It was initially attributed to Abbot Benedict of Peterborough (r. 1177–93), but Stenton, Corner, and finally Gillingham have proved beyond reasonable doubt that it is the work of Roger.[16] He began working on the *Gesta* around 1171, writing mostly contemporaneously with the events described, concluding the chronicle in 1192.[17] The text covers the years from 1170 to 1192.

Gillingham, who has worked exhaustively on establishing Roger's authorship, observes that the *Gesta* was 'a journal of his [Roger's] own travels'.[18] The *Gesta* 'followed the court when he [Roger] followed the court, but when he was away from court ... then it reflected his own journeys'.[19] This, as Gillingham argues, 'explains not only what he wrote but also what he didn't write'.[20] In some cases, Roger provided detailed accounts of minor events, such as when he provided dates and embarkation locations for Cardinal Vivian, who travelled throughout England, Ireland, and Scotland. In that case, Roger was in all likelihood present, accompanying the cardinal.[21] In other cases, he only presented the barest outlines of important events, such as those in 1186 possibly heralding war between England and France.[22]

Roger composed the *Gesta* sequentially, inserting information as it filtered through to him. He, for instance, inserted letters when he got hold of them; in contrast, he arranged them according to their date of publication in the *Chronica*.[23] With a few exceptions (Roger left blank leaves at the end of each year to be able to insert additional information),[24] the *Gesta* offers little in the way of hindsight, being supposedly drawn up within weeks or a few months after information relating to an event reached Roger. In short, the *Gesta* often possesses a narrative immediacy. As Gillingham puts it, it 'is, in a very strict sense of the words, a contemporary chronicle'.[25]

---

fin du XIIe siècle (Roger de Howden?) (Geneva: Droz, 2005), pp. 21–48; and Staunton, *The Historians*, p. 54.

[16] See Thomas Duffus Hardy, *Descriptive Catalogue of Materials Relating to the History of Great Britain and Ireland, to the End of the Reign of Henry VII*, RS (London: Longman & Co, 1865), vol. 2, pp. 494–95; *Gesta*, vol. 1, pp. l–lxiii; Antonia Gransden, *Historical Writing in England c.550–c.1307* (London: Routledge, 1974), pp. 225–30; Richard Wayne Huling, 'English Historical Writing under the Early Angevin Kings, 1170–1210' (unpublished PhD dissertation, State University of New York, Binghamton, 1981), pp. 55–57; Stenton, 'Roger of Howden'; Corner, 'The *Gesta Regis*', esp. pp. 126–31; and Gillingham, 'Roger of Howden on Crusade', esp. pp. 141–43. See also Staunton, *The Historians*, p. 53.

[17] *Gesta*, vol. 1, pp. xxii, xxiv–xxv, xliv–xlv.

[18] Gillingham, 'The Travels of Roger', p. 154.

[19] Ibid.

[20] Ibid.

[21] *Gesta*, vol. 1, pp. 118, 136–37, 166–67.

[22] Ibid., pp. 353–56.

[23] See Gillingham, 'Roger of Howden on Crusade', pp. 144–45.

[24] *Gesta*, vol. 1, pp. xlvi–xlviii; Gillingham, 'Roger of Howden on Crusade', p. 145.

[25] Gillingham, 'Roger of Howden on Crusade', p. 145.

Shortly after returning from the crusade (i.e., around 1192), Roger abandoned the *Gesta* to compose a longer but also more stringent and streamlined narrative: the *Chronica*.[26] He not only extended the coverage, beginning in 732 and ending in 1201, but he also revised and abbreviated the overlapping parts of the chronicles.[27] These reworkings offer fascinating insights into the way he viewed events over time. Roger's aim was probably to make his new chronicle more useful and readable. If so, he succeeded. Only two manuscripts of the *Gesta* have survived the ages while the *Chronica* exists in numerous copies.[28]

Historians have termed Roger an 'administrative historian' or a 'civil service historian'.[29] It is true that Roger showed a marked interest in and knowledge of royal administration and foreign connections; he was a royal clerk. However, as Michael Staunton stresses, 'an administrative historian or a civil service historian is not necessarily an official historian'.[30] Staunton argues that historians like Roger of Howden 'did not act as mouthpieces for the English kings', but instead expressed 'the perspective and concerns of the many people associated in various ways with the government of England'. This, according to Staunton, was 'an ongoing community that was loyal to the established institutions of the realm but took a long view – something akin to civil service'.[31]

Despite these assessments of Roger's motives, he remains something of a puzzle as a historian. He composed no preambles nor did he offer reasons for writing. He mentioned no patron for whom he might have written, nor is there any trace of any dedications. Roger moreover wrote in a conservative northern English annalistic tradition, effacing himself from his work.[32] As a result, his own voice can be difficult to disentangle from those of his sources. For instance, in the *Gesta*, Roger lifted the description of the Scottish incursion of 1174 nearly verbatim from another chronicle, the *Historia post obitum Bedae* (a mid-twelfth-century compilation from Durham). The *Historia*'s account did not concern the 1174 incursion, but another Scottish incursion in 1138.[33] Roger's account of King Richard's coronation is a further example. The account has the appearance of an eyewitness account, but Henry Richardson has demonstrated that Roger simply

---

[26] See Corner, 'The Earliest Surviving Manuscripts', esp. pp. 302–3.
[27] The overlapping parts of the *Gesta* and the *Chronica* are roughly 607 and 557 pages, respectively, in their modern published versions in the Rolls Series.
[28] *Chronica*, vol. 1, pp. xxi–xxvii, lxxiv.
[29] See Staunton, *The Historians*, p. 51.
[30] Ibid.
[31] Ibid., p. 52.
[32] Huling, 'English Historical Writing', p. 38.
[33] Gillingham, 'The Travels of Roger', p. 161; Staunton, *The Historians*, p. 61; *Gesta*, vol. 1, p. 64. On the *Historia post obitum Bedae*, see, e.g., Gransden, *Historical Writing*, pp. 225–26.

revised a coronation ordo, giving it the appearance of an eyewitness account.[34] Even when Roger wrote passionately about something, such as the anti-heresy mission of Peter of Pavia, cardinal-priest of S. Crisogono, and Henry of Marcy, abbot of Clairvaux (r. 1177–79),[35] his passion was lifted directly from Cardinal Peter's letter.[36] Staunton, consequently, argues for proceeding with caution if one should wish to study Roger's viewpoints.[37] Beryl Smalley goes so far as to argue that 'inconsistency did not bother him [Roger]. His mind was a rag-bag.'[38] Frank Barlow asserts that 'Roger was a trimmer', and that 'his bias accurately represents the forces exerted on him'.[39]

It is sometimes possible to deduce something about Roger's viewpoints, however, especially when comparing the *Gesta* and the *Chronica*. In the *Chronica*, at the year 1185, Roger inserted a story about a conversation with the devil. The devil expressed regret over the multitude of people taking the cross, but simultaneously hoped that the sins of the crusaders would swell the ranks of hell again. Roger commented that 'this afterwards appeared to come about' ('quod de post facto apparuit').[40] The story – absent from the *Gesta*'s longer and more detailed account of the Third Crusade (1187–92) – was written in hindsight after the (partial) failure

---

[34] Henry G. Richardson, 'The Coronation in Medieval England: The Evolution of the Office and the Oath', *Traditio* 16 (1960): 111–201, esp. pp. 181–89.

[35] On this mission, see, e.g., Beverly Mayne Kienzle, *Cistercians, Heresy and Crusade in Occitania, 1145–1229: Preaching in the Lord's Vineyard* (York: York Medieval Press, 2001), pp. 109–34. Henry of Marcy later became cardinal-bishop of Albano.

[36] Compare Roger's report with the cardinal's letter. Roger's report: 'When the Count of Toulouse and the others, who had previously heard them [the heretics] to have preached contrary to the Christian faith, provoked with vehement astonishment and inflamed with zealousness for the Christian faith, rose, and clearly convicted them to their head [faces] of having lied more flagrantly' ('Quod cum comes Tolosiæ et cæteri qui prius audierant ipsos Christianæ fidei contraria prædicasse, vehementi admiratione commoti et Christianæ fidei zelo succesi, surrexerunt, et eos plane in caput suum mentitos fuisse manifestius convicerunt'); see *Gesta*, vol. 1, p 201. The cardinal's letter (included in the *Gesta*): 'The noble man, the Count of Toulouse, and many others, both clerics and laymen, who had heard them [the heretics] preach differently, provoked with vehement astonishment and inflamed with zeal for the Christian faith, rose, and clearly convicted them to their head [faces] of having lied more flagrantly' ('Nobilis vir comes Tolosensis, et multi alii clerici et laici, qui eos audierant aliter prædicantes, vehementi admiratione commoti, et Christianæ fidei zelo succensi, surrexerunt, et eos plane in caput suum mentitos fuisse manifestius convicerunt'); see *Gesta*, vol. 1, p. 205. Roger repeated his report almost verbatim in the *Chronica*; see *Chronica*, vol. 2, p. 152.

[37] Staunton, *The Historians*, pp. 65–66.

[38] Beryl Smalley, *Historians in the Middle Ages* (London: Thames and Hudson, 1974), p. 114.

[39] Barlow, 'Roger of Howden', p. 360.

[40] *The Annals*, vol. 2, pp. 49–50; *Chronica*, vol. 2, pp. 302–3. See also Gillingham, 'Roger of Howden on Crusade', p. 150; and Gillingham, 'Writing the Biography', pp. 210–11.

of the crusade. Roger inserted the story as a moral assessment of the events. The account of King Richard's departure on crusade is another example. In the *Gesta*, Roger reported that the archbishop of Rouen handed Richard his pilgrim staff. In the *Chronica*, Roger added that when Richard leaned on the staff, it broke![41]

These examples highlight that Roger was not only a historian of the bureaucracy or a civil servant.[42] He might have written a 'passionless, colourless narrative', as Stubbs puts it,[43] but I contend that his aim was to chronicle good deeds to emulate and bad deeds to shun, like so many other medieval authors (and are law-making and administrative innovation not deeds?). Roger's immediate posterity certainly found his works useful. The *Chronica*, especially, was widely utilised by an array of authors, including abbey annalists at Burton and Peterborough as well as the chroniclers Walter of Coventry and William of Newburgh. The Lanercost Chronicle is a continuation of the *Chronica*. King Edward I (r. 1272–1307) used parts of the *Chronica* to insist on English lordship over Scotland.[44] The chroniclers Roger of Wendover and Gervase of Canterbury used the *Gesta*, while the abbey of Peterborough possessed an incomplete manuscript of the work.[45] The *Gesta* also made its way to Scotland.[46] Roger's audience, if dissemination is anything to go by, were those interested in good deeds to emulate and bad deeds to shun.

Popes, Legates, and England

Roger lived through an era of intense legatine activity. The pontificate of Alexander III, as mentioned previously, saw a massive expansion in the use of cardinal-legates. The main impetus for this development was the schism (1159–77/8) between Alexander and a number of imperial-backed antipopes. Alexander needed his cardinals to fight for him at the courts of European princes and ecclesiastical elites.

In England, the Becket case added to the complexity of the situation. Shortly after Thomas Becket's appointment as archbishop of Canterbury (1162), he and King Henry II fell out over the rights of the English Church. Henry appealed to Alexander, hoping he could sway the pope's legates to act in his favour. This act

---

[41] *Gesta*, vol. 2, p. 111; *The Annals*, vol. 2, p. 141; *Chronica*, vol. 3, pp. 36–37.
[42] See also Gillingham, 'The Travels of Roger', pp. 155–56, 161–62, 167.
[43] *Chronica*, vol. 1, p. lxix. Twentieth-century historians have generally been dismissive of the literary quality of Roger's writings; see Richard W. Southern, *Medieval Humanism and Other Studies* (Oxford: Basil Blackwell, 1970), p. 150; Barlow, 'Roger of Howden', p. 360; and Gransden, *Historical Writing*, p. 235.
[44] *Chronica*, vol. 1, pp. lxxi–lxxiii; John Gillingham, 'Two Yorkshire Historians Compared: Roger of Howden and William of Newburgh', *The Haskins Society Journal* 12 (2002): 15–37.
[45] *Gesta*, vol. 1, pp. xxix–xxxi; Gervase, vol. 1, p. xxi.
[46] Walter Bower, *Scotichronicon by Walter Bower*, ed. D. E. R. Watt, 9 vols (Aberdeen: Aberdeen University Press, 1994), vol. 4, p. xxii.

was a de facto recognition of papal jurisdiction: three successive legatine missions had tried and failed to reach a compromise in the case.[47] Roger's patron, Archbishop Roger of York, was a chief opponent of Becket.[48] With Becket out of royal favour, he had moved to strengthen his position.[49] However, all scheming and jostling for position became moot when royal knights murdered Becket in his own cathedral at the end of 1170 (the same year Roger entered royal service). The murder turned Becket into St Thomas, which forced King Henry to come to terms with the papacy and the Canterbury Church. In 1172, Theodwin and Albert, cardinal-legates, negotiated the compromise of Avranches, which strengthened the position of the Church in England and secured the right of appeal to Rome. Henry also did public penance.[50]

The conclusion of the Becket case normalised Anglo-Papal relations. Pope Alexander lifted the interdict, which he had imposed in the wake of Becket's murder. Alexander also appointed Archbishop Richard of Canterbury (r. 1173–84) as resident legate. The policy of appointing resident papal legates continued until the pontificate of Innocent III. Resident legates were acceptable and often useful to the English king. When King Richard went on crusade, he left William Longchamp, his chancellor and bishop of Ely, in charge of affairs in England, but he was only confident in William's authority once he had convinced Pope Clement III (r. 1187–91) to appoint William as legate.[51]

Popes simultaneously dispatched curial legates on a number of missions. One important area of legatine activity revolved around peace making between England and France whilst in preparation for initiating a crusade. Popes

---

[47] See Anne J. Duggan, *Thomas Becket* (London: Arnold, 2004); and Anne J. Duggan, 'Henry II, the English Church and the Papacy, 1154–76', in *Henry II: New Interpretations*, ed. Christopher Harper-Bill and Nicholas Vincent (Woodbridge: Boydell Press, 2007), pp. 154–83.

[48] Gillingham, 'The Travels of Roger', pp. 155–56.

[49] Duggan, *Thomas Becket*, pp. 36–37, 40–41, 103–4, 172–73, 181–85, 191–92, 196, 200.

[50] Anne J. Duggan, '*Alexander ille meus*: The Papacy of Alexander III', in *Pope Alexander III (1159–81): The Art of Survival*, ed. Peter D. Clarke and Anne J. Duggan (Farnham: Ashgate, 2012), pp. 13–49, at p. 32; Duggan, *Thomas Becket*, pp. 201–23; Anne J. Duggan, '*Ne in dubium*: The Official Record of Henry's Reconciliation at Avranches, 21 May 1172', *EHR* 115, no. 462 (2000): 643–58; Helene Tillmann, *Die päpstlichen Legaten in England bis zur Beendigung der Legation Gualas, 1218* (Bonn: Hch. Ludwig, 1926), pp. 68–72. Roger showed much interest in the legation of 1172, but he was not on hand to witness it; see Duggan, '*Ne in dubium*', esp. pp. 646–49. His knowledge about the compromise of Avranches derived from the official acts, which he inserted into his chronicles; see *Gesta*, vol. 1, pp. 29–34; *The Annals*, vol. 1, pp. 354–61; and *Chronica*, vol. 2, pp. 33–40.

[51] Tillmann, *Die päpstlichen Legaten*, pp. 85–87; Ilicia Jo Sprey, 'Papal Legates in English Politics, 1100–1272' (unpublished PhD dissertation, University of Virginia, Charlottesville, 1998), pp. 221–38.

dispatched a substantial number of legates to France and Normandy for this very purpose (although they often achieved little). Cardinals also intermittently visited England, but they pursued no long-term objectives. Popes instead tasked them with *ad hoc* missions, often in response to petitions.[52] Two such petitions came from King Henry himself: in 1175, Henry petitioned the pope for a legate to sort out some ambiguities in the compromise of Avranches. Alexander dispatched Cardinal Hugh Pierleoni in response.[53] In 1186, Henry also asked for legates to crown his son, John, as king of Ireland. Pope Urban III dispatched Octavian, cardinal-deacon of SS. Sergius e Bachus, and Hugh de Nonant, bishop-elect of Coventry (r. 1185–98), to comply with the king's wish. Troubles in Ireland and an imminent war with France caused them to abandon the coronation, however.[54]

Some curial legates and other papal envoys came uninvited to England, only passing through or promoting ecclesiastical business. One such was Vivian, cardinal-priest of S. Stefano al Monte Celio, who arrived in England in 1176. The king of Scotland, William I the Lion (r. 1165–1214), had probably invited him, although his legation also included Ireland and Norway.[55] In 1178, Albert de Suma and Peter di Sant'Agata entered England to promulgate summons to the Third Lateran Council. In 1180, John 'the Scot', a claimant to the see of St Andrews in Scotland, returned to Scotland with Alexius, legate and Roman subdeacon, through England. Alexius was supposed to settle the disputed election to the see of St Andrews.[56] In late 1189, Cardinal John arrived in England. John's is an interesting case. He had been in France and Normandy to procure peace, but subsequently turned his attention to a protracted dispute between Archbishop Baldwin and the archbishop's cathedral chapter at Canterbury. The chapter had petitioned for a legate, but the new king, Richard, played a waiting game. He kept the cardinal in Normandy, hastening to England himself and imposing a settlement in the case before he allowed the legate to set foot on English soil.[57]

No other cardinal-legates came to England during Richard's reign, but while

---

[52] Ian S. Robinson, *The Papacy 1073–1198: Continuity and Innovation* (Cambridge: Cambridge University Press, 1990), pp. 168–69; Sprey, 'Papal Legates', pp. 212–20.

[53] Tillmann, *Die päpstlichen Legaten*, pp. 73–77; Sprey, 'Papal Legates', pp. 215–16; Duggan, 'Henry II', pp. 178–80.

[54] Tillmann, *Die päpstlichen Legaten*, pp. 80–85; Colin Veach, 'Henry II and the Ideological Foundations of Angevin Rule in Ireland', *Irish Historical Studies* 42, no. 161 (2018): 1–25.

[55] Tillmann, *Die päpstlichen Legaten*, p. 77; Ferguson, *Medieval Papal Representatives*, pp. 53–55; Gillingham, 'The Travels of Roger', pp. 159–62; Sprey, 'Papal Legates', pp. 216–18.

[56] Tillmann, *Die päpstlichen Legaten*, pp. 78–79; Ferguson, *Medieval Papal Representatives*, pp. 55–61.

[57] Werner Maleczek, *Papst und Kardinalskolleg von 1191 bis 1216. Die Kardinäle unter Coelestin und Innocenz III.* (Vienna: Verlag der Österreichischen Akademie der Wissenschaften, 1984), pp. 70–71; Tillmann, *Die päpstlichen Legaten*, pp. 83–85.

Richard was in the Holy Land, a group of conspirators, including Richard's brother, John, expelled Richard's regent, William Longchamp, from England. Pope Celestine III dispatched cardinal-legates Octavian of Ostia and Jordan de Fossa Nova to attend to the matter. As the legates approached Normandy, however, the seneschal refused them entry, causing them to subject the whole duchy to interdict, but to no avail. Roger also lived just long enough to witness Cardinal John of Salerno's arrival at York in 1201 when the cardinal was on his way to Scotland.[58]

It was within this motley picture of legatine activity that Roger observed and addressed the receptions of papal legates. During his life, legatine activity in England was at its height. Activities and relations always fluctuated, but if any age was formative, Roger's lifetime was. The schism and the Becket affair brought matters to a head. One outcome was increased papal influence in England, as England was further integrated into the papal network of jurisdiction. However, the papacy did not exert dominance over the kingdom or the king. After the conclusion of the Becket affair, matters settled down into what might be termed 'normalcy'. Yet, there was never anything routine about a legatine visit. The relationship between the various papal legates and the king decided how Roger presented each legatine *adventus*.

Roger and the Proper Welcome

Perhaps the two most welcome papal legates in all of Roger's writings were Octavian, cardinal-deacon of SS. Sergius e Bachus, and Hugh de Nonant, bishop-elect of Coventry.[59] They landed in England at Christmas 1186. Their coming was part of King Henry II's design to institute his son, John, as king of Ireland. The legates came to crown the prince, thus providing official papal backing. It was a longstanding ambition: the king had lobbied for papal support for more than a decade, but success had only come with the election of Pope Urban III.[60] Roger was well aware of these designs, mentioning them explicitly in the *Gesta*.[61]

Roger described the arrival of the legates in both the *Gesta* and the *Chronica*. In the *Gesta*, Roger began with the news of the legates' landing reaching the king:

---

[58] Tillmann, *Die päpstlichen Legaten*, pp. 85–87, 90; Wilhelm Janssen, *Die päpstlichen Legaten in Frankreich von Schisma Anaklets II. bis zum Tode Coelestins III. (1130–1198)* (Cologne: Böhlau, 1961), pp. 139–40; Sprey, 'Papal Legates', pp. 221–38; *The Annals*, vol. 2, p. 277; *Chronica*, vol. 3, pp. 193–94; *Gesta*, vol. 2, pp. 246–47, 249–50.

[59] On Cardinal Octavian, see Maleczek, *Papst und Kardinalskolleg*, pp. 80–83.

[60] Veach, 'Henry II'.

[61] *Gesta*, vol. 1, p. 339; ibid., vol. 2, pp. 3–4.

Moreover, thereupon on the morrow of the nativity of the Lord, it reached the ears of the king that two legates, sent from the side of Urban, the highest pontiff, had landed in England at Dover ... Having heard this rumour [why the legates had come], the king sent to meet them John [Cumin], archbishop of Dublin [r. 1181–1212], and Radulf, archdeacon of Hereford: and the lord king went to London to meet them [having spent Christmas at Guildford]; and he received them on the circumcision of the lord [1 January] with a venerable procession at Westminster in the church of St Peter. With the authority of the highest pontiff, they had crosses carried in front of themselves wherever they went; and they always advanced mitred, and clothed in red garments; and they said that they were sent from the side of the lord pope to hear and decide ecclesiastical cases, if there were any such [cases] to submit to the highest pontiff.[62]

Having spent the last chapter in the company of some of the most detailed representations of the *adventus*, Roger's account might seem underwhelming. However, Roger did not write to record for posterity every detail of the reception. Rather, Roger wrote to highlight the meaning in specific details. Even brief accounts sometimes contain considerable information, meaning, and opinion.

The king, in Roger's account, recognised the legates' position and authority. This is no surprise: the legates had, after all, come on royal invitation to do the king's bidding. Roger construed the recognition in a straightforward manner: he described the prelude and the principal parts of the ceremony. Upon learning about the arrival of the legates, the king dispatched high-ranking emissaries to greet them, while he himself went to Westminster to prepare their reception. Westminster was a natural choice, but Roger made sure to mention that the church was dedicated to St Peter ('in the church of St Peter'), echoing the connection between the pope and England. Henry received the legates with a 'venerable procession' ('venerabili processione'). Roger also mentioned the legates' insignia – mitres, crosses, and red clothing – showing that he interpreted the insignia to signal authority and primacy

---

[62] *Gesta*, vol. 2, pp. 3–4: 'Ibi autem in crastino Nativitatis Domini pervenit ad aures regis quod duo legati, missi a latere Urbani summi pontificis, applicuerunt in Angliam apud Doveram ... Quo audito rumore, rex misit obviam eis Johannem Divelinensem archiepiscopum, et Radulfum Herefordensem archidiaconum: et dominus rex venit Lundonias obviam eis; et recepit eos in die Circumcisionis Domini, cum venerabili processione, apud Westmonasterium in ecclesia Sancti Petri. Ipso vero, auctoritate summi pontificis, cruces ante se portari fecerunt ubicunque ambulabant; et semper incedebant mitrati, et rubeis indumentis induti; et dicebant quod missi erant a latere domini papæ ad audiendas et terminandas causas ecclesiasticas, si quæ referendæ essent ad summum pontificem.' I am grateful to August Thomsen, cand.mag. i latin (candidate/master in Latin), for discussing the translation of this passage.

relative to other ecclesiastics. Roger's report on the extent of their authority to settle ecclesiastical cases probably echoes the reading aloud of their mandate.

At the same time, the king, according to the *Gesta*'s chain of events, retained control over the situation. The legates, for example, did not leave Dover until the king had provided them with an escort. The emissaries brought them to London to meet the king. On the one hand, this aligned with common protocol and was even expected. The courtesy rules of hospitality stipulated that lords and nobles were obliged to provide escorts to important guests.[63] On the other hand, the monarch kept control of the situation, just like the abbot in the monastic instructions. There is little reason to believe that the legates in any meaningful way could or intended to threaten Henry (either in the *Gesta*'s account or in real life), even if the king's position was not as secure as it had been during his youth. However, it never hurt to keep an eye on the legates' whereabouts or their meetings with powerful lords.

The identity of the emissaries, the archbishop of Dublin and the archdeacon of Hereford, is interesting. There is an almost direct line from London to Dublin through Hereford. In reality, this was expedient: local escorts made travel easier as they knew the lay of the land and had access to local prestige and resources.[64] The same is, to a lesser degree, true when the king chose Roger to accompany another legate, Cardinal Vivian, to Scotland in 1176. Roger was from Yorkshire and an expert on Scotland. On the other hand, even when legates were welcome, like Cardinal Octavian and Bishop-elect Hugh de Nonant, Henry presumably did not give them leeway to wander at will, but assigned dignitaries to escort and guide them through specific parts of the country.

Despite all of this, the legates never made it to Dublin; instead, Henry went to the continent, taking them with him. War with King Philip was looming, and Henry intended to use the legates in his negotiations with the king of France. This is probably the reason why the *Chronica*'s account, in contrast to the *Gesta*'s account, is brief and disinterested:

> In the same year after the birth of the Lord, Pope Urban sent into England Octavian, cardinal-subdeacon of the Holy Roman Church, and with him Hugh de Nonant, to whom he himself had committed the legateship in Ireland to crown there John, son of the king; but the lord king deferred that coronation, and brought the aforementioned legates with him to Normandy to a conference between himself and Philip, king of France.[65]

---

[63] See Julie Kerr, '"Welcome the Coming and Speed the Parting Guest": Hospitality in Twelfth-Century England', *JMH* 33, no. 2 (2007): 130–46, esp. pp. 141–42.

[64] See ibid., p. 141.

[65] *The Annals*, vol. 2, p. 63 (translation adjusted); *Chronica*, vol. 2, p. 317: 'Eodem anno post Natale Domini Urbanus papa misit in Angliam Octovianum sanctæ Romanæ ecclesiæ

The contrast between the *Gesta* and the *Chronica* is glaring. Roger excised the *adventus* from the *Chronica*. It presumably did not matter anymore. Much had changed since Henry requested the presence of the legates. In the summer of 1186, Irishmen had beheaded Hugh de Lacy, one of Henry's most important men in Ireland. In response, Henry had dispatched Prince John to Ireland. It is uncertain whether John actually arrived in Ireland at all, but if he did, he was unsuccessful.[66] At the same time, trouble with France was brewing. This was an inopportune moment for Henry to impose John as king on the rebellious Irish.[67] The arrival of the legates at the turn of 1186 can be viewed as a symbol of the failure of Henry's Irish ambitions. He had come so close: he had a crown, papal approval, and papal legates. All was ready. Henry, instead, went to the continent, taking the legates with him. In the *Gesta*, Roger recorded events as they unfolded. He could not have known that war with France and the rebellion of Duke Richard, the king's son, would keep Henry occupied until his death. However, with the abortive coronation and the death of King Henry, royal ambitions in Ireland lapsed. Accordingly, when Roger produced the *Chronica*, he found no reason to provide more than the barest outline of events.

This shows how circumstantial the significance of the *adventus* was. At the time of the event, the reception of the legates seemed important to Roger. He described how the king recognised the authority of the legates in solemn ritual form, and he implicitly emphasised the legatine insignia as bearers of primacy. Revisited years later, the significance of the event had faded in light of the failed venture and possibly also due simply to the passage of time.

Nevertheless, the performance of the ritual seemingly mattered at the time of its performance, contrary to how Philippe Buc sees it. Buc argues against using accounts of rituals to study performance and its meanings; in his view, accounts of rituals 'were [only] forces in the practice of power'.[68] According to Buc, they cannot inform us about what actually took place. He is undoubtedly right in many instances; accounts of rituals were in themselves forces in the practice of power. Roger's account in the *Gesta* certainly constructs a particular image of the power of those present at the event. However, Roger's account implies that

---

subdiaconum cardinalem, et cum eo Hugonem de Nunant, quibus ipse commisit legatiam in Hybernia ad coronandum ibi Johannem filium regis; sed dominus rex coronationem illam distulit, et prædictos legatos duxit secum in Normanniam, ad colloquium inter ipsum et Philippum regem Franciæ.'

[66] *Gesta*, vol. 1, p. 350; Sean Duffy, 'John and Ireland: The Origins of England's Irish Problem', in *King John: New Interpretations*, ed. Stephen D. Church (Woodbridge: Boydell Press, 1999), pp. 221–45, esp. pp. 228–34.

[67] See also Tillmann, *Die päpstlichen Legaten*, pp. 80–81.

[68] Philippe Buc, *The Dangers of Ritual: Between Early Medieval Texts and Social Scientific Theory* (Princeton: Princeton University Press, 2001), p. 259.

the performance *also* mattered, and that – in certain instances – it is possible to access performance (if it is possible to access anything from the past recorded in writing), and this has to do with Roger's way of recording.

The *Gesta* was likely an eyewitness account – an assessment that hinges on the acceptance of Gillingham's view of the *Gesta* as Roger's travel diary. Roger's entries suggest not only that he was in England in 1186, but also that he was with the court at Christmas. The first piece of evidence is his detailed account of the negotiations between King Henry and King William of Scotland in August and September.[69] These details point to Roger's presence. Second, Roger simultaneously neglected events on the continent, even as war with King Philip was brewing. (Roger's account of the discovery of the building of a secret French castle close to the Norman border is a notable exception.)[70] Third, although Roger's account of the last three months of 1186 leaves little indication as to his own whereabouts (the king was in England),[71] his description of Christmas at the turn of 1186 strongly suggests his physical presence at court:

> Present [at Christmas] were John, his [Henry's] son, and John Cumin, archbishop of Dublin, Geoffrey [Ridel], bishop of Ely, David, brother of the king of Scotland, earl of Huntingdon, Robert, earl of Leicester, William, earl of Arundel, [and] Earl Roger Bigod. Moreover, on that aforementioned feast day, the earls of Leicester and Arundel, as well as Roger Bigod, served at the king's table regarding the act of serving [*sic*] as befitted them at coronations and solemn feasts of the king of England.[72]

Compare this account with the Christmases of 1185 and 1187, respectively.[73]

---

[69] *Gesta*, vol. 1, pp. 347–51.

[70] Ibid., pp. 354–55.

[71] See ibid., pp. 343–61.

[72] *Gesta*, vol. 2, p. 3: 'Cui interfuit Johannes filius ejus, et Johannes Cumyn archiepiscopus Divelinensis, Gaufridus Eliensis episcopus, David frater regis Scotiæ comes de Huntedona, Robertus comes de Leycestria, Willelmus comes de Arundel, Rogerus Bigot comes. In illo vero festo prædicti comites de Leicestria et de Harundel, et Rogerus bigot servierunt ad mensam regis de servitio quod ad illos pertinebat in coronatibus et sollemnibus festis regum Angliæ.'

[73] **1185**: 'In the year 1186 [Roger began the new year at Christmas], suffering delay in Normandy, Henry, king of England, kept the solemn feast day of the nativity of the lord (which fell on the fourth weekday) at Domfront' ('Anno MCLXXXVI, Henricus rex Angliæ, moram faciens in Normannia, tenuit festum sollemne die nativitatis Dominicæ, quæ quarta feria evenit, apud Dampnifrontem'); see *Gesta*, vol. 1, p. 343. **1187**: In the year of the incarnation of the lord 1188, which is the thirty-fourth year of the reign of King Henry the second, suffering delay in Normandy, the same King Henry, son of the Empress Matilda, kept the solemn feast day of the nativity of the lord (which fell on the

Roger's knowledge of the king's whereabouts as Henry learned about the arrival of the legates, as well as Roger's account of the preparations to receive the legates, are best understood as the writings of someone who was present, especially when viewed in the context of the *Gesta* as a whole.

Moreover, reports on legatine insignia and clothing are rare, and it is highly unlikely that Roger could have obtained his information from any written source. No English chronicle then in existence (as far as I am aware) mentioned crosses, mitres, and red clothing. Roger could, at most, have picked up suggestions and imprecise details from other sources. Nor does canon law mention these items until the thirteenth century. Letters about the insignia of papal legates are, with a few exceptions, almost non-existent until the thirteenth century.[74] It cannot be ruled out, however, that Roger received a written report, or that he learned about the insignia in some other way, but the most likely explanation is that he was himself at court.

If one accepts it as an eyewitness account (which, admittedly, cannot be proven definitively), the immediacy of the report implies that the performance of the ritual was important, as was the insignia of the legates and probably the reading of their mandate. But as time passed, the event and its significance faded. In the *Chronica*, the result was a downsizing of the presence of papal and legatine authority. Yet, there is little reason to think that Roger had significantly altered his perception of the papacy. Anglo-Papal relations did not change substantially between the closing of the Becket case and the first years of the pontificate of Innocent III, suggesting that Roger's abbreviated account could be attributed to the diminished significance of the event as he viewed it retrospectively.

Roger reported on another reception of a welcome legate: Cardinal Hugh, who arrived in 1175. The cardinal was in England to clarify some matters regarding the compromise of Avranches and to mediate between the archbishops of Canterbury and York.[75] The *Gesta* and the *Chronica* contain near-identical accounts. The *Gesta*:

> And in the same year, a little before the feast of All Saints, a certain cardinal named Hugh, legate of the Apostolic See, whom the lord king had sent for to

---

Sabbath) at Caen' ('Anno ab Incarnatione Domini MCLXXXVIII, qui est annus xxxiv[tus]. regni regis Henrici secundi, idem Henricus rex, filius Matildis imperatricis, moram faciens in Normannia, tenuit festum sollemne die Nativitatis Dominicæ, quæ Sabbato evenit, apud Cadomum'); see *Gesta*, vol. 2, p. 29.

[74] See pp. 41–45.

[75] Tillmann, *Die päpstlichen Legaten*, pp. 73–77; Sprey, 'Papal Legates', pp. 215–16; Duggan, 'Henry II', pp. 178–81. On the Canterbury–York dispute, see Roy Martin Haines, 'Canterbury versus York: Fluctuating Fortunes in a Perennial Conflict', in *Ecclesia Anglicana: Studies in the English Church of the Later Middle Ages*, ed. Roy Martin Haines (Toronto: University of Toronto Press, 1989), pp. 69–105.

Rome, landed in England; and he found the lord king at Winchester. And the lord king came to meet him, and with him [came] the king his son [Henry, the young king, d. 1183], and they received him with due honour and reverence.[76]

It is possible that Roger was present. His narrative voice – the legate finding the king – may indicate that he accompanied the cardinal. Either way, it is far more curious that Roger felt no need to edit the account, and that he was satisfied simply to tick off the most important parts of the *adventus*. Roger noted that the king had sent for the legate, and that the king came with his son to meet him (the *occursus* part), before receiving the cardinal with due honour and reverence.

There is nothing intrinsically subversive about Roger's account of the reception, but it is disinterested relative to the *Gesta*'s account of the reception of Cardinal Octavian and Bishop-elect Hugh de Nonant. This might be explained by Roger's hostility towards Cardinal Hugh, which, according to Gillingham, probably derived from Hugh's acceptance of the subjection of the clergy to the forest law, depriving them of their immunity.[77] The forest law, which governed the king's extensive hunting privileges, was extremely harsh and profitable to the king – not least due to the substantial amercements for violating the king's rights.[78] Roger, at one point, called the cardinal a 'limb of Satan' ('membrum Sathanæ').[79] Roger also accused Hugh of accepting a bribe from Archbishop Richard of Canterbury on the question of Canterbury's primacy over York.[80]

Such conflicting attitudes might be the consequence of Roger's split loyalty. Cardinal Hugh was of use to Henry II, hence Roger's account of the king's acceptance of legatine authority. Roger, however, was not only a royal clerk, he was the parson of Howden, a client of the archbishop of York, and later a client of the two bishops of Durham. As Gillingham observes, 'doubtless it was not always easy [for Roger] … [because] from the beginning of his career to its end, Roger always served two masters, the king and a powerful prelate'.[81]

---

[76] *Gesta*, vol. 1, p. 104: 'Et eodem anno, paulo ante festum Omnium Sanctorum, applicuit in Anglia quidam cardinalis, nomine Hugozun, apostolicæ sedis legatus, pro quo dominus rex Romam miserat; et invenit dominum regem apud Wintoniam. Et dominus rex in obviam ei venit, et rex filius suus cum eo, et eum cum debito honore et reverentia susceperunt.' Regarding the *Chronica*'s account, see *The Annals*, vol. 1, pp. 404–5; and *Chronica*, vol. 2, p. 85.

[77] Gillingham, 'The Travels of Roger', pp. 155–56; Gillingham, 'Writing the Biography', pp. 210–11.

[78] See Charles R. Young, *The Royal Forests of Medieval England* (Philadelphia: University of Pennsylvania Press, 1979), esp. pp. 33–59.

[79] *Gesta*, vol. 1, p. 105.

[80] Ibid., pp. 113–14.

[81] Gillingham, 'The Travels of Roger', p. 167.

Roger excised much of the criticism of Cardinal Hugh from the *Chronica*, presumably to make the work less offensive. However, he kept an account of the council of London (1176), in which he related that Cardinal Hugh was driven from the council due to a brawl over the question of Canterbury's primacy over York. Roger blamed Archbishop Richard's servants for starting the fight.[82] He also kept the account of the legatine *adventus* from the *Gesta* verbatim. This account is important, as it indicates that not all receptions faded over time or lost their importance. Roger may not have liked the cardinal or agreed with his compliance towards King Henry, but he recognised that his visit and his decisions were significant. The king had invited the legate and subsequently recognised his legatine authority in ritual form with an *adventus*, and this was worth recording.

Unwelcome Papal Legates

The king's invitation was the dividing line in Roger's authorship. Uninvited legates could expect to be met with suspicion or even hostility, such as when Cardinal Vivian came to England in 1176:

> In the same year [1176], Pope Alexander sent Cardinal-Priest Vivian, legate of the Apostolic See, into Scotland and into the adjacent islands, and into Ireland, and into Norway ... When he came into England, the lord king of England sent to him Richard of Winchester and Geoffrey of Ely, bishops, and asked him on whose authority he had dared to enter his kingdom without his licence. On this interrogation, the aforementioned cardinal, greatly terrified, therefore swore to the satisfaction of the king that he himself would perform nothing in his legation contrary to his [the king's] will.[83]

In the previous year, 1175, Henry had welcomed Cardinal Hugh with an *adventus*. Cardinal Vivian, moreover, had previously been assigned to the Becket case, and according to Sprey, 'Vivian arrived in England believing that his [prior] activities with the English church ... allowed him unrestricted movement throughout the

---

[82] *Gesta*, vol. 1, pp. 112–13; *The Annals*, vol. 1, pp. 411–12; *Chronica*, vol. 2, pp. 92–93.

[83] *The Annals*, vol. 1, p. 417 (translation adjusted); *Chronica*, vol. 2, pp. 98–99: 'Eodem anno Alexander papa misit Vivianum presbyterum cardinalem, apostolicæ sedis legatum, in Scotia et in insulis circumjacentibus, et in Hybernia, et in Noreweia ... Qui cum in Angliam veniret, dominus rex Angliæ misit ad eum Ricardum Wintoniensem, et Gaufridum Eliensem episcopos, et interrogavit eum cujus auctoritate ausus erat intrare regnum suum sine licentia illius. His igitur interrogationibus prædictus cardinalis plurimum territus, de satisfactione juravit regi, quod ipse nihil ageret in legatione sua contra voluntatem illius.'

land without the consent of the king'.[84] Vivian was obviously mistaken. Roger may have exaggerated the cardinal's terror (even if Becket's murder might have given any high-ranking ecclesiastic reason to be wary), but Roger consistently presented Henry as wary of uninvited legates. The English kings also kept an eye on other foreigners in their kingdom,[85] but legatine movement was without doubt an issue of importance.

Roger reported that once the king had made his position clear, and Vivian had accepted the king's position, the king offered some hospitality. The *Gesta* recounts that Henry 'instructed the abbots and bishops of his kingdom, through whom he [Vivian] would make the crossing, that they should receive him honourably, as a cardinal' ('præcepit quod abbatiæ et episcopi regni sui, per quos transitum faceret, eum honorifice, sicut cardinalem, recepissent').[86] It was honour under supervision: Vivian was not free to roam the country as he pleased, but implicitly ordered to follow a route through and out of the kingdom. In the *Chronica*, Roger noted that Henry paid Vivian's upkeep from his own purse.[87] Sprey found the payments in the Pipe Rolls, pointing out that Henry, in all likelihood, intended to impede legatine claims to procurations. Henry had also paid Cardinal Hugh's expenses.[88]

It is noteworthy that the king, according to Roger, instructed the English prelates to receive Vivian as a cardinal, not as a legate, perhaps subtly indicating that Vivian was not a legate to England. Then again, it is unclear if there was a recognised distinction between cardinals and legates when encountering a cardinal outside Rome. King Henry actually provided Vivian with a white horse, which might be a recognition of Vivian's legatine office or simply be an expensive gift. The Pipe Rolls record the expense as a gift to 'Legate Vivian' ('Viuiani legati').[89] Nevertheless, if Henry acknowledged Vivian as a legate, he seems not to have acknowledged him as a legate to England – at least not according to Roger. Nowhere in his writings are there any indications of Henry visiting the legate in person or awarding him an *adventus*. Only the inhabitants of the Isle of Man apparently granted Vivian an *adventus*:

---

[84] Sprey, 'Papal Legates', p. 217.
[85] See Duggan, *Thomas Becket*, p. 85; and Sprey, 'Papal Legates', pp. 216–18.
[86] *Gesta*, vol. 1, p. 118.
[87] *The Annals*, vol. 1, p. 417; *Chronica*, vol. 2, p. 99.
[88] Sprey, 'Papal Legates', pp. 215–18; PR, vol. 28, Henry II (1178–79), p. 200: 'et clericorum domini legat .c. et .v. s. per breve regis'; ibid., p. 211: 'Et in passagio Hugonis legati .lxx. s. per breve regis'; PR, vol. 26, Henry II (1176–77), p. 47: 'Et pro .j. palefrido albo ad opus Viuiani legati .ij. m. et dimidia per breve regis'.
[89] PR, vol. 26, Henry II (1176–77), p. 47.

[Vivian] landed on the island, which is called Man, and there he suffered through fifteen days delay. He was received honourably and on friendly terms by the king of that island, and by the clergy and the populace.[90]

Such details, which Roger left out of the *Chronica*,[91] suggest that Roger accompanied the legate personally. Vivian later returned to England, finally meeting Henry in person. However, it was Vivian who had to go 'to the court of the king of the English' ('ad curiam regis Angliæ'), where 'he obtained his letters of protection and escort from the lord king' ('impetravit a domino rege litteras protectionis suæ et conductus').[92] Henry showed sufficient hospitality to avoid a diplomatic crisis, but very little warmth.

According to Roger, Henry treated another legate in much the same way. In 1178, two legates came to England: Peter di Sant'Agata and Albert de Suma. Their mission was to make summons to the upcoming Third Lateran Council: Albert in England, Peter in Scotland and Ireland. Albert elicited little comment from Roger, but he noted in the *Chronica* that Henry would not grant Peter leave to pass through England before he had taken an oath, 'touching the sacred Gospels, that in his legateship he would neither aspire to hurt the king nor his kingdom' ('tactis sacrosanctis evangeliis, quod in legatione sua neque regi neque regno suo malum quæreret').[93] This time, the *Gesta*'s account is muddled, perhaps because Roger was not personally present, and instead relied on information that had filtered through to him unevenly.[94]

Roger's account of Cardinal-Legate John of Anagni's reception in 1189 is particularly interesting. Pope Clement III had dispatched John to France and England in early 1189. The pope had tasked him with a range of issues, one of which was to settle a dispute between Archbishop Baldwin of Canterbury and his cathedral chapter. The archbishop planned to build a new collegiate church for secular canons, which the chapter opposed vehemently. The monks (the Canterbury chapter was monastic) were afraid that the archbishop plotted to translate the archiepiscopal see to the new church.[95] Both the *Gesta* and the *Chronica* are well

---

[90] *Gesta*, vol. 1, pp. 136–37: 'applicuit in insula quæ vocatur Man, et ibi per quindecim dies moram fecit, familiariter et honorifice susceptus ab rege illius insulæ, et a clero et populo'.

[91] See *The Annals*, vol. 1, pp. 455–56; *Chronica*, vol. 2, p. 135.

[92] *Gesta*, vol. 1, p. 166.

[93] *The Annals*, vol. 1, pp. 490–91 (translation adjusted); *Chronica*, vol. 2, p. 167. The Pipe Rolls record the king's gift of a silver cup to the 'legate of Ireland'; see PR, vol. 28, Henry II (1178–79), p. 124: 'Et pro .j. cupa argenti quam Rex dedit legato Hibernie .iiij. *l*. et .xvj. *s*. et .viij. *d*. per idem breve.'

[94] See *Gesta*, pp. 206–7, 209–10.

[95] The first study dedicated entirely to the dispute was only published recently; see James Barnaby, *Religious Conflict at Canterbury Cathedral in the Late Twelfth Century: The*

informed, each presenting, for all intents and purposes, the same narrative, even if the *Chronica*'s account is slightly more streamlined. Most of Roger's narrative is corroborated by Gervase of Canterbury's *Chronica* and the contemporary collection of letters relating to the dispute and compiled by the Canterbury chapter. The letter collection (published as the *Epistolæ Cantuarienses*) contains some fascinating eyewitness reports, such as the conversation between Cardinal John and Duke Richard, when they met in Normandy before Richard crossed to England to be crowned king.[96] This dispute will take centre stage in the next chapter.

On the face of it, King Richard awarded Cardinal John a fitting *adventus*, even if Roger does not provide many of details:

> In the same month [November], Cardinal John, legate of the Apostolic See, came to Canterbury on the mandate of the king [Richard]; and he was received in a solemn procession in the church of the Holy Trinity in Canterbury by the king and the archbishops.[97]

The legate had come 'on the mandate of the king' ('per mandatum regis'), that is, at the king's invitation. However, as Roger was quick to point out:

> He [Cardinal-Legate John] was indignant that they, in his absence, should have arranged peace and concord between the archbishop of Canterbury and the monks of the Holy Trinity in the quarrel that he was sent to England from the side (*a latere*) of the highest pontiff to settle.[98]

Richard had not given Cardinal John permission to proceed inland after landing at Dover. In the *Gesta*, Queen Eleanor (Richard's mother) acted as an emissary to the legate; in the *Chronica*, John is simply kept at Dover on the king's command.[99]

Dispute between the Monks and the Archbishops, 1184-1200 (Woodbridge: Boydell Press, 2024). Only William Stubbs had previously written extensively about the dispute in his introduction to the *Epistolæ Cantuarienses*, the Canterbury chapter's letter collection relating to the case; see William Stubbs, ed., *Epistolæ Cantuarienses, the Letters of the Prior and Convent of Christ Church, Canterbury. From A.D. 1187 to A.D. 1199*, RS (London: Longman, 1865). The introduction is reprinted in William Stubbs, *Historical Introductions to the Rolls Series*, ed. Arthur Hassall (London: Longmans, 1902), pp. 366-438.

[96] See Stubbs, *Epistolæ Cantuarienses*, no. 315, pp. 300-2.
[97] *Gesta*, vol. 2, pp. 98-99: 'Eodem mense Johannes Cardinalis, apostolicæ sedis legatus, venit Cantuariam per mandatum regis, et a rege et ab archiepiscopis cum sollemni processione receptus in ecclesia Sanctæ Trinitatis Cantuariæ.'
[98] Ibid., p. 99: 'Indigne ferebat quod in absentia ejus, qui ad litem illam dirimendan a latere summi pontificis missus erat in Angliam, pax et concordia facta esset inter Cantuariensem archiepiscopum et monachos Sanctæ Trinitatis.'
[99] Ibid., p. 97; *The Annals*, vol. 2, p. 129; *Chronica*, vol. 3, p. 23. The Canterbury letters confirm the queen's actions; see Stubbs, *Epistolæ Cantuarienses*, no. 334, pp. 321-22.

In the meantime, the king summoned the disputing parties to London to settle the dispute. One of the Canterbury monks wrote a detailed report to the Canterbury chapter about the proceedings. The report discloses how those present at the meeting debated whether to recognise the authority of Cardinal John. According to the report, Hugh de Nonant, no longer bishop-elect but now bishop of Coventry, and the bishop of Rochester, Gilbert Glanvill (r. 1185–1214), argued against recognising the legate's authority. The bishop of Bath, Reginald fitz Jocelin (r. 1174–97), spoke against them.[100]

Roger was probably not present at the meeting, and it is unclear how much he knew about the proceedings, even if his patron, Hugh de Puiset, bishop of Durham, was in attendance.[101] Roger only reported on the final settlement. The 'settlement' was in reality the king's dictate to the chapter. Despite Cardinal-Legate John's prohibition against holding any proceedings in the case before his arrival, the king and most of the episcopate had subjected the monastic delegates to intense pressure, forcing the 'settlement' on them.[102] Richard had initially kept John in Normandy, arguing that he needed to be crowned before allowing a legate into the kingdom to forestall any charges of undue papal pressure (an interesting argument, even if probably partially dishonest).[103] After his coronation, Richard had written to John that he was going to solve the dispute himself.[104] It was in response to that letter that the cardinal had forbidden the king to do anything in the case before his arrival.[105] However, the king had not heeded the legate's command.

Roger did not report on these machinations, and it is unclear how much he knew of them, but it is no wonder that Cardinal John was indignant over the matter. The legate (unbeknownst to Roger) secretly absolved the monks from adhering to the settlement, citing that they had been under duress.[106] That was all Cardinal John could do, however, because he was recalled to Rome shortly thereafter.[107] Baldwin died on the Third Crusade only a short while later, rendering the 'agreement' de facto null and void. The secret absolution did not need to be used.

All this puts into perspective the hollowness of Cardinal John's *adventus*. Roger was aware of the public scheming, and I cannot help but suspect him of deliberately mocking the legate. Or perhaps it was 'the forces exerted on him'[108] that were the origins of the mockery? Whatever the case, Roger's King Richard had hamstrung the

---

[100] Stubbs, *Epistolæ Cantuarienses*, no. 329, pp. 315–19, at p. 318.
[101] See ibid., no. 329, pp. 315–19.
[102] Barnaby, *Religious Conflict at Canterbury*, pp. 130–34.
[103] Stubbs, *Epistolæ Cantuarienses*, no. 315, pp. 300–2. King Henry had also forbidden the legate to enter England; see ibid., no. 311, pp. 295–97, at p. 296.
[104] Ibid., no. 325, pp. 310–11.
[105] See ibid., nos. 326–332, pp. 311–320.
[106] Ibid., no. 336, p. 323.
[107] Ibid., no. 333, p. 321.
[108] Barlow, 'Roger of Howden', p. 360.

meaning of the *adventus* by rendering the legate's judgement in the case irrelevant. The king, in this way, had assured his own authority over the English Church.[109]

At the same time, Richard took advantage of the presence of the legate *a latere*. Roger reported that the cardinal agreed to confirm the election of Geoffrey, Richard's half-brother, as the archbishop of York.[110] Roger was not pleased with the choice. He reported that the bishop of Durham, his patron, appealed against Geoffrey. Two prominent members of the Church of York, the treasurer and the dean, also appealed against Geoffrey, arguing that 'he [Geoffrey] was not canonically elected, both because he was a murderer, and because he was begot in adultery and born of a harlot' ('non fuisse canonice electum, tum quia homicida erat, tum quia erat in adulterio genitus et de scorto natus').[111] That is some pretty strong language directed against the son of a king. Roger did not like Geoffrey, and it is a fair bet that some of his hostility rubbed off on the legate.

Roger also displayed antipathy towards other papal legates. The king's attitude defined the reception and the relationship, but, within this framework, Roger was willing to criticise papal legates no matter their status as invited or not. One contemporary favourite was the accusation of greed,[112] with Roger following prevailing fashions. Roger's comment on Cardinal John of Salerno is an amusing example: 'the aforementioned [Legate] John, truly, did not eat meat; he did not drink wine and cider, nor anything by which he could become inebriated; but he was thirsty for gold and silver'.[113] Roger accused Cardinal Vivian of cupidity as well as oppression and plunder.[114] Roger also reported on King Richard's meeting with Cardinal Octavian on his way to the Holy Land. The king, according to Roger, hurled abuse at the cardinal, charging the Romans with simony.[115] A further insult included the aforementioned 'limb of Satan'.

---

[109] See also Christopher R. Cheney, *From Becket to Langton: English Church Government 1170–1213: The Ford Lectures Delivered in the University of Oxford in Hilary Term 1955* (Manchester: Manchester University Press, 1955), pp. 87–118, esp. pp. 88–96; and Ralph V. Turner, 'Richard Lionheart and English Episcopal Elections', *Albion* 29, no. 1 (1997): 1–13, esp. pp. 2–3.

[110] See also Turner, 'Richard Lionheart', esp. pp. 4–5.

[111] *The Annals*, vol. 2, p. 132 (translation adjusted); *Chronica*, vol. 3, p. 27. The *Gesta* makes the same accusation; see *Gesta*, vol. 2, p. 99.

[112] Robinson argues that the incessant complaints of greed levelled against papal legates is 'in fact convincing evidence of the effectiveness of the cardinal-legates as an instrument of papal government'; see Robinson, *The Papacy 1073–1198*, p. 164.

[113] *The Annals*, vol. 2, p. 532 (translation adjusted); *Chronica*, vol. 4, p. 175: 'Prædictus vero Johannes, non manducavit carnem; vinum et siceram non bibit, nec aliquid quo inebriari potuit; sed aurum et argentum sitivit.'

[114] *Gesta*, vol. 1, pp. 166–67.

[115] Ibid., vol. 2, p. 114. See also *The Annals*, vol. 2, p. 144; and *Chronica*, vol. 3, pp. 36–37.

One resident legate in particular received Roger's special ire, the aforementioned William Longchamp. In preparation for leaving on the Third Crusade, King Richard had made Longchamp chancellor, bishop of Ely, and regent of England.[116] Richard had also arranged for William's appointment as a resident papal legate (as mentioned before), threatening the pope that he might not leave on crusade unless the pope complied with his wishes.[117] One reason for Roger's antipathy might have to do with Longchamp's treatment of Roger's patron, Bishop Hugh of Durham. According to Roger, Longchamp 'seized him [Bishop Hugh] and held him until he had surrendered to him the castle of Windsor and others which the king had entrusted to him in custody' ('cepit eum et tenuit, donec reddiderat ei castellum de Vindeshoveres, et cætera quæ rex illi tradiderat in custodia').[118] Roger showed his disdain for William Longchamp in several ways, one of them was via a couple of failed *adventus* ceremonies. Longchamp came to York at Easter in 1190, expecting to be received according to his station:

> He [William Longchamp], moreover, put the clerics of the church of York, and the metropolitan itself, under interdict, because they had refused to receive him as a legate of the Apostolic See, neither with a procession nor with the peal of bells. And he had the bells of the same church placed on the ground, and he held the canons and vicars of the same church firmly under interdict all this time until all should have come to him to do penance.[119]

Longchamp was neither the first nor the last to pronounce interdict as punishment for refusing to provide an *adventus*. Refusal was a serious matter, and the Church of York had questioned Longchamp's legatine authority. Not only did this reflect badly on York, but it also reflected badly on Longchamp – and probably more so for him, as he had failed, in this instance, to command respect.[120]

---

[116] On William Longchamp, see esp. David Bruce Balfour, 'William Longchamp: Upward Mobility and Character Assassination in Twelfth-Century England' (unpublished PhD dissertation, University of Connecticut, Storrs, 1996).

[117] Sprey, 'Papal Legates', pp. 225–26.

[118] *The Annals*, vol. 2, p. 139 (translation adjusted); *Chronica*, vol. 3, p. 35. See also *Gesta*, vol. 2, p. 109; and Corner, 'The *Gesta Regis*', pp. 137–38.

[119] *Gesta*, vol. 2, pp. 108–9: 'Clericos vero ecclesiæ Eboraci, et ipsam metropolitanam sub interdicto posuit, quia noluerunt eum recipere sicut apostolicæ sedis legatum, neque cum processione neque cum sonitu campanarum. Et campanas ejusdem ecclesiæ in terram deponere fecit, et canonicos et vicarios ejusdem ecclesiæ tamdiu sub interdicto arctius tenuit donec omnes ad eum veniret ad satisfactionem.'

[120] Roger streamlined the account of the incident in the *Chronica*, but told virtually the same story; see *The Annals*, vol. 2, p. 139; *Chronica*, vol. 3, p. 35.

That message – failing to command respect – was seemingly so important that Roger was happy to repeat it when Longchamp took refuge in Paris. A group of discontented and opportunistic barons and bishops had driven Longchamp out of England, causing him to flee to Paris.[121] Roger claimed that Longchamp had disguised himself as a woman when he fled.[122] In the *Gesta*, Roger wrote:

> And proceeding thence, he [William Longchamp] arrived at Paris, and gave to Bishop Maurice [de Sully], sixty marks of silver, for that he himself received him with a solemn procession at that place in the archiepiscopal church.[123]

Given Roger's disdain, it is a wonder William did not pay thirty pieces of silver. Maybe that would have been too incredible? Perhaps it would have made the bishop of Paris look excessively bad? William did pay in silver, however, and maybe the number sixty – two times thirty – served as subtlety subversive commentary? Whatever the case, having to pay for his *adventus*, Longchamp failed to command respect in the eyes of Roger. The honour became disingenuous, sullying not only William Longchamp but also Bishop Maurice, who had agreed to receive the chancellor-legate on such terms.

Conclusion

Roger confirms the concerns outlined in the *adventus* instructions. He portrayed a world in which receiving a papal legate was fraught with peril, explaining why Roger's kings took a stance on the entry of papal legates. Uninvited legates were met with caution or outright hostility, as they posed a threat to the internal hierarchy of the kingdom. Compared to the abbot in the monastic *adventus* instructions, the king was naturally in a league of his own. In this sense, Roger's image diverges from the perspectives presented in the monastic *adventus* instructions because the asymmetry between cardinal-legates and kings was less pronounced than that between an abbot and a cardinal-legate. Nevertheless, the dynamics, dangers, and anxieties had something in common. The king endeavoured to blunt, curb, direct, and control papal legates, whether they were welcome or not. The king appointed

---

[121] See esp. Balfour, 'William Longchamp', pp. 334–401.
[122] *Gesta*, vol. 2, p. 219.
[123] Ibid., pp. 220–21: 'Et procedens inde venit Parisius, et dedit Mauricio episcopo sexaginta marcas argenti, pro eo quod ipse eum recepit ibidem in metropolitana ecclesia cum solemni processione.' Roger abbreviated the account slightly in the *Chronica*, but kept the essentials while making the sentence more stringent: 'Et procedens inde venit Parisius, et dedit Mauricio episcopo lx. marcas argenti tali conditione, ut ipse receptus esset ibi cum processione, et factum est ita.' See *Chronica*, vol. 3, p. 150; *The Annals*, vol. 2, p. 241.

trustworthy officials to monitor and manage the papal legates entering his realm, and to regulate their movement and access to other parties within England.

In instances where this strategy proved effective, Roger seldom felt the need to provide details. He only found it interesting if tensions arose in some way. Roger's account of the reception of the two papal legates at the turn of 1186 is an exception, but their mission was one of considerable significance. When that mission failed, Roger omitted the *adventus* from the *Chronica*. In contrast, Roger rarely removed or neglected to mention contentious legatine receptions. Take, for example, the case of Cardinal Vivian. In the *Gesta*, Roger mentioned King Henry's hostile reaction to the uninvited Vivian, while also noting the legate's honourable reception on the Isle of Man. Roger also offered a few details about Vivian's visit to the royal court. However, in the *Chronica*, Roger omitted Vivian's reception on the Isle of Man while retaining the king's indignant reaction to his visit.

Roger's kings might pursue different strategies, and the *adventus* of Cardinal-Legate John of Anagni is an illustrative case. While his arrival and mission were subject to contention, King Richard responded with less overt hostility than his father, the late Henry II. Henry had exhibited hostility towards several legates, apparently denying them honourable receptions and facing no consequences for these slights. Roger's Richard, for whatever reason, appeared unwilling to take such a stance. Was it due to the specific circumstances? Did Legate John's invitation by an ecclesiastical party to judge an ecclesiastical case influence Richard's approach? Or was Richard more cunning – effectively blunting the legate's authority while exploiting it for his own benefit?

Whatever the reasons, the meaning and significance of the legatine *adventus* were shaped by prevailing concerns. If my reconstruction of the legatine *adventus* of 1186 is accurate, this suggests that the actual performance held importance within the immediate context, although the significance could change. The legatine *adventus* was always part of a wider context, which imbued it with meaning, but contemporary developments could place it within a different light or even render it irrelevant.

5

The Road of St Thomas: Gervase of Canterbury and Local Adaptation

One of the intriguing facets of perspective is how what might appear trivial and unimportant to some can appear spectacular and decisive to others. In hindsight, Roger of Howden deemed the *adventus* of Octavian and Hugh de Nonant to be of little significance. Roger's account, or rather the absence thereof, in his *Chronica* even exudes a sense of disappointment. In contrast, Gervase of Canterbury wrote passionately about the *adventus* at Canterbury Cathedral.

The reception occurred not only during the heightened religious importance of Christmas, but also amid escalating tensions within the Canterbury chapter, of which Gervase was a part. The chapter at Canterbury Cathedral was Benedictine, with its abbot doubling as the archbishop of Canterbury.[1] This arrangement not only enhanced the power of the archbishop-abbot relative to the chapter, but also made it crucial for the king and the episcopate to have a say in the election of the archbishop-abbot. This was much more pronounced than if Christ Church had been just another Benedictine house, primarily concerned with the division between monastic and abbatial income (a conflict that the Canterbury monks and the archbishop-abbot also experienced). Those chosen might be more interested in the archiepiscopal office than in the abbatial office, and the archbishop was often away on business unrelated to the office of abbot. These sources of estrangement between the monastic community and the archbishop-abbot likely aggravated the clashes between the Canterbury chapter and successive archbishop-abbots over the archbishop's plans to construct a new cathedral.[2] The two legates arrived just as a fifteen-year long dispute was commencing.

---

[1] See David Knowles, *The Monastic Order in England: A History of Its Development from the Times of St Dunstan to The Fourth Lateran Council, 940–1216*, 2nd edn (Cambridge: Cambridge University Press, 1963), pp. 129–34, 619–24.

[2] See James Barnaby, *Religious Conflict at Canterbury Cathedral in the Late Twelfth Century: The Dispute between the Monks and the Archbishops, 1184–1200* (Woodbridge: Boydell Press, 2024), esp. pp. 38–40; and Everett U. Crosby, *Bishop and Chapter in Twelfth-Century England: A Study of the* Mensa Episcopalis (Cambridge: Cambridge University Press, 1994), esp. pp. 10–29, 66–105.

This backdrop greatly influenced Gervase's perception of the two papal legates. Gervase likely composed one of his works – also called the *Chronica* – amidst the ongoing dispute, interpreting the legates' arrival within this context. In his *Chronica*, Gervase employed the legates' reception as a platform to stage an attack on Archbishop Baldwin of Forde, drawing on the meaning of the *adventus* and the symbols of legatine authority. In doing so, Gervase reshaped the *adventus* to align with a Canterbury narrative dominated by the prominent figure of St Thomas. Within this narrative framework, notions of archiepiscopal legitimacy and Romanness intertwined in a distinct configuration unique to Canterbury. The outcome was a profoundly local adaptation of the legatine *adventus*. Gervase's authorship highlights the malleability not only of the *adventus* itself but of the legatine *adventus*. It reveals the extent to which local attitudes, concerns, and perspectives could significantly mould the interpretation and meaning of the legatine *adventus*. Gervase's perspective was firmly rooted in the viewpoint of the community, which longed for the might of the papacy to intervene and overthrow the oppressive rule of Archbishop-Abbot Baldwin.

Gervase of Canterbury and His Authorship

Gervase of Canterbury became a monk of Christ Church on 16 February 1163.[3] He was probably around eighteen years old at the time and likely of Kentish extraction[4] – maybe from Maidstone, as William Stubbs proposes, or from Canterbury, as William Urry and more recently Michael Staunton argue.[5] He had a brother named Thomas, whom he mentioned in the *Chronica*.[6] The scarcity of personal

---

[3] Gervase, vol. 1, p. 173.

[4] Gervase, vol. 1, pp. xi–xii; Antonia Gransden, *Historical Writing in England c.550–c.1307* (London: Routledge, 1974), p. 253; Richard Wayne Huling, 'English Historical Writing under the Early Angevin Kings, 1170–1210' (unpublished PhD dissertation, State University of New York, Binghamton, 1981), p. 192; Michael Staunton, *The Historians of Angevin England* (Oxford: Oxford University Press, 2017), p. 110; Knowles, *The Monastic Order*, p. 439–41; William Urry, *Canterbury under the Angevin Kings* (London: The Athlone Press, 1967), pp. 153, 156–57.

[5] Staunton, *The Historians*, p. 110; Urry, *Canterbury under the Angevin Kings*, p. 153; Gervase, vol. 1, pp. xi–xii, 110.

[6] Gervase, vol. 1, p. 89. See also Huling, 'English Historical Writing', p. 202 and Gransden, *Historical Writing*, p. 254. The evidence points to Brother Thomas being Gervase's biological brother, not a circumlocution for St Thomas. At one point in the *Chronica*, Gervase identified a *clericus* as 'my brother' ('fratri meo'). He bore the same name ('nominis sui') as Thomas Becket, but he was not Thomas Becket; see Gervase, vol. 1, p. 231. It is likewise possible, as Stubbs suggests, that the 'cuidam clerico nomine Thomæ' of the *Tractatus de combustione* (one of Gervase's other works), who received a vision from St Thomas, might have been Gervase's brother; see Gervase, vol. 1, pp. xxi–xxii, 18–19.

information makes it unlikely that Gervase hailed from a prominent family. Stubbs argues that Gervase died shortly after 1210, in which year one of his minor works, the *Gesta Regum*, changes stylistically, indicating another author's quill.[7]

Gervase lived through turbulent times. He joined the convent just as the relationship between Archbishop Thomas Becket (r. 1162–70) and King Henry II broke down. Some seven years were spent in anxious uncertainty as Henry and Becket clashed. As mentioned previously, the result was the murder of an archbishop, Thomas Becket, the creation of a saint, St Thomas, and a (partial) victory for the English Church and the papacy. Then, in 1174, parts of Canterbury Cathedral burned down, causing lengthy construction works to commence. Gervase also took part in the protracted disputes with archbishops Baldwin and Hubert, during which St Thomas became a rallying cry for the monks.

Gervase held some prominence in the convent in his middle and senior years. He was the sacristan during the 1190s and an authority on Canterbury customs.[8] The convent entrusted him with acting as a messenger and with writing about their tribulations during the dispute with Archbishop Baldwin. Gervase likely authored an appeal to Pope Urban III against Baldwin, delivering the appeal in person to the archbishop.[9] He wrote a couple of pamphlets addressing the arguments of the monks and the archbishop, and Gervase authored letters of complaint, which the monks circulated abroad to enlist support.[10] Gervase was also one of the representatives at Westminster in 1189 when King Richard intervened on Baldwin's behalf, imposing a 'settlement' on the monks.[11]

Gervase wrote eleven works, including a history of the archbishops of Canterbury, the *Actus pontificum*, as well as a tract on the reconstruction of the cathedral after the fire in 1174 called the *Tractatus de combustione*. He also wrote a short history of the English kings, the *Gesta Regum*, as well as the *Mappa mundi*, a topographical work on ecclesiastical institutions. Gervase's magnum opus, however, was the *Chronica*. The *Chronica* purports to chronicle the history of England from the time of King Henry I to Richard, that is, 1100–99. In reality,

---

Barnaby suggests that Gervase's brother might have been a spiritual brother rather than a biological one; see Barnaby, *Religious Conflict at Canterbury*, pp. 22–23, n. 72.

[7] Gervase, vol. 1, pp. xxx–xxxii. Gransden is unsure if Gervase worked on the *Gesta Regum* post-1199, but she accepts Stubb's date of 1210 as the *terminus post quem* for Gervase's death without realising its dependence on Gervase's authorship of the *Gesta Regum* up until 1210; see Gransden, *Historical Writing*, pp. 253–54.

[8] Gransden, *Historical Writing*, p. 254.

[9] Gervase, vol. 1, pp. xxi, 333, 343.

[10] Huling, 'English Historical Writing', pp. 197–99; Gervase, vol 1, pp. xxiii–xxiv; William Stubbs, ed., *Epistolæ Cantuarienses, the Letters of the Prior and Convent of Christ Church, Canterbury. From A.D. 1187 to A.D. 1199*, RS (London: Longman, 1865), pp. xlii–xliv.

[11] Gervase, vol. 1, pp. 464–72; Barnaby, *Religious Conflict at Canterbury*, pp. 130–34.

it centres on Christ Church and the convent's disputes with its archbishops. It is a piece of monastic history writing, presenting the world as viewed from the chapter of Christ Church.[12] Indeed, Gervase maintained that he wrote for the benefit of his fellow monks: 'I write for you, my brother Thomas, and our poor little family [the monks]' ('tibi, mi frater Thoma, et nostrae familiolae pauperculae scribo').[13] Scribes at Canterbury produced and preserved the three extant medieval manuscripts.[14]

Gervase likely began composing the *Chronica* at the convent's request sometime between January 1188 and August 1189. It was a time of intense pressure, as Baldwin had placed the monks under house arrest. According to Gervase, the townspeople were forced to smuggle food in to the monks to prevent starvation.[15] Gervase likely ceased writing the *Chronica* in 1199, recording the last years contemporaneously with events.[16] Archbishop Baldwin was dead at that point, but the new archbishop, Hubert Walter, had taken up the mantle, pursuing the same agenda as his predecessor. The dispute was still raging at the *Chronica's* conclusion.[17]

England, the Papacy, and Legates at the Time of Gervase

Gervase was likely born around 1145 during the troubled times of King Stephen (r. 1135–54), whose reign is sometimes referred to as 'the anarchy'.[18] It was a period marked by increased papal and legatine influence. King Stephen, besieged by challenges to his claim to the throne, turned to his brother, Henry of Blois, bishop of Winchester, for support. Bishop Henry served as resident papal legate and held a particularly prominent position as a source of papal authority at the time. The success of Stephen's strategy is debatable, but relying on papal-legatine authority in this manner did lead to increased acceptance of its presence and legitimacy.[19]

---

[12] Ibid., pp. 84–91; Huling, 'English Historical Writing', pp. 200–3, 210–14; Staunton, *The Historians*, pp. 114–17; Barnaby, *Religious Conflict at Canterbury*, pp. 21–26.

[13] Gervase, vol. 1, p. 89. This brother Thomas was Gervase's biological or spiritual brother, not St Thomas; see n. 6.

[14] Ibid., pp. xlix–lvi.

[15] Ibid., pp. xvi–xxii, 401–53; Huling, 'English Historical Writing', p. 203; Gransden, *Historical Writing*, pp. 253–60.

[16] See Gervase, vol. 1, pp. xxvi–xxvii.

[17] See also Barnaby, *Religious Conflict at Canterbury*, pp. 43–44, 169.

[18] Numerous studies centre on this time; see, e.g., Edmund King, *King Stephen* (New Haven: Yale University Press, 2010).

[19] Ilicia Jo Sprey, 'Papal Legates in English Politics, 1100–1272' (unpublished PhD dissertation, University of Virginia, Charlottesville, 1998), pp. 151–93; Ilicia Jo Sprey, 'Henry

The situation changed with the accession of Henry II in 1154. Henry claimed the right to interfere in ecclesiastical matters, including restricting access to appeal to Rome.[20] The Becket dispute was, in part, a result of Henry's policy. Ironically, the dispute increased the acceptance of papal authority in England, as both Henry and Becket appealed to Pope Alexander III, thereby acknowledging the pope's authority in the matter.

Alexander, however, found himself in a precarious position during the course of the dispute. He was embroiled in a schism and even at war with the emperor, causing Alexander to proceed cautiously for fear of losing support. He dispatched three unsuccessful legations to negotiate with the parties in England.[21] Eventually, Alexander sided with Becket, forcing the English monarch to formally accept a 'settlement'. By the end of 1170, the stage was set for royal knights to commit murder.[22] However, the murder backfired spectacularly, as public sympathy decisively swung towards the (now deceased) archbishop, who almost immediately became the object of saintly worship. Alexander dispatched two legates, Cardinals Albert and Theodwin, who soon negotiated a settlement mostly favourable to the Church. This settlement involved Henry rescinding his ban on appeals to Rome and granting clerical immunity from secular jurisdiction. Henry was also required to do public penance.[23] Anglo-Papal relations thereafter remained mostly amicable for the remainder of the century. The new archbishop of Canterbury, Richard of Dover (r. 1174–84), worked with the king while safeguarding the gains of the Church.[24]

From the mid-1170s until 1198, popes (Alexander III, Lucius III, Urban III, Gregory VIII, Clement III, and Celestine III) primarily relied on the archbishops of Canterbury for the legatine presence in England. Nevertheless, as mentioned in

---

of Winchester and the Expansion of Legatine Political Authority in England', *Revue d'histoire ecclésiastique* 91, nos. 3–4 (1996): 785–804.

[20] Anne J. Duggan, 'Henry II, the English Church and the Papacy, 1154–76', in *Henry II: New Interpretations*, ed. Christopher Harper-Bill and Nicholas Vincent (Woodbridge: Boydell Press, 2007), pp. 154–83.

[21] Anne J. Duggan, '*Alexander ille meus*: The Papacy of Alexander III', in *Pope Alexander III (1159–81): The Art of Survival*, ed. Peter D. Clarke and Anne J. Duggan (Farnham: Ashgate, 2012), pp. 13–49, at pp. 25–32; Anne J. Duggan, *Thomas Becket* (London: Arnold, 2004), pp. 33–100, 124–78.

[22] Duggan, *Thomas Becket*, pp. 179–200.

[23] Ibid., pp. 201–23; Duggan, '*Alexander ille meus*', p. 32; Helene Tillmann, *Die päpstlichen Legaten in England bis zur Beendigung der Legation Gualas, 1218* (Bonn: Hch. Ludwig, 1926), pp. 68–72; Anne J. Duggan, '*Ne in dubium*: The Official Record of Henry's Reconciliation at Avranches, 21 May 1172', *EHR* 115, no. 462 (2000): 643–58; Anne J. Duggan, 'Diplomacy, Status, and Conscience: Henry II's Penance for Becket's Murder', in *Forschungen zur Reichs-, Papst- und Landesgeschichte. Peter Herde zum 65. Geburtstag von Freunden, Schülern und Kollegen dargebracht*, ed. Karl Borchardt and Enno Bünz, 2 vols (Stuttgart: Hiersemann, 1998), vol. 1, pp. 265–90.

[24] Duggan, '*Alexander ille meus*', pp. 33–34.

the previous chapter, some curial legates made their way to England. War between England and France also increased legatine activity. Between them, Urban III and Clement III (1185–91) directed four legations to France to procure peace.[25] All these legations failed. One of the legates was the abovementioned Cardinal John of Anagni, who came to England from Normandy in an unsuccessful attempt at resolving the dispute between Archbishop Baldwin and the Canterbury monks.[26]

The Canterbury Dispute

Christopher Cheney argues that the records of the Canterbury dispute 'may have encouraged historians of the Church to attach overmuch importance to the episode', reasoning that 'the practical issues were comparatively trivial'.[27] Yet, for Gervase and his fellow monks, the disputes with Archbishops Baldwin and Hubert were defining moments of their lives, as James Barnaby argues.[28] Barnaby has recently written the first comprehensive study of the dispute since Stubbs examined it in 1865. Baldwin's plan was to construct a new church at Hackington, just north of Canterbury, while Hubert later chose Lambeth. Baldwin, himself a Cistercian monk, intended to follow recent trends by staffing the new church with secular canons, whom he considered better suited for the administrative tasks of the time.[29]

The extant evidence was produced almost solely by the monks of Canterbury, making it difficult to distinguish between the monks' accusations, their fears, and the archbishop's true intentions. Barnaby notes that Baldwin never intended to translate St Thomas to the new church, nor did he intend to strip Christ Church of its archiepiscopal dignity and the right of the monks to elect the archbishop. However, the monks believed that this was exactly what Baldwin intended. To them, it seemed that Baldwin was scheming to destroy Canterbury Cathedral, stripping Christ Church of its status and transferring the dignity of the archiepiscopal centre to the new church.[30]

The monks decided to resist. One result of their fight was the creation of a collection of more than 500 letters pertaining to the case (Lambeth Ms 415),

---

[25] Tillmann, *Die päpstlichen Legaten*, pp. 81–82.
[26] Ibid., p. 83.
[27] Christopher R. Cheney, *Hubert Walter* (London: Nelson, 1967), p. 135.
[28] Barnaby, *Religious Conflict at Canterbury*, esp. pp. 50–56. See also Staunton, *The Historians*, p. 113
[29] See Nigel of Whiteacre [Nigellus Wireker], *The Passion of St. Lawrence, Epigrams and Marginal Poems*, ed. Jan M. Ziolkowski (Leiden, New York, and Cologne: Brill, 1994), pp. 31–34; and Richard W. Southern, *The Monks of Canterbury and the Murder of Archbishop Becket* (Canterbury: The Friends of Canterbury Cathedral & the William Urry Memorial Trust, 1985), pp. 8–11.
[30] See Barnaby, *Religious Conflict at Canterbury*, esp. pp. 9–32, 50–56.

which Stubbs published as the *Epistolæ Cantuarienses*. According to Barnaby, these letters should be read in conjunction with Gervase's *Chronica*. Although the letter collection retains an array of unique first-hand reports documenting the ebbs and flows of the dispute, it is constructed as a narrative of monastic triumph over archiepiscopal tyranny. Some letters are edited, and others are deliberately excluded to present a streamlined narrative of monastic victory.[31] However, the most important route of resistance for the monks was an appeal to Rome. This was a costly affair; petitioners had to offer gifts, fees, and bribes without any guarantee of success.[32] In 1187, the representatives of the chapter wrote home: 'Frequently we called on our lord the pope about our business, both opportunely and importunely, both publicly and privately, and always with groans and tears'.[33]

The Canterbury representatives might have exaggerated their tribulations at the curia, but they knew that this and other reports were likely read aloud at chapter meetings in Canterbury.[34] They knew that their brethren at home followed the progress of the case closely, that they judged and assessed the costs of the case relative to the progress that they made. Being a representative in Rome was a position of trust, but also one where failure might spell disgrace. Thomas of Marlborough, who litigated in Rome in 1204 on behalf of his fellow monks of Evesham Abbey, stated in his *Chronicon* that he had resolved never to return home unless he won the case.[35]

Some of the delegates from Christ Church died in Rome, and Gervase's comments on their deaths are telling. He argued that they had fought 'for the

[31] Ibid., pp. 9–21, 26–30, 51–52, 99, 124–25, 134, 138–39.

[32] Patrick Zutshi, 'Petitioners, Popes, Proctors: The Development of Curial Institutions c.1150–1250', in *Pensiero e Sperimentazioni Istituzionali Nella 'Societas Christiana' (1046-1250): Atti della Sedicesima Settimana Internationale di Studio Mendola, 21–31 Agosto 2004*, ed. Giancarlo Andenna (Milan: Storia Ricerche, 2007), pp. 265–93; Patrick Zutshi, 'The Roman Curia and Papal Jurisdiction in the Twelfth and Thirteenth Centuries', in *Die Ordnung der Kommunikation und die Kommunikation der Ordnungen. Band 2: Zentralität: Papsttum und Orden im Europa des 12. und 13. Jahrhunderts*, ed. Christina Andenna, Klaus Herbers, and Gert Melville, Schriften der Villa Vigoni (Stuttgart: Franz Steiner Verlag, 2013), pp. 213–27; Jane E. Sayers, 'English Benedictine Monks at the Papal Court in the Thirteenth Century: The Experience of Thomas of Marlborough in a Wider Context', *Journal of Medieval Monastic Studies* 2 (2013): 109–29; Barnaby, *Religious Conflict at Canterbury*, pp. 158, 161–62.

[33] Translated by George B. Parks, *The English Traveler to Italy: The Middle Ages (to 1525)* (Rome: Edizioni di Storia e Letteratura, 1954), p. 238; Stubbs, *Epistolæ Cantuarienses*, no. 148, p. 122: 'Multoties namque dominum papam super negotio nostro opportune, importune, tum in publico, tum in occulto convenimus in gemitu et lacrymis.'

[34] See Barnaby, *Religious Conflict at Canterbury*, p. 72.

[35] Thomas of Marlborough, *History of the Abbey of Evesham*, ed. Jane E. Sayers and Leslie Watkiss, OMT (Oxford: Oxford University Press, 2003), bk. 3, pt. 3, 262, pp. 264–67.

conservation of the peace and freedom of the Church of God' ('pro pace et libertate ecclesiæ Dei conservanda').[36] He considered one of them, Prior Honorius, to belong among the martyrs, accusing Baldwin of poisoning.[37]

Despite these deaths, the efforts at the curia continued. Examining the case took time. The brief pontificates of the 1180s and 1190s did not help, not least because it resulted in curial inconsistency. Pope Urban III (r. 1185–87) supported the monks, only for Gregory VIII (r. 21 October 1187–17 December 1187) to favour Baldwin,[38] before Clement III (r. 1187–91) decided to use legatine authority to resolve the matter. However, the first cardinal-legate died en route to England, only for the second to do the same![39] Only the third legate, Cardinal John of Anagni, actually reached England. There, as seen previously, he only came in time to absolve the monks clandestinely of adhering to their forced agreement with the archbishop. He had to hurry back to Rome because of some urgent Sicilian business.[40] However, it was all rendered irrelevant when Baldwin died suddenly on the Third Crusade in 1190. The monks had de facto won the first round.[41]

The victory only lasted until the new archbishop, Hubert Walter, took up Baldwin's mantle. Although Hubert initially moved more cautiously than Baldwin, proposing various checks on the archbishop's infringement of the convent's rights, the monks would have none of it and they once again appealed to Rome. This hardened Hubert's stance.[42]

Pope Innocent III initially supported the monks, but Hubert cunningly asked the pope for leave to found a new church at Lambeth. This caused the pope to revisit the issue, referring the case to delegates in England.[43] Appeals were issued back and forth; the monks wavered, unsure about the best course of action. In the end, protracted negotiations between Hubert, the monks, and papally appointed judges-delegate produced a compromise. The settlement granted Hubert the right to build a conventual church, not a collegiate one. The deal forbade Hubert from transferring any revenues, rights, or saints. Hubert also gave various sureties

---

[36] Gervase, vol. 1, pp. 429–30, quote at p. 429.
[37] Ibid., pp. 429–30.
[38] Barnaby, *Religious Conflict at Canterbury*, pp. 50–51, 59–63, 77–102.
[39] Ibid., pp. 102–107; Tillmann, *Die päpstlichen Legaten*, pp. 83.
[40] Barnaby, *Religious Conflict at Canterbury*, pp. 107, 111–16, 119–36; Stubbs, *Epistolæ Cantuarienses*, pp. lxvii–lxxx, no. 336, p. 323; Werner Maleczek, *Papst und Kardinalskolleg von 1191 bis 1216. Die Kardinäle unter Coelestin und Innocenz III.* (Vienna: Verlag der Österreichischen Akademie der Wissenschaften, 1984), pp. 70–71; Tillmann, *Die päpstlichen Legaten*, pp. 83–85.
[41] Barnaby, *Religious Conflict at Canterbury*, pp. 136–40.
[42] Cheney, *Hubert Walter*, pp. 137–45.
[43] Barnaby, *Religious Conflict at Canterbury*, pp. 153–70; Cheney, *Hubert Walter*, pp. 141–47.

concerning the convent's rights.[44] Innocent ratified the compromise on 31 May 1201. For the rest of the Middle Ages, the archbishops of Canterbury primarily resided at Lambeth,[45] although the conflict between the monks and their archbishop-abbot would only conclude once Archbishop Pecham (1279–92) successfully founded a tiny collegiate church at Wingham.[46]

Cheney observes that 'the case is instructive because it shows the degree of respect accorded to papal authority in England in 1200'.[47] He asserts that 'without an appeal to Rome the affair would have ended differently. Royal influence would have ensured that the archbishop got all he wanted.'[48] Innocent's anonymous biographer, the author of the *Gesta Innocentii*, also congratulated the pope for having saved the monks from the twin assault of the king and the archbishop.[49]

The monks agreed that papal might was an important part of their deliverance, but St Thomas was equally responsible. Gervase viewed the dispute with Archbishop Baldwin – as well as the role of the legates in the dispute – within a divinely ordained framework. St Thomas held the framework together. He was a crucial part of the convent's self-perception. Looking back some twenty-five years, Gervase made sure to mention that 'he [St Thomas] ... granted me monkhood' ('michi ... monachatum concessit').[50] It is almost impossible to overstate the importance of the cult of St Thomas to the Canterbury monks. St Thomas attracted more pilgrims than any other saint in England, and the monks directed almost all their activities to promote his cult.[51] Even the former adversary, King Henry, recognised his sainthood. In 1174, Henry came to Canterbury in response to a major rebellion, recognising that he had to make peace with St Thomas to regain Fortune's blessing.

---

[44] Barnaby, *Religious Conflict at Canterbury*, pp. 171–76; Christopher R. Cheney, 'The Settlement between Archbishop Hubert and Christ Church Canterbury in 1200: A Study in Diplomatic', in *Mediaevalia Christiana XIe-XIIIe siècles: Hommage à Raymonde Foreville*, ed. Coloman Étienne Viola (Paris: Editions Universitaires, 1989), pp. 136–51.

[45] Cheney, *Hubert Walter*, pp. 147–50.

[46] Barnaby, *Religious Conflict at Canterbury*, pp. 177–200.

[47] Ibid., p. 151.

[48] Ibid.

[49] James M. Powell, trans., *The Deeds of Pope Innocent III by an Anonymous Author* (Washington, D.C.: The Catholic University of America Press, 2004), ch. xlii, pp. 57–58; David Richard Gress-Wright, 'The "Gesta Innocentii III": Text, Introduction and Commentary' (unpublished PhD dissertation, Bryn Mawr College, 1981), pp. 62–63.

[50] Gervase, vol. 1, p. 231.

[51] Marie-Pierre Gelin, 'Gervase of Canterbury, Christ Church and the Archbishops', *JEH* 60, no. 3 (2009): 449–63, pp. 450–51; Marie-Pierre Gelin, 'The Cult of St Thomas in the Liturgy and Iconography of Christ Church, Canterbury', in *The Cult of St Thomas Becket in the Plantagenet World, c.1170–c.1220*, ed. Paul Webster and Marie-Pierre Gelin (Woodbridge: Boydell Press, 2016), pp. 53–79; Duggan, *Thomas Becket*, pp. 216–18; C. Eveleigh Woodruff, 'The Financial Aspect of the Cult of St. Thomas of Canterbury. As Revealed by a Study of the Monastic Records', *Archaeologia Cantiana* 44 (1932): 13–32.

He humbled himself before St Thomas, while the monks, probably including Gervase, flogged him publicly. Henry then left to defeat the rebellion.[52]

At the outbreak of the dispute between the monks and Archbishop Baldwin, Gervase recorded in the *Chronica* a dream vision from St Thomas. St Thomas showed himself to a young monk: 'I am', he said, 'your Archbishop Thomas, who for this church and in this church suffered martyrdom'.[53] St Thomas further said that he wished to destroy Baldwin's scheme, drawing a sword and telling the monk to hand the sword to the prior for the defence of the church. An inscription on the sword read, 'Sword of the blessed apostle Peter' ('Gladius beati Petri apostoli').[54] There is no mistaking the message: the pope would save the church. It is also possible that the sword alludes to excommunication (even if the pope never excommunicated Baldwin).[55] Medieval authors often illustrated excommunication as the drawing of the sword of anathema. In Cardinal Boso's biography of Pope Adrian IV, Adrian 'unsheathing the sword of Peter, struck the king [King William I of Sicily (r. 1154–66)] with the sharp sword of excommunication'.[56] The young monk was hesitant at first, but after St Thomas had appeared to him three times (symbolising the trinity), he disclosed the vision to Prior Honorius.[57] The convent also mentioned the vision in its correspondence with Rome.[58]

---

[52] Anne J. Duggan, 'Becket is Dead! Long Live St Thomas', in *The Cult of St Thomas Becket in the Plantagenet World, c.1170–c.1220*, ed. Paul Webster and Marie-Pierre Gelin (Woodbridge: Boydell Press, 2016), pp. 25–51, at pp. 36–40; Frank Barlow, *Thomas Becket* (Berkeley and Los Angeles: University of California Press, 1990), pp. 269–70. Henry seemingly performed a rite of begging pardon; see Geoffrey Koziol, *Begging Pardon and Favor: Ritual and Political Order in Early Medieval France* (Ithaca, NY: Cornell University Press, 1992).

[53] Gervase, vol. 1, p. 339: '"Ego sum," inquit, "Thomas archiepiscopus vester, qui pro hac ecclesia et in hac ecclesia martyrium passus sum."'

[54] Ibid., p. 340.

[55] I am grateful to Dr Professor Jochen Johrendt, Bergische Universität, Wuppertal, for suggesting this parallel to me. On excommunication, see, e.g., Torstein Jørgensen, 'Excommunication – An Act of Expulsion from Heaven and Earth', in *The Creation of Medieval Northern Europe: Christianisation, Social Transformations, and Historiography: Essays in Honour of Sverre Bagge*, ed. Leidulf Melve and Sigbjørn Olsen Sønnesyn (Oslo: Dreyer, 2012), pp. 58–69.

[56] Cardinal Boso, '*Vita Adriani IV*/Life of Adrian IV', in *Adrian IV The English Pope (1154-1159): Studies and Texts*, ed. Brenda M. Bolton and Anne J. Duggan (Aldershot: Ashgate, 2003), pp. 214–33, at pp. 216–17: 'Petri gladium exerens ipsum regem excommunicationis mucrone percussit'.

[57] Gervase, vol. 1, pp. 338–41. See also James Barnaby, '*Becket vult*: The Appropriation of St Thomas Becket's Image During the Canterbury Dispute, 1184–1200', in *ANS XL*, ed. Elisabeth van Houts (Woodbridge: Boydell Press, 2018), pp. 63–76, at pp. 69–70.

[58] Stubbs, *Epistolæ Cantuarienses*, pp. xli–xlii, nos. 69, 294, pp. 54–57 (at p. 55), 278–79 (at p. 279).

Another vision followed in the *Chronica*. A monk saw Baldwin trying to cut off the head of St Thomas, which resulted in Baldwin's mitre – a key episcopal symbol – simply disappearing ('sed mitra ejus disparuit').[59] It is probably no coincidence that the visions are ripe with symbols from the martyrdom of St Thomas. Possibly the most iconic visual representation of the martyrdom is the moment when one of the murderers hit Thomas on his mitred head with his sword.[60] Gervase wrote that both visions were reported during a meeting. At this meeting, the prior argued that these visions pointed to St Thomas urging them to appeal to the Apostolic See. The prior immediately arranged for such an appeal, while the monks took comfort in the divine attention.[61]

The Account of the Legatine Reception in the Chronica

The *Chronica*'s account of the reception of the two legates at Canterbury Cathedral is not an isolated incident in Gervase's chronicle; rather, the reception fulfils a purpose in the wider storyline within the *Chronica*. The account of the *adventus* marks the opening blows of the dispute with Archbishop Baldwin, serving as a prophecy, a harbinger of times to come. To understand the entire narrative arc culminating in the reception of the two papal legates, it is, however, necessary to begin with the election of Baldwin upon the death of Archbishop Richard in 1184.

According to Gervase, who wrote about the election four years (or more) after it took place, the monks were hesitant to elect Baldwin, but since he had the backing of the king and the entire episcopate, they eventually conceded and elected him.[62] The election thus acts as a framework for the dispute in the *Chronica*. The king and the episcopate united against the convent of Christ Church, which struggled against the pressure.

An uneventful year then passed in the *Chronica* before Baldwin suddenly struck, seizing several of the convent's properties. Dumbfounded, the monks wanted to negotiate with Baldwin, only to be confronted with Baldwin's plans for a new church. At this point in the *Chronica*, St Thomas showed himself to the young monk, drawing the sword of St Peter.[63] The vision in which Baldwin tried to cut off the head of St Thomas followed immediately.[64] Soon, the chapter met to discuss events, deciding, as mentioned, to appeal to Rome. Emissaries from the

---

[59] Gervase, vol. 1, p. 342.
[60] See Gelin, 'The Cult of St Thomas', p. 71; and Barnaby, 'Becket vult', pp. 70–71.
[61] Gervase, vol. 1, pp. 342–44.
[62] Ibid., pp. 308–25.
[63] Ibid., pp. 325–41.
[64] Ibid., pp. 341–42.

chapter – Gervase among them – informed the archbishop about their appeal.[65] The *Chronica* asserts that the archbishop thereafter came to Canterbury shortly before Christmas, causing consternation when he suspended Prior Honorius. In response, Honorius set out for Rome to appeal to the pope. He would, according to Gervase, eventually die as a martyr in Rome. In the meantime, Baldwin retreated to Otford to celebrate Christmas. A few days later, the two papal legates arrived.[66]

The appearance of the papal legates is the preliminary culmination of the narrative on Archbishop Baldwin and his wicked machinations. The appeal to Rome is the 'point of no return' (if the narrative was written in the classic 'Hollywood model'), while the arrival of the legates is a divine portent of things to come. Gervase wrote:

> For during this vigil of the festivity two legates from the lord pope directed to Ireland landed in England at Sandwich. They were received solemnly on the day of the Lord's birth by the convent of Canterbury. Never before had such a great injury been inflicted on the archbishop of Canterbury, that any legate should proceed through the archbishop's own province, even into his own church, wearing a mitre (to say nothing of the cross). Now, however, a cardinal of the Roman church (but deacon), the second in truth suffragan of the church of Canterbury not yet even consecrated, but elect of the church of Coventry, both advancing mitred, both bearing crosses in front of themselves, held honour and reverence of legation in the province of Canterbury.[67]

According to Gervase, the papal legates landed at Sandwich, and from there they advanced to Canterbury. In Canterbury, the monks received the legates solemnly. Both legates wore mitres and both carried crosses, establishing their legation in Canterbury. Baldwin was a resident papal legate, but his legation now ostensibly lapsed.[68] One of the legates was a cardinal-deacon, the other was the bishop-elect

---

[65] Ibid., pp. 343–43.

[66] Ibid., pp. 342–46.

[67] Ibid., p. 346: 'Nam in hujus vigilia festivitatis applicuerunt in Anglia apud Sandwicum duo legati a domino papa in Hiberniam directi. Qui in die Natalis Domini a conventu Cantuariensi solempniter sunt suscepti. Non est ante hæc tempora archiepiscopo Cantuariensi talis illata injuria, ut in provincia ejusdem archiepiscopi, immo et in ecclesia, ut de cruce sileam, legatus aliquis mitratus incederet. Nunc autem quidam Romanæ ecclesiæ cardinalis quidem sed diaconus, alter vero Cantuariensis ecclesiæ suffraganeus nedum sacratus, sed Coventrensis ecclesiæ electus, ambo mitrati incedentes, ambo præ se cruces ferentes, in Cantuariensi provincia honorem et reverentiam habuerunt legationis.' I am grateful to Michael Staunton, University College Dublin, for discussing the translation of this passage.

[68] See Tillmann, *Die päpstlichen Legaten*, p. 34.

of Coventry. Gervase, interestingly, linked the legatine insignia with the authority of the legates. The insignia interfered with the rights of the archbishop.

It is a cleverly wrought account with two possible interpretations. The account can pass itself off as a defence of Archbishop Baldwin. Stubbs asserts that:

> He [Gervase] writes throughout as the champion of the cathedral convent against the whole world, and especially against the archbishop, wherever the interests of the archbishop and convent are opposed. Where there is no such opposition he is willing to act and write as the archbishop's champion, and his interest is never more vivid, or his argument stronger, than where the rights of the archbishop and convent are identical.[69]

Stubbs did not specifically refer to the account of the reception, but he may have had it in mind while writing the assessment. In the margin of the *Chronica*, Stubbs characterises the reception of the legates as an 'insult to the see of Canterbury'.[70] Robert Figueira had this reception in mind when he asserted that Gervase, who is 'ever vigilant for real or imagined slights inflicted on Christ Church … disapprovingly reports the reception of two papal legates'.[71]

On the face of it, Gervase wrote as if astonished, expressing shock at the legatine entry into the archbishop's province, even into the church. He mentioned that the legates entered the archiepiscopal province, then exclaimed 'even into his own church' ('immo et in ecclesia'). He could barely speak about the cross: 'to say nothing of the cross' ('ut de cruce sileam'). Pretending to recover from the shock, Gervase wrote as if he had resolved to repress his anger, while also revealing a willingness to lay bare the facts of the indignities suffered. These indignities included three insults to the archbishop.

The first insult concerned rank. Even if one of the legates was a cardinal, he was still only a deacon, while the other was the bishop-elect of Coventry, not even consecrated, and nominally a suffragan of Canterbury. The bishop-elect of Coventry should have deferred to the archbishop, and from this perspective, the eclipse of archiepiscopal dignity was seemingly unacceptable. The second insult concerned the lapse of the archbishop's legation. As long as these higher-ranking legates were present, Baldwin's legation was set aside. The third insult concerned the use of insignia, specifically the mitre and the cross. The mitre was originally a papal prerogative, but during the eleventh and twelfth centuries, cardinals and then bishops

---

[69] Gervase, vol. 1, p. xvi.
[70] Ibid., p. 346.
[71] Robert Charles Joseph Figueira, 'The Canon Law of Medieval Papal Legation' (unpublished PhD dissertation, Cornell University, Ithaca, NY, 1980), pp. 383–84.

appropriated it.[72] Gervase seemingly drew on the notion that the mitre was an exclusive episcopal symbol, implying that deacons should not wear mitres, even if they were cardinals and/or legates. Bishops-elect probably did not use mitres.[73]

Canterbury had a conflict-ridden history with processional crosses, particularly in its strife with the archbishop of York.[74] In 1125, Pope Honorius II (r. 1124–30) rebuked the southern English bishops for their resistance to the archbishop of York's right to have a cross borne before him.[75] Thomas Becket also clashed with Archbishop Roger of York over the use of the archiepiscopal cross.[76] During the vacancy between Baldwin and Hubert Walter (1190–93), Archbishop Geoffrey of York journeyed to London with his archiepiscopal cross carried before him. Geoffrey took up residence in London but retreated north when the bishop of London pronounced an interdict on his lodgings.[77]

In the *Chronica*, Gervase mentioned how in 1193 the newly elected Hubert Walter had asked him to investigate the archbishop-elect's right to carry a cross before receiving the pallium. Gervase, Christ Church's authority on Canterbury customs, concluded that the archiepiscopal cross could not be used without the pallium. The mention of this incident probably reflects an awareness of the symbolic significance of the cross for the archbishops of Canterbury,[78] even if this particular incident, for reasons of chronology, could not have been on Gervase's mind when he wrote about the reception of the two papal legates. Still, in the account of the legatine reception, Gervase twice asserted that the legates' use of crosses was an affront to the archbishop of Canterbury.

---

[72] Tapio Salminen, 'In the Pope's Clothes: Legatine Representation and Apostolic Insignia in High Medieval Europe', in *Roma, magistra mundi. Itineraria culturae medievalis: mélanges offerts au Père L.E. Boyle à l'occasion de son 75e anniversaire*, ed. Jacqueline Hamesse (Louvain-la-Neuve: Brepols, 1998), pp. 349–54, at pp. 352–54; Joseph S. J. Braun, *Die liturgische Gewandung im Occident und Orient: Nach Ursprung und Entwicklung, Verwendung und Symbolik* (Freiburg im Breisgau: Herdersche Verlagshandlung, 1907), pp. 447–53. The pope might grant abbots the right to wear a mitre; see Braun, *Die liturgische Gewandung*, pp. 452–57. See also p. 41 in this book.

[73] See Robert L. Benson, *The Bishop-Elect: A Study in Medieval Ecclesiastical Office* (Princeton: Princeton University Press, 1968), p. 178.

[74] See esp. Roy Martin Haines, 'Canterbury versus York: Fluctuating Fortunes in a Perennial Conflict', in *Ecclesia Anglicana: Studies in the English Church of the Later Middle Ages*, ed. Roy Martin Haines (Toronto: University of Toronto Press, 1989), pp. 69–105.

[75] Herbert Thurstan, 'The Cross and Crucifix in Liturgy', in *The Catholic Encyclopedia* (New York: Robert Appleton, 1908); available at www.newadvent.org/cathen/04533a.htm (accessed 15 April 2024).

[76] Haines, 'Canterbury versus York', pp. 78–81.

[77] Ibid., p. 84.

[78] See Gervase, vol. 1, pp. 520–22. Cf. Gransden, *Historical Writing*, p. 254; and Huling, 'English Historical Writing', p. 199. See also Staunton, *The Historians*, p. 112.

The legatine *adventus* was undoubtedly an insult to the archbishop, but was it also an injury to the convent or to Christ Church as such? It depends on the assessment of the relationship between the context of the reception, Gervase's worldview, and the narrative flow of the *Chronica*. I believe the story Gervase was telling his monastic brethren was one in which St Thomas partnered with the papacy to drive out the evil of Baldwin and to humiliate him.[79] The two papal legates and their reception were important components of this story, but it must be admitted that the two legates, Cardinal-Deacon Octavian of SS. Sergius e Bachus and Hugh de Nonant, bishop-elect of Coventry, were not friends of the convent of Christ Church.

Octavian was a distinguished member of the curia, advancing to become cardinal-bishop of Ostia in 1189, before dying in 1206.[80] After his legation to England, Octavian returned to Rome, where he encountered the representatives of Christ Church. These representatives wrote home in late 1188, calling Octavian a 'hostile man' ('inimicus homo').[81] The other legate, Hugh of Nonant, once installed as bishop, expelled his monastic chapter at the turn of 1190.[82] Gervase considered this expulsion to be horrific.[83] In 1186, Hugh witnessed a royal letter confirming Baldwin's permission to build the new church.[84] In 1189, when King Richard kept the oft-mentioned Cardinal John of Anagni away, the king took advice about the dispute. Some of the monks were present, writing a report in which they claimed Hugh had exclaimed that 'monks belong with the devils' ('monachi ad diabolos').[85]

It is impossible to pinpoint the exact time when Gervase penned the account of the reception of the two legates. The encounter with Octavian in Rome likely occurred around the time he began composing the *Chronica*. Hugh's expulsion of his monastic chapter probably happened after Gervase began writing, but only a short while later. Whatever the precise chronology, Gervase was likely aware that neither of the legates were sympathetic to the monks. This is probably the reason he did not mention the legates' names, even as he was aware of their identities, merely pointing out that one was a cardinal-deacon and the other the bishop-elect of Coventry. When the king decided to go to the continent rather than Ireland,

---

[79] See also Barnaby, *Religious Conflict at Canterbury*, esp. pp. 43–44, 57–60; and Barnaby, 'Becket vult', esp. pp. 69–70.

[80] Maleczek, *Papst und Kardinalskolleg*, pp. 80–83.

[81] Stubbs, *Epistolæ Cantuarienses*, no. 190, pp. 271–72, at p. 271.

[82] James Barnaby, 'The Coventry Dispute and Alan of Tewkesbury', *Journal of Medieval Monastic Studies* 9 (2020): 83–105.

[83] Gervase, vol. 1, pp. 461.

[84] Stubbs, *Epistolæ Cantuarienses*, no. 7, pp. 7–8.

[85] Ibid., no. 329, pp. 315–19, at p. 318.

he and the legates stopped off at Canterbury. Gervase mentioned Hugh on that occasion, not giving him the best of reviews.[86]

However, the reception of the two legates at Canterbury on Christmas Day 1186 fits perfectly within Gervase's storyline, wherein Baldwin is depicted as evil, while St Thomas and the papacy are portrayed as good. If Gervase held the personal opinions of the legates against them, he excised their persons from the account of their reception in order to use their 'papal *auctoritas*' in the way Wasner argued that such *auctoritas* transcended all other features.[87] This was a deliberate choice made by Gervase, but it also aligned with papal messaging and doctrine, as well as with the overarching story that Gervase was telling.

There is a teleological streak in the *Chronica*, especially in the part leading up to the legatine *adventus*, and it is worth emphasising this point. In the *Chronica*, the dispute begins with Baldwin's unprovoked seizure of properties belonging to the convent. The monks decide to negotiate with Baldwin, showing their good intentions, but Baldwin responds by revealing his evil scheme. The two aforementioned visions then follow. One vision is about how Baldwin intends to destroy Canterbury Cathedral and, by extension, St Thomas; the other vision reveals that St Thomas has ordained that papal might will protect them and save the church. The monks hold a meeting in which they decide to appeal to Rome. A group of monks announces the appeal to Baldwin. Baldwin then appears at Canterbury on 16 December, behaving erratically and with hostility towards the monks, and eventually suspending Prior Honorius. Shortly after, on Christmas Eve, the two papal legates make landfall at Sandwich.

The landing at Sandwich is another important part of the narrative, even if it may, strictly speaking, be untrue. As mentioned in the last chapter, Roger of Howden's *Gesta* placed the landing site of the legates at Dover. There are two reasons to believe Roger. First, Dover was the usual landing site, situated at the narrowest point of the English Channel. Second, Roger was well placed to know, likely being at court at the time and probably writing within weeks or at most months of the event.[88] Roger, furthermore, had no reason to lie about the landing site: even if he had misremembered, or been misinformed, or was simply careless – what did it matter?

It, however, did matter to Gervase. St Thomas had landed at Sandwich on that fatal, final journey home towards martyrdom. The location held symbolic significance in the St Thomas narrative as the precursor to that martyrdom. One of Becket's household clerks, Herbert of Bosham, completed a biography of St

---

[86] Gervase, vol. 1, p. 349.

[87] See Franz Wasner, 'Fifteenth-Century Texts on the Ceremonial of the Papal "Legatus a Latere"', *Traditio* 14 (1958): 295–358, p. 300.

[88] *Gesta*, vol. 2, pp. 3–4.

Thomas sometime between 1184 and 1186.[89] In the biography, he reported that 'we [Archbishop Thomas and his household] landed successfully not in the bay of the sea at Dover, as expected, but in another bay of the sea, which is called Sandwich' ('non in sinu maris Doroberniæ, ut putabatur, sed in alio maris sinu, qui vocatur Sandwiz, prospere applicuimus').[90] Herbert of Bosham was a friend of the Canterbury monks, even if he did not believe the monks could prevail against the archbishop.[91] Nevertheless, in December 1187, 'he came to Canterbury as if out of special love' ('quasi ex speciali dilectione Cantuariam accessit'), according to Gervase.[92] Staunton argues that Herbert was a great influence on Gervase's authorship. Staunton also asserts that Gervase's *Chronica* echoes the St Thomas *Lives* both linguistically and thematically. In Staunton's words: 'for Gervase, the persecutions of the monks by Baldwin and Hubert Walter were all of a piece with the earlier persecutions of Thomas and the church of Canterbury, and their struggles the same'.[93]

The landing of the papal legates at Sandwich fitted perfectly into Gervase's storyline. He knew that St Thomas had landed at Sandwich.[94] Helene Tillmann argues that Gervase's account is the most trustworthy because he was an eyewitness to the *adventus* at Canterbury.[95] However, he was no more an eyewitness to the landing than Roger of Howden had been. Roger was likely an eyewitness to the reception at Westminster. Additionally, Gervase wrote years, not weeks or months, after the event.

It cannot be conclusively determined if Gervase changed the landing site, but Sandwich fitted perfectly into his design, in which the landing site was a crucial piece of the St Thomas narrative. St Thomas had presented the monks with the sword of St Peter only days before the arrival of the legates, making it clear that St Peter's representative on Earth was to be the saviour of the convent. Then, two representatives of St Peter's successor had landed at Sandwich. If nothing else, Gervase aligned the pieces of information to tell a certain story, in which he conflated St Thomas' road to martyrdom with St Peter's protection. The legates,

---

[89] Michael Staunton, *Thomas Becket and His Biographers* (Woodbridge: Boydell Press, 2006), pp. 65–66. For an introduction to Herbert of Bosham, see Michael Staunton, ed., *Herbert of Bosham: A Medieval Polymath* (York: York Medieval Press, 2019).

[90] James Craigie Robertson and J. Brigstocke Sheppard, eds, *Materials for the History of Thomas Becket, Archbishop of Canterbury*, 7 vols, RS (London: Longmans, 1875-85), vol. 3, p. 476.

[91] Barnaby, '*Becket vult*', p. 72.

[92] Gervase, vol. 1, p. 393.

[93] Michael Staunton, 'Thomas Becket in the Chronicles', in *The Cult of St Thomas Becket in the Plantagenet World, c.1170–c.1220*, ed. Paul Webster and Marie-Pierre Gelin (Woodbridge: Boydell Press, 2016), pp. 95–111, quote at p. 107.

[94] Gervase, vol. 1, pp. xx–xxi, 222.

[95] Tillmann, *Die päpstlichen Legaten*, p. 80, n. 14. Tillmann was unaware of Roger of Howden's authorship of the *Gesta*, which was only established later.

heaven-sent, landed at Sandwich in place of St Thomas, advancing to take the rightful place of authority at Canterbury Cathedral. The Canterbury monks would be aware of the references to St Thomas. Becket's return to Canterbury via Sandwich was an addition to the usual allusions to Christ's entry into Jerusalem at *adventus* ceremonies. Sandwich was the way of 'the Canterbury saint', the road of St Thomas. In this way, the account of the reception of the two papal legates became an omen, a harbinger of better times. It was a portent of the protection offered by St Thomas and St Peter.

It does not necessarily follow that the legates went around Canterbury. Canterbury is on the road to London from Dover. However, Roger of Howden's dating of the events would have to be inaccurate for the legates to have visited Canterbury on 25 December. The *Gesta* reports that King Henry received word on the morrow after the Nativity (i.e., 26 December) about the landing at Dover. The king was at Guildford, some hundred miles west of Dover. The legates did not move inland before their escort arrived, probably on 28 or 29 December. The legates would have had to be time travellers to reach Canterbury Cathedral 'on the day of the Lord's birth' ('in die Natalis Domini').[96]

These objections highlight that Gervase's purpose was not to tell the 'material truth', but a 'higher truth'. The account of the reception is part of a teleological story about martyrdom and salvation, in which the wicked are punished and the pious are saved. The account of the reception at Canterbury follows upon numerous references to St Thomas, persecution, and martyrdom.

Gervase then moved on to the punishment of the wicked, framing it within the symbolism of the *adventus* once more. Literally the next sentence after the account of the reception at Canterbury is the following:

> They [the legates] were received honourably by King Henry and the nobles of England; they furthermore had mitres and crosses in the presence of the archbishop of Canterbury, who came unwilling and summoned by the king.[97]

It was a literary slap in the face of the archbishop, who had behaved erratically and unjustly at the cathedral mere sentences before. Three pages prior to the account of the reception (in the modern edition), Gervase had stated that Baldwin was no longer the archbishop. In the context of Prior Honorius dispatching three monks to inform Baldwin of the convent's appeal to Rome, Gervase stated that the monks

---

[96] Gervase, vol. 1, p. 346.
[97] Ibid., p. 346: 'Qui a rege Henrico et primoribus Angliæ honorifice suscepti, etiam in præsentia Cantuariensis archiepiscopi, cum a rege vocatus et invitus accederet, mitras habuerunt et cruces.'

were dispatched 'to Baldwin, no longer archbishop but a tyrant' ('Baldewino jam non archiepiscopo sed tyranno').[98] The year closes with the humiliation of Baldwin – it is the very final sentence of 1186. The new year opens with Anglo-French tensions, marking a thematic and stylistic change, and indicating a shift in the narrative arc.

Legitimate Authority at Canterbury Cathedral

Gervase's interpretation of the legatine *adventus* had its roots in a particular perception of order and authority at Canterbury Cathedral. This perception was probably hundreds of years old, but the disputes with Baldwin and Hubert drove Gervase (and the other monks) to contemplate, clarify, and rearticulate it. The crux of the matter was arguing why relocating the archiepiscopal centre was preposterous. In response, Gervase (and the other monks) construed an intimate connection between the cathedral, the monastic convent, the archbishops of Canterbury, and papal Rome. They formed a conceptual whole of legitimate authority and liturgical meaning. Baldwin's crime was his attack on this order.

Two of Gervase's other works set this idea out in detail. These are the *Actus pontificum*, probably composed *c.* 1205-10, and the *Tractatus de combustione*, probably composed in 1199. Marie-Pierre Gelin argues that Gervase (and by extension the convent) took the burial of the archbishops in the cathedral as the hub connecting the various threads of authority and liturgy. The burial in the cathedral gave the monks the opportunity to care for the religious and social remembrance of the archbishops, their *memoria*.[99] The cult of St Thomas was the impetus for this reasoning, but it helped that the monks could include him in a line of saintly Anglo-Saxon archbishops, St Dunstan (r. 959-88) and St Alphage (r. 1006-12). Both became objects of increased worship at this time.[100]

---

[98] Ibid., p. 343.

[99] Gelin, 'Gervase of Canterbury'. See also Carol Davidson Cragoe, 'Reading and Rereading Gervase of Canterbury', *Journal of the British Archaeological Association* 154 (2001): 40-53. On *memoria*, see, e.g., Truus van Bueren and Andrea van Leerdam, eds, *Care for the Here and the Hereafter: 'Memoria', Art and Ritual in the Middle Ages* (Turnhout: Brepols, 2005). Architectural historians have mined the *Tractatus* for details of medieval construction works; see, e.g., R. Willis, *The Architectural History of Canterbury Cathedral* (London: Longman & Co, 1845) and Peter Draper, 'Interpretations of the Rebuilding of Canterbury Cathedral, 1174-1186: Archaeological and Historical Evidence', *Journal of the Society of Architectural Historians* 56, no. 2 (1997): 184-203. Carol Cragoe and Gelin argue against the fruitfulness of using the *Tractatus* in this way, asserting that its details about the reconstruction are literary constructs; see Cragoe, 'Reading and Rereading Gervase' and Gelin, 'Gervase of Canterbury'.

[100] See Gelin, 'The Cult of St Thomas'.

According to Gelin, Gervase claimed that all archbishops succeeding Cuthbert (d. 760) had been buried at Christ Church. However, at least four archbishops were not buried at Christ Church, including Ælfsige (r. 958–59), Robert (r. 1051–52), Stigand (r. 1052–70), and Baldwin. The latter was buried at Acre, a fact Gervase was aware of.[101] The elections of these archbishops were either canonically dubious and/or their actions in some way disqualified them in the eyes of Gervase. Papal legates had, for instance, deposed Stigand for pluralism. Baldwin had committed crimes against St Thomas. Gelin concluded that 'Gervase ... constructs an intimate and direct relationship between the legitimacy of the archbishop and his burial in the cathedral'.[102] As mentioned, Gervase at one point asserted that Baldwin was no longer the archbishop but a tyrant.[103] The vision in which Baldwin's mitre disappeared as he tried to cut off the head of St Thomas is telling.[104] It was a clear message: Baldwin's hostility to the God-given order of Christ Church and St Thomas removed him from the archiepiscopal dynastic line. His burial at Acre was both a confirmation and a (divinely ordained) consequence of the removal.

Gervase furthermore held the opinion that archiepiscopal authority at Christ Church was in part composed of Roman authority. Pope Gregory the Great (r. 590–604) had sponsored St Augustine's mission to convert the Angles to Christianity, and it was St Augustine who had founded Christ Church.[105] In the *Tractatus*, Gervase echoed the work of another Canterbury historian, Eadmer. Gervase asserted that the cathedral destroyed in 1067 by fire 'was that very church which had been built by Romans, as Bede bears witness in his history, and which was duly arranged in some parts in imitation of the church of the Blessed Prince of Apostles, Peter'.[106]

---

[101] Gervase, vol. 2, pp. 405–6.
[102] Gelin, 'Gervase of Canterbury', p. 455.
[103] Gervase, vol. 1, p. 343.
[104] See ibid., p. 342; and above.
[105] Gelin, 'Gervase of Canterbury', p. 453. See also Jane E. Sayers, 'Peter's Throne and Augustine's Chair: Rome and Canterbury from Baldwin (1184–90) to Robert Winchelsey (1297–1313)', *JEH* 51, no. 2 (2000): 249–66. On the construction of monastic identity through history in general, see Gert Melville, 'Knowledge of the Origins: Constructing Identity and Ordering Monastic Life in the Middle Ages', in *Knowledge, Discipline and Power in the Middle Ages: Essays in Honour of David Luscombe*, edited by Joseph Canning, Edmund J. King, and Martial Staub (Leiden: Brill, 2011), pp. 41–62.
[106] Gervase, vol. 1, p. 7: 'Erat enim ipsa ecclesia ... sicut in hystoriis Beda testatur, Romanorum opere facta, et ex quadam parte ad imitationem ecclesiæ beati apostolorum principis Petri'; translated by Gelin, 'Gervase of Canterbury', p. 457. See Eadmer of Canterbury, 'Edmeri Cantvariensis Cantoris Nova Opvscvla de Sanctorum Veneratione et Obsecratione (altera pars)', ed. André Wilmart, *Revue des sciences religieuses* 15, no. 3 (1935): 354–79, p. 365, ll. 118–21; and Bede, *Bede's Ecclesiastical History of the English People*, ed. Bertram Colgrave and R. A. B. Mynors, revised edition, OMT (Oxford: Clarendon Press, 1992), bk. 2, ch. 3, pp. 142–45.

Certain features of Christ Church's architecture were deliberate imitations of St Peter's in Rome. This included the length of St Anselm's cathedral.[107] Eadmer asserted that, in the first church, the crypt under the main altar, the *confessio*, had been built in imitation of St Peter's *confessio*.[108] Furthermore, the spiral columns in St Anselm's crypt, still extant, are possibly modelled on those that supported St Peter's shrine.[109] The dedication of the cathedral to Christ also echoed the dedication of the Lateran Cathedral to the Saviour.[110]

The connection between Rome, St Peter, and Canterbury is important in light of the reception of the papal legates. Papal Rome was present at Christ Church in the architectural and spatial dimensions, and even in the sacred dynastic lineage of the archbishops. The traditional bestowal of the legateship on the archbishops of Canterbury probably fed into this notion as well. In a letter to Prior Honorius in Rome, the convent accused Baldwin of striving to introduce the constitutions of Clarendon – those very constitutions that St Thomas had fought against. According to the convent, Baldwin's aim was 'to shake off his neck from under the yoke of the holy Roman Church' ('de sub jugo sanctæ Romanæ ecclesiæ collum excutere'), making himself 'as if pope' ('quasi papa') and the English bishops 'as if cardinals' ('quasi cardinales').[111] These accusations were meant to be laid at the feet of the pope and to shock him, but they also reveal how the monks viewed Baldwin's disdain for the connection between Canterbury and papal Rome.

Finally, it is worth pointing out that Gervase was not alone. Amid all the complaints about the papacy and legatine interference, it is easy to forget that most people at the time accepted the papacy and papal authority – even if only grudgingly. One who praised papal authority was another Benedictine monk named Lucian, who was a monk at St Werburgh's Abbey, Chester. Around 1195, he penned a 396-page eulogistic comparison of the city of Chester with Rome. It is called the *Liber Luciani de laude Cestrie*. In it, Lucian extolled the Christian city of Rome, as the pagan city had previously been dead through lies, while St Peter – and by extension

---

[107] Eric Fernie, *The Architecture of Norman England* (Oxford: Oxford University Press, 2000), p. 284.

[108] Eadmer of Canterbury, 'Edmeri Cantvariensis', p. 365, ll. 128–32.

[109] H. M. Taylor, 'The Anglo-Saxon Cathedral Church at Canterbury', *The Archaeological Journal* 126, no. 1 (1969): 101–30; Fernie, *The Architecture*, pp. 284–86; Eric Fernie, 'St Anselm's Crypt', in *Medieval Art and Architecture at Canterbury before 1220* (Leeds: W. S. Maney and Son, 1982), pp. 27–38, at pp. 31–32; Deborah Kahn, *Canterbury Cathedral and Its Romanesque Sculpture* (London: Harvey Miller, 1991), pp. 75–78. See also Sayers, 'Peter's Throne', esp. pp. 249–51.

[110] See Sayers, 'Peter's Throne', p. 249; and Bede, *Bede's Ecclesiastical History*, bk. 1, ch. 33, pp. 114–17.

[111] Stubbs, *Epistolæ Cantuarienses*, no. 69, pp. 54–57 (at p. 55).

his successors – brought it back to life. The exquisite morals of the papal city were true greatness in stark contrast to the military oppression of the pagan Empire.[112]

Lucian's praise served a purpose. In the words of John Doran, Lucian argued that '[St] Peter had chosen Rome that he might teach …, but Chester that he might defend it'.[113] Lucian wrote at a time when Hugh de Nonant became bishop of Coventry. The diocese had been subject to several organisational restructurings during the eleventh and twelfth centuries; among other things, the episcopal seat had moved between Chester, Coventry, and Lichfield. It thus caused great consternation at St Werbergh's when Hugh expelled his monastic chapter; the monks feared that this might be the beginning of a wider attack on the privileges of the Benedictines in the diocese, especially themselves. The *Liber Luciani de laude Cestrie* was written as a defence of St Werburgh's and its privileges. The defence built upon the claim to a special relationship with papal Rome.[114] Lucian's reasoning was thus conceptually not very different from that of Gervase's.

Humour and Humility

There is one more layer to the account: humour. It is not immediately obvious to the modern reader, which is why the account can pass itself off as a defence of Archbishop Baldwin, as Stubbs and Figueira have interpreted it. However, humour was not unknown at Canterbury.

The cathedral library contained the works of classical satirists such as Juvenal and Horace.[115] John of Salisbury, who, among other things, served as Becket's secretary, composed satire;[116] the library at Canterbury had a copy of his *Entheticus*.[117]

---

[112] See esp. John Doran, 'Authority and Care: The Significance of Rome in Twelfth-Century Chester', in *Roma Felix: Formation and Reflections of Medieval Rome*, ed. Éamonn Ó Carragain and Carol Neuman de Vegvar (Aldershot: Ashgate, 2007), pp. 307–32.

[113] Ibid., pp. 314–15.

[114] Ibid., pp. 328–29. See also C. P. Lewis, 'Communities, Conflict and Episcopal Policy in the Diocese of Lichfield, 1050–1150', in *Cathedrals, Communities and Conflict in the Anglo-Norman World*, ed. Paul Dalton, Charles Insley, and Louise J. Wilkinson (Woodbridge: Boydell Press, 2011), pp. 61–76. For the papal privileges, see James Tait, ed., *The Chartulary or Register of the Abbey of St. Werburgh Chester*, 2 vols (Manchester: The Chetham Society, 1920), vol. 1, nos. 61, 70, pp. 109–12, 115–16.

[115] Montague Rhodes James, *The Ancient Libraries of Canterbury and Dover* (Cambridge: Cambridge University Press, 1903), pp. xxxiii–xxxiv.

[116] See, e.g., Ronald E. Pepin, 'John of Salisbury's Entheticus and the Classical Tradition of Satire', *Florilegium* 3 (1981): 215–27. On John of Salisbury, see, e.g., Christophe Grellard and Frédérique Lachaud, eds, *A Companion to John of Salisbury* (Leiden and Boston, MA: Brill, 2014).

[117] James, *The Ancient Libraries of Canterbury and Dover*, p. xxxiv.

In fact, satirical writing was booming in Europe in the second half of the twelfth century, and nowhere more so than in England.[118]

Gervase spent around thirty years at Christ Church with one of the most important satirists of the late twelfth century, Nigel of Whiteacre.[119] Nigel was a monk at Christ Church from around 1170 to the beginning of the thirteenth century.[120] Nigel was a productive author, writing poetry and hagiography, but he is best known for his *Speculum stultorum* (Mirror of Fools), a satirical work that became highly popular shortly after its production. The work retained its allure throughout the Middle Ages.[121] Nigel probably composed the *Speculum* between 1190 and 1193, that is, at a time when Baldwin's shadow still loomed large and when Gervase was writing the *Chronica*.[122] Jill Mann argues that Nigel left thinly veiled comments on Baldwin's evil plans in the *Speculum*.[123] Nigel also wrote a poem in honour of Prior Honorius, who died in Rome, fighting Archbishop Baldwin. Like Gervase, Nigel regarded him as a martyr.[124] St Thomas also mattered profoundly to Nigel.[125]

---

[118] See Rodney M. Thomson, 'The Origins of Latin Satire in Twelfth Century Europe', *Mittellateinisches Jahrbuch* 13 (1978): 73–83. See also Katrin Beyer, 'Wit and Irony – Rhetorical Strategies and Their Performance in Political and Learned Communication in England (c.1066–1259)', in *Networks of Learning: Perspectives on Scholars in Byzantine East and Latin West, c.1000–1200*, ed. Sita Steckel, Niels Gaul, and Michael Grünbart (Berlin: LIT Verlag, 2014), pp. 147–59; and J. A. Yunck, *The Lineage of Lady Meed. The Development of Medieval Venality Satire* (Notre Dame, IN: University of Notre Dame Press, 1963).

[119] Nigel is known under several surnames, including 'of Canterbury', 'de Sarneis', and 'of Longchamp', of which the latter has been used extensively in modern literature, despite Nigel having nothing to do with the Longchamp family; see A. G. Rigg, 'Nigel of Canterbury: What Was His Name?', *Medium Aevum* 56, no. 2 (1987): 304–7.

[120] Nigel of Whiteacre, *The Passion of St. Lawrence*, pp. 6–13, 38–42; Jill Mann, 'Does an Author Understand His Own Text? Nigel of Longchamp and the *Speculum stultorum*', *Journal of Medieval Latin* 17 (2007): 1–37.

[121] Nigel of Whiteacre [Nigel de Longchamps], *Speculum stultorum*, ed. John H. Mozley and Robert R. Raymo (Berkeley and Los Angeles: University of California Press, 1960), pp. 1–2, 8–9. See also Nigel of Whiteacre, *The Passion of St. Lawrence*, pp. 1–3. For a broader analysis of the poem, see Jill Mann, 'Nigel of Longchamp's *Speculum stultorum*', in *From Aesop to Reynard: Beast Literature in Medieval Britain* (Oxford: Oxford University Press, 2009), pp. 98–148.

[122] Mann, 'Does an Author Understand', passim. See also Mann, 'Nigel of Longchamp's *Speculum stultorum*', pp. 142–47.

[123] See Mann, 'Does an Author Understand', pp. 28–34. Nigel is mentioned in two letters pertaining to the dispute; see Stubbs, *Epistolæ Cantuarienses*, nos. 326, 329, pp. 312, 315–17. Nigel probably composed letter no. 322 at pp. 306–7; see ibid., pp. lxxxv–lxxxvi, n. 2; and Mann, 'Nigel of Longchamp's *Speculum stultorum*', n. 101. Nigel may have composed other letters as well.

[124] Nigel of Whiteacre, *The Passion of St. Lawrence*, epigr. 11, pp. 260–63; Gervase, vol. 1, pp. 429–30.

[125] Nigel of Whiteacre, *The Passion of St. Lawrence*, pp. 11–13.

If we can trust Gerald of Wales (c. 1146–1220 × 1223), clerk and archdeacon of Brecon, Canterbury was alive with jesting and humour. Sitting at high table in 1180, Gerald observed that 'he [Gerald] seemed to be seated at a stage-play or among actors and jesters' ('ad ludos scenicos aut inter histriones et joculatores sibi videretur constitutus').[126] Although Gerald made the observation in his *De Rebus a se Gestis*, which he composed between 1208 and 1216,[127] he likely described a real Canterbury spirit of liveliness and jocularity.[128]

I suggest that the spirit of humour at Canterbury and the presence of satirists, especially Nigel of Whiteacre, influenced Gervase, even if the *Chronica* itself is not particularly humorous or satirical as such. Gransden asserts that Gervase 'had not the same temptation to eulogize the king as the romance historians had. Neither did he try to satirize the king and magnates.'[129] I agree, but I suggest that in this instance, Gervase used humour to mock Archbishop Baldwin. If one interprets the account within such a frame, it finds its place within a carefully constructed narrative.

There is a villain in this narrative, Baldwin, who persecutes the monks of Christ Church. Might one call the monks martyrs? The monks are the guardians of St Thomas, who himself is a defender of ecclesiastical liberty. St Thomas supports the monks against Baldwin, revealing himself to a member of the convent and investing their struggle against Baldwin with divine approval. St Thomas points the monks to the protector and defender of God's order on Earth, the Apostolic See.

When Archbishop Baldwin arrives at Canterbury immediately after the visions, he behaves erratically and unjustly before he scorns the cathedral chapter and withdraws to Otford. While he is absent, two legates – representatives of papal authority – arrive at Canterbury, where the monks receive them solemnly. In this way, the monks ritually and symbolically invite and welcome papal authority. The archbishop is absent due to his own unjust behaviour, his faults divesting

---

[126] Gerald of Wales, 'De Rebus a se Gestis', in *Giraldi Cambrensis Opera*, ed. J. S. Brewer, RS (London: Longman, 1861), vol. 1, pp. 1–122, bk. 2, ch. 5, p. 51; translated by H. E. Butler, *The Autobiography of Giraldus Cambrensis* (London: Jonathan Cape, 1937), p. 71. Gerald often referred to himself in the third person. I am grateful to William Kynan-Wilson, The Open University, for directing my attention to this account.

[127] See Robert Bartlett, *Gerald of Wales: A Voice of the Middle Ages*, 2nd edn (Stroud: Tempus, 2006), p. 178.

[128] Scholars commenting on the account include Nigel of Whiteacre, *The Passion of St. Lawrence*, p. 21; Knowles, *The Monastic Order*, pp. 463–65; Reginald Anthony Lendon Smith, *Canterbury Cathedral Priory: A Study in Monastic Administration* (Cambridge: Cambridge University Press, 1943), pp. 41–43; and Peter J. A. Jones, 'Gerald of Wales's Sense of Humour', in *Gerald of Wales: New Perspectives on a Medieval Writer and Critic*, ed. Georgia Henley and A. Joseph McMullen (Cardiff: University of Wales Press, 2018), pp. 147–63, at p. 148.

[129] Gransden, *Historical Writing*, p. 257.

him from his attachment to the cathedral, which is the fount of archiepiscopal authority and legitimacy.

In this light, Gervase's indignation on the archbishop's behalf is feigned. Instead, Gervase's comments are sarcastic and ironic – like someone who has suffered mistreatment at the hands of an oppressor only to see the oppressor slighted and humiliated. The mistreated feigns horror but gloats inwardly at the oppressor's misfortune. Gervase's exaggerated horror at the legates' arrival becomes comical; his feigned recovery from the shock of seeing the legates enter the cathedral becomes ironic. In this way, Gervase inverted the moral meaning of the event. Instead of reproaching legatine – and by extension papal – authority, Gervase embraced it. Instead of defending the archbishop, Gervase expressed severe criticism of Baldwin.

The humour moved the account into a 'different reality', in David Warner's phrase,[130] where the content made little sense in itself or, read literally, misinformed the audience. Only those in possession of sufficient contextual knowledge would understand the information – like the monks of Christ Church for whom Gervase was writing. This is the case with all information, but there is a qualitative distinction between (competently executed) symbolic communication and quotidian information. Humour – joking – speaks to shared experiences and perceptions; it loses potency if it requires explanation. A joke leaves the audience to connect the dots and organise the information into a coherent picture. A joke forces an audience to draw on preconceived notions and ideas, while the narrator of the joke strives to arrange the dots in such a way that the audience connects the dots according to the narrator's agenda. Too little information leaves the audience confused; too much spoils the joke.

For a joke to work, a narrator needs to entice the audience to (re)create the premises upon which to understand the information. For instance, when Gervase could barely write about the cross at the reception of the two legates – 'to say nothing of the cross' ('ut de cruce sileam') – the premise of his exclamation, among other things, rested upon the knowledge of the meaning of processional crosses, particularly Canterbury's history with them, even if Gervase did not explicitly tell his audience so. The Canterbury monks, however, were capable of drawing upon their repertoire of knowledge and selecting the pieces of information about processional crosses that were relevant to Gervase's exclamation. The monks, in their minds, put the pieces of relevant information together, effectively creating a pool of information whose exact composition was the result of Gervase's narration.

---

[130] David A. Warner, 'Ritual and Memory in the Ottonian Reich: The Ceremony of Adventus', *Speculum* 76, no. 2 (2001): 255–83, pp. 256–57. See pp. 6–7 for further exposition of this phrase.

Creating such a pool of information encourages an audience to gain a proprietary interest in the joke, having had a personal investment in it. In this way, joking may create a powerful emotional response – precisely what Gervase strove to create. He wanted his audience, the Canterbury monks, to feel that they had divine support for their cause; he wanted them to laugh at Baldwin and his evil scheme; he wanted them to gloat when the two papal legates cut short Baldwin's powers merely with their presence. For Gervase, this was part of a strategy to comfort and assure the monks, to make them laugh together, and in this way, experience unity and togetherness against a shared enemy.

Not everyone had this experience. There were dissenters among the monks.[131] Gervase used two strategies to deal with such dissenters. One strategy was to portray the convent as unified. Gervase claimed that the decision to resist Baldwin's scheme was unanimous, leaving no room for dissenting voices.[132] The other strategy Gervase used was to excise dissenters. Gervase opened his account of the house arrest with a warning against false brothers ('falsis fratribus').[133] Such branding was not uncommon amongst Gervase's contemporaries. Nigel of Whiteacre warned against 'false brothers' ('falsis fratribus') in a passage of the *Speculum* dedicated to denigrating the Cistercians (Baldwin's order).[134] Thomas of Marlborough branded some Evesham monks as 'falsi fratres' because they wanted to give in to the demands of Bishop Mauger of Worcester (r. 1199/1200–12).[135]

Barnaby identifies at least eight dissenting monks,[136] but two in particular drew the ire of Gervase. The first was Roger Norreys, who deserted the convent to join Archbishop Baldwin.[137] Baldwin and King Richard imposed him as prior, only for the monks to remove him later.[138] The other monk was Osbert, who had also deserted the convent. Gervase dismissed him as a 'non-monk' ('non monachus'), labelling him haughty, hateful, contumacious, and more.[139] Osbert was also later imposed on the convent as prior, but the monks demoted him and held him in confinement.[140]

In a letter from May 1189, one of the convent's representatives reported home about his meeting with Archbishop Baldwin and the 'apostate monks' ('apostatas

---

[131] Barnaby, *Religious Conflict at Canterbury*, pp. 41–43, 52, 77, 85–88, 99–100, 112–14, 126–27, 133–39.
[132] Gervase, vol. 1, p. 353.
[133] Ibid., p. 404.
[134] Nigel of Whiteacre, *Speculum stultorum*, vv. 2160–80, p. 79.
[135] Thomas of Marlborough, *History of the Abbey of Evesham*, bk. 3, pt. 2, 256, pp. 260–61.
[136] Barnaby, *Religious Conflict at Canterbury*, p. 113.
[137] Gervase, vol. 1, p. 404. See also Thomas of Marlborough, *History of the Abbey of Evesham*, bk. 3, pt. 1, 185, pp. 188–91.
[138] Barnaby, *Religious Conflict at Canterbury*, pp. 41, 85–87, 99–100, 126–33.
[139] Gervase, vol. 1, pp. 443–44.
[140] Ibid., pp. 495–96. See also Barnaby, *Religious Conflict at Canterbury*, pp. 112–14, 126, 135–39.

monachos').[141] He did not disclose the number of 'apostate monks', but the usage of plural descriptors reveals what Gervase was loath to admit: they were not unified in their struggle. Gervase wrote to hold the convent together, discountenancing any breach of unity. For Gervase, mocking Baldwin was a way to stiffen communal resistance.

Comparisons with other accounts of receptions of papal legates highlight how the legatine *adventus* at Canterbury at Christmas was unique. One example is the account of the reception of the oft-mentioned Cardinal John of Anagni:

> John of Anagni, legate of the Apostolic See, therefore came to Canterbury, and he was received solemnly by the bishops of England and likewise by the convent of Canterbury.[142]

There is nothing 'wrong' with this summary of the event, but it is not particularly inspired either. Gervase considered the reception worth recording but otherwise had no real interest in it. This was the case despite the fact that Cardinal John of Anagni had supported the monks. However, the cardinal ultimately failed to deliver, leaving in a hurry with only a secret absolution to show for his visit. Gervase presumably saw no reason to cultivate the account of his reception.

Hugh Pierleoni, cardinal-deacon of S. Angelo, is a further example. When Hugh arrived in England in 1175, Gervase remarked that 'he [the legate] was received honourably by the king [Henry II] and the nobles of England' ('a rege et a primoribus Angliæ honorifice susceptus est').[143] While this reception was evidently worth mentioning, apart from providing bare facts, Gervase tellingly offered no further details.

This lack of interest had nothing to do with a lack of understanding of the importance of such ritualised receptions. Gervase reported that the convent offered to receive Archbishop Baldwin with a procession upon the archbishop's return to England in 1189.[144] The offer took place in the shadow of the dispute; hence, this offer implicitly argued that the monks were willing to deal with the archbishop as good faith actors (which cannot be taken at face value). Gervase's reporting on the offer shows that Gervase was aware of the meaning of such receptions.

The *Chronica* reports on other ceremonial receptions, including those of Archbishops Richard and Hubert Walter.[145] Gervase considered both *adventus*

---

[141] Stubbs, *Epistolæ Cantuarienses*, no. 307, pp. 290–93, at p. 291.
[142] Gervase, vol. 1, pp. 481–82: 'Venit igitur Cantuariam Johannes Anagninus, apostolicæ sedis legatus, et ab episcopis Angliæ simul et conventu Cantuariensi solenniter susceptus est.'
[143] Ibid., p. 256.
[144] Ibid., pp. 451–52. A letter in the monks' dossier confirms the offer to receive the archbishop with a procession; see Stubbs, *Epistolæ Cantuarienses*, no. 314, pp. 298–30.
[145] Gervase, vol. 1, pp. 251, 522, 545.

ceremonies worth mentioning. All of the *adventus* ceremonies in the *Chronica* have their own stories to tell, but none of them stands out to the same extent in terms of symbolic messaging as the 1186 Christmas *adventus*. Gervase devoted special attention to that particular *adventus*.

The account of the reception at Christmas 1186 is also part of a homiletic narrative. Gervase was a Benedictine monk, and the Rule of St Benedict prescribes that, 'Whoever exalts himself shall be humbled, and whoever humbles himself shall be exalted [Luke 14:11]'.[146] Humility is a key Benedictine virtue. Holzherr, in his comments on the Rule of St Benedict, observes that 'the didactic opening part of the entire Rule of St Benedict finds its climax in this chapter [7] on humility'.[147] Within medieval literature, humility is a pervasive precondition for holding office, and thirteenth-century canon law lists lack of ambition as a prerequisite for the validity of a candidate's election to episcopal office.[148] Gervase relied on such notions of humility. His account, from Baldwin's election to the beginning of the dispute and further on to the reception of the two papal legates, is a teleological narrative. Within this narrative, legatine and papal power, in accord with St Thomas and divine approval, will eventually humble the proud Bishop Baldwin and elevate the humble monks.

Conclusion

If Roger of Howden's perspective primarily centred around the head of the monastery (in a manner of speaking), then Gervase of Canterbury viewed the legatine *adventus* from the point of view of one who yearned for papal legates to challenge the internal hierarchy of the monastery – quite literally. At the top of this hierarchy stood Archbishop-Abbot Baldwin, who received the main portion of Gervase's ire. However, Baldwin was not the only one. To the monks of Christ Church, the powers of England appeared aligned against them. The king supported the archbishop-abbot's attempt to destroy his own church and his own convent. Additionally, Gervase likely commenced writing the *Chronica* while suffering

---

[146] *Rule of Benedict*, ch. 7, 1, translation at p. 138, Latin at p. 135: 'Omnis qui se exaltat humiliabitur et qui se humiliat exaltabitur.'

[147] Ibid., p. 142.

[148] See Björn K. U. Weiler, 'The *Rex Renitens* and the Medieval Idea of Kingship, ca. 900–ca. 1250', *Viator* 31 (2000): 1–42; Emil Lauge Christensen, 'Justifying Episcopal Pluralism: The Negotiation between Suitability and Legitimacy in the Narrative of Saxo Grammaticus', in *Dominus Episcopus: Medieval Bishops between Diocese and Court*, ed. Anthony John Lappin and Elena Balzamo (Stockholm: Kungl. Vitterhets Historie och Antikvitets Akademien, 2018), pp. 100–30, esp. pp. 118–22; and Katherine Harvey, *Episcopal Appointments in England, c. 1214–1344: From Episcopal Election to Papal Provision* (Burlington, VT: Ashgate, 2014), pp. 11–45, esp. pp. 40–41.

house arrest alongside his fellow monks. No wonder the *Chronica* at times resonates with strong emotions, anxiety, deep-felt religiosity, apprehension, and hope.

Gervase's depiction of the legatine *adventus* at Canterbury during the Christmas of 1186 echoes some of the notions found in the *adventus* instructions: the solemn reception serves as a literary device for introducing the external dignitary to the concerns and interests of the host community. In Gervase's description of the reception, it is of course not one but two dignitaries, and they were not just any random lords, but embodiments of apostolic authority.

The *Chronica*'s message, however, was directed towards fellow members of the monastic community. Gervase was telling the monks that their salvation lay with the papacy, and he instructed them to include the pope in their cares and to make an ally out of him. Gervase's text was thus in an intimate relationship with the world around Canterbury, because Gervase strove to depict real events in a manner that both influenced his fellow monks and resonated emotionally with them. In Gervase's depiction of the Christmas *adventus*, he deliberately ignored the two papal legates' unsympathetic stance towards the monks as insignificant. Gervase was aware of the legates' antipathy towards the monks, but in his account of the reception, the office of papal legate mattered much more than any personal animosities that the two papal legates might have had. In the *Chronica*, the reception of the two papal legates was part of a deliberate narrative strategy. Structurally, in Gervase's narrative, the reception set the stage for the impending clashes with Archbishop Baldwin in the *Chronica*. The villain had made his first move, the protagonists had resolved to battle it out, and then, having received another blow from the antagonist (the suspension of Prior Honorius), the legates arrived.

In the *Chronica*, the arrival of the two papal legates primarily represented the arrival of the power of Rome: the Sword of the blessed apostle Peter. However, Gervase also ensured that the account of the *adventus* alluded to broader themes, such as order and disorder, and included a range of intertwining symbols associated with the traditions of Canterbury, St Thomas, Christ, and papal-legatine authority. A sense of humour, a characteristic often present at Christ Church, is also palpable. The legates played the role of good omens in the tale, signalling to the monks that St Thomas, the pope, and even God were watching over them, ready to drive out the tyrannical archbishop and restore the proper order of the church. In the *Chronica*, the reception amalgamated distinct Canterbury perspectives with features of the *adventus*. Gervase custom-tailored the *adventus* to fit Christ Church, incorporating elements such as the road of St Thomas, as well as the cross and the mitre. These latter two symbols were both legatine and (archi) episcopal insignia. It was this duality that enabled Gervase to integrate them into a Canterbury setting.

Gervase appropriated messages emanating from Rome. He willingly accepted that legatine insignia denoted and carried the presence of the papacy. However, the viewpoints and beliefs at Canterbury simultaneously directed him to adjust the message to suit the particular needs of his church. Gervase embraced papal authority because it was meaningful to him. Archbishop Baldwin was also a papal legate, but Gervase's wrath remained immune to the archbishop's legatine office. For Gervase, Baldwin's actions completely overshadowed his legatine dignity. Gervase shaped his view of legatine authority and the legatine *adventus* with at least one eye intensely fixed on the interests and cares of the convent of Christ Church, Canterbury.

6

Treason and Slavery: Roger of Wendover and the Plight of England

Gervase of Canterbury and Roger of Wendover shared certain similarities. Both were Benedictine monks and chroniclers. Their social backgrounds were probably quite similar. Historically, Christ Church and St Albans maintained certain connections such as Lanfranc's Monastic Constitutions, which Lanfranc composed for both Canterbury and St Albans. Nevertheless, the views of Roger and Gervase on the papacy and its legates stood worlds apart. English criticism of the papacy was not novel,[1] but Roger took it to a new level. The world had changed since Gervase wrote his *Chronica*: King John had offered up England as a fief to the pope.

In 1213, King John had found himself in deep trouble. Excommunicated by the pope for his stance on the Stephen Langton affair, facing rebellion, and expecting a French invasion, John had capitulated to Pope Innocent III to curry favour and offered England as a fief to the pope.[2] Roger found this manoeuvre outrageous. He accused the king of selling his country and his people into slavery. The pope, in the same vein, was a traitor in Roger's eyes because he had accepted the offer. Innocent became the feudal lord of England, John, receiving England as a fief, his vassal. Roger viewed this arrangement as a momentous shift in Anglo-Papal relations. It greatly affected his outlook on the legatine *adventus*. While he, like Gervase, viewed the legatine *adventus* as the ceremonial affirmation of papal-legatine authority, he interpreted the implications in a radically different way.

The most notable instance of a legatine *adventus* within Roger of Wendover's writings is the reception in the autumn of 1213 of Legate Nicholas, cardinal-bishop of Tusculum. This was the same Nicholas whose missive recounted his arrival in England and bemoaned his limited room for manoeuvre and his mandate's lack of clarity. It was not an uncertain Nicholas whom Roger depicted, however. On the contrary, Nicholas arrived in the immediate aftermath of the enfeoffment, being the first papal legate to set foot on English soil since the subjugation of England.

---

[1] See pp. 20–21.
[2] See pp. 169–70.

Roger did not merely view Cardinal Nicholas as a papal legate; he regarded him as an extension of the feudal lord of England, the pope. But the pope was not a benevolent, altruistic lord: he was a tyrant. Nicholas came to take possession of England and to plunge its inhabitants into slavery and despair. Roger viewed Nicholas' *adventus* from the vantage point of the English community, focusing particularly on the clergy's perspective. He viewed the *adventus* with equal parts despair and rage, as the papacy colluded with the king to oppress the English and disregard Christian virtues.

The Historian Roger of Wendover

Not much is known about Roger of Wendover. He was a monk at the abbey of St Albans, before being promoted to prior of Belvoir (a cell of St Albans) sometime before 1217, only to be later deposed by Abbot William of Trumpington (r. 1214–35) between 1225 and 1226, at which point Roger returned to St Albans as a monk.[3] Roger composed one work, the *Flores Historiarum* (Flowers of History), which he probably began writing in the late 1220s after his return to St Albans. He concluded his work in 1234, dying in 1236.[4] Aside from these details, everything else pertaining to Roger is conjecture. It is impossible to date his birth or his entry into monastic life. It can, however, be inferred that he came from the town of Wendover in Buckinghamshire. Altogether this lack of concrete personal information suggests that Roger was of humble extraction.

The *Flores Historiarum* begins at the Creation, with the work concluding in the year 1234. Aside from a few separate brief annals, Roger's work is the primary literary source for several crucial decades of English history – a history Roger was well placed to chronicle. St Albans was a major hub of communication, being located only a day's travel from London and lodging many of the major figures of power.[5] The abbey even built the so-called 'queen's chamber', which only housed

---

[3] *Flores Historiarum*, vol. 3, pp. vii–x; David Crook, 'Roger of Wendover, Prior of Belvoir, and the Implementation of the Charter of the Forest, 1225–7', in *The Growth of Royal Government under Henry III*, ed. David Crook and Louise J. Wilkinson (Woodbridge: Boydell Press, 2015), pp. 166–78, at pp. 167–69; Matthew Paris, 'Gesta Abbatum', in *Gesta abbatum monasterii Sancti Albani, a Thoma Walsingham, regnante Ricardo Secundo, ejusdem ecclesiæ præcentore, compilata*, ed. Henry Thomas Riley, 3 vols, RS (London: Longmans, 1867), vol. 1, pp. 3–324, at p. 270.

[4] Richard Kay, 'Wendover's Last Annal', *EHR* 84, no. 333 (1969): 779–85; Crook, 'Roger of Wendover'. See also Antonia Gransden, *Historical Writing in England c.550–c.1307* (London: Routledge, 1974), p. 359; J. C. Holt, *The Northerners: A Study in the Reign of King John* (Oxford: Clarendon Press, 1961), p. 3; and Michael Staunton, *The Historians of Angevin England* (Oxford: Oxford University Press, 2017), p. 182.

[5] Richard Vaughan, *Matthew Paris* (Cambridge: Cambridge University Press, 1958), pp. 11–17.

royal and distinguished women, and was unique to St Albans.[6] How much Roger interacted with such guests is unknown, but his successor as chronicler, Matthew Paris, conversed with many notabilities, including the king.[7]

Scholars have, nevertheless, shown little interest in the *Flores*. W. L. Warren dismisses Roger's work as 'an edifying pot-pourri'; worse yet, his 'account bears the hallmarks of worthless gossip'.[8] Vivian Galbraith asserts that 'the dignity of authorship is perhaps too high for the compiler of such a book', although he recognises the importance of the last thirty-five years of the *Flores*, but only because of a 'lack of [other] sources'.[9] This assessment is widespread.[10] Roger, on the other hand, wrote with a clear purpose of mind. He worked to provide a store of *exempla* of good and bad deeds:

> Now we would have such persons [who disregard history] know that the lives of good men in past times are set forth for the imitation of succeeding times; and that the examples of evil men, when such occur, are not to be followed but shunned.[11]

It was not an unusual position, but if his motivations for writing are clear, his audience is not. Roger never mentioned his audience, forcing modern scholars (those who have bothered, anyway) to speculate. Complicating matters further is the fact

---

[6] Julie Kerr, *Monastic Hospitality: The Benedictines in England, c.1070–c.1250* (Woodbridge: Boydell Press, 2007), p. 82.

[7] Vaughan, *Matthew Paris*, pp. 11–20.

[8] W. L. Warren, *King John*, 3rd edn (New Haven: Yale University Press, 1996), p. 13 and p. 12, respectively.

[9] Vivian H. Galbraith, 'Roger Wendover and Matthew Paris', in *Kings and Chroniclers: Essays in English Medieval History*, ed. Christopher Hill (London: The Hambledon Press, 1944), X: 5–48, p. 15.

[10] See, e.g., Frederick Maurice Powicke, 'Roger of Wendover and the Coggeshall Chronicle', *EHR* 21, no. 82 (1906): 286–96; Gransden, *Historical Writing*, pp. 359–60, 368–69; and Sean McGlynn, 'Roger of Wendover and the Wars of Henry III, 1216–1234', in *England and Europe in the Reign of Henry III (1216–1272)*, ed. Björn K. U. Weiler and Ifor W. Rowlands (Aldershot: Ashgate, 2002), pp. 183–206, at pp. 183–84. See also Björn K. U. Weiler, 'How Unusual Was Matthew Paris? The Writing of Universal History in Angevin England', in *Universal Chronicles in the High Middle Ages*, ed. Michele Campopiano and Henry Bainton (York: York Medieval Press, 2017), pp. 199–222, at p. 209.

[11] Roger of Wendover, *Rogeri de Wendover Chronica, sive Flores Historiarum*, ed. Henry O. Coxe, vol. 1 (London: English Historical Society, 1841), p. 1: 'Noverint isti bonos mores et vitas præcedentium, ad imitationem subsequentium proponi; malorum vero exempla, non ut imitentur, sed ut potius evitentur, describi.' Translated by Warren, *King John*, p. 13. Lacking a critical edition of the *Flores Historiarum* in its entirety, one has to turn to Henry Coxe's edition. The Rolls Series edition only begins at the year 1154. A new critical edition is needed.

that a proper critical edition of the *Flores* is lacking, as the Rolls Series edition only begins at the year 1154.[12] Nor does it help that only two manuscripts have survived, indicating that the *Flores* did not disseminate widely.[13] Roger's severe criticism of the papacy and the contemporary kings, John and Henry III, rules out support from that quarter. The subject matter of the *Flores* – world history and national politics – was mainly suitable for a learned audience. I suggest that the audience most prominently on his mind was his own convent, but that he also thought of other learned men (and women).

One of the few modern scholars to appreciate the *Flores* is Claude Jenkins.[14] He observes that Roger wrote 'comparative history … [in] itself a significant element in the English history of the period'.[15] He also produced 'a serious attempt at parallelism', wherein, for instance, 'Moses and the Exodus synchronize with the end of the reign of Cecrops at Athens … [moreover] Brutus was in Britain while Saul was in Judæa'.[16] This, I would argue, is an important key to interpret Roger's narratives. Circumstantial evidence supports that parallelism was important to Roger's way of messaging, as Björn Weiler has showed that Matthew Paris, Roger's continuator, often employed 'implicit yet open [contrasts] … to judge and evaluate the events which he described'.[17] Matthew was heavily indebted to Roger for his viewpoints and writing style.[18] Roger paralleled and contrasted events from all of human history, likely having planned the writing of the *Flores* meticulously.

The transition from the reign of King Richard to the reign of King John constitutes an important shift in the *Flores* – and an opportunity for Roger to compare and contrast. Richard and John represented two opposites: Richard's reign was good, John's was bad. It is tempting to speculate (and it is only speculation) that Cain and Abel were a (sub)conscious inspiration. Roger portrayed a sharp shift between the reigns of the two kings, being able to lay out their differences meticulously because he viewed both reigns from the vantage point of hindsight. Roger put quill to parchment only at the beginning of the reign of Henry III. His views are especially clear when he is independent of other narrators, such as when he

---

[12] See Weiler, 'How Unusual', p. 209.
[13] Bodleian Library, Douce MS 207 (from the thirteenth century) and British Museum, Cotton MS Otho B.v. (from the fourteenth century); see *Flores Historiarum*, vol. 1, p. viii.
[14] To be fair, Sean McGlynn and David Crook have appreciated some traits of the *Flores*; see McGlynn, 'Roger of Wendover and the Wars'; and Crook, 'Roger of Wendover'.
[15] Claude Jenkins, *The Monastic Chronicler and the Early School of St. Albans: A Lecture* (London: Macmillan, 1922), p. 51.
[16] Ibid., p. 52.
[17] Björn K. U. Weiler, 'Matthew Paris on the Writing of History', *JMH* 35, no. 3 (2009): 254–78, p. 273.
[18] See pp. 187–90.

reported on a vision in which Richard left purgatory for heaven in 1232.[19] Roger wrote that King Richard had 'respected all ordained prelates and especially religious men' ('prælatos omnes ordinatos, et præcipue viros religiosos, honoravit').[20] A good trait in a king, but one, he implied, sorely lacking in the present age. In the *Flores*, Richard's reign became an ideal by which to compare later and less prosperous times, even if the thrust of his narrative was not entirely consistent due to the influence of his sources (most notably Ralph of Coggeshall, Roger of Howden, and Ralph de Diceto).

In the *Flores*, the contrast between kings Richard and John extended to how they received papal legates. This included the account of the frequently mentioned Cardinal John of Anagni. Relying heavily on Roger of Howden's *Gesta* for the years between 1188 and 1192, often reproducing the *Gesta* verbatim and structurally, Roger of Wendover lifted the events surrounding the legate's arrival in England from the *Gesta*.[21] However, whereas the *Gesta* included an account of the reception of the cardinal,[22] Roger omitted it entirely from the *Flores*. Instead, he continued as if nothing had happened, mentioning, like the *Gesta*, Richard's

---

[19] *Flowers of History*, vol. 2, p. 547; *Flores Historiarum*, vol. 3, pp. 21–22.

[20] *Flowers of History*, vol. 2, p. 549 (translation adjusted); *Flores Historiarum*, vol. 3, p. 25.

[21] Roger of Howden (*Gesta*, vol. 2, p. 97, my emphasis): *Eodem mense Novembri, Johannes cardinalis applicuit in Angliam apud Dover; et prohibitum* fuit *ei ex parte Alienor reginæ, ne ulterius procederet, nisi per mandatum regis* filii sui; et ita factum est. Eodem mense Ricardus rex venit Cantuariam, et *fecit pacem* et *finalem* concordiam *inter* Baldewinum archiepiscopum et monachos Sanctæ Trinitatis Cantuariæ *in hunc modum* ....

Roger of Wendover (*Flores Historiarum*, vol. 1, p. 171, my emphasis): *Eodem mense Novembris Johannes,* Anagniæ *cardinalis, applicuit in Angliam apud* Doveram, et, quia rex in partibus aquilonis, *prohibitum* est *ei ex parte Alienor reginæ, ne ulterius procederet nisi per mandatum regis*; unde per dies tredecim ibidem substitit sumptibus archiepiscopi, donec de capella de Akintuna *pax inter archiepiscopum et monachos* Cantuariæ firmaretur. Sed rex sapientissimus Richardus a partibus vocatus accessit et *eodem mense* Novembris *finalem inter* eos concordiam *in hunc modum fecit* ....

Translation of the *Gesta*: In the same month of November, Cardinal John landed in England at Dover, and it was forbidden to him by Queen Eleanor, not to proceed further unless by her son the king's mandate; and thus it was done. In the same month, King Richard came to Canterbury, and he made peace and a final settlement between Archbishop Baldwin and the monks of the Holy Trinity of Canterbury in this manner ....

Translation of the *Flores Historiarum*: In the same month of November, John, Cardinal of Anagni, landed in England at Dover, and, because the king was in the northern parts, it was forbidden to him by Queen Eleanor, not to proceed further unless by the king's mandate; for which reason he remained there for thirteen days at the expense of the archbishop, until peace between the archbishop and the monks of Canterbury was established concerning the chapel of Hackington. However, the most wise King Richard, recalled from the [northern] parts, came and in the same month of November made a final settlement between them in this manner ....

[22] See p. 126; *Gesta*, vol. 2, pp. 98–99.

grants to his brother, John, and his mother, Queen Eleanor.[23] Editing Richard's reign in this way helped create the contrast between his reign and later reigns, particularly John's. It denormalised legatine receptions and legatine authority.

The purpose was to reject papal-legatine authority (in secular matters). Take Roger's account of Richard's meeting with Cardinal-Legate Peter of Capua in 1198. The pope had dispatched the cardinal to act as a peace broker between Richard and King Philip Augustus of France.[24] Peter and Richard met; however, Roger never mentioned the manner in which the king received the cardinal, leaving the impression that he did not receive him ceremoniously. It is not even clear where Richard and Peter met. The only mention of their meeting is a brief phrase: 'and coming to the king of the English' ('veniensque ad regem Anglorum').[25] The context of the report suggests that they met somewhere in the Angevin continental lands, but the manner of the cardinal-legate's reception can only be guessed at. The wording may imply some disrespect for the cardinal. The text, read literally, suggests that Richard did not perform an *occursus*, but simply received the cardinal as if he were another subject seeking an audience. The king still listened to the legate's proposal but replied 'with indignation' ('cum indignatione'), saying, as paraphrased by Roger, that 'by law, the pope himself could not make him [Richard] be held to do anything' ('se de jure non teneri pro ipso papa quicquam facere').[26]

Roger held up King Richard's hostile rejection of papal-legatine authority as a model for emulation. King John, on the other hand, openly declared his subjection to the pope:

> The king [John] openly declared before them all [at a gathering in 1215] that the kingdom of England by right of dominion belonged to the Church of Rome, and therefore he could not and ought not without the knowledge of our lord the pope to make any new arrangements or alter anything in the kingdom to the detriment of that pontiff.[27]

Roger viewed this as a perversion of the natural order. When Cardinal Guala stopped off at the court of King Philip in 1216, Roger placed the following view of the vassalage into the collective mouths of the French nobles:

---

[23] Ibid., p. 99; *Flowers of History*, vol. 2, p. 86; *Flores Historiarum*, vol. 1, p. 172.
[24] On Peter of Capua, see Werner Maleczek, *Papst und Kardinalskolleg von 1191 bis 1216. Die Kardinäle unter Coelestin und Innocenz III.* (Vienna: Verlag der Österreichischen Akademie der Wissenschaften, 1984), pp. 117–24.
[25] *Flowers of History*, vol. 2, p. 176; *Flores Historiarum*, vol. 1, p. 281.
[26] *Flowers of History*, vol. 2, p. 176 (translation adjusted); *Flores Historiarum*, vol. 1, p. 281.
[27] *Flowers of History*, vol. 2, p. 329; *Flores Historiarum*, vol. 2, p. 138: 'idem rex publice protestatus est coram eis, regnum Angliæ ratione dominie ad Romanam ecclesiam specialiter pertinere, unde nec potuit nec debuit præter conscientiam domini papæ de novo aliquid statuere vel quicquam in ejus præjudicium in regno immutare.'

Then all the [French] magnates likewise with one mouth began to call out that they would resist that article to the death, namely that a king or a prince by his singular will could surrender or make tributary a kingdom, by which the nobles of the kingdom would become slaves.[28]

A Time of Tumultuous Change?

The relationship between England and the papacy changed during Roger's (probable) lifetime. King Richard kept curial legates at arm's length, but he simultaneously recognised the value of the legatine office to royal government. Richard effected the appointments of William Longchamp, bishop of Ely, and Archbishop Hubert Walter as papal legates. They ruled England while Richard was abroad.[29] However, when Lothar of Segni became pope in 1198 as Innocent III, he refused to appoint resident legates, instead dispatching curial legates on short-term legations.[30] Curiously, this applied only to England: Innocent appointed resident legates elsewhere.[31] He never explained his position, but Christopher Cheney has hypothesised that Innocent simply refused to renew Hubert's commission due to the ongoing dispute between the archbishop and his cathedral chapter.[32] However, this does not explain why Innocent maintained his policy after he had ratified the settlement between the archbishop and the cathedral chapter in 1201.

Whatever Innocent's reasons for refusing to appoint resident legates to England, this policy, different from that of his predecessors, is discernible in the number of curial legations. Popes dispatched two legations to England during Richard's reign, while a third stayed from the reign of Henry II into that of Richard.[33] In contrast, from John's accession (1199) to the outbreak of the 'Stephen Langton dispute' in 1207, the pope dispatched five legations to England, while one legate stayed from

---

[28] *Flowers of History*, vol. 2, p. 362 (translation adjusted); *Flores Historiarum*, vol. 2, p. 177: 'Tunc quoque magnates omnes uno ore clamare cæperunt quod pro isto articulo starent usque ad mortem, ut videlicet rex vel princeps per solam voluntatem suam posset regnum dare vel tributarium facere, unde nobiles regni efficerentur servi.'

[29] Ilicia Jo Sprey, 'Papal Legates in English Politics, 1100–1272' (unpublished PhD dissertation, University of Virginia, Charlottesville, 1998), pp. 223–41; Christopher R. Cheney, *Hubert Walter* (London: Nelson, 1967), esp. pp. 115–25.

[30] Sprey, 'Papal Legates', pp. 240–42.

[31] See Heinrich Zimmermann, *Die päpstliche Legation in der ersten Hälfte des 13. Jahrhunderts: Vom Regierungsantritt Innocenz' III. bis zum Tode Gregors IX. (1198–1241)* (Paderborn: Ferdinand Schöningh, 1913), pp. 66–71.

[32] Cheney, *Hubert Walter*, pp. 122–23.

[33] Sprey, 'Papal Legates', p. 292.

Richard's reign into John's.[34] In effect, the pope denied John the legatine instrument Richard had possessed, making legates into external figures once more.

In 1205, Archbishop Hubert Walter died. Two irregular elections followed until, on papal request, a delegation of Canterbury monks elected Stephen Langton, cardinal-priest of San Crisogono, as archbishop.[35] The election did not receive John's recognition, causing a crisis in Anglo-Papal relations. Innocent pronounced interdict on England in 1208, excommunicating John in 1209. Most bishops went into exile, while the English king turned on the clergy still loyal to the pope, confiscating their estates, collecting their revenues, or forcing them to pay fines.[36] In 1212, a baronial plot against the king was discovered, and by 1213 the French stood poised to invade England with papal backing. Besieged by enemies both at home and abroad, John capitulated to the pope. He not only promised to accept Stephen Langton and pay reparations, but also offered England to the pope, receiving the kingdom back from the pope as a fief. This last move bought John Innocent's support. When Innocent dispatched Cardinal Nicholas to finalise the peace, the pope had probably already set his eyes on a future crusade rather than on the painstakingly difficult negotiations between John and the English Church.[37]

Innocent's turnabout made it possible for John to attempt a reconquest of the continental provinces, which he had lost to King Philip in 1204. The campaign began in early 1214 but lasted no more than eight months, as King Philip decisively defeated John and his allies. This was a catastrophe for John. For years, John had imposed heavy taxation on the English with reconquest in mind, but all was for naught.[38] John's subjects were fed up: his issue of Magna Carta only delayed the

[34] Ibid.
[35] Paul Webster, 'Crown, Cathedral and Conflict: King John and Canterbury', in *Cathedrals, Communities and Conflict in the Anglo-Norman World*, ed. Paul Dalton, Charles Insley, and Louise J. Wilkinson (Woodbridge: Boydell Press, 2011), pp. 204–19, at pp. 211–19; Christopher R. Cheney, 'A Neglected Record of the Canterbury Election of 1205–6', *Bulletin of the Institute of Historical Research* 21 (1948): 233–38; David Knowles, 'The Canterbury Election of 1205–6', *EHR* 53, no. 210 (1938): 211–20.
[36] See Christopher R. Cheney, 'King John and the Papal Interdict', in *The Papacy and England 12th–14th Centuries: Historical and Legal Studies* (London: Variorum Reprints, 1982), IX: 295–317; and Christopher R. Cheney, 'King John's Reaction to the Interdict on England', in ibid., X: 129–50.
[37] For an instructive overview, see Christopher Harper-Bill, 'John and the Church of Rome', in *King John: New Interpretations*, ed. Stephen D. Church (Woodbridge: Boydell Press, 1999), pp. 289–315. For the peace treaty, see Christopher R. Cheney and W. H. Semple, ed. and trans., *Selected Letters of Pope Innocent III Concerning England (1198–1216)* (London: Thomas Nelson and Sons, 1953), no. 67, pp. 177–83.
[38] See Jane Frecknall Hughes and Lynne Oats, 'King John's Tax Innovations – Extortion, Resistance, and the Establishment of the Principle of Taxation by Consent', *The Accounting Historians Journal* 34, no. 2 (2007): 75–107.

ensuing civil war by a few months. Soon, the rebellious barons invited Prince Louis of France to take the English crown. The pope, on the other hand, dispatched Cardinal Guala Bicchieri as legate to England to buttress the royal cause. The legate arrived only months prior to the deaths of John and Innocent, but Pope Honorius III immediately recommissioned him, giving him a free hand.[39] Together with the regent, William Marshall (1146/7–1219), Guala gathered support for the succession of John's nine-year-old son, Henry III. They succeeded, and in 1218 the pope replaced Guala with Pandulf, papal nuncio, whose legation terminated in 1221.[40]

Depending on one's perspective, the outcome of these events was either momentous or negligible, positive or upending. David Carpenter comments that 'the role played by the pope and his legates was as remarkable as it was usually constructive'.[41] In a way, nothing changed: England was a vassal state but the pope did not attempt to govern the country. When Pandulf's legation terminated, England was at peace and Henry III soon came of age, leaving England to reclaim its pre-civil war status.[42]

But something had indeed changed. During the minority, William Marshal had realised that 'any position that he [William Marshal] held would be worthless unless it derived from the general will'.[43] A central feature of the regent's rule was therefore 'the convening of great councils and the conferral of common consent'.[44] This royal policy of consultation with the crown's subjects created precedents, emboldening the baronage to demand more influence. Henry's minority did not preordain anything, nor was any one factor the sole cause of later developments, but Henry already had to face a (minor) rebellion from Richard Marshall early in his reign (1233–34).[45] Carpenter calls Richard Marshal 'a precursor of Simon de

---

[39] Warren, *King John*, pp. 233–55; Stephen Church, *King John: England, Magna Carta and the Making of a Tyrant* (Basingstoke: Macmillian, 2015), pp. 244–52.

[40] David A. Carpenter, *The Minority of Henry III* (Berkeley: University of California Press, 1990), pp. 5–262. See also Maleczek, *Papst und Kardinalskolleg*, pp. 141–46; and Nicholas Vincent, ed., *The Letters and Charters of Cardinal Guala Bicchieri, Papal Legate in England, 1216–1218* (Woodbridge: Boydell Press, 1996), pp. xxxi–lxxxviii.

[41] David A. Carpenter, *The Struggle for Mastery: Britain, 1066–1284* (London: Penguin, 2003), p. 431.

[42] Fred A. Cazel, Jr., 'The Legates Guala and Pandulf', in *TCE II*, ed. P. R. Coss and S. D. Lloyd (Woodbridge: Boydell Press, 1988), pp. 15–21; Rose Catherine Clifford, 'England as a Papal Fief: The Role of the Papal Legate in the Early Period, 1216–1241' (unpublished PhD dissertation, University of California, Los Angeles, 1978), esp. pp. 354–59. See also Benedict Wiedemann, *Papal Overlordship and European Princes, 1000–1270* (Oxford: Oxford University Press, 2022), pp. 95–118, esp. pp. 95–109.

[43] Carpenter, *The Minority of Henry III*, p. 14.

[44] Ibid.

[45] David A. Carpenter, *Henry III: The Rise to Power and Personal Rule 1207–1258* (New Haven: Yale University Press, 2020), pp. 125–64. See also C. H. Lawrence, *St Edmund*

Montfort',[46] the rebel leader in the Second Barons' War (1264–67), in which the rebels would attempt to replace the kingship with some form of parliamentary government.[47] Henry III, furthermore, believed (perhaps rightly) that he owed his crown to the papacy, and he reversed more than fifty years of policy that had previously kept foreign papal legates at arm's length. Henry instead welcomed direct papal authority, striving throughout the 1230s to have a cardinal dispatched to England to help him navigate various troubles.[48]

The events and the vassalage also changed the composition of the English Church. These changes began with King John distributing benefices to the cardinalate to purchase support. Upon the conclusion of the civil war, Cardinal Guala deposed rebel clergy, appointing Italians in their stead.[49] Papal nominees increasingly took possession of English benefices. Frederick Powicke estimates (with some uncertainty) that curial candidates held as much as 10 per cent of the income of the English Church by the 1250s.[50] The papacy awarded benefices to non-resident clergy, sometimes as pensions (allowing pluralism), while papal executors reserved the right to the most valuable livings for papal candidates under pain of excommunication, violating the rights of patrons. In 1231 and 1232, discontent boiled over, resulting in a series of attacks against foreign clergy. The numbers and influence of the perpetrators were on such a magnitude that King Henry and the pope chose leniency in response to the attacks.[51]

---

of Abingdon: A Study in Hagiography and History (Oxford: Clarendon Press, 1960), pp. 124–38; and Frederick Maurice Powicke, *King Henry III and the Lord Edward: The Community of the Realm in the Thirteenth Century*, 2nd edn, 2 vols (Oxford: Clarendon Press, 1966), vol. 1, pp. 123–38.

[46] Carpenter, *Henry III: The Rise to Power*, p. 152.

[47] See Adrian Jobson, *The First English Revolution: Simon de Montfort, Henry III and the Barons' War* (London: Bloomsbury, 2012).

[48] See Adam Davies, 'The Appointment of Cardinal-Deacon Otto as Legate in Britain (1237)', in *TCE XI*, ed. Björn K. U. Weiler et al. (Woodbridge: Boydell Press, 2007), pp. 147–58. See also pp. 194–97 in this book.

[49] Christopher R. Cheney, *Pope Innocent III and England* (Stuttgart: Hiersemann, 1976), pp. 91–6; Vincent, *The Letters and Charters*, pp. lxi–lxxiv.

[50] Powicke, *King Henry III*, vol. 1, pp. 274–89, esp. pp. 278–79. For a measured assessment of the development of papal provisions (the system of papal appointment), see Thomas W. Smith, 'The Development of Papal Provisions in Medieval Europe', *History Compass* 13, no. 3 (2015): 110–21.

[51] Hugh MacKenzie, 'The Anti-Foreign Movement in England, 1231–1232', in *Anniversary Essays in Medieval History by Students of Charles Homer Haskins Presented on His Completion of Forty Years of Teaching*, ed. Charles H. Taylor and John Life La Monte (Boston, MA: Houghton Mifflin Company, 1929), pp. 183–203; Oscar Albert Marti, 'Popular Protest and Revolt against Papal Finance in England from 1226 to 1258', *The Princeton Theological Review* (1927): 610–29.

Roger wrote the history of King John's reign under the influence of these immediate events. Reporting on the anti-foreign attacks, Roger quoted a document in which the anonymous instigators justified their actions. Whether genuine or not, the document surely reflected Roger's view of things:

> How the Romans and their legates have hitherto behaved themselves towards us and other ecclesiastics of England, we are sure is no secret to you [audience of the letter], and how you have conferred the benefices of the kingdom on their followers, at their pleasure, to the great prejudice and injury of yourselves and all others of the kingdom ...[52]

Cardinal Nicholas and His Legatine Mission

Cardinal Nicholas remains a figure of some obscurity. No records disclose his family or his education, but he was close to Pope Innocent, signing many of his privileges. Innocent elevated Nicholas to cardinal-bishop of Tusculum in 1204.[53] Writing to the English magnates in 1213, the pope recommended Nicholas as 'a man pleasing to God and acceptable to men, and one whom we love with a special affection among our brethren for his piety and integrity'.[54] Nicholas had, however, no previous legatine experience nor was his task easy: England was in a state of tension and excitement.

The English Church had, figuratively speaking, bled for the pope. The English prelates had upheld the interdict, suffering exile and financial losses. Now they wanted reparations and free elections to ecclesiastical offices.[55] Eager to wind things down, however, the pope's handling of the situation was disastrously tone-deaf. Innocent had been extremely displeased with John, giving the king's initial peace offers a frosty reception. Only John's offer to become a papal vassal had

---

[52] *Flowers of History*, vol. 2, p. 544 (translation adjusted); *Flores Historiarum*, vol. 3, pp. 16–17: 'Qualiter circa nos et alias personas ecclesiasticas Angliæ hactenus se habuerint Romani et eorum legati, vestram non dubitamus latere discretionem, beneficia regni suis secundum quod eis placet, conferendo in vestrum et omnium aliorum regni intolerabile præjudicium et gravamen ...'. See also *Flowers of History*, vol. 2, pp. 466–68, 471–72; *Flores Historiarum*, vol. 2, pp. 295–97, 302.

[53] Maleczek, *Papst und Kardinalskolleg*, pp. 147–48. Early modern historiography awarded Nicholas the surname *de Romanis*, but medieval sources do not substantiate it.

[54] Cheney and Semple, *Selected Letters*, no. 55, p. 154: 'virum utique gratum deo et acceptum hominibus, quem inter alios fratres nostros merito sue religionis et honestatis speciali diligimus caritate.'

[55] Harper-Bill, 'John and the Church of Rome', pp. 308–9.

worked – and 'worked like a charm', according to Warren.[56] This 'brilliant diplomatic stroke'[57] (Warren, again) made Innocent appreciate that 'we [Innocent] ought to show diligent care and concern for our well-beloved son in Christ, John, illustrious king of the English'.[58] This 'care and concern' extended to cutting short Nicholas' negotiations about reparations to the English Church. Innocent settled for a compensation of 100,000 marks: 40,000 marks to be paid upfront, the rest payable in instalments which never materialised.[59]

Free elections were not forthcoming. The pope instructed Nicholas to fill vacant churches with men 'who should not only be distinguished by their life and learning but also loyal to the king, profitable to the kingdom, and capable of giving counsel and help – the king's assent having been requested'.[60] Innocent later moderated the instruction,[61] but the king still had his way. Warren argues that 'men who had unblushingly stayed in John's service through the years of interdict were now by an arbitrary exercise of papal power promoted to the richest prizes'.[62] In 1215, Innocent remarked that John 'has beyond expectation made amends to God and the Church'.[63] It is highly unlikely that the English prelates agreed.

Innocent's hopes for English royal participation in a crusade likely influenced his approach towards John. The pope at one point asserted that one of his 'desires of our heart' ('desiderabilia cordis nostri') was 'to recover the Holy Land' ('ad recuperationem ... terre sancte').[64] Innocent had announced plans for a crusade in April

---

[56] Warren, *King John*, p. 209. See also Cheney, *Pope Innocent III and England*, pp. 343–44.
[57] John W. Baldwin, *The Government of Philip Augustus: Foundations of French Royal Power in the Middle Ages* (Berkeley: University of California Press, 1991), p. 210.
[58] Cheney and Semple, *Selected Letters*, no. 60, p. 164: 'de carissimo in Christo, filio nostro I. illustri Anglorum rege ... nos curam et sollicitudinem gerere diligentem'.
[59] Cheney, *Pope Innocent III and England*, pp. 348–56; Cheney, 'King John's Reaction', p. 129; Harper-Bill, 'John and the Church of Rome', p. 308; Cheney and Semple, *Selected Letters*, nos. 64, 70, pp. 171–72, 188–90.
[60] Cheney and Semple, *Selected Letters*, no. 62, p. 166 (translation adjusted): 'que non solum vita et scientia sint preclare, verum etiam regi fideles et regno utiles, necnon ad consilium et auxilium efficaces, assensu regio requisito.' In 1215, in the face of mounting opposition, John actually granted a charter of free elections; see ibid., no. 76, pp. 198–201.
[61] Christopher R. Cheney and Mary G. Cheney, eds, *The Letters of Pope Innocent III (1198–1216) Concerning England and Wales: A Calendar with an Appendix of Texts* (Oxford: Clarendon Press, 1967), no. 968, p. 161.
[62] Warren, *King John*, p. 212.
[63] Cheney and Semple, *Selected Letters*, no. 80, p. 207: 'supra spem deo et ecclesie satisfecerit'. The letter is dated 7 July 1215. It admonishes Innocent's chief agents in England for failing to support King John, who was experiencing opposition against his rule; and it pronounces interdict on all 'disturbers' ('perturbatores') of the kingdom. Innocent was not aware of Magna Carta when he issued the letter.
[64] Ibid., no. 51, pp. 144–47.

1213, and he was already issuing crusade instructions to Cardinal Nicholas in the autumn of 1213, even as the negotiations in England were proving difficult.[65] When war broke out between King John and King Philip, Innocent wrote worriedly that 'it is preventing the aid to the Holy Land' ('impediatur terre sancte succursus').[66]

Nicholas' task was impossible. On the one hand, he was to ensure episcopal support for the king; on the other hand, the pope instructed the legate to deprive the bishops of compensation and curtail their rights of appointment to benefices.[67] The pope recalled Nicholas at the end of 1214. He died in either 1218 or 1219.[68]

The Monastic Tour

There is, however, another side to the story. Cardinal Nicholas visited several monasteries during his stay in England. Some of the monasteries were happy to receive the legate. Among these were the monks of Bury St Edmunds, who in 1213 were in the middle of a succession crisis. Abbot Samson had recently died, but King John had refused to confirm Hugh as abbot-elect, prompting one faction of monks to push for a new election, while another faction supported Hugh.[69] The knowledge of these events comes primarily from a detailed work known as the *Electio Hugonis*. This is the work of a certain Master Nicholas of Dunstable, a monk at Bury St Edmunds, who composed the text in the late 1220s.[70] In the *Electio*, Master Nicholas reported how the 'venerable Legate Nicholas' ('uenerabilibus N(icholao) legato')[71] came to the abbey at Christmas 1213:

> The lord legate, then, arrived before Christmas, on the day of St Thomas the apostle, and was received with due honour by a procession at the church door, the precentor leading in the singing of the *Summae Trinitati*.[72]

---

[65] Ibid., no. 58, pp. 159–60.
[66] Ibid., no. 68, p. 184.
[67] Cheney, *Pope Innocent III and England*, pp. 159–70, 344–55.
[68] Ibid., pp. 363–64; Maleczek, *Papst und Kardinalskolleg*, p. 150.
[69] Rodney M. Thomson, ed., *The Chronicle of the Election of Hugh, Abbot of Bury St. Edmunds and Later Bishop of Ely*, OMT (Oxford: Clarendon Press, 1974), esp. pp. xxi–xlvii. See also Cheney, *Pope Innocent III and England*, p. 161; and Helene Tillmann, *Die päpstlichen Legaten in England bis zur Beendigung der Legation Gualas, 1218* (Bonn: Hch. Ludwig, 1926), pp. 105–7.
[70] Thomson, *The Chronicle of the Election*, pp. xv–xxi.
[71] Ibid., pp. 24–25.
[72] Ibid., pp. 26–27 (translation adjusted): 'Veniente quidem domino legato die sancti Thome apostoli ante Natale, honorifice ad processionem susceptus est ad portam ecclesie, precentore incipiente *Summe Trinitati*.'

The *Summae Trinitati* was sung at the reception of kings and queens.[73] Although Cardinal Nicholas did not confirm Hugh's election, Master Nicholas described him as sympathetic. The *Electio* is also favourable towards the legate's reforming measures at the abbey.[74] Papal judges-delegate would later confirm Hugh as abbot.[75]

The monks of Evesham Abbey received Cardinal Nicholas even more joyfully. In 1190, Archbishop Baldwin and King Richard had imposed Roger Norreys (d. 1223 × 1225) as abbot on the monks of Evesham. He was one of those 'false brothers' that Gervase of Canterbury had denounced during the dispute with Baldwin, and the monks at Evesham did not like him either.[76] Feeling the heavy oppression of the abbot, the monks put their faith in God, according to Thomas of Marlborough,[77] who chronicled the chain of events in his *Chronicon abbatiae de Evesham*. Thomas composed his chronicle sometime between 1218 and 1229.[78] He reported that 'we said special prayers every day for help to be sent us from Heaven' ('speciales cotidie fecimus orationes ut mitteretur nobis auxilium de celo').[79] Finally, the 'Lord took pity' ('misertus est Dominus') and 'the Dayspring from on high visited us [Luke 1:78], for the Lord pope sent Lord Nicholas, bishop of Tusculum, and legate of the Apostolic See, to England' ('uisitante nos oriente ex alto, missus est in Angliam a domino papa dominus Nicholaus Tusculan episcopus, apostolice sedis legatus').[80] With the legate in England, Thomas was sent to speak with Nicholas on a number of occasions, during which the legate learned about the state of affairs at Evesham. One time, Thomas met and spoke with the legate at Bruern Abbey, at which occasion the legate decided to visit Evesham. Thomas reported that 'around nine o'clock the next morning, the lord legate arrived [at Evesham], and he was received in solemn procession'.[81] The account

---

[73] See Frank Ll. Harrison, *Music in Medieval Britain* (London: Routledge, 1958), p. 259, n. 1.

[74] Thomson, *The Chronicle of the Election*, pp. 25–29, 50–53. See also Antonia Gransden, *A History of the Abbey of Bury St Edmunds 1182–1256: Samson of Tottington to Edmund Walpole* (Woodbridge: Boydell Press, 2007), pp. 199–200.

[75] Thomson, *The Chronicle of the Election*, pp. 72–173.

[76] James Barnaby, *Religious Conflict at Canterbury Cathedral in the Late Twelfth Century: The Dispute between the Monks and the Archbishops, 1184–1200* (Woodbridge: Boydell Press, 2024), pp. 41, 85–87, 99–100, 126–33; David Knowles, *The Monastic Order in England: A History of Its Development from the Times of St Dunstan to The Fourth Lateran Council, 940–1216*, 2nd edn (Cambridge: Cambridge University Press, 1963), pp. 331–45; G. G. Coulton, *Five Centuries of Religion. Volume II: The Friars and the Dead Weight of Tradition, 1200–1400 A.D.* (New York: Octagon Books, 1927), pp. 347–78.

[77] Thomas of Marlborough, *History of the Abbey of Evesham*, ed. Jane E. Sayers and Leslie Watkiss, OMT (Oxford: Oxford University Press, 2003), bk. 3, pt. 5, 446, pp. 428–29.

[78] Ibid., pp. xxi, xxiii–xxv.

[79] Ibid., bk. 3, pt. 5, 446, pp. 428–29.

[80] Ibid.

[81] Ibid., bk. 3, pt. 5, 459, pp. 438–39 (translation adjusted): 'In crastino uero circa horam terciam uenit dominus legatus, et recepto eo cum sollempni processione.'

of the *adventus* is brief, but Thomas was delighted that the cardinal demoted Abbot Roger.[82] Thomas painted a picture of a fearsome and powerful man, who commanded his surroundings and knew how to make men obey.[83]

The story of Nicholas' visit to St Albans in November 1214 was very different. The monks had just elected a new abbot, William of Trumpington. William had been obliged to agree to sign a charter that limited his abbatial powers;[84] however, once elected, he refused to honour the charter.[85] It was at this moment that Nicholas appeared on the stage. According to Roger's continuator, Matthew Paris, Nicholas supported the abbot, reminding the monks of their duty of obedience, before 'he tore the charter into small pieces' ('chartam ... in particulas dilaceravit').[86]

Roger mentioned the passing of Abbot John of Wallingford (r. 1195–1214) and the election of William of Trumpington,[87] but he never mentioned the legate's visit to St Albans. He was not obliged to, but it is inconceivable that he was unaware of the visit, even if he might not have been present. Matthew Paris only took the monastic habit some three years after the event, penning the account of the visit sometime in the 1240s or 1250s. The senior monks remembered how the legate tore their charter into pieces, and Roger must have been one of them.

It was, furthermore, Abbot William who would go on to demote Roger from his priorate at Belvoir. Roger never mentioned his demotion. Henry Hewlett observes that 'some excuse for resentment had undoubtedly been given to the ex-Prior of Belvoir by the Abbot's severity ... [however,] his account of Trumpington's official career nevertheless displays no trace whatever of unkindly feeling'.[88] Hewlett argues that this was a mark of self-restraint and magnanimity. He believes Roger had only stopped writing when he died in May 1236, more than a year after William's death.[89] However, Richard Kay shows that Roger stopped writing in 1234, before William's death.[90] Without assessing the details of the censorship at St Albans, it seems likely that Roger was not in a position to write whatever he pleased. He could not malign Abbot William, but it is reasonable to presume that he held some animosity against both Cardinal-Legate Nicholas and the abbot. This animosity would go some way to explain his hostility towards legates, including Nicholas, as will become clear in

---

[82] Ibid., bk. 3, pt. 5, 493, p. 462–63. See also pp. 86–87 in this book.
[83] Thomas of Marlborough, *History of the Abbey of Evesham*, bk. 3, pt. 5, 447–504, pp. 428–73.
[84] Cheney, *Pope Innocent III and England*, pp. 363–64; F. T. Wethered, ed., *St. Mary's, Hurley, in the Middle Ages: Based on Hurley Charters and Deeds* (London: Bedford Press, 1898), no. 45, pp. 105–6.
[85] Matthew Paris, 'Gesta Abbatum', pp. 253–56.
[86] Ibid., p. 257.
[87] *Flowers of History*, vol. 2, pp. 297, 304; *Flores Historiarum*, vol. 2, pp. 104, 112.
[88] *Flores Historiarum*, vol. 3, p. xviii.
[89] Ibid.
[90] Kay, 'Wendover's Last Annal'.

the next section. Writing the *Flores Historiarum* in the late 1220s and early 1230s, it was likely less controversial to malign Legate Nicholas and his kind than it was to mention Abbot William's abuses and his collusion with the legate.

Finally, it is possible (but speculative) that Roger wrote to counter the interpretations of the character of Cardinal Nicholas emerging from Evesham and Bury St Edmunds. I have found no way to ascertain if Roger read the accounts of the *Electio Hugonis* or Thomas of Marlborough, but the abbeys of St Albans, Evesham, and Bury St Edmunds were sufficiently close to be in regular contact. The abbots of these houses officiated together at the Benedictine general chapter at Oxford in 1218 and 1219.[91]

The Reception of Legate Nicholas

Roger of Wendover's account of the reception of Cardinal-Legate Nicholas is as follows:

> In the same year [1213], around the feast of St Michael [Michaelmas, 29 September], Nicholas, bishop of Tusculum and legate of the Apostolic See, came into England in order to amend the dissensions between the kingship and the priesthood with apostolic authority, and although the country had been under interdict, he was however received honourably everywhere with a solemn procession and musical song and festive clothing; and when he had arrived at Westminster, he immediately demoted Abbot William whose monks accused him of wastefulness and unchastity.[92]

The account consists of two parts: a prelude and a reception. The prelude spans from the first lines from 'In the same year' ('Eodem anno') to 'with apostolic authority' (in the Latin, the sentence concludes with 'reformaret', 'to amend' or 'to reform'). The prelude is connected by 'and' ('et') to the reception, the second part, which continues from there to the legate's arrival at Westminster.

---

[91] William Abel Pantin, ed., *Documents Illustrating the Activities of the General and Provincial Chapters of the English Black Monks 1215–1540*, 3 vols (London: Butler & Tanner, 1931), vol. 1, p. 7.

[92] *Flowers of History*, vol. 2, p. 289 (translation adjusted); *Flores Historiarum*, vol. 2, pp. 93–94: '[prelude:] Eodem anno, circa festum sancti Michaelis, venit in Angliam Nicolaus, Tusculanensis episcopus et apostolicæ sedis legatus, ut dissensiones inter regnum et sacerdotium auctoritate apostolica reformaret, et, [reception:] licet terra interdicta fuisset, ubique tamen cum processione solemni et cantuum modulis et indumentis festivis honorifice receptus est; cumque ad Westmonasterium pervenisset, Willelmum abbatem, de dilapidatione et incontinentia a monachis suis accusatum, illico degredavit.'

The prelude sets the stage for Nicholas' authority and mission. He held the position of 'legate of the Apostolic See' ('apostolicæ sedis legatus'). His mission was to 'amend' ('reformaret') the dissension between the 'kingship' ('regnum') and the 'priesthood' ('sacerdotium'), which he had apostolic authority to do: 'with apostolic authority' ('auctoritate apostolica'). Roger portrayed Nicholas as a representative of peace, unity, and order, in contrast to the then present state of discord, dissension, and disunion.

In the second part, Roger demonstrates the recognition of Nicholas' authority: the legate was received honourably everywhere with processions, song, and festive garments. Roger described an *adventus*, 'ticking off' the most important components: special clothing, processions, and singing. These details were all distinctly visual and audible traits, those that a spectator was most likely to notice, and they were also the most overtly ritualistic features, particularly suited to convey meaning and message.

It is unlikely that Roger relied on an *adventus* instruction to compose his account. His continuator, Matthew Paris, mentioned the St Albans copy of Lanfranc's Monastic Constitutions.[93] If Matthew could find it, presumably so could Roger, but there is no indication that he used it. What is striking about Roger's account is the way he summarised and highlighted distinctive traits of the *adventus* to convey a certain message: the account is a prime example of corrosive sarcasm. Roger may have made Nicholas into a representative of peace, unity, and order, but his message was the opposite. To a certain extent, Roger was critical of King John, but his real target was Pope Innocent and his legate. This is abundantly clear from Nicholas' actions in England, as narrated by Roger, and from the way Roger paraphrased some of Innocent's letters, mocking Innocent's claims.

Upon entering England, Nicholas immediately set about increasing his retinue, according to Roger. He came into England 'with only seven horsemen', but he 'in a short time advanced with fifty and was surrounded closely by an excessively great household'.[94] Medieval writers often complained about the size of legatine retinues.[95] Any clergyman would have shuddered at the thought of entertaining a retinue as numerous as the figure provided by Roger. Moreover, the size of Cardinal Nicholas' retinue, as recorded by Roger, blatantly disregarded canon

[93] Matthew Paris, 'Gesta Abbatum', p. 52. Matthew claimed (probably incorrectly) that it was an autograph from Lanfranc's hand; see *The Monastic Constitutions*, pp. xxxiii–xxxiv.

[94] *Flowers of History*, vol. 2, p. 290 (translation adjusted); *Flores Historiarum*, vol. 2, p. 94: 'cum septem tantum equitaturis … quinquaginta in brevi et familia multa nimis stipatus incessit'.

[95] See Ian S. Robinson, *The Papacy 1073–1198: Continuity and Innovation* (Cambridge: Cambridge University Press, 1990), pp. 162–63.

law. Pope Innocent had decreed in the summons to the Fourth Lateran Council less than a year before Cardinal Nicholas' legatine mission that 'you will observe such moderation in your retinue and equipage as has been appointed by the [Third] Lateran Council'.[96] Cardinals were restricted to twenty-five horses.[97] Roger mentioned the limitation in his summary of the Third Lateran.[98]

The legate also alienated the English clergy. During the peace talks, Nicholas was annoyed that the bishops wanted to deliberate on the terms, 'from which it was immediately suspected that the legate agreed more equally with the royal side'.[99] Roger played a trump card: 'with the legate showing favour to the king, he accepted the postponement of all payment'.[100]

Roger accused the legate and the pope of supporting the appointment of the king's men to vacant benefices. He quoted Innocent's order to Nicholas to appoint the king's men to vacant churches.[101] Then:

> The legate, on receiving this authority from the pope, rejected the advice of the archbishop and bishops of the kingdom and, going to the vacant churches with the clerks and agents of the king, presumed to make appointments to them, according to the evil old custom of England, of persons little suited to those offices. Some indeed, of various orders, who, on manifest detriment, appealed to the hearing of the supreme pontiff, he suspended and sent to the court of Rome, and to them, he showed himself so destitute of humanity that he did not allow them even one penny out of their own money to pay their expenses on the journey. Moreover, he distributed the parochial churches which were vacant in various places amongst his own clerks without asking the consent of the patrons, for which he deserved the maledictions of many instead of their benediction, since he changed justice into injury and judgement into pre-judging.[102]

---

[96] Cheney and Semple, *Selected Letters*, no. 51, p. 146: 'personarum et evectionum mediocritate servata quam Lateranense concilium diffinivit'.

[97] Norman P. Tanner, ed., *Decrees of the Ecumenical Councils, Vol. 1: Nicaea I to Lateran V*, 2 vols (London: Sheed & Ward, 1990), c. 4, p. 213.

[98] *Flowers of History*, vol. 2, p. 45; *Flores Historiarum*, vol. 1, p. 119.

[99] *Flowers of History*, vol. 2, p. 290 (translation adjusted); *Flores Historiarum*, vol. 2, p. 94: 'unde protinus suspicatum est, legatum plus æquo parti regiæ consentire.'

[100] *Flowers of History*, vol. 2, p. 291; *Flores Historiarum*, vol. 2, p. 96: 'sed, legato regi favorem præbente, solutio omnium dilationem accepit.'

[101] *Flowers of History*, vol. 2, pp. 291–92; *Flores Historiarum*, vol. 2, p. 96; equivalent to Cheney and Semple, *Selected Letters*, no. 62, pp. 166–67.

[102] *Flowers of History*, vol. 2, p. 292 (translation adjusted); *Flores Historiarum*, vol. 2, pp. 96–97: 'Legatus quoque, cum hujus authenticum a domino papa accepisset, spreto archiepiscopi et episcoporum regni consilio, cum clericis regis et ministris ad vacantes

Nor would Cardinal Nicholas aid the clergy, whose properties and revenues King John had damaged during the interdict:

> The legate, however, in reply to this multitude of complainants, said that no mention had been made in the pope's letters of their losses and injuries, wherefore he ought not and could not lawfully go beyond the bounds of the apostolic mandate; but he nevertheless advised them to lay a complaint about their losses and injuries before the pope and to ask for full justice to be shown to them.[103]

'On hearing this', Roger wrote, 'the whole of that assembly of prelates, having no hope of better luck, returned again to their homes'.[104] Roger knew what the English Church had been through during the interdict,[105] so his presentation of events was designed to convey how the pope and the legate had betrayed the English prelates.

Instances in the *Flores* show that Roger occasionally copied or paraphrased papal letters.[106] Roger's account of the entry of Legate Nicholas shows signs of him having paraphrased papal letters on Nicholas as well as Anglo-Papal relations. One example is the similarity between Roger's phrase 'ut dissensiones inter regnum et sacerdotium auctoritate apostolica reformaret' and Innocent's remark that 'vera pax et plena concordia sit inter regnum et sacerdotium in Anglia reformata'.[107]

> accedens ecclesias, ordinationes earum secundum antiquum Angliæ abusum de personis minus idoneis celebrare præsumpsit; nonnullos vero diversi ordinis, pro gravamine manifesto ad audientiam summi pontificis appellantes, suspensos ad curiam Romanam destinavit, quibus se adeo inhumanum exhibuit, quod de rebus propriis nec quidem denarium unum ad expensas itineris portare permisit. Parochiales insuper ecclesias in locis diversis vacantes clericis suis distribuit, patronorum consensu minime requisito; unde multorum maledictionem pro benedictione promeruit, dum justitiam in injuriam, judicium in præjudicium, commutavit.'

[103] *Flowers of History*, vol. 2, p. 297; *Flores Historiarum*, vol. 2, pp. 103–4: 'Legatus vero universæ multitudini conquerentium ita respondit, quod, videlicet, de damnis eorum et injuriis in literis domini papæ nulla mentio facta fuerat, unde nec debuit nec de jure potuit mandati apostolici fines præterire; sed tamen consilium dedit, ut de injuriis et damnis comram domino papa querelam deponerent, et peterent sibi justitiæ plenitudinem exhiberi.'

[104] *Flowers of History*, vol. 2, p. 297; *Flores Historiarum*, vol. 2, p. 104: 'his ... auditis, universitas illa conquerentium prælatorum sine spe melioris boni ad propria sunt reversi.' See also Cheney, *Pope Innocent III and England*, pp. 353–55.

[105] *Flowers of History*, vol. 2, pp. 245–47, 250–51, 259–60; *Flores Historiarum*, vol. 2, pp. 45–48, 52–53, 63–64.

[106] For copying, see, e.g., *Flowers of History*, vol. 2, pp. 241–44; *Flores Historiarum*, vol. 2, pp. 41–44, equivalent to Cheney and Semple, *Selected Letters*, no. 29, pp. 86–90. For paraphrasing, see, e.g., *Flowers of History*, vol. 2, p. 245; *Flores Historiarum*, vol. 2, pp. 44–45. It is a paraphrasing of Cheney and Semple, *Selected Letters*, no. 34, pp. 102–3.

[107] Cheney and Semple, *Selected Letters*, no. 57, p. 157: 'in order to amend the dissension

Innocent addressed the letter to all Irish prelates and laymen, including the 'people' ('populis'), informing them that John was back in Innocent's good grace. Other expressions from Innocent's letters that Roger may have paraphrased include 'ad reconciliationem regis ac regni venerabilem fratrem nostrum Tusculanum episcopum, apostolice sedis legatum, quasi pacis et salutis angelum destinemus' and 'ut bonum pacis tam regno quam sacerdotio maxime necessarium feliciter consummetur'.[108] The letter (no. 55) is part of a series of near-identical letters in which the pope commended Cardinal Nicholas to King John (no. 53) and the bishops of England (no. 54). At the very least, Roger embedded echoes of Innocent's statements in his own account. Roger, however, went one step further by twisting these statements into mocking puns: he presented Cardinal Nicholas as an apostolic saviour at the *adventus*, but he simultaneously derided Innocent's picture of the legate as a benevolent apostolic prince. Roger composed a narrative in which all the English received Nicholas honourably and devotedly, only to eventually realise that they had received a wolf instead of a shepherd. Nicholas should have been a benevolent lord, but he instead sowed dissension and caused scandal.

The *adventus* also contained a possession-taking aspect. Through their presence and participation, the English had acknowledged Nicholas' authority. Roger, who was aware of the vassalage,[109] constructed his account of the reception in such a way as to make the possession-taking and Nicholas' authority as comprehensive as possible. Roger chose his words and his phrases carefully.

Roger also stretched time and space. He reported that the 'country' ('terra') had been under interdict, but that the legate was received honourably 'everywhere' ('ubique'). 'Everywhere' was 'everywhere on the way to Westminster', but it suggested more than that. 'Everywhere' was blurry and imprecise, creating an impression of a wider reception across the country.

Roger used the same narrative strategy when describing the recipients of the legate. The legate 'was received honourably' ('honorifice receptus est') – note the use of passive voice, with the passive construction blurring the identities of those doing the receiving. Again, Roger was obviously referring to those along

---

between the kingship and the priesthood with apostolic authority' and 'true peace and full harmony have been restored between the kingdom and priesthood in England', respectively.

[108] Cheney and Semple, *Selected Letters*, no. 55, p. 154: 'to reconcile king and kingdom, we are sending as legate of the Apostolic See a very angel of peace and salvation, our venerable brother the bishop of Tusculum' and 'so that the blessing of peace which is most necessary both for the kingdom and the priesthood may be happily attained', respectively.

[109] *Flowers of History*, vol. 2, pp. 258–59, 264–65, 268–70, 273–75, 290–91; *Flores Historiarum*, vol. 2, pp. 62–63, 69–70, 74–77, 80–82, 95–96.

the road to Westminster, but his textual indistinctness creates an impression of comprehensiveness. Nicholas reported to Innocent that he landed at Dover, where Archbishop Stephen received him. They travelled to London together, where the king came out to meet the cardinal,[110] most likely making the journey in a matter of days. The Waverley Annals place Nicholas' arrival on 27 September and his convening of a council in London on 30 September.[111] Nicholas reported that Archbishop Stephen met him at Dover 'with the necessary horses' ('cum equis necessariis').[112] The distance from Dover to London via Canterbury is around 70–75 miles, which was probably doable in a matter of days. Nicholas' letter is also in line with what most chroniclers usually reported: single receptions at specific places.

Together, the blurriness of distance, space, and participants alluded to a wider English acceptance of legatine authority, as distance, area, and crowd size were important elements of the *adventus*. Cardinal Boso employed a similar strategy in his account of the travels of the three cardinal-legates. His message was also one of possession-taking, although his account of it was more positive than Roger's. A few carefully chosen words or strategically placed omissions of specific locations can generate a particular narrative thrust. Sometimes the lack of specificity is just that – holding no meaning for the narrative or indicative of the writer being unaware of certain details – but when these details impact a significant ritual of power, it is worth considering their implications. In this case, the vagueness worked in Roger's favour, enticing his audience – rather than forcefully insisting – to accept his view of events.

The demotion of Abbot William of Westminster at the conclusion of the *adventus* symbolised a demotion of royal authority. Since 1066, Westminster had been the royal church of coronation. In that year, both claimants to the English crown, Harold Godwinson (r. 1066) and William the Conqueror, had in turn used Westminster for their coronations. Both had chosen Westminster because it was the burial place of King Edward (r. 1042–66), the last undisputed king. Coronations still take place at Westminster. Though the Angevins had little regard for Westminster, King John least of all (throwing some interpretative caution into the equation),[113] it is difficult to perceive the demotion as anything but a symbolic

---

[110] Angelo Mercati, 'La Prima Relazione del Cardinale Nicolò de Romanis sulla sua legazione in Inghilterra', in *Essays in History Presented to Reginald Lane Poole*, ed. H. W. C. Davis (Oxford: Clarendon Press, 1927), pp. 274–89, at pp. 277–78.

[111] Henry Richards Luard, ed., 'Annales de Waverleia', in *AM*, 5 vols, RS (London: Longman, 1865), vol. 2, pp. 129–411, at p. 277.

[112] Mercati, 'La prima relazione', p. 277.

[113] See Emma Mason, *Westminster Abbey and Its People, c.1050–c.1216* (Woodbridge: Boydell Press, 1996), pp. 269–87; and Barbara Harvey, *Westminster Abbey and Its Estates in the Middle Ages* (Oxford: Clarendon Press, 1977), p. 25. Henry III spent enormous

attack on John's regality. At a previous point in the *Flores*, Roger had even claimed that John was no longer king from the moment he offered England to the papacy.[114]

Roger's account of the demotion of Abbot William of Westminster also contains some stretching of the time. Nicholas did not actually demote the abbot until three months after his arrival, not immediately ('illico') as Roger reported.[115] This compression of time conveyed a certain impression about the legate's exercise of his powers. After taking possession of England, the legate immediately began making significant decisions without seeking advice or following due process.

The name of the abbot was not William, but Ralph Arundel. It was probably a mistake on Roger's part, as both the successor and predecessor at Westminster were named William.[116] However, it is tempting to speculate (and only that) as to whether this was also a Freudian slip. Another abbot named William, William of Trumpington, demoted Roger. Roger may have wished that the legate had actually demoted William of Trumpington.

A perhaps surprising implication of Roger's narrative is the overt recognition of legatine authority. The *Flores* emphatically acknowledges the English recognition of the legate's authority and powers, even if there is a note of despair in it, especially in the reports on Nicholas' actions in England. Roger's description of the English clergy's reaction to the cardinal can best be described as resignation in the face of the overwhelming powers of the legate and the pope. Given Roger's hostility to those powers, it would perhaps have seemed more natural if he had minimised their influence or glossed over them, but he chose to double down on the misfortune that had befallen England. Notably, he had the French nobles exclaim that they would oppose a king's right to make his kingdom tributary, 'by which the nobles of the kingdom would become slaves' ('unde nobiles regni efficerentur servi').[117] Roger genuinely believed that the English nobles had become *servi*, slaves or, interpreted in a slightly more positive light, servants or serfs. Altogether this made Roger's sarcasm more acrid and more transgressive. Roger bemoaned that Nicholas did not, in reality, come 'in order to amend the dissensions between the kingship and the priesthood' ('ut dissensiones inter regnum et

---

sums on Westminster, but only from the 1240s onwards; see Suzanne Lewis, 'Henry III and the Gothic Rebuilding of Westminster Abbey: The Problematics of Context', *Traditio* 50 (1995): 129–72.

[114] This is the point of the convoluted story of Peter the Hermit; see *Flowers of History*, vol. 2, pp. 258, 264–65, 270; *Flores Historiarum*, vol. 2, pp. 62, 68–70, 77.

[115] See Mason, *Westminster Abbey and Its People*, pp. 131–32; and Harvey, *Westminster Abbey and Its Estates*, pp. 83–84.

[116] See David Knowles, Christopher Nugent Lawrence Brooke, and Vera C. M. London, *The Heads of Religious Houses, England and Wales*, 2nd edn (Cambridge: Cambridge University Press, 2001), vol. 1, p. 77; and Mason, *Westminster Abbey and Its People*, pp. 67–78.

[117] *Flowers of History*, vol. 2, p. 362; *Flores Historiarum*, vol. 2, p. 177

sacerdotium ... reformaret').[118] The pope could have dispatched a legate to 'amend the dissensions', but he did not. In this way, Roger's account also evolved into a direct attack on the self-perception of the papacy.

Papal monarchy revolved around authority – of course – but pastoral care mattered as well, as Brenda Bolton has shown.[119] In a letter to King John, dated 4 November 1213, Pope Innocent asserted that 'in the heart of the Supreme Pontiff ... are punitive severity and delightful goodwill'. The pope went on: 'he [the pope] visits sternness upon the rebellious and stubborn while showing kindness to the lowly and repentant'.[120] Roger never mentioned this letter nor quoted from it, but even if he knew nothing about the letter, it did not express an exclusive papal attitude to authority and pastoral care: the letter aligned with Benedictine notions. The Rule of St Benedict prescribed a duality between sternness and care. Chapter 2 of the Rule ordained that 'he [the abbot] must vary with circumstances, threatening and coaxing by turns, stern as a taskmaster, devoted and tender as only a father can be'.[121] Moreover:

> With the undisciplined and restless, he [the abbot] will use firm argument; with the obedient and docile and patient, he [the abbot] will appeal for greater virtue; but as for the negligent and disdainful, we [St Benedict] charge him [the abbot] to use reproof and rebuke.[122]

Gransden argues that Matthew Paris, Roger's continuator, 'regarded the ideas he had as a Benedictine as equally applicable to all parts [of society]'. Accordingly, 'monastery, kingdom and papacy represented the same static pattern of government on a progressively large scale'.[123] Matthew presumably adopted this notion from Roger, if it was not simply a widespread Benedictine attitude. If nothing else, Roger projected the values of the Benedictine abbot on to the pope, judging the pope and his legate accordingly.

---

[118] *Flowers of History*, vol. 2, p. 289; *Flores Historiarum*, vol. 2, pp. 93–94.

[119] See, e.g., Brenda M. Bolton, *Innocent III: Studies on Papal Authority and Pastoral Care* (Aldershot: Variorum, 1995).

[120] Cheney and Semple, *Selected Letters*, no. 63, p. 168 (translation adjusted): 'in pectore summi pontificis ... rigor districtionis et favor dulcedinis continentur' and 'in rebelles et induratos severitatem exerceat quod benignitatem exhibeat erga humiles et correctos.'

[121] *Rule of Benedict*, ch. 2, 24, translation at p. 61, Latin at p. 59: 'miscens temporibus tempora, terroribus blandimenta, dirum magistri, pium patris ostendat affectum.' See also Clark, *The Benedictines*, pp. 113–14.

[122] Ibid., ch. 2, 25, translation at p. 61, Latin at p. 59: 'id est indisciplinatis et inquietos debet durius arguere, oboedientes autem et mites et patientes ut in melius proficiant obsecrare, neglegentes et contemnentes ut increpat et corripiat admonemus.'

[123] Gransden, *Historical Writing*, p. 373.

The pope and the legate were found wanting. Roger quoted one of Innocent's letters to John about the Langton affair. In it, the pope encouraged John to show humility, one of the most important Benedictine (and Christian) virtues:[124] 'we [Pope Innocent], moreover, if you [John] with proper humility acquiesce in our wishes, will take care that no injury shall happen to you in this matter'.[125] But Roger did not believe John was humble. He was 'negligent and disdainful', while the English ecclesiastics were 'obedient and docile and patient'. The papal legate (as an extension of the pope) was the abbot of Roger's projection, and when he arrived, the English showed him due honour: 'he was honourably received' ('honorifice receptus est'). A worthy abbot would have exalted the humble and humbled the self-exalted. Instead, Cardinal Nicholas exalted the wicked and trampled on the humble and downtrodden. He failed the English, who had received him as the ruler of the land. Instead of arriving as a benevolent prince, the legate had come as a tyrant. Seen through the eyes of Roger, there is a hollow ring to Innocent's assertion that Nicholas was an 'angel of peace and salvation'.[126]

Conclusion

Roger of Wendover framed his perspective on the legatine *adventus* and the circumstances surrounding it within a complex web of experiences and historical themes. These included the actions of Abbot William and Cardinal-Legate Nicholas, the contrasts between the reigns of Richard and John, and the initial lack of awareness among the English regarding the collusion between the king and the pope.

Roger penned his account of Nicholas' reception some fifteen years after the event. While it is impossible to know the state of Roger's mind in 1213, it is reasonable to assume that hindsight influenced his presentation of the past. Hindsight allowed Roger to apply a thought-through interpretative framework to the events. Interestingly, the initial unawareness of the papal-legatine miscarriage of justice among the English, in Roger's account, might very well reflect a historical reality: the English clergy had bled for the pope, metaphorically, and they expected to be rewarded for their sacrifices, only to be disappointed. Roger wove this notion into the portrayal of Cardinal Nicholas' reception. He depicted the event as predominantly shaped by social consensus, yet left subtle hints that not everything was as it seemed.

The St Albans experience with Cardinal-Legate Nicholas might also have influenced the framework of Roger's narrative. Cardinal Nicholas had arrived at St

---

[124] See *Rule of Benedict*, ch. 7, pp. 135–71.
[125] *Flowers of History*, vol. 2, p. 244 (translation adjusted); *Flores Historiarum*, vol. 2, p. 44: 'nos autem, si nobis humiliter adquieveris, sufficienter tibi et tuis providere curabimus, ne super hoc valeat vobis aliquid præjudicium generari.'
[126] Cheney and Semple, *Selected Letters*, no. 55, p. 154: 'pacis et salutis angelum'.

Albans abbey in the midst of strife between the monks and the abbot about the abbot's powers and authority. The legate had sided with the abbot. Moreover, Abbot William had been the one to demote Roger from his priorate at Belvoir. The parallels between these dynamics at St Albans and the broader situation in England are hard to overlook, especially considering Roger's inclination to organise the world in parallels. In both instances, an external figure of power (a legate) arrived at a political unit (England and St Albans, respectively) and sided with the head of the community (the king and the abbot, respectively) against the ordinary members of the community (the English clergy and the monks of St Albans, respectively). In both instances, the members of the community had reason to expect otherwise, as they had justice on their side (as they saw it). In both instances, it was even the same cardinal-legate. While it is impossible to substantiate this hypothesis, it fits the broader narrative.

Within this framework, Roger positioned himself among the clergy, witnessing the subjugation of England to the pope. The head of the community, the king, conspired with the dignitary, the legate/pope, to make slaves of the community, the English. This solidarity at the top aligned with the priorities of the *adventus* instructions. Roger indirectly critiqued the notion that upholding the hierarchy was a paramount concern – at least if the hierarchy was corrupt and oppressive.

Roger's writings elucidate the importance of narrative strategy, experience, and history in shaping interpretations of the legatine *adventus*. In that sense, his authorship is similar to that of Gervase, but their divergent perspectives lead to radically different conclusions. Gervase viewed the papacy as a force for righteousness and justice in the world. In his Benedictine tale, the papacy would elevate the humble monks and discipline the proud archbishop. In Roger's Benedictine story, it was the opposite. The papacy elevated the proud and wicked, while trampling on the humble and patient.

Roger aligned with the curial understanding of the legatine *adventus* in so far as he saw it as a validation of legatine authority, even a possession-taking of England on behalf of the pope. Roger did not dispute that this had de facto occurred, but he twisted the legatine *adventus* into a mockery of its original meaning and intention. The legate had promised healing and cooperation, yet delivered only abuses and oppression. The account of Legate Nicholas arriving to heal England, travelling the land and being 'received honourably everywhere', is dripping with corrosive sarcasm.

7

Choosing Submission: Matthew Paris and the Foolishness of the English

Matthew Paris was the literary heir of Roger of Wendover, whom he spent around a decade with at St Albans.[1] Matthew inherited Roger's view of the vassalage, his use of parallels and contrasts, and his inclination towards exaggeration and the use of hyperbole. However, Matthew was far more than a mere successor and continuator. He extended the condemnation of the papacy and the English clergy well beyond Roger's scope. Matthew's condemnation of the nature of the Anglo-Papal relationship reached unprecedented heights, and his view of King Henry III bordered on the treasonous.

All this came to the forefront as Matthew reported on the reception of Legate Otto de Tonengo, cardinal-deacon of S. Nicola in Carcere. Otto arrived in England in the summer of 1237, and did not depart until January 1241. Matthew viewed the mere anticipation of Otto's arrival as a catalyst for the kingdom becoming 'divided and dismantled' ('divisum et dissipatum').[2] However, Matthew did not only blame the papacy for this rupture; forces within England shared in the blame.

Matthew viewed the reception of the legate from the point of view of the English dissidents – those who declined to welcome the legate and to acknowledge his authority. This, as will be seen below, was likely an illusion, in the sense that Matthew employed the dissident perspective to engineer a division within the English community that did not exist or only existed on the fringes of the English polity. This dissident perspective facilitated his attack on the king and the English prelates, whose acceptance of the legate he regarded as a voluntary act of unnatural submission. The acceptance highlighted their spineless response to papal demands. Not only did Matthew deride and ridicule the pope and the legate, but he also took aim at the English prelates and their king. Matthew's account of the arrival of Legate Otto underlines how the legatine *adventus* could be construed not only as a commentary on the legate, but primarily as a comment on those

---

[1] See pp. 189–90.
[2] Matthew Paris, *CM*, vol. 3, p. 395.

welcoming him. While Roger of Wendover focused on the papacy and the legate, Matthew centred his attention on the king and the English prelates.

Matthew Paris and His Authorship

Matthew Paris was probably born around 1200, taking the monastic habit at St Albans in 1217. He died in 1259. Beyond these details, not much personal information about him has survived. No information about his family exists. Scholars previously believed that his patronym, *Parisiensis* or *de Parisius* (of Paris), referred to his birthplace, but Richard Vaughan has shown that it is very unlikely to be the case.[3]

Matthew made a name for himself within his convent and among the powerful people of the age. He never held any monastic office, but his work as a historian and chronicler was prestigious. Like Roger, Matthew was well placed to gather information and survey developments in England and abroad.[4] He mingled with many dignitaries, including King Henry, who often frequented St Albans. Queen Eleanor (r. 1236–72) at one point sent him a present.[5] Vaughan identifies forty-six contacts, including Robert Grosseteste, bishop of Lincoln (r. 1235–53), Earl Richard (1209–72), the king's half-brother, and Isabella, countess of Arundel.[6] Matthew was a specialist in banking and finance, at one point travelling to Norway to help turn around the fortunes of the debt-ridden abbey of Nidarholm.[7]

Matthew composed several chronicles, including the *Chronica Majora* (his magnum opus), the *Historia Anglorum*, the *Flores Historiarum* (not to be confused with Roger's work of the same name), and the *Abbreviatio Chronicarum*. He collected documents (the *Liber Additamentorum*) and composed a history of the abbots of St Albans (the *Gesta Abbatum*) as well as several Latin and Anglo-Norman saints' lives.[8] He wrote the 'Life of St Edward' for Queen Eleanor.[9]

---

[3] Richard Vaughan, *Matthew Paris* (Cambridge: Cambridge University Press, 1958), pp. 1–11.
[4] See Julie Kerr, *Monastic Hospitality: The Benedictines in England, c.1070–c.1250* (Woodbridge: Boydell Press, 2007), pp. 80–85; and Vaughan, *Matthew Paris*, p. 11.
[5] Vaughan, *Matthew Paris*, pp. 11–20, 137, 143, 261–65; Matthew Paris, *CM*, vol. 6, p. 391.
[6] Vaughan, *Matthew Paris*, pp. 12–17.
[7] See Björn K. U. Weiler, 'Matthew Paris in Norway', *Revue Bénédictine* 122, no. 1 (2012): 153–81.
[8] For a succinct overview, see Björn K. U. Weiler, 'Matthew Paris on the Writing of History', *JMH* 35, no. 3 (2009): 254–78, pp. 254–56.
[9] Rebecca Reader, 'Matthew Paris and Women', in *TCE VII*, ed. Michael Prestwich, Richard Britnell, and Robin Frame (Woodbridge: Boydell Press, 1999), pp. 153–59, at p. 157; Antonia Gransden, *Historical Writing in England c.550–c.1307* (London: Routledge, 1974), pp. 357–59.

Matthew was also a superb artist and cartographer, producing what Björn Weiler describes as some of the 'foremost examples of English Gothic manuscript art'.[10]

As a historian, Matthew was the heir to Roger of Wendover, whom he must have known personally: they lived together at St Albans for around ten years.[11] Perhaps Roger instructed Matthew in the chronicler's trade? Like Roger, Matthew considered history to be a record of pious deeds to emulate and sinful deeds to shun.[12] The purpose behind historical writing was moral instruction and spiritual benefits:

> For it is good, to the praise of God, to preserve in writing the events of notable things, in order that those coming after by reading may be warned to avoid evil things, which deserve punishment, and encouraged to do good things, which God will fully reward.[13]

Matthew's Benedictine vocation informed his worldview in much the same way as it informed his predecessor. According to Antonia Gransden, Matthew believed that one could infer the condition of every organisation from the Benedictine monastery. A king should listen to his councillors, just as an abbot should take the advice of his monks: they were micro/macrocosms of each other. This was true for the papacy as well. The pope, like the king and the abbot, should live off his own property, and taxation was unlawful unless agreed to freely. Abbeys and kingdoms were autonomous units. An abbey was (partially) subject to the diocesan – customs and liberties regulated the exact relationship – while a kingdom was autonomous in matters temporal. The pope held authority in matters spiritual, but he should exercise authority with due respect to customs and liberties.[14]

Matthew's most important work was the *Chronica Majora*. It began as a continuation of Roger's *Flores Historiarum*, but later evolved into a separate work

---

[10] Weiler, 'Matthew Paris on the Writing of History', pp. 255–56. On his art, see Suzanne Lewis, *The Art of Matthew Paris in the Chronica Majora* (Berkeley and Los Angeles: University of California Press, 1987).

[11] Gransden, *Historical Writing*, pp. 368–69.

[12] See Weiler, 'Matthew Paris on the Writing of History', pp. 257–63.

[13] Matthew Paris, 'Abbreviatio Chronicorum Angliæ', in *Matthæi Parisiensis, monachi Sancti Albani, Historia Anglorum, sive, ut vulgo dicitur, Historia Minor. Item, ejusdem Abbreviatio Chronicorum Angliæ*, ed. Frederic Madden, RS (London: Longmans, 1869), vol. 3, pp. 151–348, at p. 319: 'Bonum quippe est ad Dei laudem eventus rerum notabilium scribendo perpetuare, ut subsequentes legendo castigentur, mala quae digna sunt ultione devitando, et bona quæ Dominus plene remunerat operando.' Translated by David A. Carpenter, 'Chronology and Truth: Matthew Paris and the *Chronica Majora*', in *Matthew Paris Essays*, ed. James Clark, forthcoming, p. 10; available at https://fine-rollshenry3.org.uk/redist/pdf/Chronologyandtruth3.pdf (accessed 15 August 2023).

[14] Gransden, *Historical Writing*, pp. 371–74.

in its own right. Building on the work of Miriam Weiss,[15] Nathan Greasley has recently reconsidered the compositional history of the *Chronica*. He argues that the traditional understanding of the composition of the *Chronica* as a two-stage process is wrong – it was a three-stage process. Matthew first revised Roger's *Flores Historiarum* slightly, inserting a few additional pieces of information. This was probably done before 1237. Matthew only returned to it in 1247, expanding greatly upon the work, turning it into the *Chronica Majora*. He closed the *Chronica* contemporaneously with events in 1250. He then produced a number of abbreviations and revisions, that is, his other chronicles, before returning to the *Chronica* for the third time some years later, writing as events unfolded when he died in April 1259.[16] The traditional perception of the composition, mostly the work of Vaughan,[17] combines stages one and two, setting a date for the beginning of the composition to the first half of the 1240s, but is otherwise in line with Greasley. For the purpose of this study, the main takeaway is that Matthew viewed the reception of Otto and his legatine mission in hindsight, whatever reconstruction of the compilation process one believes.

The *Chronica* is primarily a chronicle of England and the English, even if Matthew was conscious of England as part of Christendom.[18] The text covers a variety of subjects, but two issues are especially important: the aliens in English politics and the subjection to the papacy.[19] The first issue was not only about papal nominees to English benefices but also about King Henry's policy of extending patronage to his French wife's relatives and their connections. This policy led to intense competition between a recurrent influx of foreigners and the English

---

[15] See Miriam Weiss, *Die* Chronica maiora *des* Matthaeus Parisiensis (Trier: Kliomedia, 2018).

[16] Nathan Greasley, 'Revisiting the Compilation of Matthew Paris's *Chronica Majora*: New Textual and Manuscript Evidence', *JMH* 47, no. 2 (2021): 230–56.

[17] Vaughan, *Matthew Paris*, esp. pp. 52–63, 66–67, 102–3, 112–13.

[18] See Björn K. U. Weiler, 'How Unusual Was Matthew Paris? The Writing of Universal History in Angevin England', in *Universal Chronicles in the High Middle Ages*, ed. Michele Campopiano and Henry Bainton (York: York Medieval Press, 2017), pp. 199–222, esp. pp. 209–11.

[19] Examples of studies on various subjects include Hans-Eberhard Hilpert, 'Zu den Prophetien im Geschichtswerk des Matthaeus Paris', *Deutsches Archiv für Erforschung des Mittelalters* 41, no. 1 (1985): 175–91; Rebecca Reader, 'Matthew Paris and the Norman Conquest', in *The Cloister and the World: Essays in Medieval History in Honour of Barbara Harvey*, ed. John Blair and Brian Golding (Oxford: Clarendon Press, 1996), pp. 118–47; Paul Binski, 'The Faces of Christ in Matthew Paris's Chronica Majora', in *Tributes in Honour of James H. Marrow: Studies in Painting and Manuscript Illumination of the Late Middle Ages and Northern Renaissance*, ed. Jeffrey Hamburger and Anne Korteweg (London: Harvey Miller, 2006), 85–92; Daniel K. Connolly, *The Maps of Matthew Paris: Medieval Journeys through Space, Time and Liturgy* (Woodbridge: Boydell Press, 2009); and Zsuzsanna Papp Reed, *Matthew Paris on the Mongol Invasion in Europe* (Turnhout: Brepols, 2022).

baronage.[20] Embittered by the competition, the barons mounted a coup in 1258.[21] Matthew feared the outbreak of civil war, but still sided with the barons.[22] Nothing underlines Matthew's disdain for King Henry more than this.

Matthew also abhorred the enfeoffment of England. In the *Gesta Abbatum*, he wrote that King John had rendered himself 'wretchedly tributary' ('infeliciter tributarium').[23] Even in the *Historia Anglorum*, which he likely composed for a royal audience,[24] Matthew opined that the charter of submission 'should be detested for all time' ('omnibus seculis detestandam').[25] Matthew was particularly outspoken in the *Chronica*, asserting that King Henry allowed himself to be under the papacy's undue influence:

> But the king, however, as he had begun, spurning his [Earl Richard's] advice as that of his other natural men, raved more and more; and he assigned himself so much to the volition of the Romans, especially the legate [Cardinal Otto], whom he had ill-advisedly summoned, that he seemed almost to worship his footsteps; declaring himself both in public and private, that he could arrange, change, or alienate nothing concerning the kingdom without the consent of his lord the pope or the legate [Otto], that he might be said not to be a king but a vassal of the pope.[26]

---

[20] Huw W. Ridgeway, 'King Henry III and the "Aliens", 1236–1272', in *TCE II*, ed. P. R. Coss and S. D. Lloyd (Woodbridge: Boydell Press, 1988), pp. 81–92; Huw W. Ridgeway, 'Foreign Favourites and Henry III's Problems of Patronage, 1247–1258', *EHR* 104, no. 412 (1989): 590–610; Margaret Howell, *Eleanor of Provence: Queenship in Thirteenth-Century England* (Oxford: Blackwell, 1998), pp. 22–26, 30–70; Harold S. Snellgrove, *The Lusignans in England 1247–1258*, vol. 2 (Albuquerque: University of New Mexico Press, 1950); David A. Carpenter, *The Reign of Henry III* (London: The Hambledon Press, 1996), pp. 261–80; David A. Carpenter, *Henry III: The Rise to Power and Personal Rule 1207–1258* (New Haven: Yale University Press, 2020), pp. 672–99, esp. pp. 688–99. See also Eugene L. Cox, *The Eagles of Savoy: The House of Savoy in Thirteenth-Century Europe* (Princeton: Princeton University Press, 1974).

[21] Carpenter, *Henry III: The Rise to Power*, pp. 675–99; Adrian Jobson, *The First English Revolution: Simon de Montfort, Henry III and the Barons' War* (London: Bloomsbury, 2012), pp. 5–27; J. R. Maddicott, *Simon de Montfort* (Cambridge: Cambridge University Press, 1994), esp. pp. 147–72.

[22] Carpenter, 'Chronology and Truth', pp. 15–22.

[23] Matthew Paris, 'Gesta Abbatum', in *Gesta abbatum monasterii Sancti Albani, a Thoma Walsingham, regnante Ricardo Secundo, ejusdem ecclesiæ præcentore, compilata*, ed. Henry Thomas Riley, 3 vols, RS (London: Longmans, 1867), vol. 1, pp. 3–324, at p. 229.

[24] Weiler, 'Matthew Paris on the Writing of History', pp. 276–77; Vaughan, *Matthew Paris*, pp. 123–24.

[25] Matthew Paris, *Matthæi Parisiensis, monachi Sancti Albani, Historia Anglorum, sive, ut vulgo dicitur, Historia Minor. Item, ejusdem Abbreviatio Chronicorum Angliæ*, ed. Frederic Madden, 3 vols, RS (London: Longmans, 1866), vol. 2, p. 135.

[26] Matthew Paris, *EH*, vol. 1, p. 68 (translation adjusted); Matthew Paris, *CM*, vol. 3, p. 412:

Historians disagree on the *Chronica*'s target audience. Matthew's outspokenness, particularly the attacks on King Henry, made the *Chronica* practically unexportable,[27] prompting Carpenter to argue that 'the monks of St Albans were clearly the first and primary audience'.[28] This is a belief given some credence by Matthew's assertion at the *Chronica*'s original conclusion that he had written it 'out of love for God and for the honour of St Alban, the English protomartyr'.[29] Weiss, on the other hand, argues that Matthew might have had a wider English audience in mind, perhaps all English secular and ecclesiastical literates.[30] Furthermore, erasures and changes in the text indicate that Matthew might have changed his mind during the process of composition.[31] Whomever Matthew had in mind, it is likely that most literates at the time would have understood his allusions, scriptural references, and ritual subversions.

England and the Papacy at the Time of Matthew Paris

Matthew grew up during a time of political turmoil. Most cross-channel possessions were lost in 1204, the Stephen Langton affair broke out in 1207, and King John enfeoffed England to the papacy in 1213. Military disaster in France led to civil war and invasion, which culminated in the year Matthew joined St Albans (1217). The legates Nicholas, Guala, and Pandulf were heavily involved in these affairs.[32] Archbishop Stephen Langton, himself a cardinal, apparently grew so tired of the legatine involvement that he made Pope Honorius III, according to the Annals of Dunstable, promise that he would dispatch no new legates to England within Langton's lifetime once Pandulf's legation terminated.[33] When in 1225 the pope set in motion plans for a new financial scheme, he dispatched Otto de Tonengo as

---

'Sed rex, tam ejus quam aliorum naturalium hominum suorum spreto consilio, magis ac magis, ut incepit, deliravit; et se voluntati Romanorum præcipue legati, quem inconsultius advocaverat, mancipavit adeo, ut videretur quasi vestigia sua adorare; affirmans se tam in publico quam secreto, sine domini sui Papæ vel legati consensu, nil posse de regno disponere, transmutare, vel alienare, ut non rex, sed feodarius Papæ diceretur.'

[27] Vaughan, *Matthew Paris*, pp. 49–61, 64–65, 117–24, 153–54; Gransden, *Historical Writing*, pp. 370–71; Carpenter, 'Chronology and Truth', pp. 13–15.

[28] Carpenter, 'Chronology and Truth', p. 14.

[29] Matthew Paris, *EH*, vol. 1, p. 121 (translation adjusted); Matthew Paris, *CM*, vol. 3, p. 476: 'Dei pro amore et beati Albani Anglorum prothomartyris honore'.

[30] Weiss, *Die* Chronica maiora, pp. 181–88.

[31] See Vaughan, *Matthew Paris*, pp. 117–20; and Carpenter, 'Chronology and Truth', pp. 12–14.

[32] See pp. 168–74.

[33] Henry Richards Luard, ed., 'Annales de Dunstaplia', in *AM*, 5 vols, RS (London: Longman, 1866), vol. 3, pp. 3–408, at p. 74.

nuncio to England, but Cardinal-Deacon Romanus as legate *a latere* to France.[34] Neither Honorius nor Gregory IX appointed any resident legates to England.[35] Sixteen years would pass from the termination of Pandulf's legation (1221) until Cardinal-Legate Otto came to England. This was the longest continuous period without legatine presence since the Norman invasion.[36] Legates, in the meantime, travelled mainly to Germany (to ease tensions with the emperor) and France (to combat the Albigensian heresy).[37]

In England, resentment towards the papacy grew. As mentioned, Italian and other foreign clergy were subjected to a range of attacks in 1231 and 1232.[38] Papal taxation also became an issue. Traditionally, the only papal tax on England had been Peter's pence, paid by the king annually.[39] Another tax of 1,000 marks annually had been added on the king as a result of the vassalage. The payments had fallen into arrears during the civil war (1215–17), but even after Henry III had finally cleared the debt in 1225, he continuously struggled to pay.[40] From the time of Pope Alexander III, the papacy also slowly began taxing the English Church. Taxation began inconspicuously with a request for a subsidy in 1173. These payments were analogous to the aids subjects contributed to their lord in times of need.[41] Another request followed in 1184. In 1199, Pope Innocent III imposed a

---

[34] On Romanus' mission to France, see Richard Kay, *The Council of Bourges, 1225: A Documentary History* (Aldershot: Ashgate, 2002).

[35] Heinrich Zimmermann, *Die päpstliche Legation in der ersten Hälfte des 13. Jahrhunderts: Vom Regierungsantritt Innocenz' III. bis zum Tode Gregors IX. (1198–1241)* (Paderborn: Ferdinand Schöningh, 1913), pp. 100–3, 134–40.

[36] See Helene Tillmann, *Die päpstlichen Legaten in England bis zur Beendigung der Legation Gualas, 1218* (Bonn: Hch. Ludwig, 1926), pp. 5–120.

[37] See Zimmermann, *Die päpstliche Legation*, pp. 72–140. On the Albigensians (the Cathars), see, e.g., Malcolm Lambert, *The Cathars* (Oxford: Blackwell, 1998).

[38] Hugh MacKenzie, 'The Anti-Foreign Movement in England, 1231–1232', in *Anniversary Essays in Medieval History by Students of Charles Homer Haskins Presented on His Completion of Forty Years of Teaching*, ed. Charles H. Taylor and John Life La Monte (Boston, MA: Houghton Mifflin Company, 1929), pp. 183–203; Oscar Albert Marti, 'Popular Protest and Revolt against Papal Finance in England from 1226 to 1258', *The Princeton Theological Review* (1927): 610–29; Frederick Maurice Powicke, *King Henry III and the Lord Edward: The Community of the Realm in the Thirteenth Century*, 2nd edn, 2 vols (Oxford: Clarendon Press, 1966), vol. 1, pp. 274–89, esp. pp. 278–79. See also Carpenter, *The Reign of Henry III*, pp. 260–80.

[39] William E. Lunt, *Financial Relations of the Papacy with England to 1327* (Cambridge, MA: The Mediaeval Academy of America, 1939), pp. 3–84. For the discretionary nature of papal finance, see Benedict Wiedemann, 'The Character of Papal Finance at the Turn of the Twelfth Century', *EHR* 133, no. 562 (2018): 503–32.

[40] Lunt, *Financial Relations*, pp. 134–48.

[41] Ibid., pp. 175–76.

one-off tax on ecclesiastical revenue.[42] He would only ask again in 1215, but then demands and requests followed in 1217, 1226, 1228, and possibly 1229.[43] In 1225, Otto, not yet a cardinal, came to England as a papal nuncio to make an offer to the English clergy: all major churches would set aside prebends and income for the papacy; in return, litigation at the curia would be free of charge. The English rejected the suggestion (as did the French, who received a similar offer).[44] Papal demands and requests followed in 1238, in 1239, in 1241, twice in 1244, and in 1245, at which point the English prelates protested vehemently.[45] They argued that taxation might lead to the lapse of divine service, starvation, murder, and theft.[46] The pope ordered another subsidy in 1246, but then, probably as a result of the victory against Emperor Frederick II and the improvement of the papal finances, demands for subsidies eased.[47]

Matthew wrote against this backdrop. He commented on Earl Richard's (short-lived) rebellion in 1238:[48]

> And it was really hoped then, that Earl Richard himself [King Henry's brother] would free the land from the wretched slavery with which it was oppressed by the Romans and other foreigners; and all from boys to old men continuously heaped blessings upon him.[49]

Matthew wanted the Romans gone.

Cardinal Otto and England

King Henry did not want the Romans gone. He requested the dispatch of a legate in 1230, ostensibly (the details are unclear) for the legate to participate in the peace talks between himself and King Louis IX of France (r. 1226–70). Henry's justiciar, Hubert de Burgh (c. 1170–1243), persuaded the king to recall the messenger.[50]

---

[42] Ibid., pp. 176–77, 240–42.
[43] Ibid., pp. 177–78, 187–93, 242–49.
[44] Ibid., pp. 178–86. Roger of Wendover alternately calls Otto *nuncio* and legate during his visit in 1225; see *Flowers of History*, vol. 2, pp. 461–62, 466–68, 471–72; *Flores Historiarum*, vol. 2, pp. 289–90, 295–97, 302.
[45] Lunt, *Financial Relations*, pp. 194–220, 250–55.
[46] Ibid., pp. 250–55.
[47] Ibid., pp. 220–39.
[48] See, e.g., Carpenter, *Henry III: The Rise to Power*, pp. 200–3.
[49] Matthew Paris, *EH*, vol. 1, p. 121 (translation adjusted); Matthew Paris, *CM*, vol. 3, p. 476: 'Et sperabatur certissime tunc, quod ipse comes Ricardus esset liberaturus terram tam a Romanorum quam aliorum alienigenarum misera, qua premebatur, servitute; et omnes a puero usque ad homninem senem crebras in ipsum benedictiones congresserunt.'
[50] Björn K. U. Weiler, *Henry III of England and the Staufen Empire, 1216–1272* (Woodbridge:

In 1233, Henry perhaps requested the presence of a legate to help him combat Richard Marshal's rebellion. The only source for the request is from Roger of Wendover, who mentions this in his *Flores Historiarum*, using the request as a smear against the king and the pope.[51] Given Roger's hostility, some doubt about the veracity of his claim is unavoidable. In 1235, Pope Gregory suggested dispatching a legate to Ireland, but Henry rejected it, wanting a legate in England.[52] Henry kept up his lobbying, appointing proctors to the curia in May 1236, only to have the pope refuse their requests.[53] In late January 1237, Henry dispatched Walter de Cantilupe, bishop-elect of Worcester, with another request.[54] According to Carpenter, Henry's reason for requesting a legate was his desire to have a 'prop' to help him govern.[55] Government issues included Henry's worsening financial situation – at the January parliament of 1237, the barons had angrily refused Henry's request for additional taxes – and the deteriorating relationship with King Alexander II of Scotland (r. 1214–49). War was looming.[56]

Adam Davies argues that the timeline does not add up. Henry dispatched Walter de Cantilupe in late January; on 12 February, the pope appointed Cardinal Otto legate to England, Wales, and Ireland.[57] Walter could not have reached the

---

Boydell Press, 2006), pp. 20–24; Adam Davies, 'The Appointment of Cardinal-Deacon Otto as Legate in Britain (1237)', in *TCE XI*, ed. Björn K. U. Weiler et al. (Woodbridge: Boydell Press, 2007), 147–58, pp. 148–49; Walter Waddington Shirley, ed., *Royal and Other Historical Letters Illustrative of the Reign of Henry III*, 2 vols (London: Longman, 1862), vol. 1, no. 310, pp. 379–80.

[51] *Flowers of History*, vol. 2, p. 579; *Flores Historiarum*, vol. 3, p. 69. Matthew reproduced it; see Matthew Paris, *CM*, vol. 3, p. 261.

[52] *CCR, 1234–37*, pp. 166–67.

[53] Shirley, *Royal and Other Historical Letters*, vol. 2, no. 422, pp. 13–14; *CPR, 1232–1247*, p. 147; Lucien Auvray, ed., *Les registres de Grégoire IX: recueil des bulles de ce pape*, 4 vols (Paris: Albert Fontemoing, 1896–1955), vol. 2, nos. 3298–299, cols. 467–68.

[54] *CPR, 1232–1247*, p. 173; Henry Richards Luard, ed., 'Annales de Theokesberia', in *AM*, 5 vols, RS (London: Longman, 1864), vol. 1, pp. 43–180, at p. 104.

[55] Carpenter, *Henry III: The Rise to Power*, p. 197.

[56] Robert C. Stacey, *Politics, Policy, and Finance under Henry III 1216–1245* (Oxford: Clarendon Press, 1987), pp. 93–118; Howell, *Eleanor of Provence*, pp. 9–21; Dorothy M. Williamson, 'The Legate Otto in Scotland and Ireland 1237–1240', *The Scottish Historical Review* 28, no. 105 (1949): 12–30, pp. 12–18; *CCR, 1234–37*, p. 529.

[57] Auvray, *Les registres de Grégoire IX*, vol. 2, no. 3509, col. 563. Otto did not leave the curia at once; Dorothy Williamson places him at Viterbo on 13 April; see Dorothy M. Williamson, 'Some Aspects of the Legation of Cardinal Otto in England, 1237–41', *EHR* 64, no. 251 (1949): 145–73, p. 172. However, her reference to August Potthast, ed., *Regesta Pontificum Romanorum: Inde ab a. post Christum natum MCXCVIII ad a. MCCCIV*, 2 vols (Berlin: Rudolphi de Decker, 1874–75), no. 10,887, is a document dated 29 May 1240. I have not found Otto around April 1237 in either Auvray, *Les registres de Grégoire IX* or Potthast, *Regesta Pontificum Romanorum*.

curia by then.[58] The pope, in Davies' interpretation, took the initiative to dispatch Cardinal Otto to England without a formal request on the table. Having rejected the request of May 1236, Davies maintains, the pope changed his mind because of the deteriorating papal–imperial relationship. In 1239, the pope would excommunicate Frederick, launching a fight that would not cease until the death of the emperor in 1250. Henry was Frederick's brother-in-law, but he was also a papal vassal and ally. His position was uncertain. It may have been prudent to humour Henry with the dispatch of a legate, as Davies explains.[59] Such considerations likely influenced the pope, but Pascal Montaubin shows that in 1236, the pope did not reject the king's request outright; instead, he postponed the appointment of a suitable legate due to staffing shortages.[60] He honoured 'your petition' ('petitioni tuo'),[61] referring to Henry's 1236 petition, in his letter of credence to the king, issued on 13 February 1237. The addition of the Scottish question to Otto's commission on 24 March of the same year was the result of Walter de Cantilupe's arrival, updating the curia on the king's needs.[62]

Otto de Tonengo (d. 1250/1) was an experienced legate. He had, as mentioned, been a nuncio in England (1225–26), before Pope Gregory elevated him to the cardinalate in 1227.[63] Otto had participated in or headed three legations, before being appointed legate to England in 1237.[64] He had received legal training at Bologna sometime in the 1210s; he had been papal chaplain between 1219 and 1225, and he had been in charge of resolving disputes about contradictory written evidence at some point (*auditor litterarum contradictarum*).[65] In brief, Otto was a

---

[58] Davies, 'The Appointment', pp. 148–49.
[59] Ibid., pp. 149–53, 156–58. See also Weiler, *Henry III of England*, pp. 45–67; and Michael Lower, *The Baron's Crusade: A Call to Arms and Its Consequences* (Philadelphia: University of Pennsylvania Press, 2005), pp. 133–36.
[60] Pascal Montaubin, 'De Petits papes en voyage: les légats en France et en Angleterre au XIIIe siècle', in *Se déplacer du moyen âge à nos jours: actes du 6e colloque européen de Calais, 2006-2007*, ed. Stéphane Curveiller and Laurent Buchard (Calais: Les amis du Vieux Calais, 2009), pp. 58–70, at p. 62.
[61] Auvray, *Les registres de Grégoire IX*, vol. 2, no. 3510, col. 564.
[62] See also Williamson, 'The Legate Otto', pp. 17–18; Auvray, *Les registres de Grégoire IX*, vol. 2, no. 3578, col. 605.
[63] Zimmermann, *Die päpstliche Legation*, p. 104; Frances Ann Underhill, 'Papal Legates to England in the Reign of Henry III (1216–1272)' (unpublished PhD dissertation, Indiana University, Bloomington, 1965), pp. 138–42; Lunt, *Financial Relations*, pp. 178–86.
[64] Zimmermann, *Die päpstliche Legation*, pp. 104, 107–9; Underhill, 'Papal Legates', pp. 142–44.
[65] Jane E. Sayers, *Papal Government and England during the Pontificate of Honorius III (1216-1227)* (London: Cambridge University Press, 1984), pp. 38–40. For more information about the *audientia litterarum contradictarum*, see Peter Herde, *Audientia litterarum contradictarum: Untersuchungen über die päpstlichen Justizbriefe und die*

man of standing at the curia. The pope told the English to receive Otto 'with due reverence and honour' ('cum debita reverentia et honore').[66]

Otto's activities in England were many and varied.[67] He procured peace between England and Scotland, he worked for an extension of the peace treaty between England and France, he helped ease tension with Wales, and he mediated between King Henry and Earl Richard, Henry's brother. Richard had rebelled in 1238 because Henry had clandestinely arranged the marriage of Eleanor, their sister, to Simon de Montfort.[68] Otto also promulgated a range of reforming statutes. The most notable are the statutes issued at the council at St Paul's in London in November 1237.[69] These statutes survive in more than sixty manuscripts.[70] Otto probably promulgated comparable statutes in Scotland. He also engaged in reforming the English Benedictines.[71]

Otto's legation was unusual from a twelfth-century perspective, both for its length and for the freedom of movement Otto enjoyed. His long stay (around three and a half years) gave the English clergy easy access to papal justice. Williamson points out that this was widely appreciated, and that the legate's court worked to meet the demand.[72] However, the Plantagenets of the twelfth century would never have entrusted a curial legate with so much power and autonomy. Since then, however, papal legates had played a prominent role in English government and politics during the civil war and during Henry's minority. By 1237, it perhaps seemed uncontroversial to have a cardinal-legate roaming the English countryside – at least to Henry.

Modern assessments of Otto's legation have largely been negative. Frederick Powicke asserts that 'Otto was a tactful and able man', but 'he was not welcome'.[73]

---

päpstliche Delegationsgerichtsbarkeit vom 13. bis 16. Jahrhundert, 2 vols (Tübingen: Max Niemeyer, 1970).

[66] Auvray, *Les registres de Grégoire IX*, vol. 2, no. 3509, col. 563.
[67] The most comprehensive study of Otto's activities in England is Rose Catherine Clifford, 'England as a Papal Fief: The Role of the Papal Legate in the Early Period, 1216-1241' (unpublished PhD dissertation, University of California, Los Angeles, 1978), esp. pp. 240-351.
[68] Clifford, pp. 266-70; Williamson, 'The Legate Otto', pp. 18-20; Stacey, *Politics, Policy, and Finance*, pp. 118-128; Thomas Rymer, ed., *Foedera, Conventiones, Litteræ, et cujuscunque generis Acta Publica, inter Reges Angliæ et Alios quosvis Imperatores, Reges, Pontifices, Principes, vel Communitates*, revised by the Record Commission (London, 1816), vol. 1, pt. 1, pp. 233-34.
[69] Clifford, 'England as a Papal Fief', pp. 271-79; Williamson, 'Some Aspects', pp. 159-67.
[70] Williamson, 'Some Aspects', pp. 159-60; F. M. Powicke and C. R. Cheney, eds, *Councils & Synods with Other Documents Relating to the English Church*, 2 vols (Oxford: Clarendon Press, 1964), vol. 2, pt. 1, p. 239.
[71] Williamson, 'Some Aspects', pp. 167-70; Williamson, 'The Legate Otto', pp. 21-24; Clifford, 'England as a Papal Fief', pp. 283-90.
[72] Williamson, 'Some Aspects', pp. 149-56.
[73] Powicke, *King Henry III*, vol. 1, quotes at p. 353 and p. 352, respectively.

Ilicia Sprey argues that the English, having experienced Guala and Pandulf, saw Otto as a time-server, because they did not understand the restrictions on his authority.[74] Although dispatched 'from our side' ('de latere nostro') 'with the full office of legate' ('plene legationis officio'),[75] Otto referred all major issues back to Rome, including the disputed episcopal elections at Winchester, Durham, and Norwich.[76] Frances Underhill argues that Otto's tax collecting alienated the English Church[77] – Pope Gregory ordered him to levy the subsidy of 1239[78] – while Williamson asserts that Otto's presence 'intensified the dislike and mistrust with which the agents of the Roman church were regarded'.[79]

Matthew's conclusion on Otto's activities in England is not exactly rosy:

> On the day after the Epiphany [i.e., 7 January], the legate, after receiving an embrace and kisses from the king, took ship at Dover, and, laying aside the insignia of his legateship, turned his back on England, leaving no one except the king, and those whom he had fattened on the property of the kingdom, to lament his departure.[80]

An incident in 1238 between the legate and some Oxford scholars confirms that Matthew was not a lonely voice. The incident took place at Oseney Abbey, where Otto was lodging when the Oxford scholars came to visit him. Matthew wrote in vivid detail about how members of the legatine retinue insulted the scholars, prompting the scholars to physically attack the legate's retinue and Otto himself, killing at least one. The Tewkesbury Annals corroborate the incident.[81] The legate had to flee to the king, who clamped down on the attackers. The intercession of the English bishops re-established the peace.[82] It is a good thing the Oxford dons of today only fight verbally.

Nevertheless, it is probably unwise to regard this one incident as representing the feelings of the English en bloc, even if the *Chronica* is overflowing with claims

---

[74] Ilicia Jo Sprey, 'Papal Legates in English Politics, 1100–1272' (unpublished PhD dissertation, University of Virginia, Charlottesville, 1998), pp. 262–71.

[75] Auvray, *Les registres de Grégoire IX*, vol. 2, no. 3509, col. 563.

[76] See Williamson, 'Some Aspects', pp. 147–48.

[77] Underhill, 'Papal Legates', pp. 184–87.

[78] Lunt, *Financial Relations*, pp. 197–205.

[79] Williamson, 'Some Aspects', p. 145.

[80] Matthew Paris, *EH*, vol. 1, p. 319; Matthew Paris, *CM*, vol. 4, p. 84: 'Igitur in crastino Epiphaniæ, apud Doveram legatus navem ascendens, post regales amplexus et oscula, legationis deposuit insigni, et transfretans apporriatam Angliam a tergo salutavit, nullo præter regem, et quos idem legatus bonis regni saginaverat, de recessu suo condolente.'

[81] Luard, 'Annales de Theokesberia', p. 107.

[82] See David L. Sheffler, 'An Early Oxford Riot: Oseney Abbey, 1238', in *History of Universities*, ed. Mordechai Feingold and Jane Finucane, vol. 21 (Oxford: Oxford University Press, 2006), pp. 1–32.

about Otto's greed, asserting at one point, for instance, that he preferred 'to reap where he had not sown' ('metere ubi non seminavit').[83]

However, even Matthew occasionally praised Otto:

> The legate Otto ... by conducting himself prudently and with moderation, refusing, in a great measure, the valuable presents offered to him (contrary to the usual custom of the Romans), calmed the angry feelings which had been conceived against him by the clergy as well as the soldiery by his well-ordered conduct.[84]

Otto conducted himself prudently, contrary to the usual customs of the Romans. The praise was backhanded, but it was praise.

Evidence from Bury St Edmunds and the highly esteemed Robert Grosseteste, bishop of Lincoln, is interesting. At Bury, the monks were in dispute with the Franciscans and the Dominicans about the settlement of the friars on the abbey's properties. Otto ruled in favour of Bury – to the delight of the monks.[85] Conversely, the Franciscans and the Dominicans were probably not pleased. During his stay in England, Otto corresponded often with Bishop Robert Grosseteste, who employed a friendly and respectful tone.[86] In 1243, the chapter of Canterbury excommunicated Bishop Grosseteste, presuming archiepiscopal authority due to the vacancy at that time. Grosseteste wrote to Otto, who was at the curia at the time.[87]

In sum, Otto's standing with the English was complex. It is probably fair to say that opinions differed. The English frowned on some of Otto's actions, particularly his tax collection, but it is also obvious that some of them respected Otto and valued his accomplishments and presence.

---

[83] Matthew Paris, *EH*, vol. 1, p. 119; Matthew Paris, *CM*, vol. 3, p. 473. The pope did really recall Otto in 1238, but it was the king who objected; see *CPR, 1232–47*, p. 235.

[84] Matthew Paris, *EH*, vol. 1, pp. 61–62 (translation adjusted); Matthew Paris, *CM*, vol. 3, p. 403: 'Dominus autem Otho legatus ... prudenter ac modeste se gerens, munera pretiosissima sibi oblata in magna parte respuens, contra consuetudinem Romanorum, indignationem in toto regno conceptam tam clero quam militia ... per gestum suum ordinatum temperavit.'

[85] Antonia Gransden, ed. and trans., *The Chronicle of Bury St Edmunds, Chronica Buriensis, 1212–1301* (London: Nelson, 1964), pp. 9–10.

[86] F. A. C. Mantello and Joseph Goering, trans., *The Letters of Robert Grosseteste, Bishop of Lincoln* (Toronto: University of Toronto Press, 2010), nos. 49, 52, 60, 61, 74, 76, 79, 82, 104, 105, 110, pp. 172–74, 179–82, 208–13, 262–64, 266–68, 271–80, 281–83, 329–32, 341–45; Henry Richards Luard, ed., *Roberti Grosseteste episcopi quondam lincolniensis Epistolæ*, RS (London: Longman, 1861), nos. 49, 52, 60, 61, 74, 76, 79, 82, 104, 105, 110, pp. 144–46, 151–54, 182–88, 241–43, 245–47, 250–53, 262–64, 311–14, 324–28.

[87] Mantello and Goering, *The Letters of Robert Grosseteste*, no. 110, pp. 341–45; Henry Richards Luard, *Roberti Grosseteste episcopi quondam lincolniensis Epistolæ*, nos. 110, pp. 324–28.

Reporting and Authorial Voice

Cardinal-Legate Otto came to England in the summer of 1237. Matthew reported on his arrival as follows:

> [Prelude:] In the same year, too, around the feast of the apostles Peter and Paul, no one knowing why, Lord Otto, cardinal-deacon of San Nicola in Carcere, came into England through the summons of the Lord King [Henry III] without the knowledge of the magnates of the kingdom. Whence many conceived great indignation against the king, saying, 'the king corrupts everything – the law, trust, promises; he transgresses in each. Indeed, he has now united himself in marriage to a foreigner [Queen Eleanor] without the council of his friends and natural men; now he has secretly summoned a legate, a changer of the whole kingdom; now he gives his own, now he desires to recall that which is given.' Thus, day by day, in such a way, just as the Gospel said, divided and dismantled in itself, the kingdom was enormously desolate [paraphrasing Matthew 12:25]. However, it is said that the archbishop of Canterbury, Edmund, reproved the king for doing such things, especially concerning the invitation of the legate, knowing that thenceforth, to the prejudice of his dignity, great loss for the kingdom was imminent. But the king, having spurned his advice as much as that of his other [councillors], by no means wanted to revoke what he had conceived in his mind. [Reception:] The aforesaid legate, therefore, came in great apparel and great power. And the renowned bishops and clerics went all the way to the coast to meet him; and some went to meet him by sailing in boats, applauding and offering invaluable gifts. Even, indeed, in Paris, messengers of various bishops offered scarlet cloth and expensive cups to meet him. For which act they deserved so greatly to be rebuked by many, both for the gift and for the manner of giving, because by the cloth and its colour, the office of the legate and the arrival was seen to be accepted. Arriving, however, he did not accept all the offered gifts, but some; but those he did not accept, he ordered to be reserved for himself. Moreover, he liberally distributed vacant revenue [benefices] to his men, whom he had brought with him, deserving and undeserving. The king also went all the way to the edge of the sea to meet him, and bowing his head to his knees, he dutifully escorted [Otto] all the way to the interior of the kingdom. And the arriving bishops, with the abbots and other prelates of the churches, received him with all honour and reverence – with processions and the peal of bells and expensive gifts – as is seemly and more than seemly.[88]

---

[88] Matthew Paris, *EH*, vol. 1, pp. 54–55 (translation adjusted); Matthew Paris, *CM*, vol. 3, pp. 395–396: 'Eodem quoque anno, nesciebatur ad quid, circa festum Apostolorum Petri

This is one of the longest and most detailed narrative accounts of a legatine reception. It is split into two parts: a prelude and a reception. I have marked both in the quote. The prelude takes the place of the preparations, setting the scene for the reception. The reception adheres to the '*adventus* template': the English prelates moved out to receive Otto (*occursus*); they met him outside of their home area (*susceptio*); and they conducted him back into their home (*ingressus*). There is little to suggest that Matthew based his account on any one written model, even though he had certainly encountered many written accounts of the *adventus* (there is a fair number in Roger of Wendover's *Flores Historiarum*). He knew St Albans had a copy of Lanfranc's Monastic Constitutions.[89] Matthew undoubtedly had personal experience, such as when the St Albans monks welcomed Otto on his visit to their abbey in 1239. Matthew mentioned no *adventus* on that occasion, but it is inconceivable that the St Albans monks did not receive the legate appropriately (Otto would probably have excommunicated them otherwise).[90]

One observation from the *Chronica*'s account is that King Henry and the English prelates acknowledged the authority of the legate and received him accordingly. Matthew was aware of this reality. He reported the same in the *Historia Anglorum*:

> et Pauli, dominus Otto Sancti Nicholai in carcere Tulliano diaconus cardinalis per mandatum domini regis venit legatus in Angliam, nescientibus regnu magnatibus. Unde plures adversus regem magnam conceperunt indignationem, dicentes; "Omnia rex pervertit, jura, fidem, promissa, in omnibus transgreditur. Nunc enim matrimonio se sine suorum amicorum et hominum naturalium [consilio] alienigenæ copulavit; nunc legatum, regni totius immutatorem, clam vocavit; nunc sua dat, nunc data cupit revocare." Sic sicque de die in diem, juxta dictum evangelium, in se divisum et dissipatum regnum est enormiter desolatum. Dictum est autem, quod archiepiscopus Cantuariensis Ædmundus regem talia facientem increpavit, præcipue de vocatione legati, sciens inde in suæ dignitatis præjudicium magnam regno imminere jacturam. Sed rex, spreto tam suo quam aliorum suorum consilio, quod concepit animo nullatenus voluit propositum revocare. Venit igitur in magno apparatu legatus prænominatus et potentia magna. Et occurrerunt ei episcopi et clerici famosi usque ad litus; et aliqui in naviculis navigando obviarunt ei, applaudentes et munera impretiabilia offerentes. Immo etiam Parisius in obviam ei obtulerunt telas escarleti et vasa pretiosa nuntii diversorum episcoporum. In quo facto nimis a multis meruerunt reprehendi, tum pro dono et pro dandi modo, quia in panno et ejus colore videbatur legationis officium et adventum acceptari. Adveniens autem munera oblata omnia non accepit, sed aliqua; sed quæ non recepit, jussit sibi reservari. Redditus autem vacantes suis, quos secum adduzit, dignis et indignis largiter distribuit. Rex autem ei usque ad confinium maris occurrit, et inclinato ad genua ejus capite, usque ad interiora regni deduxit officiose. Et adventantes episcopi, cum abbatibus et aliis ecclesiarum prælatis, eum cum omni honore et reverentia, cum processionibus et campanarum classico et pretiosis muneribus, ut decuit et plus quam decuit, receperunt.'

[89] See Matthew Paris, 'Gesta Abbatum', p. 52.
[90] Matthew Paris, *EH*, vol. 1, pp. 195–96; Matthew Paris, *CM*, vol. 3, pp. 568–69.

This legate [Otto] coming into England, in accordance with the lord king's petition and desire, was received with the greatest honour and reverence by the lord king himself, by the archbishop of Canterbury, Edmund, and by all the bishops, abbots, priors, and other prelates of the Church, and also the magnates.[91]

However, even though both the *Chronica* and the *Historia* report on the English acceptance of legatine authority, their narrative thrusts differ substantially. The *Chronica* mentions 'great indignation' ('magnam … indignationem'), the 'desolation' ('desolatum') of the kingdom, Archbishop Edmund, who 'reproved the king for doing such things' ('regem talia facientem increpavit'), and gift-giving to the legate being 'more than seemly' ('plus quam decuit'), among other things. The *Historia* provides fewer details, but it projects a far more positive spin on the *adventus*: 'he was received with the greatest honour and reverence' ('cum summo honore et reverentia est receptus'). It also includes a wider selection of participants. In the *Chronica*, the king and the English prelates are present, seemingly excluding Archbishop Edmund. In the *Historia*, the king, the magnates, the prelates, and Archbishop Edmund are all present. It is a united England, welcoming the legate confidently and honourably.

The differences between the two accounts are revealing. They highlight Matthew's authorial voice. The purpose of the *Historia* was, according to Björn Weiler and Lars Kjær, to educate the royal court on moral issues.[92] This required some tact. Accordingly, Matthew framed the event in honourable terms. Conversely, in the *Chronica*, Matthew wrote what he considered the moral truth. Neither the *Historia* nor the *Chronica* contain 'objective' accounts of the event, but they reveal some of the sentiments and optics at stake.

The king, who had lobbied extensively for the presence of a cardinal-legate, probably received Otto with enthusiasm. The thoughts of each individual noble or prelate at the reception are, of course, impossible to know, but, as mentioned above, the evidence suggests that the general mood in England towards Otto was ambivalent. Nevertheless, it is difficult to imagine the English boycotting the reception – that would have been extremely hostile. The *Historia* likely comes closest to reflecting the actual optics of the event. When Otto was leaving England

---

[91] Matthew Paris, *Historia Anglorum*, vol. 2, p. 398: 'Qui veniens in Angliam legatus, juxta domini regis petitionem et desiderium, ab ipso domino rege, ab archiepiscopo, Cantuariensi Æ[dmundo], et ab omnibus episcopis, abbatibus, prioribus, et aliis ecclesiæ prælatis, necnon et magnatibus, cum summo honore et reverentia est receptus.'

[92] Weiler, 'Matthew Paris on the Writing of History', pp. 256, 276–77; Lars Kjær, 'Matthew Paris and the Royal Christmas: Ritualised Communication in Text and Practice', in *TCE XIV*, ed. Janet Burton, Phillipp Schofield, and Björn K. U. Weiler (Woodbridge: Boydell Press, 2013), pp. 141–54, at p. 147.

in a sort of reverse *adventus*,[93] Bishop Grosseteste wrote to apologise to Otto because he could not personally escort him to the sea, citing bad health, dispatching one of his clerks instead.[94] Matthew's problem was that the English undoubtedly received the legate with due honour and decorum. Matthew's own abbot might have been present for the occasion. As the head of one of the most prestigious and important abbeys in the kingdom, the abbot's presence would probably have been expected. The royal records place Otto's landfall at Dover.[95] It required some travel to reach Dover, but nothing that a wealthy abbey like St Albans could not arrange.

Weiler observes that Matthew 'rarely made up things entirely'.[96] Kjær agrees that Matthew 'did not go so far as to "invent" rituals that had not taken place, nor did he recycle purely literary tropes'.[97] Instead, according to Weiler, Matthew's 'desire to offer a moral interpretation … required him to present events in a manner that made their deeper meaning, their ethical value and message, discernable to his readers'.[98] Kjær agrees, arguing that 'what he [Matthew] did was to take the events … and present them in a manner that aligned itself with his various authorial agendas'.[99] Matthew did not want to gloss over or minimise the importance of the event in the *Chronica*; he wished to present the event in such a way that its moral significance became obvious.

The Prelude

The prelude began with the announcement of the legate's arrival 'around the feast of the apostles Peter and Paul' ('circa festum Apostolorum Petri et Pauli'), that is, 29 June. Matthew bookended it with the king's decision to receive the legate, despite the warnings of his councillors. This set the tone and framed the event. Right from the beginning some of the details are suspect, including the date of the arrival. The royal records show that Otto arrived sometime between 16 July and 3 August.[100] In the *Flores Historiarum*, Matthew's dating fell within this interval: on the feast of Mary Magdalene, 22 July.[101] Why the discrepancy? Saints could bestow

---

[93] See Julie Kerr, '"Welcome the Coming and Speed the Parting Guest": Hospitality in Twelfth-Century England', *JMH* 33, no. 2 (2007): 130–46, pp. 139–42.
[94] Mantello and Goering, *The Letters of Robert Grosseteste*, no. 105, pp. 330–2; Henry Richards Luard, *Roberti Grosseteste episcopi quondam lincolniensis Epistolæ*, no. 106, pp. 313–14.
[95] *CCR, 1234–37*, pp. 541–42.
[96] Weiler, 'Matthew Paris on the Writing of History', p. 274.
[97] Kjær, 'Matthew Paris and the Royal Christmas', p. 154.
[98] Weiler, 'Matthew Paris on the Writing of History', p. 274.
[99] Kjær, 'Matthew Paris and the Royal Christmas', p. 154.
[100] *CCR, 1234–1237*, pp. 478–9, 541–2.
[101] Matthew Paris, *Flores Historiarum*, ed. Henry Richards Luard, 3 vols, RS (London: Eyre

meaning to dates. The Tewkesbury annalist dated the legate's arrival to 'around the feast of St Kenelm' ('circa festum beati Kenelmi'), 17 July.[102] Tewkesbury is located in Gloucestershire, where St Kenelm was held in special veneration.[103] Matthew's reasons for dating the arrival of the legate to the feast of Peter and Paul probably had to do with mockery by comparison: targeting both the king and the legate.[104] The legate was nothing like those papal saints, Peter and Paul; he came 'in great apparel and great power' ('in magno apparatu ... potentia magna'). He was an expression of the modern-day papacy, not of those saints. King Henry should have known better – but he did not.

The core argument of the prelude is that Henry was a wilful, incompetent king, unwilling to listen to the advice of 'his friends and natural men' ('suorum amicorum et hominum naturalium'), that is, the magnates of the realm (presumably both lay and ecclesiastical). A king was supposed to take advice.[105] The prelude was more focused on Henry than either the legate or the papacy. A papal legate might not be a force for good in the world – he was a 'changer of the whole kingdom' ('regni totius immutatorem') – but it was Henry who had summoned and welcomed the legate without proper consultation.

Archbishop Edmund tried to warn the king. According to Matthew, 'it is said that the archbishop of Canterbury, Edmund, reproved the king for doing such things, especially concerning the invitation of the legate'.[106] Edmund was an extremely important figure: he was not only the archbishop of Canterbury; he was a saint. Edmund was only canonised at the turn of 1246, but if Greasley's redating of the compositional history of the *Chronica* is correct, Matthew would have known about the canonisation at the time of writing. If Greasley's redating is

---

and Spottiswoode, 1890), vol. 2, p. 223; Matthew Paris [Matthew of Westminster], *The Flowers of History: Especially Such as Relate to the Affairs of Britain; from the Beginning of the World to the Year 1307*, trans. Charles Duke Yonge, 2 vols (London: Henry G. Bohn, 1853), vol. 2, p. 183.

[102] Luard, 'Annales de Theokesberia', p. 105.

[103] See Francesca Tinti, *Sustaining Belief: The Church of Worcester from c. 870 to c. 1100* (Farnham: Ashgate, 2010), pp. 251–52.

[104] The conflicting dates bewildered Williamson; see Williamson, 'The Legate Otto', p. 18. The Annals of Winchester and those of Oseney date the arrival to August, while the chronicle of Bury St Edmunds mentions 10 July; see Henry Richards Luard, ed., 'Annales de Wintonia', in *AM*, 5 vols, RS (London: Longman, 1865), vol. 2, pp. 3–125, at p. 87; 'Annales de Oseneia', ibid., vol. 4, pp. 3–352, at p. 83; and Gransden, *Chronica Buriensis*, p. 9.

[105] See, e.g., Björn K. U. Weiler, 'William of Malmesbury on Kingship', *History* 90, no. 297 (2005): 3–22.

[106] Matthew Paris, *EH*, vol. 1, p. 55 (translation adjusted); Matthew Paris, *CM*, vol. 3, p. 395: 'Dictum est ..., quod archiepiscopus Cantuariensis Ædmundus regem talia facientem increpavit, præcipue de vocatione legati.'

incorrect, Matthew would still have heard rumours of Edmund's sanctity, which spread within a year of his death in 1240.[107] Matthew went on to compose a Life of St Edmund (1247 × 1253), first in Latin and later in Anglo-French.[108] In the *Chronica*, Matthew claimed that the king and the legate drove Edmund into exile. He repeated the allegation in his Life of St Edmund. It was pure fabrication, but Matthew used the exile to evoke both explicit and implicit memories of Thomas Becket. In the *Chronica*, Matthew claimed that Edmund had gone into exile 'for the same cause' ('ob similem causam') as St Thomas.[109] Matthew did not mention the presence of Edmund at the reception (the only identifiable figures at the *adventus* were King Henry and Legate Otto), but he used Edmund to impart a powerful indirect commentary. It bolstered Matthew's argument that it was a figure of Edmund's high standing who voiced the criticism.[110] The king, nevertheless, would not listen.

The king's recklessness had immediate repercussions: the division and devastation of the kingdom. Matthew reported that the magnates were angry because of the impending arrival of the legate, whom the king had summoned clandestinely. The imminent arrival of this 'changer of the whole kingdom' ('regni totius immutatorem') caused 'many' ('plures') to remember and air their old grievances. The king was deceitful: he violated the law, married a foreigner (Queen Eleanor) without proper consultation, and recalled gifts already given. It got so bad, according to Matthew, that 'day by day, in such a way, just as the Gospel said, divided and dismantled in itself, the kingdom was enormously desolate' ('sicque de die in diem, juxta dictum evangelium, in se divisum et dissipatum regnum est enormiter desolatum'). It was a paraphrase of Matthew 12:25, in which Christ uttered that 'every kingdom divided against itself shall be made desolate: and every city or house divided against itself shall not stand' ('omne regnum divisum contra se desolatur et omnis civitas vel domus divisa contra se non stabit').[111] England faced a dire future thanks to the king's incompetence and stupidity.

---

[107] See C. H. Lawrence, *St Edmund of Abingdon: A Study in Hagiography and History* (Oxford: Clarendon Press, 1960), pp. 14–15, 19–20.

[108] Vaughan argues for a composition around 1247, Lawrence for a composition around 1253; see Vaughan, *Matthew Paris*, pp. 161–81; and Matthew Paris, *The Life of St Edmund*, ed. and trans. C. H. Lawrence (Oxford: Alan Sutton, 1996), pp. 115–16. The Life is published in Lawrence, *St Edmund of Abingdon*. For the Anglo-French text, see A. T. Baker, 'La Vie de Saint Edmond, archevêque de Cantorbéry', *Romania* 55 (1929): 332–81.

[109] Matthew Paris, *EH*, vol. 1, p. 310; Matthew Paris, *CM*, vol. 4, p. 74. For the account of the exile in the Life of St Edmund, see Matthew Paris, *The Life of St Edmund*, pp. 146–62, esp. pp. 149–52; Lawrence, *St Edmund of Abingdon*, pp. 257–78, esp. pp. 261–65.

[110] See also Weiler, 'Matthew Paris on the Writing of History', pp. 273–74.

[111] *The Holy Bible, Douay-Rheims Version: Translated from the Latin Vulgate*, revised by Richard Challoner (1752), Matthew 12:25; Robert Weber and Bonifatius Fischer, eds, *Biblia Sacra: iuxta vulgatem versionem*, 3rd edn (Stuttgart: Deutsche Bibelgesellschaft, 1983), Matthew 12:25.

The Reception

The account of the reception is a well-crafted rhetorical piece, in which Matthew utilised a specific structure and certain themes to best convey his messages. He scattered time, space, and themes (such as gift-giving) across the account with little apparent regard for chronology or completion. Nonetheless, his structure creates an effective narrative flow, integral to the way he delivered his messages.

The account of the reception begins with the legate arriving 'in great apparel and great power' ('in magno apparatu ... et potentia magna'). Matthew then stated that the English clergy went to the coast to meet Otto, some went out in boats, and some dispatched messengers all the way to Paris. In this way, Matthew jumped in time and space – from the coast, to the Channel, to Paris. At Paris, the messengers offered gifts. In the next sentence, Otto is 'arriving' ('adveniens'), accepting some gifts but not others. But where and when did it happen? It is unclear. Then Otto distributed revenue to his men – presumably English benefices – but following the *Chronica*'s narrative structure, Otto had not even arrived in England at this point. Maybe it is a general comment on Otto's behaviour?

Matthew thereafter abruptly jumped to the coast again. The king had at this point arrived, bowing to Otto at the edge of the sea ('confinium maris'). He then escorted Otto 'all the way to the interior of the kingdom' ('usque ad interiora regni'). Only then did the prelates arrive on the scene, 'arriving' ('adventantes') and receiving Otto with the peal of bells, processions, and gifts. Did it happen at the seashore? Or was it an all-encompassing *adventus* journey along the lines of the accounts of Boso and Roger of Wendover? For the reader, it is, again, left unclear.

Breaking the account down into these 'illogical' jumps in time and space reveals how considered the account was. It is not confusing to read the account; it is only once you think about time and space that the disorder becomes clear. The account has a tightly structured disorder. The purpose of the jumps had to do with the *adventus*. The *adventus* was an orderly ceremony, in which one thing is happening after another. However, in Matthew's account, it becomes disjointed, confused, and disordered, while at the same time retaining enough of its defining features to remain recognisable. It is, in a wider sense, a symbol of the disorder of papal-legatine authority inflicted on England.

Within this structure, the key message was the asymmetrical relationship of power between the English and the legate, not only as a de facto condition, but as something the English prelates foolishly and willingly submitted to. These prelates were happy, servile subjects, and Matthew mocked them mercilessly for their idiocy.

Matthew illustrated this through various themes and narrative strategies, one being the elongation of the *adventus*. Matthew began with the prelates going 'all the way to the coast' ('usque ad litus'), only to have some of them meeting the legate in small boats ('naviculis') in the Channel. He exclaimed that some 'even, indeed' ('immo etiam') dispatched messengers to Paris to meet the legate. Taken altogether, these narrative jumps created an impression of deterioration. It went from bad (the coast) to worse (the Channel) to catastrophe (Paris). The *adventus* became excessively elongated, stretching from Paris to the English coast and perhaps even beyond, as the king conducted Otto 'all the way to the interior of the kingdom' ('usque ad interiora regni'). This vague reference to the interior of the kingdom served to create an impression of comprehensiveness. As previously discussed, *adventus* ceremonies usually took place at specific locations and at specific times, but by stretching the *adventus* to an unreasonable length and having the king escort the legate into the unspecified interior of England, Matthew's account conveyed an extreme asymmetry between Cardinal Otto and the English hosts. Otto's authority became excessive.

The English prelates, however, not only responded to Otto's excessive authority with eager submissiveness, but they were also co-creators of their own submission, trying to outdo each other with child-like eagerness. The 'renowned' ('famosi') ecclesiastics – a sarcastic comment, if ever there was one – applauded ('applaudentes') the legate onboard their small ships in the Channel. The English clergy seemingly could not honour the legate enough.

The gift-giving to the legate followed the same line of thinking. Matthew was not averse to gift-giving as such.[112] Gift-giving was an integral part of medieval culture, but it was filled with all kinds of pitfalls and dangers.[113] The curia was aware of the optics of gift-giving. The *Gesta Innocentii* relates a story about how one disobedient bishop, Conrad of Hildesheim, tried to placate Pope Innocent III with gifts of expensive silverware. The *Gesta* recounts how the gifts left Innocent 'hesitating whether he should accept or rather refuse them' ('hesitans utrum deberet illa recipere an potius refutare').[114] Accepting them could be construed as a bribe, not accepting them implied that Innocent could not forgive Conrad.

---

[112] See also Lars Kjær, *The Medieval Gift and the Classical Tradition: Ideals and the Performance of Generosity in Medieval England, 1100–1300* (Cambridge: Cambridge University Press, 2019), esp. pp. 85–97.

[113] Medieval scholarship on gift-giving is enormous, but in this context, see especially Kjær, *The Medieval Gift*, pp. 66–97, 172–83; and Benjamin Linley Wild, 'A Gift Inventory from the Reign of Henry III', *EHR* 125, no. 514 (2010): 529–69. See also, e.g., Barbara H. Rosenwein, *To Be the Neighbor of Saint Peter: The Social Meaning of Cluny's Property, 909–1049* (Ithaca, NY: Cornell University Press, 1989); and Arnoud-Jan A. Bijsterveld, 'The Medieval Gift as Agent of Social Bonding and Political Power: A Comparative Approach', in *Medieval Transformations: Texts, Power and Gifts in Context*, ed. Esther Cohen and Mayke B. de Jong (Leiden: Brill, 2001), pp. 123–56.

[114] David Richard Gress-Wright, 'The "Gesta Innocentii III": Text, Introduction and Commentary' (unpublished PhD dissertation, Bryn Mawr College, 1981), p. 66.

The pope opted to reciprocate Conrad's gifts with a golden cup, worth much more than the silverware. In this way, Innocent showed his magnanimity, acting with good will, but not letting himself be corrupted.[115] Matthew, elsewhere, cited Seneca: 'to receive all presents offered is greedy; none, rebellious; some, friendly'.[116] It was actually one of the few times Matthew praised Otto, as he admitted that Otto adhered to Seneca's advice, choosing moderation in gift-giving.

The English prelates did not choose moderation. From Paris to the seashore and even beyond, the prelates offered 'invaluable gifts' ('munera impretiabilia') in a manner that was 'more than seemly' ('plus quam decuit'). Not a shred of corroborating evidence for these assertions in Matthew's text exists, though it is reasonable to believe that the prelates offered some gifts. This was what King Henry did. According to the royal records, Henry offered a trickle of gifts to Otto during his stay in England, including supplies of deer, firewood, wine, oak timber, money, and a gyrfalcon. The king also offered some silverware to Otto on two occasions, but Otto rejected the silverware both times.[117] Otto accepted the consumables, but not the high-status silverware. Other gifts undoubtedly went unrecorded. Nevertheless, the records not only document trickles rather than cascades of presents, but they also capture what Matthew admitted only grudgingly: that Otto was aware of the optics of gift-giving – that it could be construed as bribery and corruption – and was careful about what he accepted.

That was not how Matthew portrayed the legate at the *adventus*. According to Matthew, 'he [Otto] did not accept all the offered gifts' ('munera oblata omnia non accepit'), but 'those he did not accept, he ordered to be reserved for himself' ('quæ non recepit, jussit sibi reservari'). The meaning of this self-contradictory statement must be that Otto refused to receive some gifts as gifts, that is, with the usual moral attachments, but still kept them as tribute. This showed the asymmetrical relationship between Otto and the English: social equals or near equals were supposed to reciprocate each other's gifts. Only lords made demands on their subjects without reciprocating – Cardinal Otto acted as the lord of England.[118] In the next sentence, Matthew claimed that 'he [Otto] moreover liberally distributed

---

[115] *The Deeds of Pope Innocent III by an Anonymous Author*, trans. James M. Powell (Washington, D.C.: The Catholic University of America Press, 2004), ch. xliv, pp. 59-60; Gress-Wright, 'Gesta Innocentii', pp. 64-66.

[116] Matthew Paris, *EH*, vol. 1, p. 69 (translation adjusted); Matthew Paris, *CM*, vol. 3, p. 412: 'Omnia oblata recipere, avarum est; nulla, rebelle; aliqua, sociale.' On the use of classical authors in medieval thought about gift-giving, see Kjær, *The Medieval Gift*.

[117] Accepted gifts: *CCR, 1234-1237*, pp. 478-79, 480; *CCR, 1237-1242*, pp. 19, 36, 55, 98, 105, 167, 183, 205; *CPR, 1232-1247*, p. 191, 241. The silverware: *CCR, 1234-1237*, p. 508; *CCR, 1232-1247*, pp. 33-34.

[118] See also David Graeber, *Debt: The First 5,000 Years*, 2nd edn (Brooklyn: Melville House, 2014), pp. 109-13.

vacant revenue [benefices] to his men' ('redditus autem vacantes suis ... largiter distribuit'). Otto, thus, not only refused to reciprocate those gifts that he had just received from the English, but proceeded to hand out vacant revenue, that is, benefices, to the men he had brought with him. In short, Otto kept taking and demanding. His actions were also a jab at the increasing number of papal nominees in English benefices – a development Matthew detested.[119]

The worst of it was that the English prelates eagerly accepted the legate's lordship. At Paris, messengers from 'various bishops' ('diversorum episcoporum') presented the legate with 'scarlet cloth and expensive cups' ('telas escarleti et vasa pretiosa'). Matthew opined that they 'deserved so greatly to be rebuked by many, both for the gift and for the manner of giving, because by the cloth and its colour, the office of legate and the arrival was seen to be accepted'.[120] The colour of the cloth implied acceptance of the legatine office. Scarlet was not a colour in medieval classification; it was an expensive type of cloth, distinguished by its fabrication.[121] Matthew, nevertheless, was clearly thinking of red, a colour associated with the pope and his legates, and one the Fourth Lateran had forbidden the clergy to wear outside of their churches.[122] Matthew was probably aware of the prohibition. A Scottish council reiterated the prohibition in 1225, while the Council of Worcester repeated the ban in 1240.[123] At the council at St Pauls in November 1237, Otto promulgated a statute on clerical dress, which did not mention the prohibited colours, but made unambiguous reference to the prohibitions of the Fourth Lateran. Matthew reproduced the statutes in the *Chronica*.[124] Red clothing set the pope and his legates apart visually. Presenting Otto with cloth that only he among the clergy might wear in all settings constituted a recognition of Otto's legatine authority. The English prelates, once again, willingly and foolishly submitted themselves to Otto's authority.

---

[119] See Thomas W. Smith, 'The Development of Papal Provisions in Medieval Europe', *History Compass* 13, no. 3 (2015): 110–21, pp. 111–13.

[120] '… nimis a multis meruerunt reprehendi, tum pro dono et pro dandi modo, quia in panno et ejus colore videbatur legationis officium et adventum acceptari.'

[121] See John H. Munro, 'Scarlet', in *Encyclopedia of Dress and Textiles in the British Isles c. 450–1450*, ed. Gale R. Owen-Crocker, Elizabeth Coatsworth, and Maria Hayward (Leiden: Brill, 2012), pp. 477–81. I am grateful to Maureen Miller, UC Berkeley, for drawing my attention to this fact.

[122] Antonio García y García, ed., *Constitutiones Concilii quarti Lateranensis una cum commentariis glossatorum*, Monumenta iuris canonici, A: Corpus glossatorum 2 (Vatican City: Biblioteca Apostolica Vaticana, 1981), c. 16, pp. 64–65.

[123] See Thomas M. Izbicki, 'Forbidden Colors in the Regulation of Clerical Dress from the Fourth Lateran Council (1215) to the Time of Nicholas of Cusa (d. 1464)', *Rutgers University Community Repository* (2005): 105–14, pp. 108–9.

[124] Matthew Paris, *EH*, vol. 1, p. 83; Matthew Paris, *CM*, vol. 3, pp. 429–30.

Henry, too, was a fool – probably the biggest of them all. He 'went all the way to the edge of the sea to meet him [Otto] …, bowing his head to his knees' ('ei usque ad confinium maris occurrit …, inclinato ad genua ejus capite'). There are two possible readings of this remark: either Henry bowed his head to his own knees or to those of the legate, the latter being the more plausible, although the Latin is a bit ambiguous. Bowing the head to one's knees is unquestionably an image of ridiculousness as well as subjection.[125] The same is true if one imagines the king bowing his head to the legate's knees, but this also implies submission in a more formal and prescribed way. The so-called Long Ceremonial of Avignon contains a description of the curial ritual on Ash Wednesday. During the festivities, the head of the cardinalate was obliged to place his head between the pope's knees in a gesture of complete submission.[126] Is it possible that Matthew alluded to something similar? He did not know the Long Ceremonial; it was still a century in the future, but perhaps the gesture was not invented in the fourteenth century?[127] The gesture, in any case, signalled submissiveness and self-ridicule – not least because Otto did not reciprocate.

Henry, finally, 'dutifully escorted [Otto] all the way to the interior of the kingdom' ('usque ad interiora regni deduxit officiose'). It was common to escort a visitor into one's home,[128] but the vagueness of 'all the way to the interior' made it appear absurdly extended, signalling an all-encompassing authority over England as a form of a possession-taking. Matthew, moreover, placed the word 'officiose' ('dutifully') last in the sentence for maximum effect. If the chronicler in question had not been Matthew Paris, it might have been possible to assume that this was simply a way to say that the king was a good host. However, it is evident that Matthew used 'officiose' to refer to Henry's position as a papal vassal. Henry was depicted as the subject receiving his lord. As mentioned above, Matthew later declared 'that he [Henry] might be said not to be a king but a vassal of the pope'.[129]

---

[125] See also J. A. Burrow, *Gestures and Looks in Medieval Narrative* (Cambridge: Cambridge University Press, 2002), p. 18.

[126] Marc Dykmans, ed., *Le cérémonial papal de la fin du Moyen-Âge à la Renaissance: Les textes avignonnais jusqu'à la fin du grand schisme d'occident*, 4 vols, Bibliothèque de l'Institut historique belge de Rome 26 (Brussels: Institut historique belge de Rome, 1983), vol. 3, nos. 33–34, p. 189: 'Et deposita mitra pape per diaconum cardinalem sibi assistentem a dextris, prior episcoporum cardinalium, si presens est, sin autem subprior episcoporum cardinalium, stando, et nihil dicendo, imponit cineres super caput pape ad modum crucis. Deinde idem prior genuflexus ponit caput suum inter genua pape, et papa eodem modo ponit cinerem super caput eius, dicens: «Memento homo», etc.; postea osculatur genu dextrum pape.' See also Agostino Paravicini-Bagliani, *The Pope's Body*, trans. David S. Peterson (Chicago and London: University of Chicago Press, 2000), p. 26.

[127] The front cover of this book is a woodcarving from around 1563, which shows Henry kneeling in front of the legate.

[128] Kerr, 'Welcome the Coming', pp. 131–33.

[129] Matthew Paris, *EH*, vol 1, p. 68 (translation adjusted); Matthew Paris, *CM*, vol. 3, p. 412: 'ut non rex, sed feodarius Papæ diceretur'.

The Choice of Submission

Matthew argued that it did not have to be that way – that England did not have to be a vassal state of the papacy. Submission to the papacy was a choice King Henry had made; he had welcomed a papal legate as an oppressor of the kingdom. Roger of Howden had claimed that King Henry I negotiated the right to deny entry to papal legates,[130] and Matthew wrote as if this were a matter of course for Henry III as well.[131] For instance, when reporting on Pope Innocent IV's dispatch of legates across Europe in 1247 to propagandise against Emperor Frederick II, Matthew asserted that those entering England were sent 'without insignia, lest he [the pope] should appear to violate the manifest privilege of the lord king' ('sine insignibus, ne videretur manifeste privilegium domini regis infringere').[132] This privilege must refer to the king's right to deny legates entry into England. Accordingly, King Henry III could have denied Cardinal Otto entry into England; instead, Otto came to England 'through the summons [or mandate] of the lord king' ('per mandatum domini regis'). The king had voluntarily brought a papal legate upon himself and the English. Henry was, therefore, to blame for England's misfortunes.

Weiler argues that one of Matthew's favourite techniques to convey moral meaning was through an 'implicit, yet open' contrast.[133] He noted that 'such parallels are ... integral to Matthew's method of writing'.[134] In this case, the King of Scotland, Alexander II, served as a model of how it should be done. After mediating between Henry III and Alexander II at a meeting at York in September 1237, Otto expressed interest in visiting Scotland. According to Matthew, Alexander replied in the following manner:

> I do not remember having seen a legate in my land, nor that it has been necessary for one to be summoned there, thanks to God, and there is not now any need of one, for all goes on well. Besides, neither was any legate allowed ingress during the time of my father or any of my ancestors, nor will I, as long as I am in possession of myself [i.e., able or sane], tolerate it ...'[135]

---

[130] *The Annals*, vol. 1, p. 212; *Chronica*, vol. 1, p. 176.
[131] Also mentioned previously; see pp. 47–48.
[132] Matthew Paris, *CM*, vol. 4, p. 612.
[133] Weiler, 'Matthew Paris on the Writing of History', p. 273.
[134] Ibid. See also Kjær, 'Matthew Paris and the Royal Christmas', p. 151.
[135] Matthew Paris, *EH*, vol. 1, p. 70 (translation adjusted); Matthew Paris, *CM*, vol. 3, p. 414: 'Non me memini legatum in terra mea vidisse, nec opus esse aliquem esse vocandum, Deo gratias; nec adhuc opus est, omnia bene se habent. Nec etiam tempore patris mei vel alicujus antecessorum meorum visus est aliquis legatus introitum habuisse, nec ego, dum mei compos fuero, tolerabo ....'

There is no reason to believe that Alexander actually threatened Otto in this way; moreover, the assertions that Matthew put into Alexander's mouth were not even true: Alexander II was king in 1221 when Master James, papal penitentiary and chaplain, arrived in Scotland as a legate.[136] The papal registers record that the pope dispatched Master James 'from his side' ('de latere suo').[137] Had Alexander not been sane at the time? Furthermore, Otto would visit Scotland in 1239 and promulgate a range of statutes.[138] However, the veracity (or lack thereof) of Matthew's claims is not the point. Matthew used his account of Alexander's stern rejection as an implicit contrast to Henry's servile reverence.[139]

Returning to the meeting at York in 1237, Matthew claimed that Alexander threatened the legate. According to Matthew, Alexander said that if Otto were to enter Scotland, he could not guarantee his safety, because 'fierce and untamed men live there, thirsting after human blood' ('indomiti … et silvestres homines ibi habitant, humanum sanguinem sitientes').[140] The legate abandoned his plans to enter Scotland, 'but a certain Italian, a relative of the legate, remained with the king of Scotland, whom the king honoured with a soldierly belt [knighthood], and also conferring land [on him], lest he [Alexander] was to appear thoroughly rebellious'.[141] This, Matthew implied, served as a model for cultivating a proper relationship between the papacy and secular rulers (and probably between other rulers as well): have relatives dwell in each other's courts to foster relationships and networks.

Matthew's point here was that the situation was King Henry's fault. Henry was a fool to have invited an oppressor to his kingdom, and he was a fool for allowing the legate entry. Henry fuelled Otto's authority, and the English prelates, disgracefully, played along. Roger of Wendover had implied that the English prelates in good faith had expected a benevolent lord in Cardinal Nicholas. It was not the fault of the prelates that Nicholas turned out to be a traitorous tyrant. Matthew Paris made no allowance for 'good faith': the English prelates knew what it meant to receive a legate, and there was no need to receive him with sycophantic servility.

---

[136] On his mission, see Paul Craig Ferguson, *Medieval Papal Representatives in Scotland: Legates, Nuncios, and Judges-Delegate, 1125–1286* (Edinburgh: The Stair Society, 1997), pp. 85–88.

[137] Potthast, *Regesta Pontificum Romanorum*, vol. 1, no. 6316, p. 552; Pietro Pressutti, ed., *Regesta Honorii Papae III*, 2 vols (Rome: Typographica Vaticana, 1888–95), vol. 1, nos. 2590, 2591, pp. 429–430.

[138] See Williamson, 'The Legate Otto', esp. pp. 18–26; and Ferguson, *Medieval Papal Representatives*, pp. 89–96.

[139] Matthew Paris, *EH*, vol. 1, p. 195; Matthew Paris, *CM*, vol. 3, p. 568.

[140] Matthew Paris, *EH*, vol. 1, p. 70 (translation adjusted); Matthew Paris, *CM*, vol. 3, p. 414.

[141] Matthew Paris, *EH*, vol. 1, p. 70 (translation adjusted); Matthew Paris, *CM*, vol. 3, p. 414: 'Remansit autem cum rege Scotiæ quidam Italicus legati consanguineus, quem rex cingulo militari, terram etiam conferendo, ne penitus rebellis videretur, nobilitavit.'

Is it possible that Matthew was projecting some of his own failings onto the English clergy? In 1247, Matthew witnessed the translation of the relic of the Holy Blood at Westminster, one of King Henry's prestige projects. Matthew mentioned that Henry, upon the conclusion of the ceremony, had recognised him in the crowd, inviting Matthew to sit at his throne and to dine with him.[142] Was there, as Weiler phrases it, 'a degree of infatuation'?[143] Still, Matthew demeaned Henry in the *Chronica*. Matthew dedicated the Life of St Edward to Queen Eleanor, and she sent him a present at one point. However, in the *Chronica*'s account of the reception of Legate Otto, Matthew also included Eleanor in the magnates' list of grievances, referring disdainfully to her as the king's foreign wife.

It is a pitiful image: Matthew, sitting in the scriptorium, pouring out vitriol on the pages of the *Chronica* to soothe feelings of self-loathing. It is, of course, speculative to what degree Matthew's own failings drove his attacks, defamations, and moral judgements, but whatever the case, Matthew chose to exaggerate and mock. The *adventus* of Cardinal-Legate Otto became a microcosm of everything that was wrong with England and its relationship with the papacy.

Conclusion

Matthew Paris concludes our journey through the English chroniclers. It has been a bumpy ride, especially with Matthew's steering. This is not because his narrative strategy is perplexing – reading his account is not confusing – but rather due to his extreme hostility and bellicose message. Matthew stood on the sideline, watching in disbelief as the dignitary (the legate), the head of the community (the king), and the members of the community (the clergy and the prelates) acted out the *adventus*. Matthew positioned himself among those who refused to participate and accept the legatine *adventus*, identifying these dissenters both explicitly and implicitly as Archbishop Edmund and the English magnates. They were, explicitly, dissenting voices to the king, the legate, and the *adventus* in the prelude to the *adventus*. Moreover, Archbishop Edmund and the English magnates are suspiciously absent from the *Chronica*'s account of the *adventus* itself. Matthew was on the side of these dissenters. His view was extreme: even Roger of Wendover had positioned himself as part of the community welcoming Legate Nicholas (whether he had actually been present or not is irrelevant in this context). Roger sympathised with the English, particularly the clergy. Matthew did not. While Roger of

---

[142] Matthew Paris, *EH*, vol. 2, pp. 242–43; Matthew Paris, *CM*, vol. 4, pp. 644–45. See also Nicholas Vincent, *The Holy Blood: King Henry III and the Westminster Blood Relic* (Cambridge: Cambridge University Press, 2001), esp. pp. 1–19.

[143] Weiler, 'Matthew Paris on the Writing of History', p. 263.

Wendover had penned his account from the perspective of someone opposing the state of affairs, Matthew's viewpoint was closer to that of the rebel.

Matthew saw the English prelates casting aside all shame and dignity, overzealous in their eagerness to please the legate. The prelates applauded, they offered gifts – both in excess and of symbolic value – and they competed to honour and flatter Otto the most. These prelates came in procession; they met Otto with the peal of bells, and they elongated the *occursus* in servile eagerness. The king, too, was a subservient fool – the biggest of them all. It had, after all, been at his request that the legate had come to England. Henry only played a limited role at the reception, but it was one of comical ridiculousness. Wherever Henry put his head, it was an image ridiculed. Henry conducted the legate into the interior of the kingdom to help him take possession of England on behalf of the pope.

Otto's response was one of indifference. He remained passive throughout the entire scene, save for one notable exception. Admittedly, he was not expected to do much during the *adventus*, apart from 'being received', but when he did act, he distributed English benefices to his men. The English had just recognised his authority by the giving of special clothing, and Otto's response was to utilise that authority to reward his own men, showing no regard for the English. Matthew wondered why the king and the English prelates failed to recognise the legate's indifference to them, instead willingly submitting to the papacy. Accordingly, Matthew's interpretation and depiction of the legatine *adventus* revealed remarkable acumen through his recognition of how power and authority were shaped by popular projection. The English – both the king and the prelates – granted Otto his authority, and their acknowledgement of his authority was the foundation for the exercise of his legatine powers. Submission was a choice.

Conclusion

With the rise of the reform papacy, a distinctive vision of papal monarchy and supremacy emerged. Its origins and causes are complex and somewhat obscure, but the age of the reform papacy and papal monarchy stands as distinct and significant. A particular image of the papacy shone increasingly brighter from Rome, permeating Latin Christendom. When the papacy dispatched its legates, these legates had to capture the light of the papacy to position themselves as extensions of the pope. The most pivotal moment for a legate to express his papal identity was during his reception and entry into his province: his *adventus*.

This study has examined how Anglo-Norman commentators processed this important ceremony, focusing on their receptions, interpretations, and adaptations of the meaning of the legatine *adventus* within each one's framework and agenda. It has demonstrated the variety with which English commentators approached this topic. This study has also enhanced our understanding of the papacy's perspective on the reception of its legates. Moreover, it has contributed to our comprehension of the intricacy of the *adventus* as both a performance and a message. Performance, message, and interpretation were intricately interwoven. The study has revealed the anxieties and cares of recipient communities, providing insight into the diverse perspectives surrounding legatine *adventus* ceremonies. Such insights will enable us, in this conclusion, to peel back some of the layers of the supposed consensus that the legatine *adventus* was intended to elicit, and to delve into the underlying dynamics.

The *adventus* has a long history, with numerous variations existing throughout time. At its core, the ceremony conveyed and asserted the lordship of a ruler and the acknowledgement of the ruler's authority by his or her subjects. To convey its message effectively, the curia devised a distinct legatine *adventus*. The ceremony was distinctive not because it required a specific performance, but rather because, through it, the curia propagated its own view of the ideal reception of a papal legate. While we may lack a detailed papal programme, available evidence strongly indicates the existence of a relatively coherent tradition throughout the period under consideration. The legatine *adventus* was about papal authority. The pope was obligated to govern the Church and attend to its needs, and papal legates were effectively extensions of the pope, entrusted with the responsibility of governing the Church in their designated provinces on his behalf. Receiving a papal legate with an *adventus* signified a recognition of the divinely ordained papal hierarchy. Moreover, the legate's presence recreated the presence of St Peter, Rome, the pope, and, to some degree, Christ.

Studying any reception as an actual event is extremely difficult, if not impossible in most instances. Nevertheless, surviving evidence strongly suggests that legates received an *adventus* when granted entry into England. The monastic *adventus* instructions, in particular, offer proof of the richness and elaborate nature of the ceremony: communities might employ bells, incense, Scripture, singing, praying, processions, space, and more. Although the monastic communities who produced these instructions were the experts in such ceremonies, there is no basis for assuming that kings, bishops, and other lords were incapable of orchestrating elaborate receptions. In the same vein, there is little reason to believe that the insights gained from studying the monastic *adventus* instructions are confined solely to monastic communities.

The *adventus* instructions devote considerable attention to performance, outlining in meticulous detail the procedures for preparing and receiving a dignitary in an appropriate manner. Archbishop Lanfranc's instruction stands out for its level of detail. Lanfranc described the duties of each participant: how the monks were to dress, where they should meet to prepare, what they should prepare, how they should walk in procession, what they should sing, what liturgical processional items to use, where to pray, where to kneel, etc.

Lanfranc's instruction was designed to navigate the welcoming of a dignitary in a way most beneficial to the community. The ceremony aimed to minimise disruptions, foster community cohesion, and underscore the internal hierarchical divisions. The intention behind the ceremony was to welcome dignitaries, to familiarise such individuals with the monastic community, and to establish closer bonds of friendship between him and the community.

The Cistercian and Gilbertine instructions shared similar objectives and employed related strategies. However, divergences and adaptations show how a host community, by altering various parts of the ritual, could convey considerably different messages: performance and message were closely intertwined. Commentators used descriptions of performances to articulate their own views, with Matthew Paris' elongation of the *occursus* being the most conspicuous illustration of this interplay.

The *adventus* instructions also reveal the apprehensiveness experienced by communities facing the approach of a powerful dignitary. The relationships of power obviously varied significantly between various communities and lords, yet the *adventus* instructions still elucidate the differing interests at stake within a reception, whether the recipients of a papal legate were a monastic community, a bishop, or a king. Authors of the instructions took great care to shield the head of the community from the potentially disruptive powers of an arriving dignitary. Safeguarding the internal hierarchy was important.

This emphasis on protecting the community's internal hierarchy unveils three perspectives: that of the visiting dignitary, that of the head of the community, and that of the ordinary members of the community. One can readily envisage numerous subdivisions, and, in fact, Matthew Paris described such a (sub)division within the community. He depicted a divided England during Cardinal-Legate Otto's reception, wherein the dignitary (Legate Otto), the head of the community (the king), and parts of the community (the prelates) aligned on one interpretation of the legatine *adventus*, but another part of the community (Archbishop Edmund and the English secular magnates) held a different opinion.

Taken altogether, this raises questions about the degree of social and political consensus present during such receptions. Genuine consensus only occurred when all interpretations converged. However, unanimity was not always necessary for the *appearance* of consensus. As Kim Esmark argues (previously mentioned in chapter 2), 'actors and audiences did not need to believe wholeheartedly in the sincerity of everything that went on in a particular ceremony … as long as they agreed to, or accepted the need for, participation, it worked'.[1] The objective behind such ceremonies was to attain a level of social and political consensus, within which the outward appearance of order and stable hierarchies might be upheld. The challenge for recipients of papal legates was that the nature of papal legation militated against even this degree of consensus, although it did not render it impossible. The popes reinvigorated papal legation to bring reform to the provinces: legates challenged established hierarchies, degrading bishops and imposing the reform agenda upon the local churches. The dispatch of a legate was often a response to a dispute or an emergency.

It did not help recipients that papal legation was ambiguous and everchanging. The cardinal-legates *a latere* only emerged during the pontificate of Alexander III, a period marked by protracted schisms and by clashes with the emperor. These circumstances propelled the cardinal-legates onto the stage as unequivocally the most powerful extensions of the pope. Yet, the popes persistently redefined their spheres of authority and autonomy, always using legates *a latere* in an *ad hoc* fashion. It is impressive that the canonists were able to present a relatively coherent picture of the legatine offices.

---

[1] Kim Esmark, 'Just Rituals: Masquerade, Manipulation, and Officialising Strategies in Saxo's Gesta Danorum', in *Rituals, Performatives, and Political Order in Northern Europe, c. 650–1350*, ed. Wojtek Jerzierski et al. (Turnhout: Brepols, 2015), pp. 237–67, at p. 243.

Although papal legates *a latere* wielded considerable dominion over the local ecclesiastical hierarchy, it could be difficult to draw the line. Cardinal Nicholas' desperate plea to Pope Innocent III merits repetition: 'I beg your Holiness, for the avoidance of every kind of ambiguity, to let me know your will by letter, clearly and distinctly, and give me power to act notwithstanding earlier letters obtained from the Apostolic See'.[2] Popes expected cardinal-legates to promote, communicate, and argue for the papal world order (in addition to carrying out their missions), but that world order ended at the feet of the pope, not in the itinerant legatine court. In this sense, papal communication of legatine authority was inherently ambiguous. In 1237, Pope Gregory IX directed the English to receive Cardinal Otto 'as if our person' ('tanquam personam nostram'),[3] yet he never gave Otto the freedom to act as if he were the pope. Uncertainty surrounded the relationship and the precise boundaries between the authority of the legate and the powers residing in the legatine province, especially the king. The execution of legatine authority hinged on interactions with the subjects of the legatine provinces. Was the legate welcome? Did he possess the social and diplomatic acumen required to navigate intricate political issues? As the legate drew closer to his province, the first major test awaited: his reception, his *adventus*.

The legatine *adventus* drew the attention of commentators, albeit primarily when accompanied by some form of dispute. Although this bias by the commentators, unfortunately, skews the evidence for modern historians, it is at the same time evident that the appearance of consensus was convincing enough to sustain the 'system' for hundreds of years – a remarkable accomplishment. Not every participant may have believed wholeheartedly in all that went on, but enough accepted the ceremony as meaningful. However, it is equally intriguing to look beyond the outward appearance of consensus to explore the disputes and perspectives that conveyed subversive opinions. Doing so provides insights into challenges against consensus.

The interpretations of the legatine *adventus* ceremonies were contested because the *adventus* was about power. Even the core message of the ceremony – the idea that granting an *adventus* signified the recognition of the authority of the

---

[2] Angelo Mercati, 'La Prima Relazione del Cardinale Nicolò de Romanis sulla sua legazione in Inghilterra', in *Essays in History Presented to Reginald Lane Poole*, ed. H. W. C. Davis (Oxford: Clarendon Press, 1927), pp. 274–89, at p. 285: 'quare uestre obnixe supplico sanctitati quatinus ad amouendam ambiguitatem omnimodam clare distincte et aperte per uestras litteras uestram mihi aperiatis de omnibus uoluntatem, mandantes ut non obstantibus litteris hactenus a sede apostolica impetratis rite procedere ualeam in predictis.' Translated by Christopher R. Cheney, *Pope Innocent III and England* (Stuttgart: Hiersemann, 1976), p. 350.

[3] Lucien Auvray, ed., *Les registres de Grégoire IX: recueil des bulles de ce pape*, 4 vols (Paris: Albert Fontemoing, 1896–1955), vol. 2, no. 3509, col. 563.

individual being received – was susceptible to manipulation. Roger of Howden's depiction of the reception of Cardinal-Legate John of Anagni comes to mind. Although there was nothing formally to fault in Roger's presentation of the legatine *adventus*, Roger simultaneously portrayed the *adventus* as mirage, as King Richard curbed John's ability to act, while at the same time exploiting the authority of the legate to his advantage.

The challenges to the legatine *adventus* in Roger of Howden's writings thus mainly came from the king. It was also from this monarchical vantage point, the head of the community, that Roger viewed the legatine *adventus*. Roger contended that papal assertions of authority carried weight only when endorsed by the king. The king, consequently, extended *adventus* ceremonies to legates who entered the kingdom on his invitation, whereas he reacted angrily when faced with uninvited legates. Roger's standpoint aligned so well with the royal stance that it likely mirrored the king's views in most instances.

Roger's portrayal of the legatine *adventus* unveils how conditional consensus could be. Consensus only materialised – deepfelt or not – when the interests and perspectives of the head of the community, the king, converged with those of the pope and the legate. The reception of the two papal legates at the turn of 1186 is a case in point. Yet, Roger's portrayal of the king's actions towards even those whom he welcomed betrays a crucial aspect of the interpretation of the legatine *adventus*. According to Roger, the king displayed an awareness of the arriving papal legates' assertions of authority. In response, akin to the head of the community in the *adventus* instructions, the king sought to control access to the visiting legate by appointing guides and escorts. The job of these guides and escorts was to ensure that the legate's actions aligned with the king's wishes, demonstrating that the king did not accept papal claims of authority to govern the English Church. While this is not groundbreaking news, it does shed light on the king's strategy for navigating papal assertions. With the disclaimer that Roger may have misrepresented the royal view, however unlikely in this instance, it is clear that the king did not believe wholeheartedly in the underlying message of the legatine *adventus*; yet as long as he could exert control over the outcomes and exploit legatine authority to his advantage, the king played along. Roger's depiction of King Henry II's hostility towards uninvited legates underscores the conditional nature of his cooperativeness.

Gervase of Canterbury offers another perspective. He recorded a number of legatine *adventus* ceremonies, often without explicit commentary, suggesting that a shared understanding was in place. However, one reception held significant importance for him: the arrival of two papal legates at Canterbury Cathedral on Christmas Day. Gervase viewed this event through the lens of community members who yearned for the papal legates to oust the head of the community, who, according to Gervase, had committed crimes against the cathedral and its protector, St Thomas. Gervase saw these legates as extensions of the pope, and while he accepted their authority, he also tailored the ceremony to accommodate a distinctive Canterbury agenda.

Gervase's interpretation was circumstantial. While he drew upon existing ideas, Gervase reconfigured them to suit his immediate objectives. The landing at Sandwich was a form of St Thomas imitation, tying the legates to St Thomas' fight for the freedom of the Church. However, Gervase did not apply this motif universally: there is, for instance, no trace of John of Anagni landing at Sandwich. Similar claims could be made regarding the legatine symbols: the mitre and the cross. Gervase only cared about the insignia of the two papal legates entering the cathedral on Christmas Day, because it highlighted the expulsion of false archiepiscopal authority from Christ Church. This circumstantial interpretation is also evident in Gervase's record of Archbishop Baldwin's discomfort when summoned to partake in the reception of the two papal legates at Westminster. Gervase recorded no corresponding disquiet at the reception of John of Anagni.

Gervase's account of the Christmas *adventus* of 1186 exhibits a degree of certainty of purpose and a trust in the unity of the Canterbury chapter, which suggests that the opposite was indeed the case. Gervase recounted how the Christ Church monks received the two legates, implying the presence of the entire monastic community. The veracity of his claim is irrelevant: more importantly, Gervase had crafted a narrative that projected a sense of unity within the chapter, with the mere act of physical attendance generating the appearance of consensus. A closer examination of the *Chronica*, however, reveals that dissident voices existed within the convent – noting the presence of monks who had fled in support of Baldwin. Gervase advanced an interpretation in which, according to his Benedictine outlook, the humble monks would be exalted and the proud archbishop-abbot brought low. Papal power was an important part of Gervase's story, leading him to argue for a specific interpretation of the legatine *adventus*. This interpretation was circumstantial and distinctly localised, but it was also one that was not unanimously accepted, even within his own chapter.

Roger of Wendover remained with the recipient community, albeit another recipient community. Roger purportedly spoke on behalf of all the English, particularly the clergy, but not the king. How many he actually spoke for cannot be determined, though the attacks on foreign clergy in England suggests a degree of alignment between Roger's views and those held by some powerful Englishmen.

Roger's perspective was informed by the enfeoffment of England to the papacy. This shift in Anglo-Papal relations decisively shaped his view of the legatine *adventus*. Roger accepted the core meaning of the *adventus* as an acknowledgement of authority, possibly even to the extent of a possession-taking of England. He even portrayed, tongue in cheek, the reception of Cardinal-Legate Nicholas as an event seemingly met with accord. However, the appearance of unity was only a result of deception: Nicholas was not the saviour of English concordance. In Roger's narrative, the legate and the pope (the 'dignitary') aligned with the king (the head of the community) against the English (the community). The English only realised too late that the legate and the pope had colluded with the king to undermine both justice and Christian values.

The primary subversive thrust of Roger's interpretation rested on his view of the papal world order as one characterised by disorder. In contrast to his namesake, Roger of Howden, who mainly disputed the extent of papal-legatine authority, Roger of Wendover challenged the papacy's self-perception as a force for good in this world. Papal lordship was supposed to be benevolent, but was instead abusive. According to Roger, the papacy failed to discern the true nature of humility and arrogance. Roger did not contest that the papacy had taken possession of England, but he questioned the pope's right to do so and, by extension, the legitimacy of the legatine *adventus*.

Matthew Paris shared certain aspects of interpretation and moral judgement with Roger of Wendover, particularly concerning the abhorrent conditions of the vassalage. However, his perspective diverged in one crucial way: in his *Chronica Majora*, Matthew saw the reception of Legate Otto from the perspective of those within the community who refused to welcome the legate. According to Matthew, this group included Archbishop Edmund and the English magnates, introducing a division within the community that was not present in Roger's accounts. While the veracity of Matthew's claim (that they refused to receive the legate) is highly doubtful, his view remains significant, revealing Matthew's disagreement with the papal stance on the pope's right to attend to the cares of the churches. If the papacy had deviated from the right path – according to Matthew's position – it was then morally justifiable to oppose its legates.

Matthew's intention was to demonstrate the absurdity of the official English position. The king had the right to refuse Cardinal-Legate Otto access to England. However, not only did the king not refuse Otto access, he instead openly invited the legate. Receiving the legate with an *adventus* was tantamount to willing submission. Yet, both King Henry and the English prelates (excluding Archbishop Edmund) received the legate with sycophantic enthusiasm. In contrast, Matthew adeptly crafted his descriptions to convey the event's farcical nature as he saw it. Matthew stretched and exaggerated and transformed decorous deeds such as processions and gift-giving into absurdities. The legate only took; he never gave. This reflected Matthew's own perception of the contemporary papacy.

***

Receiving a papal legate with an *adventus* meant different things to different people. The curia propagated a narrative that needed to be outwardly embraced to establish working relations with the papacy. Just as the legate himself functioned as an agent of reform, the legatine *adventus* acted as a strategic tool for the papacy to assert its authority throughout Latin Christendom. Extending an *adventus* to a legate signified recognition of the papal governance of the Church. However, much like the challenge of pinpointing the causes of papal reform, it is impossible to disentangle the legatine *adventus* from domestic politics.

Cardinal-legates *a latere* were usually invited, their arrivals often the result of someone in England being willing to accept the papal interpretation of the legatine *adventus*. As a direct consequence of this, the legatine *adventus* became entangled within domestic politics, which explains the range of available interpretations – which included different commentators adapting the ritual to suit their particular circumstances. The *adventus* could be integrated into a local setting, assigned an alternative meaning, or rejected altogether as illegitimate. Interpreting a legatine *adventus* was a means to further or counter interests within the polity.

Nonetheless, the legatine *adventus* was not merely a tool for domestic politicians; rather, by becoming entwined with domestic politics, the *adventus* emerged as a significant aspect of the papacy's involvement in England and Christendom. This development serves to elucidate the ceremony's importance and provides a plausible explanation for hosts' and legates' insistence on its performance. The reception of a legate with an *adventus* signified tacit acceptance of the ritual's meaning, while silence implied consent. The ritual potentially had the power to 'capture' dissenters by their mere presence. It became, in short, an articulation of power. Such factors explain why Matthew omitted Archbishop Edmund and the English magnates from the reception of Cardinal-Legate Otto, as their presence would have conferred their consent.

These considerations offer likely explanations for why the legatine *adventus* endured, with chroniclers frequently finding themselves compelled to comment on the reception of a papal legate *a latere*. Obviously, chroniclers not only commented on the legatine *adventus* but on other variants of the ritual as well. However, papal legates, as powerful dignitaries from afar, differed from other lords who primarily itinerated within their own lordships. The nature of papal legation set the legatine *adventus* apart, as it centred on the manner in which the papacy was invited into the kingdoms and polities of Europe.

Much remains unexplored by modern historians. Further, in-depth explorations into the perspectives on and interpretations of the legatine *adventus*, and ideally the actual receptions of papal legates *a latere*, have the potential to reveal insights into the role of the papacy in shaping domestic politics. Such studies could illuminate the reach and extent of papal authority, not just in England, but across the entirety of Christendom.

v

Appendix 1

In his *Commentaria/Lectura* (completed just before 1271), Cardinal Hostiensis glossed canon five of the Fourth Lateran Council. He noted that legates used 'vestibus rubeis, palefredo albo freno et calcaribus deauratis, et similibus'.[1] This statement has been subject to different interpretations, and thus requires a detailed discussion. All scholars agree that 'vestibus rubeis' refers to red clothing or garments (and that 'similibus', i.e., 'similar things', tells us little more). The disagreements are about the passages 'palefredo albo freno' and 'calcaribus deauratis'. There are two different interpretations: that of Karl Rueß, and that of Figueira, Salminen, and Rennie.[2]

Rueß interprets the passage 'palefredo albo freno' as two separate things, 'a white horse' and 'reins', respectively. The others interpret it as 'a horse with white reins'. Both interpretations have their merits, and there are no compelling internal or grammatical reasons to favour one above the other: only circumstantial evidence provides some clues.

The interpretation 'a horse with white reins' assumes that the legate's horse only approached the appearance of the papal horse – this is possible. The legate, after all, was not the pope. The legate rode a horse of some other colour, but used white reins to mark his association with the pope.[3] Rueß's interpretation ('a white horse'

---

[1] Cited in Robert Charles Joseph Figueira, 'The Canon Law of Medieval Papal Legation' (unpublished PhD dissertation, Cornell University, Ithaca, NY, 1980), p. 380.

[2] See Figueira, 'The Canon Law', p. 380; Tapio Salminen, 'In the Pope's Clothes: Legatine Representation and Apostolic Insignia in High Medieval Europe', in *Roma, magistra mundi. Itineraria culturae medievalis: mélanges offerts au père L.E. Boyle à l'occasion de son 75e anniversaire*, ed. Jacqueline Hamesse, Textes et Études Du Moyen Age 10 (Louvain-la-Neuve: Brepols, 1998), pp. 349–54, at p. 350; Kriston Robert Rennie, 'The Ceremonial Reception of Medieval Papal Legates', *JEH* 69, no. 2 (2018): 1–20, p. 8; and Karl Rueß, *Die rechtliche Stellung der päpstlichen Legaten bis Bonifaz VIII.* (Paderborn: Ferdinand Schöningh., 1912), pp. 204–5.

[3] Agostino Paravicini-Bagliani has noted that the cardinals covered their horses with white cloth during the papal inauguration-procession in Rome at the time of Gregory X (r. 1271–76); see Agostino Paravicini-Bagliani, *The Pope's Body*, trans. David S. Peterson (Chicago and London: University of Chicago Press, 2000), pp. 83–84. However, the

and 'reins'), on the other hand, assumes that the legate's horse closely resembled the pope's horse, which intuitively seems more convincing, given the purpose of legatine insignia. The idea that the legate's horse would strongly emulate the papal horse supports the intended visual connection between the legate and the pope. However, this interpretation raises the question of why the reins are specifically mentioned. If the reins held no particular significance, their mention seems redundant, as most riders presumably used some form of harness to ride.

There are two pieces of circumstantial evidence to counter this reservation. The first is that later *ordines* (fifteenth century) incontrovertibly recognised the legate's right to a white horse.[4] The other is that King Henry II, according to the Pipe Rolls, provided Cardinal-Legate Vivian with a white horse.[5] The gift implied not only that Legate Vivian was allowed to ride a white horse but that the king recognised it as a mark of legatine dignity (even if he did not recognise Vivian as a legate to England).

In the end, making a definitive choice is not possible. However, I find Rueß's interpretation to be the most plausible because it makes the most sense in light of the purpose of legatine insignia. A white horse in a procession would stand out relative to, say, a brown horse with white reins, especially if there were a substantial number of spectators watching the procession at some distance. Finally, it is possible that both the horse and the reins were white.

Next in line are the words 'calcaribus deauratis'. Most scholars interpret them as 'gilded shoes'. Rueß, on the other hand, interprets them as 'gilded spurs'. The most straightforward translation of *calcar* is spur, and the context only reinforces this interpretation – Hostiensis had just mentioned the white horse. Canon sixteen of the Fourth Lateran Council provides circumstantial corroborating evidence for Rueß's interpretation. The canon forbade certain clerical clothes and also mentioned 'calcaribus deauratis' in a context in which the meaning was clearly 'gilded spurs':[6]

> ... let them not enjoy cloth of red or green nor long sleeves or shoes with embroidery or peaked toes, saddles, harness, breastplates and gilded spurs, or wearing another superfluity.

---

presence of the pope curtailed everyone's ceremonial rights, including cardinals, making the observation untransferable.

[4] Franz Wasner, 'Fifteenth-Century Texts on the Ceremonial of the Papal "Legatus a Latere"', *Traditio* 14 (1958): 295–358, p. 330.

[5] PR, vol. 26, Henry II (1176–77), p. 47: 'ten [probably marks or pounds] for the white horse for the use of the legate Vivian' ('et pro .j. palefrido albo ad opus Viuiani legati').

[6] Antonio García y García, ed., *Constitutiones Concilii quarti Lateranensis una cum commentariis glossatorum*, Monumenta iuris canonici, A: Corpus glossatorum 2 (Vatican City: Biblioteca Apostolica Vaticana, 1981), c. 16, pp. 64–65.

[… pannis rubeis aut viridibus, necnon manicis aut sobtularibus consutitiis seu rostratis, sellis, frenis, pectoralibus et calcaribus deauratis aut aliam superfluitatem gerentibus non utantur.]

Considering that the canon had just mentioned 'shoes with embroidery or peaked toes', it would be odd if it then mentioned several other items, only to return to the shoes of the clergy. 'Calcaribus deauratis' are, moreover, mentioned together with items related to riding. Thus, the Fourth Lateran most likely forbade clerics from using gilded spurs. Hostiensis, glossing the canons of the Fourth Lateran, used the same expression, 'calcaribus deauratis', to describe a type of legatine insignia. It is reasonable to presume that he referred to the same, that is, 'gilded spurs'.

Appendix 2

This appendix provides a comparison of the *adventus* instructions of the Gilbertine and Cistercian orders by presenting the respective instruction texts in parallel. It also discusses one other item related to the instructions. The italics indicate differences between the two texts.

The Gilbertine instruction[1]	The Cistercian instruction (Dijon recension)[2]
Ad suscipiendum episcopum, convocentur *omnes* in chorum campana. Tunc sumat aliquis aquam benedictam nutu cantoris; quo præcedente, sequatur *prior*; deinde conventus et novicii bini et bini, sacerdotibus praeuntibus, eo ordine quo in choro stant. Cunctisque egressis et stantibus ordinatim ante fores monasterii; portarius vel alius quislibet ad hoc ydoneus, à *priore* jussus interim obviam eis adducat episcopum. Quo appropinquante, flectant omnes genua ante eum. Quibus erectis, porrigat *prior* episcopo spersorium osculans ei manum; *deinde textum ad osculandum. Quo thurificato*, incipiat cantor vel *alius responsorium*, Honor	Ad suscipiendum episcopum convocentur *fratres* in chorum campana. Tunc sumat aliquis aquam benedictam nutu cantoris. quo precedente sequatur *abbas*. deinde conventus et novicii bini et bini. sacerdotibus preeuntibus eo ordine quo in choro stant. Cunctisque egressis et stantibus ordinatim ante fores monasterii. portaris vel alius quilibet ad hoc idoneus ab *abbate* iussus interim obvium eis adducat episcopum. Quo appropinquante flectant omnes genua ante eum. Quibus erectis porrigat *abbas* episcopo sparsorium. osculans ei manum. Et incipiente cantore vel AUDI ISRAEL. *si unus*. vel SINT LUMBI. *si plures fuerint episcopi* :

---

[1] William Dugdale, ed., *Monasticon Anglicanum: A History of the Abbies and Other Monasteries, Hospitals, Frieries, and Cathedral and Collegiate Churches, with Their Dependencies in England and Wales; Also of All Such Scotch, Irish, and French Monasteries, as Were in Any Manner Connected with Religious Houses in England*, 2nd edn, 6 volumes in 8 vols (London: James Bohn, 1846), vol. 6:2, p. xxxvi.

[2] *Ecclesiastica Officia*, ch. 86, p. 246.

virtus, vel Summæ Trinitati, vel Sint Lumbi, vel Cives apostolorum. Et incipiente cantore responsorium revertatur conventus ad ecclesiam, quam introeant primùm novicii; deinde cæteri, laicis *canonicis* præeuntibus, ita ut prior eat posterior manutenens episcopum. Cum autem venerint in chorum episcopo incumbente orationi, *prior stans juxta eum*, cæteris post eum sicut ad missam ordinatis; percantato verð responsorio *dicat prior versum, Salvum fac servum tuum Domine. Oremus. Omnipotens sempiterne Deus, miserere huic famulo tuo N. episcopo nostro, et dirige eum, &c. Postea prior erigens episcopum, et data benedictione osculetur eum: post quem omnes alii, si osculum eis obtulerit. Deinde ducatur in capitulum, sermonem facturus si voluerit, vel ad suum hospitium, si capitulum intrare noluerit.* Sciendum autem, quod ad nullum recipiendum vadit conventus, nisi ad proprium episcopum et archiepiscopum, et sedis apostolicæ legatos, et regem et dominum papam *et magistrum de novo creatum*. Nulli horum omnium nisi domino papæ. Plusquam semel hæc fit processio *nisi proprio episcopo, à transmarinis reverso.*

introeant primum novicii. deinde ceteri. laicis *monachis* preeuntibus. ita ut *abbas* eat posterior. manu tenens episcopum. Cum autem venerint in chorum. episcopo incumbente orationi *abbas veniat in locum suum.* ceteris post eum sicut ad missam ordinatis. Percantato vero responsorio *abbas* erigens episcopum *ducat in capitulum. ubi cunctis ordine residentibus accepta benedictione ab episcopo legat lectionem cui cantor innuerit. Qua finita. dicto BENEDICITE. osculetur abbas episcopum et comites eius. nisi prius episcopus voluerit aliquid dicere pro edificatione. Deinde surgentes omnes et inclinantes ad benedictionem episcopi. quam abbas debet requirere nisi antea in oratorio dederit. responso AMEN egrediantur. et deducatur episcopus ad hospitium.* Sciendum autem quod ad nullum recipiendum vadit conventus. nisi ad proprium episcopum et archiepiscopum. et sedis apostolice legatos. et regem. et domnum papam. *et proprium abbatem.* Nulli horum omnium nisi domno pape plusquam semel hec fit processio.

Brian Golding has emphasised that 'the king alone amongst the laity was permitted by the [Gilbertine] Rule to be met in procession, an honour which canon law granted to the *patronus*'. Golding linked this right to the fact that 'the king could be regarded as the [Gilbertine] order's paramount patron'.[3] However, this permission is part of the near-verbatim recycling, in the Gilbertine instruction, of the Cistercian instruction's final clause, including the *sciendum autem* part

---

[3] Brian Golding, *Gilbert of Sempringham and the Gilbertine Order, c.1130–c.1300* (Oxford: Clarendon Press, 1995), p. 312.

(the 'also to be known' part). The Cistercians had composed this prior to Pope Clement III's ruling on the right of the patron. It is therefore debatable to what extent the instruction reflected Gilbertine concerns. Compare the relevant parts of the two instructions:

The Cistercian instruction:

> Sciendum autem quod ad nullum recipiendum vadit conventus. nisi ad proprium episcopum et archiepiscopum. et sedis apostolice legatos. et regem. et domnum papam. et proprium abbatem.[4]

The Gilbertine instruction:

> Sciendum autem, quod ad nullum recipiendum vadit conventus, nisi ad proprium episcopum et archiepiscopum, et sedis apostolicæ legatos, et regem et dominum papam et magistrum de novo creatum.[5]

What seemingly mattered to the Gilbertines was not just the ceremonial rights of the king, but the replacement of the ceremonial rights of the abbot (Gilbertine houses were not abbatial communities) with the ceremonial rights of the master, the leader of their order.[6]

---

[4] *Ecclesiastica Officia*, ch. 86, 11, p. 246.
[5] Dugdale, *Monasticon Anglicanum*, p. xxxvi.
[6] On Pope Clement's ruling, see *Liber Extravagantium Decretalium*, ed. Emil Friedberg, 2 vols, Corpus Iuris Canonici 2 (reprint, Leipzig; Graz: Bernhard Tauchnitz; Akademische Druck u. Verlagsanstalt, 1959), vol. 2, X 3.38.15; available at www.hs-augsburg.de/~harsch/Chronologia/Lspost13/GregoriusIX/gre_0000.html (accessed 15 April 2024).

Bibliography

Primary Sources

Aelred of Rievaulx. *Aelredi Rievallensis Opera omnia*, edited by A. Hoste and C. H. Talbot. 7 vols. CCCM 1. Turnhout: Brepols, 1971.

——*Spiritual Friendship*, edited by Marsha L. Dutton, translated by Lawrence C. Braceland. Collegeville, MN: Liturgical Press, 2010.

Auvray, Lucien, ed. *Les registres de Grégoire IX: recueil des bulles de ce pape*. 4 vols. Paris: Albert Fontemoing, 1896–1955.

Baker, A. T. 'La Vie de Saint Edmond, archevêque de Cantorbéry'. *Romania* 55 (1929): 332–81.

Baldric of Florennes [Baldericus]. 'Gesta Alberonis Archiepiscopi'. In *Chronica et gesta aevi Salici*, edited by Georg Heinrich Pertz, 243–60. MGH: SS 8. Hannover: Hahn, 1848.

Bede. *Bede's Ecclesiastical History of the English People*, edited by Bertram Colgrave and R. A. B. Mynors. Revised edition. OMT. Oxford: Clarendon Press, 1992.

Berger, Élie, ed. *Les registres d'Innocent IV: Recueil des bulles de ce pape*, vol. 2. Paris: Ernest Thorin, 1887.

Bernard of Pavia. *Bernardi Papiensis, Faventini Episcopi, Summa Decretalium*, edited by Bernard Ernst Adolph Laspeyres. Regensburg: G. Iosephum Manz, 1860.

Butler, H. E., ed. *The Autobiography of Giraldus Cambrensis*. London: Jonathan Cape, 1937.

Calendar of the Patent Rolls, 1232–1247. London: Mackie and Co., 1891.

Cardinal Boso. *Boso's Life of Alexander III*, translated by G. M. Ellis. Oxford: Basil Blackwell, 1973.

——'Vita Adriani IV/Life of Adrian IV'. In *Adrian IV The English Pope (1154–1159): Studies and Texts*, edited by Brenda M. Bolton and Anne J. Duggan, 214–33. Aldershot: Ashgate, 2003.

Caspar, Erich, ed. *Das Register Gregors VII. (Gregorii VII Registrum)*. 2 vols. MGH: Epp. Sel. 2. Berlin: Weidmannsche Buchhandlung, 1920–23.

Cawley, Martinus, trans. *The Ancient Usages of the Cistercian Order*. Lafayette, OR: Guadalupe Translations, 1998.

Cheney, Christopher R., and Mary G. Cheney, eds. *The Letters of Pope Innocent III (1198–1216) Concerning England and Wales: A Calendar with an Appendix of Texts*. Oxford: Clarendon Press, 1967.

Cheney, Christopher R., and W. H. Semple, eds and trans., *Selected Letters of*

Pope Innocent III Concerning England (1198–1216). London: Thomas Nelson and Sons, 1953.

Choisselet, Danièle, and Placide Vernet, eds. *Les 'Ecclesiastica Officia' cisterciens du XIIème siècle*. Reiningue: Documentation Cistercienne, 1989.

Clark, John Willis, ed. *The Observances in Use at the Augustinian Priory of S. Giles and S. Andrew at Barnwell, Cambridgeshire*. Cambridge: Macmillan and Bowes, 1897.

Close Rolls of the Reign of Henry III. Preserved in the Public Record Office. A.D. 1234–1237. London: Mackie and Co., 1908.

Close Rolls of the Reign of Henry III. Preserved in the Public Record Office. A.D. 1237–1242. London: The Hereford Times, 1911.

Cowdrey, H. E. J., ed. and trans. *The* Epistolae Vagantes *of Pope Gregory VII*. OMT. Oxford: Clarendon Press, 1972.

—ed. and trans. *The Register of Pope Gregory VII: An English Translation*. Oxford: Oxford University Press, 2002.

Craster, H. H. E., and M. E. Thornton, eds. *The Chronicle of St Mary's Abbey, York: From Bodley MS. 39*. Durham: Andrews & Co., 1934.

The Customary of the Benedictine Abbey of Bury St Edmunds in Suffolk (from Harleian MS. 1005 in the British Museum), edited by Antonia Gransden. Chichester: Moore and Tillyer, The Regnum Press, 1966.

The Customary of the Benedictine Abbey of Eynsham in Oxfordshire, edited by Antonia Gransden. Siegburg: Franciscum Schmitt, 1963.

The Customary of the Cathedral Priory Church of Norwich, edited by J. B. L. Tolhurst. London: Harrison and Sons, 1948.

Daniel of Beccles. *The Book of the Civilised Man: An English Translation of the* Urbanus Magnus *of Daniel of Beccles*, translated by Fiona Whelan, Olivia Spenser, and Francesca Petrizzo. London: Routledge, 2019.

—*Urbanus Magnus Danielis Becclesiensis*, edited by J. Gilbert Smyly. Dublin: Dublin University Press, 1939.

Duchesne, L., ed. *Le Liber Pontificalis: texte, introduction et commentaire*. 2 vols. Paris: Thorin, 1892.

Dugdale, William, ed. *Monasticon Anglicanum: A History of the Abbies and Other Monasteries, Hospitals, Frieries, and Cathedral and Collegiate Churches, with Their Dependencies in England and Wales; Also of All Such Scotch, Irish, and French Monasteries, as Were in Any Manner Connected with Religious Houses in England*. 2nd edn. 6 vols. in 8. London: James Bohn, 1846.

Durand, William. *Speculum iuris Gulielmi Durandi, episcopi Mimatensis, I.V.D. cum Io. And. Baldi de Vbaldis, aliorumque aliquot praestantiss. iurisc. theorematibus. Nunc denuo ab innumeris, quibus antea scatebat, erroribus atque mendis summa industria, & labore repurgatum. Pars prima quarta*. Venice, 1602.

Dykmans, Marc, ed. *Le cérémonial papal de la fin du Moyen-Âge à la Renaissance: Les textes avignonnais jusqu'à la fin du grand schisme d'occident*. 4 vols. Brussels: Institut historique belge de Rome, 1983.

Eadmer of Canterbury. 'Edmeri Cantvariensis Cantoris Nova Opvscvla de

Sanctorum Veneratione et Obsecratione (altera pars)', edited by André Wilmart. *Revue des Sciences Religieuses* 15, no. 3 (1935): 354–79.

——'Historia Novorum in Anglia'. In *Eadmeri Historia Novorum in Anglia, et Opuscula Duo de Vita Sancti Anselmi et Quibusdam Miraculus Ejus*, edited by Martin Rule, 1–302. RS. London: Longman, 1884.

——*Lives and Miracles of Saints Oda, Dunstan, and Oswald*, edited by Andrew J. Turner and Bernard J. Muir. OMT. Oxford: Clarendon Press, 2006.

Friedberg, Emil, ed. *Decretum magistri Gratiani*. Corpus Iuris Canonici 1. Leipzig: Tauchnitz, 1879, available at https://geschichte.digitale-sammlungen.de/decretum-gratiani/online/angebot (accessed 15 April 2024).

——ed. *Liber Extravagantium Decretalium*. Reprint. 2 vols. Corpus Iuris Canonici 2. Leipzig; Graz: Bernhard Tauchnitz; Akademische Druck u. Verlagsanstalt, 1959, available at www.hs-augsburg.de/~harsch/Chronologia/Lspost13/GregoriusIX/gre_0000.html (accessed 15 April 2024).

García y García, Antonio, ed. *Constitutiones Concilii quarti Lateranensis una cum commentariis glossatorum*. Monumenta iuris canonici, A: Corpus glossatorum 2. Vatican City: Biblioteca Apostolica Vaticana, 1981.

Gerald of Wales. 'De Rebus a se Gestis'. In *Giraldi Cambrensis opera*, edited by J. S. Brewer, 1:1–122. RS. London: Longman, 1861.

Gerhoch of Reichersberg. 'De Investigatione Antichristi'. In *Libelli de lite imperatorum et pontificum*, edited by Ernst Dümmler and Ernst Sackur, 305–95. MGH: Ldl 3. Hannover: Hahn, 1897.

Gertz, M. Cl., ed. 'Vita Gvnneri episcopi Vibergensis'. In *Scriptores Minores Historiæ Danicæ Medii Ævi*, 2:265–78. Copenhagen: Selskabet for udgivelse af kilder til dansk historie, 1970.

Gervase of Canterbury. *The Historical Works of Gervase of Canterbury*, edited by William Stubbs. 2 vols. RS. London: Longman, 1879–80.

Goiffon, Étienne, ed. *Bullaire de l'abbaye de Saint-Gilles*. Nîmes: P. Jouve, 1882.

Gransden, Antonia, ed. and trans. *The Chronicle of Bury St Edmunds, Chronica Buriensis, 1212–1301*. London: Nelson, 1964.

The Great Roll of the Pipe for the Twenty-Third Year of the Reign of King Henry the Second, 1176–1177. Vol. 26. London: Spottiswoode & Co., 1905.

The Great Roll of the Pipe for the Twenty-Fifth Year of the Reign of King Henry the Second, 1178–1179. Vol. 28. London: Arthur Doubleday, 1907.

Gregory Nazianzen [S. P. N. Gregorii Theologi Archiepiscopi Constantinopolitani]. 'In laudem magni Athanasii episcopi Alexandrini'. In *Patrologia Graeca*, edited by Jacques-Paul Migne, vol. 35, 1: cols. 1081–1128. Paris: Imprimerie Catholique, 1857.

——'Select Orations'. In *A Select Library of the Nicene and Post-Nicene Fathers of the Christian Church*, edited and translated by Charles Gordon Browne and James Edward Swallow, Second Series, vol. 7, pp. 185–498. Series editors Philip Schaff and Henry Wace. New York: The Christian Literature Co., 1894; repr. Edinburgh: T & T Clark, 1996.

Guigo [Guigues]. 'Consuetudines'. In *PL*, vol. 153, cols. 631–760. Paris, 1854.

Harvey, Barbara F., ed. *Documents Illustrating the Rule of Walter de Wenlock, Abbot of Westminster, 1283–1307*. London: Butler & Tanner, 1965.

Hildegard of Bingen. *Explanation of the Rule of Benedict*, translated by Hugh Feiss. Eugene, OR: Wipf & Stock, 2000.

Hildegard of Bingen [Hildegardis]. 'Regulæ S. Benedicti Explanatio'. In *PL*, 2nd edn, vol. 197, cols. 1053–66. Paris: Garnier Printing, 1882.

Hjermind, Jesper, and Kristian Melgaard, eds. 'Vita Gunneri episcopi Vibergensis'. In *Gunner: Bisp i Viborg 1222–1251*, 10–27. Løgstrup: Forlaget Viborg, 2010.

Holtzmann, Walther, ed. *Papsturkunden in England*. 3 vols. Berlin: various publishers, 1930–52.

The Holy Bible, Douay-Rheims Version: Translated from the Latin Vulgate, revised by Richard Challoner, 1752.

Innocentii III Romani Pontificis Opera Omnia. *PL*, vol. 214. Paris, 1855.

James, Montague Rhodes, ed. *The Ancient Libraries of Canterbury and Dover*. Cambridge: Cambridge University Press, 1903.

Jocelin of Brakelond. *Cronica Jocelini de Brakelonda de rebus gestis Samsonis, Abbatis Monasterii Sancti Edmundi*, edited and translated by H. E. Butler. Medieval Classics. London: Thomas Nelson and Sons, 1949.

John of Salisbury. *Metalogicon*, translated by J. B. Hall. Corpus Christianorum in Translation 12. Turnhout: Brepols, 2013.

——[Ioannes Saresberiensis]. *Metalogicon*, edited by J. B. Hall and Katharine S. B. Keats-Rohan. CCCM 98. Turnhout: Brepols, 1991.

Lanfranc. *Beati Lanfranci archiepiscopi Cantuariensis Opera quae supersunt omnia*, edited by J. A. Giles. 2 vols. Oxford: Paul Renouard, 1844.

——*The Monastic Constitutions of Lanfranc*, edited by David Knowles and Christopher Nugent Lawrence Brooke. OMT. Oxford: Clarendon Press, 2002.

Luard, Henry Richards, ed. 'Annales de Dunstaplia'. In *AM*, 3:3–408. RS. London: Longman, 1866.

——ed. 'Annales de Oseneia'. In *AM*, 4:3–352. RS. London: Longman, 1869.

——ed. 'Annales de Theokesberia'. In *AM*, 1:43–180. RS. London: Longman, 1864.

——ed. 'Annales de Waverleia'. In *AM*, 2:129–411. RS. London: Longman, 1865.

——ed. 'Annales de Wintonia'. In *AM*, 2:3–125. RS. London: Longman, 1865.

——ed. *Roberti Grosseteste episcopi quondam lincolniensis Epistolæ*. RS. London: Longman, 1861.

Mantello, F. A. C, and Joseph Goering, trans. *The Letters of Robert Grosseteste, Bishop of Lincoln*. Toronto: University of Toronto Press, 2010.

Matthew Paris. 'Abbreviatio Chronicorum Angliæ'. In *Matthæi Parisiensis, monachi Sancti Albani, Historia Anglorum, sive, ut vulgo dicitur, Historia Minor. Item, ejusdem Abbreviatio Chronicorum Angliæ*, edited by Frederic Madden, 3:151–348. RS. London: Longmans, 1869.

——*Flores Historiarum*, edited by Henry Richards Luard. 3 vols. RS. London: Eyre and Spottiswoode, 1890.

——[Matthew of Westminster]. *The Flowers of History: Especially Such as Relate to the Affairs of Britain; from the Beginning of the World to the Year 1307*, translated by Charles Duke Yonge. 2 vols. London: Henry G. Bohn, 1853.

——'Gesta Abbatum'. In *Gesta abbatum monasterii Sancti Albani, a Thoma*

Walsingham, regnante Ricardo Secundo, ejusdem ecclesiæ præcentore, compilata, edited by Henry Thomas Riley, 1:3–324. RS. London: Longmans, 1867.
——*The Life of St Edmund*, edited and translated by C. H. Lawrence. Oxford: Alan Sutton, 1996.
——*Matthaei Parisiensis, monachi Sancti Albani, Chronica Majora*, edited by Henry Richards Luard. 7 vols. RS. London: Longman, 1872–83.
——*Matthæi Parisiensis, monachi Sancti Albani, Historia Anglorum, sive, ut vulgo dicitur, Historia Minor. Item, ejusdem Abbreviatio Chronicorum Angliæ*, edited by Frederic Madden. 3 vols. RS. London: Longmans, 1866.
——*Matthew Paris's English History: From the Year 1235 to 1273*, translated by J. A. Giles. 3 vols. London: George Bell & Sons, 1889.
Mercati, Angelo, ed. 'La Prima Relazione del Cardinale Nicolò de Romanis sulla sua legazione in Inghilterra'. In *Essays in History Presented to Reginald Lane Poole*, edited by H. W. C. Davis, 274–89. Oxford: Clarendon Press, 1927.
Munier, Charles, ed. *Concilia Africae, A. 345–A.525*. Corpus Christianorum, Series Latina 149. Turnhout: Brepols, 1974.
Nelson, Janet L., trans. *The Annals of St-Bertin*. Manchester: Manchester University Press, 1991.
Nigel of Whiteacre [Nigellus Wireker]. *The Passion of St. Lawrence, Epigrams and Marginal Poems*, edited by Jan M. Ziolkowski. Leiden: Brill, 1994.
——[Nigel de Longchamps]. *Speculum stultorum*, edited by John H. Mozley and Robert R. Raymo. Berkeley and Los Angeles: University of California Press, 1960.
Pantin, William Abel, ed. *Documents Illustrating the Activities of the General and Provincial Chapters of the English Black Monks 1215–1540*. 3 vols. London: Butler & Tanner, 1931.
Peter of Blois. *Petri Blesensis Bathoniensis Archidiaconi, Opera Omnia*, edited by J. A. Giles. 4 vols. RS. Oxford: I. H. Parker, 1846–47.
Potthast, August, ed. *Regesta Pontificum Romanorum: Inde ab a. post Christum natum MCXCVIII ad a. MCCCIV*. 2 vols. Berlin: Rudolphi de Decker, 1874–75.
Powell, James M., trans. *The Deeds of Pope Innocent III by an Anonymous Author*. Washington, D.C.: The Catholic University of America Press, 2004.
Powicke, F. M., and C. R. Cheney, eds. *Councils & Synods with Other Documents Relating to the English Church*. 2 vols. Oxford: Clarendon Press, 1964.
Pressutti, Pietro, ed. *Regesta Honorii Papae III*. 2 vols. Rome: Typographica Vaticana, 1888–95.
Robertson, James Craigie, and J. Brigstocke Sheppard, eds. *Materials for the History of Thomas Becket, Archbishop of Canterbury*. 7 vols. RS. London: Longmans, 1875–85.
Roger of Howden. *The Annals of Roger de Hoveden. Comprising the History of England and of Other Countries of Europe from A.D. 732 to A.D. 1201*, translated by Henry T. Riley. 2 vols. London: H. G. Bohn, 1853.
——*Chronica magistri Rogeri de Houedene*, edited by William Stubbs. 4 vols. RS. London: Longmans, 1868–71.
[Roger of Howden]. *Gesta Regis Henrici Secundi Benedicti Abbatis*, edited by William Stubbs. 2 vols. RS. London: Longmans, 1867.

Roger of Wendover. *Roger of Wendover's Flowers of History*, translated by J. A. Giles. 2 vols. London: Henry G. Bohn, 1849.

——*Rogeri de Wendover Chronica, sive Flores Historiarum*, edited by Henry O. Coxe. Vol. 1., 4 vols. London: English Historical Society, 1841.

——*Rogeri de Wendover liber qui dicitur Flores Historiarum ab anno Domini MCLIV. Annoque Henrici anglorum regis secundi primo*, edited by Henry G. Hewlett. 3 vols. RS. London: Longman, 1886–89.

Rymer, Thomas, ed. *Foedera, Conventiones, Litteræ, et cujuscunque generis Acta Publica, inter Reges Angliæ et Alios quosvis Imperatores, Reges, Pontifices, Principes, vel Communitates*, revised by the Record Commission. Vol. 1, pt. 1. London, 1816.

Saint Augustine. *The Monastic Rules*, edited by Boniface Ramsey, translated by Agatha Mary and Gerald Bonner. New York: New City Press, 2004.

Saint Benedict. *The Rule of Benedict: An Invitation to the Christian Life*, edited by Georg Holzherr, translated by Mark Thamert. Cistercian Publications. Collegeville, MN: Liturgical Press, 2016.

Salimbene de Adam. *Chronica*, edited by Giuseppe Scalia. 2 vols. CCCM 125. Turnhout: Brepols, 1998–99.

Seegrün, Wolfgang, and Theodor Schieffer, eds. *Provincia Hammaburgo-Bremensis*. Göttingen: Vandenhoeck & Ruprecht, 1981.

Shirley, Walter Waddington, ed. *Royal and Other Historical Letters Illustrative of the Reign of Henry III*. 2 vols. London: Longman, 1862.

Stevenson, Joseph, ed. *Chronicon Monasterii de Abingdon*. 2 vols. RS. London: Longman, 1858.

Stubbs, William, ed. *Epistolæ Cantuarienses, the Letters of the Prior and Convent of Christ Church, Canterbury. From A.D. 1187 to A.D. 1199*. RS. London: Longman, 1865.

Tait, James, ed. *The Chartulary or Register of the Abbey of St. Werburgh Chester*. 2 vols. Manchester: The Chetham Society, 1920.

Tanner, Norman P., ed. *Decrees of the Ecumenical Councils. Vol. 1: Nicaea I to Lateran V*. 2 vols. London: Sheed & Ward, 1990.

Thangmar of Hildesheim. 'Vita Bernwardi episcopi Hildesheimensis'. In *Annales, chronica et historiae aevi Carolini et Saxonici*, edited by Georg Heinrich Pertz, 754–82. MGH: SS 4. Hannover: Hahn, 1841.

Thibodeau, Timothy M., trans. *The Rationale Divinorum Officiorum of William Durand of Mende: A New Translation of the Prologue and Book One*. New York: Columbia University Press, 2007.

Thomas of Marlborough. *History of the Abbey of Evesham*, edited by Jane E. Sayers and Leslie Watkiss. OMT. Oxford: Oxford University Press, 2003.

Thomson, Rodney M., ed. *The Chronicle of the Election of Hugh, Abbot of Bury St. Edmunds and Later Bishop of Ely*. OMT. Oxford: Clarendon Press, 1974.

Urbani II Pontificis Romani Epistolæ, Diplomata, Sermones. PL, vol. 151. Paris, 1853.

Vincent, Nicholas, ed. *The Letters and Charters of Cardinal Guala Bicchieri, Papal Legate in England, 1216–1218*. Woodbridge: Boydell Press, 1996.

Waitz, G., ed. *Annales Bertiniani*. MGH: SS rer. Germ. 5. Hannover: Hahn, 1883.

Walter Bower. *Scotichronicon by Walter Bower*, edited by D. E. R. Watt. 9 vols. Aberdeen: Aberdeen University Press, 1994.

Wasner, Franz. 'Fifteenth-Century Texts on the Ceremonial of the Papal "Legatus a Latere"'. *Traditio* 14 (1958): 295–358.

——'"Legatus a Latere": Addenda Varia'. *Traditio* 16 (1960): 405–16.

Weber, Robert, and Bonifatius Fischer, eds. *Biblia Sacra: iuxta vulgatem versionem*. 3rd edn. Stuttgart: Deutsche Bibelgesellschaft, 1983.

William of Malmesbury. *Historia Novella: The Contemporary History*, edited by Edmund King, translated by K. R. Potter. OMT. Oxford: Clarendon Press, 1998.

William of Tyre. *A History of Deeds Done Beyond the Sea*, translated by Emily Atwater Babcock and A. C. Krey. 2 vols. New York: Columbia University Press, 1943.

——[Willelmvs Tyrensis]. *Chronicon*, edited by R. B. C. Huygens, H. E. Mayer, and G. Rösch. 2 vols. CCCM 63. Turnhout: Brepols, 1986.

Williamson, E. W., ed. *The Letters of Osbert of Clare, Prior of Westminster*. Oxford: Oxford University Press, 1929.

Published Secondary Sources

Bachmann, Johannes. *Die päpstlichen Legaten in Deutschland und Skandinavien (1125–1159)*. Berlin: Matthiesen Verlag, 1913.

Baldwin, John W. *The Government of Philip Augustus: Foundations of French Royal Power in the Middle Ages*. Berkeley: University of California Press, 1991.

Barlow, Frank. 'Roger of Howden'. *EHR* 65, no. 256 (1950): 352–60.

——*Thomas Becket*. Berkeley and Los Angeles: University of California Press, 1990.

Barnaby, James. '*Becket vult*: The Appropriation of St Thomas Becket's Image During the Canterbury Dispute, 1184–1200'. In *ANS XL*, edited by Elisabeth van Houts, 63–76. Woodbridge: Boydell Press, 2018.

——'The Coventry Dispute and Alan of Tewkesbury'. *Journal of Medieval Monastic Studies* 9 (2020): 83–105.

——*Religious Conflict at Canterbury Cathedral in the Late Twelfth Century: The Dispute between the Monks and the Archbishops, 1184–1200*. Woodbridge: Boydell Press, 2024.

Bartlett, Robert. *Gerald of Wales: A Voice of the Middle Ages*. 2nd edn. Stroud: Tempus, 2006.

Bates, David. *William the Conqueror*. New Haven: Yale University Press, 2016.

Beattie, B. R. *Angelus Pacis: The Legation of Cardinal Giovanni Gaetano Orsino, 1326–1334*. Leiden: Brill, 2007.

Bell, Catherine. *Ritual Theory – Ritual Practice*. Oxford: Oxford University Press, 1992.

Benson, Robert L. *The Bishop-Elect: A Study in Medieval Ecclesiastical Office*. Princeton: Princeton University Press, 1968.

Benzinger, Josef. *Invectiva in Romam: Romkritik im Mittelalter vom 9. bis zum 12. Jahrhundert*. Lübeck and Hamburg: Matthiesen Verlag, 1968.

Berman, Constance Hoffman. *The Cistercian Evolution: The Invention of a Religious Order in Twelfth-Century Europe*. Philadelphia and Oxford: University of Pennsylvania Press, 2000.

Beskow, Per. *Rex Gloriae: The Kingship of Christ in the Early Church*, translated by Eric J. Sharpe. Eugene, OR: Wipf & Stock, 1962.

Beyer, Katrin. 'Wit and Irony – Rhetorical Strategies and Their Performance in Political and Learned Communication in England (c.1066–1259)'. In *Networks of Learning: Perspectives on Scholars in Byzantine East and Latin West, c.1000–1200*, edited by Sita Steckel, Niels Gaul, and Michael Grünbart, 147–59. Berlin: LIT Verlag, 2014.

Bijsterveld, Arnoud-Jan A. *Do ut des: Gift-Giving, Memoria, and Conflict Management in the Medieval Low Countries*. Hilversum: Verloren, 2007.

——'The Medieval Gift as Agent of Social Bonding and Political Power: A Comparative Approach'. In *Medieval Transformations: Texts, Power and Gifts in Context*, edited by Esther Cohen and Mayke B. de Jong, 123–56. Leiden: Brill, 2001.

Billett, Jesse D. 'The Liturgy of the "Roman" Office in England from the Conversion to the Conquest'. In *Rome Across Time and Space: Cultural Transmission and the Exchange of Ideas c.500–1400*, edited by Claudia Bolgia, Rosamond McKitterick, and John Osborne, 84–110. Cambridge: Cambridge University Press, 2011.

Binski, Paul. 'The Faces of Christ in Matthew Paris's Chronica Majora'. In *Tributes in Honour of James H. Marrow: Studies in Painting and Manuscript Illumination of the Late Middle Ages and Northern Renaissance*, edited by Jeffrey Hamburger and Anne Korteweg, 85–92. London: Harvey Miller Publishers, 2006.

Bolton, Brenda M. *Innocent III: Studies on Papal Authority and Pastoral Care*. Aldershot: Variorum, 1995.

——*The Medieval Reformation*. London: Edward Arnold, 1983.

——'Too Important to Neglect: The Gesta Innocentii PP III'. In *Church and Chronicle in the Middle Ages: Essays Presented to John Tayler*, edited by Ian Wood and G. A. Loud, 87–99. London: The Hambledon Press, 1991.

Braun, Joseph S. J. *Die liturgische Gewandung im Occident und Orient: Nach Ursprung und Entwicklung, Verwendung und Symbolik*. Freiburg im Breisgau: Herdersche Verlagshandlung, 1907.

——'Mitre'. In *The Catholic Encyclopedia*. Vol. 10. New York: Robert Appleton, 1911, available at www.newadvent.org/cathen/10404a.htm (accessed 15 April 2024).

Brett, M. *The English Church under Henry I*. Oxford: Oxford University Press, 1975.

Brühl, Carlrichard. 'Zur Geschichte der procuratio canonica vornehmlich im 11. und 12. Jahrhundert'. In *Le istituzioni ecclesiastiche della 'societas christiana' dei secoli XI–XII*, 419–31. Milan: Vita e pensiero, 1974.

Brundage, James A. *Medieval Canon Law*. London: Longman, 1995.

Bryant, L. M. 'The Medieval Entry Ceremony at Paris'. In *Coronations: Medieval and Early Modern Monarchic Ritual*, edited by János M. Bak, 88–118. Berkeley: University of California Press, 1990.

Buc, Philippe. *The Dangers of Ritual: Between Early Medieval Texts and Social Scientific Theory*. Princeton: Princeton University Press, 2001.
——'The Monster and the Critics: A Ritual Reply'. *Early Medieval Europe* 15, no. 4 (2007): 441–52.
——'Ritual and Interpretation: The Early Medieval Case'. *Early Medieval Europe* 9, no. 2 (2000): 183–210.
van Bueren, Truus, and Andrea van Leerdam, eds. *Care for the Here and the Hereafter: 'Memoria', Art and Ritual in the Middle Ages*. Turnhout: Brepols, 2005.
Burrow, J. A. *Gestures and Looks in Medieval Narrative*. Cambridge: Cambridge University Press, 2002.
Burton, Janet. 'Past Models and Contemporary Concerns: The Foundation and Growth of the Cistercian Order'. In *Revival and Resurgence in Christian History*, edited by Kate Cooper and Jeremy Gregory, 27–45. Woodbridge: Boydell Press, 2008.
Burton, Janet, and Julie Kerr. *The Cistercians in the Middle Ages*. Woodbridge: Boydell Press, 2011.
Carpenter, David A. 'Chronology and Truth: Matthew Paris and the *Chronica Majora*'. In *Matthew Paris Essays*, edited by James Clark, forthcoming, available at https://finerollshenry3.org.uk/redist/pdf/Chronologyandtruth3.pdf (accessed 15 August 2023).
——*Henry III: The Rise to Power and Personal Rule 1207–1258*. New Haven: Yale University Press, 2020.
——*The Minority of Henry III*. Berkeley: University of California Press, 1990.
——*The Reign of Henry III*. London: The Hambledon Press, 1996.
——*The Struggle for Mastery: Britain, 1066–1284*. London: Penguin, 2003.
Cazel, Jr., Fred A. 'The Legates Guala and Pandulf'. In *TCE II*, edited by P. R. Coss and S. D. Lloyd, 15–21. Woodbridge: Boydell Press, 1988.
Cheney, Christopher R. *Episcopal Visitation of Monasteries in the Thirteenth Century*. 2nd edn. Manchester: Manchester University Press, 1983.
——*From Becket to Langton: English Church Government 1170–1213: The Ford Lectures Delivered in the University of Oxford in Hilary Term 1955*. Manchester: Manchester University Press, 1955.
——*Hubert Walter*. London: Nelson, 1967.
——'King John and the Papal Interdict'. In *The Papacy and England 12th–14th Centuries: Historical and Legal Studies*, IX: 295–317. London: Variorum Reprints, 1982.
——'King John's Reaction to the Interdict on England'. In *The Papacy and England, 12th–14th Centuries: Historical and Legal Studies*, X: 129–150. London: Variorum Reprints, 1982.
——'A Neglected Record of the Canterbury Election of 1205–6'. *Bulletin of the Institute of Historical Research* 21 (1948): 233–38.
——*Pope Innocent III and England*. Stuttgart: Hiersemann, 1976.
——'The Settlement between Archbishop Hubert and Christ Church Canterbury in 1200: A Study in Diplomatic'. In *Mediaevalia Christiana XIe-XIIIe siècles:*

Hommage à Raymonde Foreville, edited by Coloman Étienne Viola, 136–51. Paris: Editions Universitaires, 1989.

Christensen, Emil Lauge. 'Justifying Episcopal Pluralism: The Negotiation between Suitability and Legitimacy in the Narrative of Saxo Grammaticus'. In *Dominus Episcopus: Medieval Bishops between Diocese and Court*, edited by Anthony John Lappin and Elena Balzamo, 100–30. Stockholm: Kungl. Vitterhets Historie och Antikvitets Akademien, 2018.

Church, Stephen. *King John: England, Magna Carta and the Making of a Tyrant*. Basingstoke: Macmillian, 2015.

Clark, James G. *The Benedictines in the Middle Ages*. Woodbridge: Boydell Press, 2011.

——'The Rule of Saint Benedict'. In *A Companion to Medieval Rules and Customaries*, edited by Krijn Pansters, 37–76. Leiden: Brill, 2020.

Cochelin, Isabelle. 'Customaries as Inspirational Sources'. In *Consuetudines et Regulae: Sources for Monastic Life in the Middle Ages and the Early Modern Period*, edited by Carolyn Marino Malone and Clark Maines, 27–72. Turnhout: Brepols, 2014.

Coleman, Edward. '"A City to Be Built for the Glory of God, St Peter, and the Whole of Lombardy": Alexander III, Alessandria and the Lombard League in Contemporary Sources'. In *Pope Alexander III (1159–81): The Art of Survival*, edited by Anne J. Duggan and Peter D. Clarke, 127–52. Farnham: Ashgate, 2012.

Connolly, Daniel K. *The Maps of Matthew Paris: Medieval Journeys through Space, Time and Liturgy*. Woodbridge: Boydell Press, 2009.

Constable, Giles. 'Review of *The Cistercian Evolution: The Invention of a Religious Order in Twelfth-Century Europe* by Constance Hoffman Berman'. *EHR* 115, no. 464 (2000): 1267–68.

Cooper, Richard. 'Legate's Luxury: The Entries of Cardinal Allesandro Farnese to Avignon and Carpentras, 1553'. In *French Ceremonial Entries in the Sixteenth Century: Event, Image, Text*, edited by Nicolas Russel and Hélène Visentin, 133–61. Toronto: Centre for Reformation and Renaissance Studies, 2007.

Corner, David. 'The Earliest Surviving Manuscripts of Roger of Howden's "Chronica"'. *EHR* 98, no. 387 (1983): 297–310.

——'The *Gesta Regis Henrici Secundi* and *Chronica* of Roger, Parson of Howden'. *Bulletin of the Institute of Historical Research* 56, no. 134 (1983): 126–44.

Cotts, John D. *The Clerical Dilemma: Peter of Blois and Literate Culture in the Twelfth Century*. Washington, D.C.: The Catholic University of America Press, 2009.

Coulton, G. G. *Five Centuries of Religion. Volume II: The Friars and the Dead Weight of Tradition, 1200–1400 A.D.* New York: Octagon Books, 1927.

Cowdrey, H. E. J. *Lanfranc: Scholar, Monk, Archbishop*. Oxford: Oxford University Press, 2003.

——*Pope Gregory VII, 1073–1085*. Oxford: Clarendon Press, 1998.

Cox, Eugene L. *The Eagles of Savoy: The House of Savoy in Thirteenth-Century Europe*. Princeton: Princeton University Press, 1974.

Cragoe, Carol Davidson. 'Reading and Rereading Gervase of Canterbury'. *Journal of the British Archaeological Association* 154 (2001): 40–53.

Crook, David. 'Roger of Wendover, Prior of Belvoir, and the Implementation of the Charter of the Forest, 1225–7'. In *The Growth of Royal Government under Henry III*, edited by David Crook and Louise J. Wilkinson, 166–78. Woodbridge: Boydell Press, 2015.

Crosby, Everett U. *Bishop and Chapter in Twelfth-Century England: A Study of the* Mensa Episcopalis. Cambridge: Cambridge University Press, 1994.

Cushing, Kathleen G. *Reform and the Papacy in the Eleventh Century*. Manchester: Manchester University Press, 2005.

Dalché, Patrick G. *Du Yorkshire à l'Inde: une 'geographie' urbaine et maritimie de la fin du XIIe siècle (Roger de Howden?)*. Geneva: Droz, 2005.

Davies, Adam. 'The Appointment of Cardinal-Deacon Otto as Legate in Britain (1237)'. In *TCE XI*, edited by Björn K. U. Weiler, Janet Burton, Phillipp Schofield, and Karen Stöber, 147–58. Woodbridge: Boydell Press, 2007.

Davis, R.H.C. *The Medieval Warhorse: Origin, Development and Redevelopment*. London: Thames and Hudson, 1989.

Dictionary of Medieval Latin from British Sources, available at https://logeion. uchicago.edu/induere (accessed 15 August 2023).

Donkin, Lucy. 'Roman Soil and Roman Sound in Irish Hagiography'. In *The Papacy and Communication in the Central Middle Ages*, edited by Iben Fonnesberg-Schmidt, William Kynan-Wilson, Gesine Elisabeth Oppitz-Trotman, and Emil Lauge Christensen. *JMH* 44, no. 3 (2018): 365–79.

Donovan, Joseph P. *Pelagius and the Fifth Crusade*. Philadelphia: University of Pennsylvania Press, 1950.

Doran, John. 'Authority and Care: The Significance of Rome in Twelfth-Century Chester'. In *Roma Felix: Formation and Reflections of Medieval Rome*, edited by Éamonn Ó Carragain and Carol Neuman de Vegvar, 307–32. Aldershot: Ashgate, 2007.

——'Remembering Pope Gregory VII: Cardinal Boso and Alexander III'. *Studies in Church History* 49 (2013): 87–98.

Dotzauer, Winfried. 'Die Ankunft des Herrshers: Der fürstliche "Einzug" in die Stadt (bis zum Ende des Alten Reichs)'. *Archiv für Kulturgeschichte* 55, no. 2 (1973): 245–88.

Draper, Peter. 'Interpretations of the Rebuilding of Canterbury Cathedral, 1174–1186: Archaeological and Historical Evidence'. *Journal of the Society of Architectural Historians* 56, no. 2 (1997): 184–203.

Duchesne, L. *Christian Worship: Its Origin and Evolution: A Study of the Latin Liturgy up to the Time of Charlemagne*, translated by M. L. McLure. 4th edn. London: Society for Promoting Christian Knowledge, 1912.

Duffy, Sean. 'Ireland's Hastings: The Anglo-Norman Conquest of Dublin'. In *ANS XX*, edited by Christopher Harper-Bill, 69–85. Woodbridge: Boydell Press, 1997.

——'John and Ireland: The Origins of England's Irish Problem'. In *King John: New Interpretations*, edited by Stephen D. Church, 221–45. Woodbridge: Boydell Press, 1999.

Duggan, Anne J. '*Alexander ille meus*: The Papacy of Alexander III'. In *Pope Alexander III (1159–81): The Art of Survival*, edited by Peter D. Clarke and Anne J. Duggan, 13–49. Farnham: Ashgate, 2012.

——'Becket is Dead! Long Live St Thomas'. In *The Cult of St Thomas Becket in the Plantagenet World, c.1170–c.1220*, edited by Paul Webster and Marie-Pierre Gelin, 25–51. Woodbridge: Boydell Press, 2016.

——'The Benefits of Exile'. In *Pope Eugenius III (1145–1153): The First Cistercian Pope*, edited by Iben Fonnesberg-Schmidt and Andrew Jotischky, 171–95. Amsterdam: Amsterdam University Press, 2018.

——'Diplomacy, Status, and Conscience: Henry II's Penance for Becket's Murder'. In *Forschungen zur Reichs-, Papst- und Landesgeschichte. Peter Herde zum 65. Geburtstag von Freunden, Schülern und Kollegen dargebracht*, edited by Karl Borchardt and Enno Bünz, 1:265–90. Stuttgart: Hiersemann, 1998.

——'The English Exile of Archbishop Øystein of Nidaros (1180–83)'. In *Exile in the Middle Ages*, edited by Laura Napran and Elisabeth van Houts, 109–30. Turnhout: Brepols, 2004.

——'Henry II, the English Church and the Papacy, 1154–76'. In *Henry II: New Interpretations*, edited by Christopher Harper-Bill and Nicholas Vincent, 154–83. Woodbridge: Boydell Press, 2007.

——'*Ne in dubium*: The Official Record of Henry's Reconciliation at Avranches, 21 May 1172'. *EHR* 115, no. 462 (2000): 643–58.

——*Thomas Becket*. London: Arnold, 2004.

Duncan, Archibald A. 'Roger of Howden and Scotland, 1187–1201'. In *Church, Chronicle and Learning in Medieval and Early Renaissance Scotland: Essays Presented to Donald Watt on the Occasion of the Completion of the Publication of Bower's Scotichronicon*, edited by Barbara E. Crawford, 135–59. Edinburgh: Mercat Press, 1999.

Dutton, Marsha L., ed. *A Companion to Aelred of Rievaulx (1110–1167)*. Leiden: Brill, 2017.

Edbury, Peter W., and John Gordon Rowe. *William of Tyre: Historian of the Latin East*. Cambridge: Cambridge University Press, 1988.

Eichbauer, Melodie Harris. 'Gratian's Decretum and the Changing Historiographical Landscape'. *History Compass* 11, no. 12 (2013): 1111–25.

Emerick, Judson J. 'Building *More Romano* in Francia during the Third Quarter of the Eighth Century: The Abbey Church of Saint-Denis and Its Model'. In *Rome Across Time and Space: Cultural Transmission and the Exchange of Ideas c.500–1400*, edited by Claudia Bolgia, Rosamond McKitterick, and John Osborne, 127–50. Cambridge: Cambridge University Press, 2011.

Engelmann, Otto. *Die päpstlichen Legaten in Deutschland bis zur Mitte des 11. Jahrhunderts*. Marburg: Chr. Schaaf, Spezialdruckerei für Dissertationen, 1913.

Esmark, Kim. 'Farlige ritualer – Middelalderens politiske kultur mellem antropologiske og tekstlige vendinger'. *Passepartout* 13, no. 25 (2005): 56–67.

——'Just Rituals: Masquerade, Manipulation, and Officialising Strategies in Saxo's Gesta Danorum'. In *Rituals, Performatives, and Political Order in Northern Europe, c. 650–1350*, edited by Wojtek Jerzierski, Lars Hermanson, Hans Jacob Orning, and Thomas Småberg, 237–67. Turnhout: Brepols, 2015.

Fassler, Margot E. '*Adventus* at Chartres: Ritual Models for Major Processions'. In *Ceremonial Culture in Pre-Modern Europe*, edited by Nicholas Howe, 13–62. Notre Dame, IN: University of Notre Dame Press, 2007.

Ferguson, Paul Craig. *Medieval Papal Representatives in Scotland: Legates, Nuncios, and Judges-Delegate, 1125–1286*. Edinburgh: The Stair Society, 1997.

Fernie, Eric. *The Architecture of Norman England*. Oxford: Oxford University Press, 2000.

——'St Anselm's Crypt'. In *Medieval Art and Architecture at Canterbury before 1220*, 27–38. Leeds: W. S. Maney and Son, 1982.

Figueira, Robert Charles Joseph. 'Papal Reserved Powers and the Limitations on Legatine Authority'. In *Popes, Teachers and Canon Law in the Middle Ages*, edited by James Ross Sweeney and Stanley Chodorow, 191–211. Ithaca, NY: Cornell University Press, 1989.

Fonnesberg-Schmidt, Iben, and William Kynan-Wilson. 'Smiling, Laughing and Joking in Papal Rome: Thomas of Marlborough and Gerald of Wales at the Court of Innocent III (1198–1216)'. *Papers of the British School at Rome* 86 (2018): 1–29.

Freed, John. *Frederick Barbarossa: The Prince and the Myth*. New Haven: Yale University Press, 2016.

Friedländer, Ina Feinberg. *Die päpstlichen Legaten in Deutschland und Italien am Ende des XII Jahrhunderts (1181–1198)*. Berlin: Matthiesen Verlag, 1928.

Frijhoff, Willem. 'The Kiss Sacred and Profane: Reflections on a Cross-Cultural Confrontation'. In *A Cultural History of Gesture: From Antiquity to the Present Day*, edited by Jan Bremmer and Herman Roodenburg, 210–36. Cambridge: Polity Press, 1993.

Galbraith, Vivian H. 'The East Anglian See and the Abbey of Bury St Edmunds'. *EHR* 40, no. 158 (1925): 222–28.

——'Roger Wendover and Matthew Paris'. In *Kings and Chroniclers: Essays in English Medieval History*, edited by Christopher Hill, X: 5–48. London: The Hambledon Press, 1944.

Gardner, Julian. 'Legates, Cardinals, and Kings: England and Italy in the Thirteenth Century'. In *L'Europa e l'arte italiana*, edited by Max Seidel, 75–94. Venice: Marsilio, 2000.

Garms-Cornides, Elisabeth. 'Review of *Der Reitende Papst*'. *The Art Bulletin* 55, no. 3 (1973): 451–56.

Gelin, Marie-Pierre. 'The Cult of St Thomas in the Liturgy and Iconography of Christ Church, Canterbury'. In *The Cult of St Thomas Becket in the Plantagenet World, c.1170–c.1220*, edited by Paul Webster and Marie-Pierre Gelin, 53–79. Woodbridge: Boydell Press, 2016.

——'Gervase of Canterbury, Christ Church and the Archbishops'. *JEH* 60, no. 3 (2009): 449–63.

Gelting, Michael H. 'Skånske Lov og Jyske Lov: Danmarks første kommisionsbetænkning og Danmarks første retsplejelov'. In *Jura & Historie: Festskrift til Inger Dübeck som forsker*, edited by Finn Taksøe-Jensen, 43–80. Copenhagen: Jurist- og Økonomforbundets Forlag, 2003.

Gibson, Margaret. *Lanfranc of Bec*. Oxford: Clarendon Press, 1978.

Gillingham, John. 'From Civilitas to Civility: Codes of Manners in Medieval and Early Modern England'. *Transactions of the Royal Historical Society* 12 (2002): 267–89.
——*Richard I*. Revised edition. New Haven: Yale University Press, 1999.
——'Roger of Howden on Crusade'. In *Richard Coeur de Lion: Kingship, Chivalry and War in the Twelfth Century*, 141–53. London: The Hambledon Press, 1994.
——'The Travels of Roger of Howden and His Views of the Irish, Scots and Welsh'. In *ANS XX*, edited by Christopher Harper-Bill, 151–69. Woodbridge: Boydell Press, 1998.
——'Two Yorkshire Historians Compared: Roger of Howden and William of Newburgh', edited by Stephen Morillo. *The Haskins Society Journal* 12 (2002): 15–37.
——'Writing the Biography of Roger of Howden, King's Clerk and Chronicler'. In *Writing Medieval Biography, 750–1250: Essays in Honour of Professor Frank Barlow*, edited by David Bates, Julia Crick, and Sarah Hamilton, 207–20. Woodbridge: Boydell Press, 2006.
Gittos, Helen. *Liturgy, Architecture, and Sacred Places in Anglo-Saxon England*. Oxford: Oxford University Press, 2013.
Gjerlöw, Lilli. *Adoratio Crucis: The Regularis Concordia and the Decreta Lanfranci: Manuscript Studies in the Early Medieval Church of Norway*. Oslo: Norwegian Universities Press, 1961.
Godfrey, John. *The Church in Anglo-Saxon England*. New York: Cambridge University Press, 1962.
Golding, Brian. *Gilbert of Sempringham and the Gilbertine Order, c.1130–c.1300*. Oxford: Clarendon Press, 1995.
Goodson, Caroline J., and John Arnold. 'Resounding Community: The History and Meaning of Medieval Church Bells'. *Viator* 43, no. 1 (2012): 99–130.
Graeber, David. *Debt: The First 5,000 Years*. 2nd edn. Brooklyn: Melville House, 2014.
Graham, Rose. 'A Papal Visitation of Bury St. Edmunds and Westminster in 1234'. *EHR* 27, no. 108 (1912): 728–39.
Graham-Leigh, Elaine. *The Southern French Nobility and the Albigensian Crusade*. Woodbridge: Boydell Press, 2005.
Gransden, Antonia. *Historical Writing in England c.550–c.1307*. London: Routledge, 1974.
——*A History of the Abbey of Bury St Edmunds 1182–1256: Samson of Tottington to Edmund Walpole*. Woodbridge: Boydell Press, 2007.
Greasley, Nathan. 'Revisiting the Compilation of Matthew Paris's *Chronica Majora*: New Textual and Manuscript Evidence'. *JMH* 47, no. 2 (2021): 230–56.
Grellard, Christophe, and Frédérique Lachaud, eds. *A Companion to John of Salisbury*. Leiden and Boston, MA: Brill, 2014.
Gussone, Nikolaus. 'Adventus-Zeremoniell und Translation von Reliquien. Victricius von Rouen, De laude sanctorum'. *Frühmittelalterliche Studien* 10 (1976): 125–33.
Haines, Roy Martin. 'Canterbury versus York: Fluctuating Fortunes in a Perennial Conflict'. In *Ecclesia Anglicana: Studies in the English Church of the*

Later Middle Ages, edited by Roy Martin Haines, 69–105. Toronto: University of Toronto Press, 1989.

Hamilton, Bernard. 'The Impact of Crusader Jerusalem on Western Christendom'. *The Catholic Historical Review* 80, no. 4 (1994): 695–713.

Hardy, Thomas Duffus. *Descriptive Catalogue of Materials Relating to the History of Great Britain and Ireland, to the End of the Reign of Henry VII*. Vol. 2. RS. London: Longman & Co, 1865.

Harper-Bill, Christopher. 'John and the Church of Rome'. In *King John: New Interpretations*, edited by Stephen D. Church, 289–315. Woodbridge: Boydell Press, 1999.

Harrison, Frank Ll. *Music in Medieval Britain*. London: Routledge, 1958.

Harvey, Barbara. *Westminster Abbey and Its Estates in the Middle Ages*. Oxford: Clarendon Press, 1977.

Harvey, Katherine. *Episcopal Appointments in England, c. 1214–1344: From Episcopal Election to Papal Provision*. Burlington, VT: Ashgate, 2014.

——'The First Entry of the Bishop: Episcopal *Adventus* in Fourteenth-Century England'. In *Fourteenth Century England VIII*, edited by J. S. Hamilton, 43–58. Woodbridge: Boydell Press, 2014.

Heinzelmann, Martin. *Translationsberichte und andere Quellen des Reliquienkultes*. Turnhout: Brepols, 1979.

Hen, Yitzhak. 'The Romanization of the Frankish Liturgy: Ideal, Reality and the Rhetoric of Reform'. In *Rome Across Time and Space: Cultural Transmission and the Exchange of Ideas c.500–1400*, edited by Claudia Bolgia, Rosamond McKitterick, and John Osborne, 111–23. Cambridge: Cambridge University Press, 2011.

Herde, Peter. *Audientia litterarum contradictarum: Untersuchungen über die päpstlichen Justizbriefe und die päpstliche Delegationsgerichtsbarkeit vom 13. bis 16. Jahrhundert*. 2 vols. Tübingen: Max Niemeyer, 1970.

Hess, Hamilton. *The Early Development of Canon Law and the Council of Serdica*. 2nd edn. Oxford: Oxford University Press, 2002.

Hilpert, Hans-Eberhard. 'Zu den Prophetien im Geschichtswerk des Matthaeus Paris'. *Deutsches Archiv für Erforschung des Mittelalters* 41, no. 1 (1985): 175–91.

Hinschius, Paul. *System des Katholischen Kirchenrechts: Mit besonderer Rücksicht auf Deutschland*. 6 vols. Berlin: Verlag von I. Guttentag, 1869.

Holt, J. C. *The Northerners: A Study in the Reign of King John*. Oxford: Clarendon Press, 1961.

Howell, Margaret. *Eleanor of Provence: Queenship in Thirteenth-Century England*. Oxford: Blackwell, 1998.

Hughes, Jane Frecknall, and Lynne Oats. 'King John's Tax Innovations – Extortion, Resistance, and the Establishment of the Principle of Taxation by Consent'. *The Accounting Historians Journal* 34, no. 2 (2007): 75–107.

Izbicki, Thomas M. 'Forbidden Colors in the Regulation of Clerical Dress from the Fourth Lateran Council (1215) to the Time of Nicholas of Cusa (d. 1464)'. *Rutgers University Community Repository* (2005): 105–14.

Jakobs, Hermann. 'Rom und Trier 1147: Der *adventus papae* als Ursprungszeugnis der rheinischen Stadtsiegel'. In *Stadt und Bistum in Kirche und Reich des Mittelalters: Festschrift für Odilo Engels zum 65. Geburtstag*, edited by Hanna Vollrath and Stefan Weinfurter, 349–65. Cologne: Böhlau Verlag, 1993.

Jamroziak, Emilia. 'The Cistercian Customaries'. In *A Companion to Medieval Rules and Customaries*, edited by Krijn Pansters, 77–102. Leiden: Brill, 2020.

Janssen, Wilhelm. *Die päpstlichen Legaten in Frankreich von Schisma Anaklets II. bis zum Tode Coelestins III. (1130–1198)*. Cologne: Böhlau, 1961.

Jenkins, Claude. *The Monastic Chronicler and the Early School of St. Albans: A Lecture*. London: Macmillan, 1922.

Jobson, Adrian. *The First English Revolution: Simon de Montfort, Henry III and the Barons' War*. London: Bloomsbury, 2012.

Jones, Peter J. A. 'Gerald of Wales's Sense of Humour'. In *Gerald of Wales: New Perspectives on a Medieval Writer and Critic*, edited by Georgia Henley and A. Joseph McMullen, 147–63. Cardiff: University of Wales Press, 2018.

Jørgensen, Torstein. 'Excommunication – An Act of Expulsion from Heaven and Earth'. In *The Creation of Medieval Northern Europe: Christianisation, Social Transformations, and Historiography: Essays in Honour of Sverre Bagge*, edited by Leidulf Melve and Sigbjørn Olsen Sønnesyn, 58–69. Oslo: Dreyer, 2012.

Kahn, Deborah. *Canterbury Cathedral and Its Romanesque Sculpture*. London: Harvey Miller, 1991.

Kalous, Antonín. *Late Medieval Papal Legation: Between the Councils and the Reformation*. Rome: Viella, 2017.

——'Through the Gates and the Streets of the City: Cardinals and Their Processions in Rome in the Late Fifteenth and Early Sixteenth Centuries'. In *Ritualizing the City: Collective Performances as Aspects of Urban Construction from Constantine to Mao*, edited by Ivan Foletti and Adrien Palaldino, 29–44. Rome: Viella, 2017.

Kamp, Hermann. 'Tugend, Macht, und Ritual: Politisches Verhalten beim Saxo Grammaticus'. In *Zeichen – Rituale – Werte*, edited by Gerd Althoff, 179–200. Münster: Rhema, 2004.

Kantorowicz, Ernst Hartwig. 'The "King's Advent" and the Enigmatic Panels in the Doors of Santa Sabina'. *The Art Bulletin* 26, no. 4 (1944): 207–31.

Kay, Richard. *The Council of Bourges, 1225: A Documentary History*. Aldershot: Ashgate, 2002.

——'Wendover's Last Annal'. *EHR* 84, no. 333 (1969): 779–85.

Keenan, Charles. 'The Limits of Diplomatic Ritual: The Polish Embassy of Giovanni Francesco Commendone (1572–1573) and Criticism of Papal Legates in Early Modern Europe'. *Royal Studies Journal* 3, no. 2 (2016): 90–111.

Keene, Derek. 'Towns and the Growth of Trade'. In *The New Cambridge Medieval History, IV c. 1024–c. 1198, Part I*, ed. David Luscombe and Jonathan Riley-Smith, 47–85. Cambridge: Cambridge University Press, 2004.

Kerr, Julie. *Life in the Medieval Cloister*. London: Continuum, 2009.

——*Monastic Hospitality: The Benedictines in England, c.1070–c.1250*. Woodbridge: Boydell Press, 2007.

——'The Open Door: Hospitality and Honour in Twelfth/Early Thirteenth-Century England'. *History* 87, no. 287 (2002): 322–35.

—'"Welcome the Coming and Speed the Parting Guest": Hospitality in Twelfth-Century England'. *JMH* 33, no. 2 (2007): 130–46.
Kienzle, Beverly Mayne. *Cistercians, Heresy and Crusade in Occitania, 1145–1229: Preaching in the Lord's Vineyard*. York: York Medieval Press, 2001.
King, Edmund. *King Stephen*. New Haven: Yale University Press, 2010.
Kipling, Gordon. *Enter the King: Theatre, Liturgy, and Ritual in the Medieval Civic Triumph*. Oxford: Clarendon Press, 1998.
Kjær, Lars. 'Food, Drink and Ritualised Communication in the Household of Eleanor de Montfort, February to August 1265'. *JMH* 37, no. 1 (2011): 75–89.
—'Matthew Paris and the Royal Christmas: Ritualised Communication in Text and Practice'. In *TCE XIV*, edited by Janet Burton, Phillipp Schofield, and Björn K. U. Weiler, 141–54. Woodbridge: Boydell Press, 2013.
—*The Medieval Gift and the Classical Tradition: Ideals and the Performance of Generosity in Medieval England, 1100–1300*. Cambridge: Cambridge University Press, 2019.
Klukas, Arnold William. 'The Architectural Implications of the Decreta Lanfranci'. In *ANS VI*, edited by R. Allen Brown, 136–71. Woodbridge: Boydell Press, 1984.
Knowles, David. 'The Canterbury Election of 1205–6'. *EHR* 53, no. 210 (1938): 211–20.
—*The Monastic Order in England: A History of Its Development from the Times of St Dunstan to The Fourth Lateran Council, 940–1216*. 2nd edn. Cambridge: Cambridge University Press, 1963.
Knowles, David, Christopher Nugent Lawrence Brooke, and Vera C. M. London. *The Heads of Religious Houses, England and Wales*. 2nd edn. Vol. 1. Cambridge: Cambridge University Press, 2001.
Koziol, Geoffrey. *Begging Pardon and Favor: Ritual and Political Order in Early Medieval France*. Ithaca, NY: Cornell University Press, 1992.
—'Review Article: The Dangers of Polemic: Is Ritual Still an Interesting Topic of Historical Study?'. *Early Medieval Europe* 11 (2002): 367–88.
Kuhrt, Amélie. 'Usurpation, Conquest and Ceremonial: From Babylon to Persia'. In *Rituals of Royalty: Power and Ceremonial in Traditional Societies*, edited by David Cannadine and Simon Price, 20–55. Cambridge: Cambridge University Press, 1987.
Kynan-Wilson, William. 'Roman Identity in William of Malmesbury's Historical Writings'. In *Discovering William of Malmesbury*, edited by Rodney M. Thomson, Emily Dolmans, and Emily A. Winkler, 81–91. Woodbridge: Boydell Press, 2017.
Kynan-Wilson, William, and John Munns, eds. *Henry of Blois: New Interpretations*. Woodbridge: Boydell Press, 2021.
Lambert, Malcolm. *The Cathars*. Oxford: Blackwell, 1998.
Lampen, Angelika. 'Der Einzug des Herrschers in seine Stadt – der *Adventus Domini* als Bühne bürgerlicher und städtischer Repräsentation'. In *Europäische Städte im Mittelalter*, edited by Ferdinand Opll and Christoph Sonnlechner, 267–80. Innsbruck: Studien Verlag, 2010.

Lawrence, C. H. *St Edmund of Abingdon: A Study in Hagiography and History*. Oxford: Clarendon Press, 1960.

Lewis, C. P. 'Communities, Conflict and Episcopal Policy in the Diocese of Lichfield, 1050–1150'. In *Cathedrals, Communities and Conflict in the Anglo-Norman World*, edited by Paul Dalton, Charles Insley and Louise J. Wilkinson, 61–76. Woodbridge: Boydell Press, 2011.

Lewis, Suzanne. *The Art of Matthew Paris in the Chronica Majora*. Berkeley and Los Angeles: University of California Press, 1987.

——'Henry III and the Gothic Rebuilding of Westminster Abbey: The Problematics of Context'. *Traditio* 50 (1995): 129–72.

Lower, Michael. *The Baron's Crusade: A Call to Arms and Its Consequences*. Philadelphia: University of Pennsylvania Press, 2005.

Lunt, William E. *Financial Relations of the Papacy with England to 1327*. Cambridge, MA: The Mediaeval Academy of America, 1939.

Maccarrone, Michele. *Vicarius Christi: storia del titolo papale*. Rome: Facultas Theologica Pontificii Athenaei Lateranensis, 1952.

MacCormack, Sabine G. *Art and Ceremony in Late Antiquity*. Berkeley: University of California Press, 1981.

——'Change and Continuity in Late Antiquity: The Ceremony of "Adventus"'. *Historia: Zeitschrift für Alte Geschichte* 21, no. 4 (1972): 721–52.

MacDonald, Allan John. *Lanfranc: A Study of His Life, Work and Writing*. 2nd edn. London: Society for Promoting Christian Knowledge, 1944.

MacKenzie, Hugh. 'The Anti-Foreign Movement in England, 1231–1232'. In *Anniversary Essays in Medieval History by Students of Charles Homer Haskins Presented on His Completion of Forty Years of Teaching*, edited by Charles H. Taylor and John Life La Monte, 183–203. Boston, MA: Houghton Mifflin Company, 1929.

Maddicott, J. R. *Simon de Montfort*. Cambridge: Cambridge University Press, 1994.

Maleczek, Werner. 'Die Kardinäle von 1143 bis 1216. Exklusive Papstwähler und erste Agenten der päpstlichen *plenitudo potestatis*'. In *Geschichte des Kardinalats im Mittelalter*, edited by Jürgen Dendorfer and Ralf Lützelschwab, 95–154. Stuttgart: Hiersemann, 2011.

——*Papst und Kardinalskolleg von 1191 bis 1216. Die Kardinäle unter Coelestin und Innocenz III*. Vienna: Verlag der Österreichischen Akademie der Wissenschaften, 1984.

Mann, Jill. 'Does an Author Understand His Own Text? Nigel of Longchamp and the *Speculum stultorum*'. *Journal of Medieval Latin* 17 (2007): 1–37.

——'Nigel of Longchamp's *Speculum stultorum*'. In *From Aesop to Reynard: Beast Literature in Medieval Britain*, 98–148. Oxford: Oxford University Press, 2009.

Marti, Oscar Albert. 'Popular Protest and Revolt against Papal Finance in England from 1226 to 1258'. *The Princeton Theological Review* (1927): 610–29.

Mason, Emma. *Westminster Abbey and Its People, c.1050–c.1216*. Woodbridge: Boydell Press, 1996.

Mauss, Marcel. *The Gift*, translated by Jane I. Guyer. Expanded edition. Chicago: Hau Books, 2016.

McCormick, Michael. *Eternal Victory: Triumphal Rulership in Late Antiquity, Byzantium, and the Early Medieval West*. Cambridge: Cambridge University Press, 1986.
McGlynn, Sean. 'Roger of Wendover and the Wars of Henry III, 1216–1234'. In *England and Europe in the Reign of Henry III (1216–1272)*, edited by Björn K. U. Weiler and Ifor W. Rowlands, 183–206. Aldershot: Ashgate, 2002.
McGuire, Brian Patrick. 'Bernard's Concept of a Cistercian Order: Vocabulary and Context'. *Cîteaux: Commentarii Cistercienses* 54, nos. 3–4 (2003): 225–49.
Melville, Gert. 'Knowledge of the Origins: Constructing Identity and Ordering Monastic Life in the Middle Ages'. In *Knowledge, Discipline and Power in the Middle Ages: Essays in Honour of David Luscombe*, edited by Joseph Canning, Edmund J. King and Martial Staub, 41–62. Leiden: Brill, 2011.
Merton, Robert K. *On the Shoulders of Giants: A Shandean Postscript*. New York: Free Press, 1965.
Miller, Maureen C. 'Clothing as Communication? Vestments and Views of the Papacy c.1300'. In *The Papacy and Communication in the Central Middle Ages*, edited by Iben Fonnesberg-Schmidt, William Kynan-Wilson, Gesine Elisabeth Oppitz-Trotman, and Emil Lauge Christensen. *JMH* 44, no. 3 (2018): 280–93.
——*Clothing the Clergy: Virtue and Power in Medieval Europe, c. 800–1200*. Ithaca, NY: Cornell University Press, 2014.
——'The Crisis in the Investiture Crisis Narrative'. *History Compass* 7, no. 6 (2009): 1570–80.
——'The Florentine Bishop's Ritual Entry and the Origins of the Medieval Episcopal *Adventus*'. *Revue d'histoire ecclésiastique* 98 (2003): 5–28.
——'Why the Bishop of Florence Had to Get Married'. *Speculum* 81, no. 4 (2006): 1055–91.
Mittag, Peter Franz. '*Processus Consularis*, *Adventus* und Herrschaftsjubiläum. Zur Verwendung von Triumphsymbolik in der mittleren Kaiserzeit'. *Hermes* 137, no. 4 (2009): 447–62.
Montaubin, Pascal. 'De Petits papes en voyage: les légats en France et en Angleterre au XIIIe siècle'. In *Se déplacer du moyen âge à nos jours: actes du 6e colloque européen de Calais, 2006–2007*, edited by Stéphane Curveiller and Laurent Buchard, 58–70. Calais: Les amis du Vieux Calais, 2009.
——'Qu'advient-il du cérémonial papal hors de Rome (milieu XIe–milieu XVe siècles)?' In *Rituels et transgressions de l'antiquité à nos jours*, edited by Geneviève Hoffmann and Antoine Gaillot, 109–19. Amiens: Encrage, 2009.
Moore, R. I. *The First European Revolution, c. 970–1215*. Oxford: Blackwell, 2000.
Morris, Colin. *The Papal Monarchy: The Western Church from 1050 to 1250*. Oxford: Clarendon Press, 1989.
Müller, Harald. 'Generalisierung, dichte Beschreibung, kontrastierende Einzelstudien? Stand und Perspektiven der Erforschung delegierter Gerichtsbarkeit des Papstes im Hochmittelalter'. In *Rom und die Regionen: Studien zur Homogenisierung der lateinischen Kirche im Hochmittelalter*, edited by Jochen Johrendt and Harald Müller, 145–56. Göttingen: De Gruyter, 2012.
——'The Omnipresent Pope: Legates and Judges Delegate'. In *A Companion to the Medieval Papacy: Growth of an Ideology and Institution*, edited by Keith Sisson and Atria A. Larson, 199–219. Leiden: Brill, 2016.

Munro, John H. 'Scarlet'. In *Encyclopedia of Dress and Textiles in the British Isles c. 450–1450*, edited by Gale R. Owen-Crocker, Elizabeth Coatsworth, and Maria Hayward, 477–81. Leiden: Brill, 2012.

Newman, Martha G. *The Boundaries of Charity: Cistercian Culture and Ecclesiastical Reform 1098–1180*. Stanford, CA: Stanford University Press, 1996.

Nicholls, Jonathan. *The Matter of Courtesy: Medieval Courtesy Books and the Gawain-Poet*. Cambridge: D.S. Brewer, 1985.

Ó Carragain, Éamonn. 'The Periphery Rethinks the Centre: Inculturation, "Roman" Liturgy and the Ruthwell Cross'. In *Rome Across Time and Space: Cultural Transmission and the Exchange of Ideas c.500–1400*, edited by Claudia Bolgia, Rosamond McKitterick, and John Osborne, 63–83. Cambridge: Cambridge University Press, 2011.

Ohnsorge, Werner. *Päpstliche und gegenpäpstliche Legaten in Deutschland und Skandinavien 1159–1181*. Berlin: E. Ebering, 1928.

Oksanen, Eljas. 'Trade and Travel in England during the Long Twelfth Century'. In *ANS XXXVII*, edited by Elisabeth van Houts, 181–204. Woodbridge: Boydell Press, 2015.

Otte, James K. 'Church Reform in the Holy Roman Empire and Reform of the Papacy: Cluny or Henry III?' In *Medieval Germany: Associations and Delineations*, edited by Nancy van Deusen, 63–69. Ottawa: Institute of Mediaeval Music, 2000.

Pansters, Krijn, ed. *A Companion to Medieval Rules and Customaries*. Leiden: Brill, 2020.

Paravicini-Bagliani, Agostino. 'Innocent III and the World of Symbols of the Papacy', translated by Gesine Elisabeth Oppitz-Trotman. In *The Papacy and Communication in the Central Middle Ages*, edited by Iben Fonnesberg-Schmidt, William Kynan-Wilson, Gesine Elisabeth Oppitz-Trotman, and Emil Lauge Christensen. *JMH* 44, no. 3 (2018): 261–79.

——*The Pope's Body*, translated by David S. Peterson. Chicago and London: University of Chicago Press, 2000.

Parks, George B. *The English Traveler to Italy: The Middle Ages (to 1525)*. Rome: Edizioni di Storia e Letteratura, 1954.

Paro, Gino. *The Right of Papal Legation*. Washington, D.C.: The Catholic University of America Press, 1947.

Pasciuta, Beatrice. 'Speculum Iudiciale (A Mirror of Procedure): 1271–1276/1296, Ed. Pr. 1474. Guilelmus Durantis (Guillaume Durand/Durant; William Durand, the Elder) (1240/1232–1296)'. In *The Formation and Transmission of Western Legal Culture: 150 Books that Made the Law in the Age of Printing*, edited by Serge Dauchy, Georges Martyn, Anthony Musson, Heikki Pihlajamäki, and Alain Wijffels, 37–40. Cham: Springer, 2016.

Pennington, Kenneth. 'Henricus de Segusio (Hostiensis)'. In *Popes, Canonists, and Texts, 1150–1550*, XVI: 1–12. Aldershot: Variorum, 1993.

——'Johannes Teutonicus and Papal Legates'. *Archivum Historiae Pontificiae* 21 (1983): 183–94.

Pennington, Kenneth, and Wolfgang P. Müller. 'The Decretists: The Italian School'. In *The History of Medieval Canon Law in the Classical Period, 1140–*

1234: From Gratian to the Decretals of Pope Gregory IX, edited by Kenneth Pennington and Wilfried Hartmann, 121–73. Washington, D.C.: The Catholic University of America Press, 2008.

Pentcheva, Bissera V. *The Sensual Icon: Space, Ritual, and the Senses in Byzantium*. Philadelphia: The Pennsylvania State University Press, 2010.

Pepin, Ronald E. 'John of Salibury's Entheticus and the Classical Tradition of Satire'. *Florilegium* 3 (1981): 215–27.

Perrin, John W. '"Legatus" in Medieval Roman Law'. *Traditio* 29 (1973): 357–78.

Peterson, E. 'Die Einholung des Kyrios'. *Zeitschift für systematische Theologie* 7 (1930): 682–702.

Petkov, Kiril. *The Kiss of Peace: Ritual, Self and Society in the High and Late Medieval West*. Leiden: Brill, 2003.

Petrus de Marca, *Dissertationum de Concordia Sacerdotii et Imperii, seu de Libertatibus Ecclesiae Gallicanae, Libri Octo: Quibus accesserunt eiusdem auctoris Dissertationes Ecclesiasticae Varii Argumenti*, edited by Stephanus Baluzius. Roboreti [Rovereto, Italy]: Societatis, 1742.

Pomarici, Francesca. 'Papal Imagery and Propaganda: Art, Architecture, and Liturgy'. In *A Companion to the Medieval Papacy: Growth of an Ideology and Institution*, edited by Keith Sisson and Atria A. Larson, 85–120. Leiden: Brill, 2016.

Pössel, Christina. 'The Magic of Early Medieval Ritual'. *Early Medieval Europe* 17, no. 2 (2009): 111–25.

Powell, James M., ed. *Innocent III: Vicar of Christ or Lord of the World?* 2nd edn. Washington, D.C.: The Catholic University of America Press, 1994.

Powicke, Frederick Maurice. *King Henry III and the Lord Edward: The Community of the Realm in the Thirteenth Century*. 2nd edn. 2 vols. Oxford: Clarendon Press, 1966.

——'Roger of Wendover and the Coggeshall Chronicle'. *EHR* 21, no. 82 (1906): 286–96.

Quillet, Jeannine. 'I – Community, Counsel and Representation'. In *The Cambridge History of Medieval Political Thought c.350–c.1450*, edited by James Henderson Burns, 520–72. Cambridge: Cambridge University Press, 1988.

Reader, Rebecca. 'Matthew Paris and the Norman Conquest'. In *The Cloister and the World: Essays in Medieval History in Honour of Barbara Harvey*, edited by John Blair and Brian Golding, 118–47. Oxford: Clarendon Press, 1996.

——'Matthew Paris and Women'. In *TCE VII*, edited by Michael Prestwich, Richard Britnell, and Robin Frame, 153–59. Woodbridge: Boydell Press, 1999.

Reed, Zsuzsanna Papp. *Matthew Paris on the Mongol Invasion in Europe*. Turnhout: Brepols, 2022.

Rennie, Kriston Robert. 'The Ceremonial Reception of Medieval Papal Legates'. *JEH* 69, no. 2 (2018): 1–20.

——*The Foundations of Medieval Papal Legation*. New York: Palgrave Macmillan, 2013.

——'Hugh of Die and the Legatine Office under Gregory VII: On the Effects of a Waning Administration'. *Revue d'histoire ecclésiastique* 103, no. 1 (2008): 27–49.

——'*Imbutus divinis dogmatibus*: Some Remarks on the Legal Training of

Gregorian Legates'. *Revue historique de droit français et étranger* 85, no. 2 (2007): 301–13.

——'The "Injunction of Jeremiah": Papal Politicking and Power in the Middle Ages'. *JMH* 40, no. 1 (2014): 108–22.

——'"Uproot and Destroy, Build and Plant": Legatine Authority under Pope Gregory VII'. *JMH* 33, no. 2 (2007): 166–80.

Reuter, Timothy. 'Pre-Gregorian Mentalities'. In *Medieval Polities and Modern Mentalities*, edited by Janet L. Nelson, 89–99. Cambridge: Cambridge University Press, 2006.

Reyerson, Kathryn L. 'Commerce and Communications'. In *The New Cambridge Medieval History, V, c. 1198–1300*, edited by David Abulafia, 50–70. Cambridge: Cambridge University Press, 1999.

Reynolds, Roger E. 'The Drama of Medieval Liturgical Processions'. *Revue de musicologie* 86, no. 1 (2000): 127–42.

Richardson, Henry G. 'The Coronation in Medieval England: The Evolution of the Office and the Oath'. *Traditio* 16 (1960): 111–201.

Ridgeway, Huw W. 'Foreign Favourites and Henry III's Problems of Patronage, 1247–1258'. *EHR* 104, no. 412 (1989): 590–610.

——'King Henry III and the "Aliens", 1236–1272'. In *TCE II*, edited by P. R. Coss and S. D. Lloyd, 81–92. Woodbridge: Boydell Press, 1988.

Rigg, A. G. 'Nigel of Canterbury: What Was His Name?' *Medium Aevum* 56, no. 2 (1987): 304–7.

Robinson, Ian S. *The Papacy 1073–1198: Continuity and Innovation*. Cambridge: Cambridge University Press, 1990.

Robinson, J. Armitage. 'Lanfranc's Monastic Constitutions'. *The Journal of Theological Studies* 10, no. 39 (1909): 375–88.

Rollo-Koster, Joëlle. *Raiding Saint Peter: Empty Sees, Violence, and the Initiation of the Great Western Schism (1378)*. Leiden: Brill, 2008.

Rosenwein, Barbara H. *To Be the Neighbor of Saint Peter: The Social Meaning of Cluny's Property, 909–1049*. Ithaca, NY: Cornell University Press, 1989.

Rozier, Charles C. 'Between History and Hagiography: Eadmer of Canterbury's Vision of the *Historia novorum in Anglia*'. *JMH* 45, no. 1 (2019): 1–19.

Rueß, Karl. *Die rechtliche Stellung der päpstlichen Legaten bis Bonifaz VIII*. Paderborn: Ferdinand Schöningh., 1912.

Sägmüller, J. B. *Die Thätigkeit und Stellung der Cardinale bis Papst Bonifaz VIII. Historisch-canonistisch untersucht und dargestellt*. Freiburg im Breisgau: Herdersche Verlagshandlung, 1896.

Salminen, Tapio. 'In the Pope's Clothes: Legatine Representation and Apostolic Insignia in High Medieval Europe'. In *Roma, magistra mundi. Itineraria culturae medievalis: mélanges offerts au père L.E. Boyle à l'occasion de son 75e anniversaire*, edited by Jacqueline Hamesse, 349–54. Louvain-la-Neuve: Brepols, 1998.

Sayers, Jane E. 'English Benedictine Monks at the Papal Court in the Thirteenth Century: The Experience of Thomas of Marlborough in a Wider Context'. *Journal of Medieval Monastic Studies* 2 (2013): 109–29.

——*Innocent III, Leader of Europe, 1198–1216*. London: Longman, 1994.

——*Papal Government and England during the Pontificate of Honorius III (1216–1227)*. London: Cambridge University Press, 1984.
——*Papal Judges Delegate in the Province of Canterbury, 1198–1254: A Study in Ecclesiastical Jurisdiction and Administration*. Oxford: Oxford University Press, 1971.
——'Peter's Throne and Augustine's Chair: Rome and Canterbury from Baldwin (1184–90) to Robert Winchelsey (1297–1313)'. *JEH* 51, no. 2 (2000): 249–66.
Schein, Sylvia. *Gateway to the Heavenly City: Crusader Jerusalem and the Catholic West (1099–1187)*. London and New York: Routledge, 2016.
Schieffer, Theodor. *Die päpstlichen Legaten in Frankreich vom Vertrage von Meersen, 870, bis zum Schisma von 1130*. Berlin: Verlag Dr. Emil Ebering, 1935.
Schmutz, Richard Antone. 'Medieval Papal Representatives: Legates, Nuncios and Judges-Delegate'. *Studia Gratiana* 15 (1972): 441–63.
Schumann, Otto. *Die päpstlichen Legaten in Deutschland zur Zeit Heinrichs IV. und Heinrichs V. (1056–1125)*. Marburg: Universitäts-Buchdruckerei von Joh. Aug. Koch, 1912.
Shagrir, Iris. '*Adventus* in Jerusalem: The Palm Sunday Celebration in Latin Jerusalem'. *JMH* 41, no. 1 (2015): 1–20.
Sheffler, David L. 'An Early Oxford Riot: Oseney Abbey, 1238'. In *History of Universities*, edited by Mordechai Feingold and Jane Finucane, vol. 21, no. 1, 1–32. Oxford: Oxford University Press, 2006.
Smalley, Beryl. *Historians in the Middle Ages*. London: Thames and Hudson, 1974.
Smith, David Norman. 'Faith, Reason, and Charisma: Rudolf Sohm, Max Weber, and the Theology of Grace'. *Sociological Inquiry* 68, no. 1 (1998): 32–60.
Smith, Katherine Allen. *War and the Making of Medieval Monastic Culture*. Woodbridge: Boydell Press, 2011.
Smith, Reginald Anthony Lendon. *Canterbury Cathedral Priory: A Study in Monastic Administration*. Cambridge: Cambridge University Press, 1943.
Smith, Thomas W. 'The Development of Papal Provisions in Medieval Europe'. *History Compass* 13, no. 3 (2015): 110–21.
Snellgrove, Harold S. *The Lusignans in England 1247–1258*. Vol. 2. Albuquerque: University of New Mexico Press, 1950.
Soria, Myriam. 'Alexander III and France: Exile, Diplomacy and the New Order'. In *Pope Alexander III (1159–81): The Art of Survival*, edited by Peter D. Clarke and Anne J. Duggan, 181–201. Farnham: Ashgate, 2012.
Southern, Richard. W. *Medieval Humanism and Other Studies*. Oxford: Basil Blackwell, 1970.
——*The Monks of Canterbury and the Murder of Archbishop Becket*. Canterbury: The Friends of Canterbury Cathedral & the William Urry Memorial Trust, 1985.
——*Saint Anselm: A Portrait in a Landscape*. Cambridge: Cambridge University Press, 1990.
Sprey, Ilicia Jo. 'Henry of Winchester and the Expansion of Legatine Political Authority in England'. *Revue d'histoire ecclésiastique* 91, nos. 3–4 (1996): 785–804.

Stacey, Robert C. *Politics, Policy, and Finance under Henry III 1216–1245*. Oxford: Clarendon Press, 1987.

Staunton, Michael, ed. *Herbert of Bosham: A Medieval Polymath*. York: York Medieval Press, 2019.

——*The Historians of Angevin England*. Oxford: Oxford University Press, 2017.

——*Thomas Becket and His Biographers*. Woodbridge: Boydell Press, 2006.

——'Thomas Becket in the Chronicles'. In *The Cult of St Thomas Becket in the Plantagenet World, c.1170–c.1220*, edited by Paul Webster and Marie-Pierre Gelin, 95–111. Woodbridge: Boydell Press, 2016.

Stenton, Doris M. 'Roger of Howden and Benedict'. *EHR* 68, no. 269 (1953): 574–82.

Stubbs, William. *Historical Introductions to the Rolls Series*, edited by Arthur Hassall. London: Longmans, 1902.

Štulrajterová, Katarína. 'Convivenza, Convenienza and Conversion: Islam in Medieval Hungary (1000–1400 CE)'. *Journal of Islamic Studies* 24, no. 2 (2013): 175–98.

Sweeney, James Ross. 'Innocent III, Hungary and the Bulgarian Coronation: A Study in Medieval Papal Diplomacy'. *Church History* 42 (1973): 320–34.

Taylor, H. M. 'The Anglo-Saxon Cathedral Church at Canterbury'. *The Archaeological Journal* 126, no. 1 (1969): 101–30.

Tenfelde, Klaus. '*Adventus*. Zur historischen Ikonologie des Festzugs'. *Historische Zeitschrift* 235, no. 1 (1982): 45–84.

Thomson, Rodney M. 'The Origins of Latin Satire in Twelfth Century Europe'. *Mittellateinisches Jahrbuch* 13 (1978): 73–83.

——*William of Malmesbury*. 2nd edn. Woodbridge: Boydell Press, 2003.

Thomson, Rodney M., Emily Dolmans, and Emily A. Winkler, eds. *Discovering William of Malmesbury*. Woodbridge: Boydell Press, 2017.

Thurstan, Herbert. 'The Cross and Crucifix in Liturgy'. In *The Catholic Encyclopedia*. Vol. 4. New York: Robert Appleton, 1908, available at www.newadvent.org/cathen/04533a.htm (accessed 15 April 2024).

Tierney, Brian. *Foundations of the Conciliar Theory: The Contribution of the Medieval Canonists from Gratian to the Great Schism*. Cambridge: Cambridge University Press, 1955.

Tillmann, Helene. *Die päpstlichen Legaten in England bis zur Beendigung der Legation Gualas, 1218*. Bonn: Hch. Ludwig, 1926.

Tinti, Francesca. *Sustaining Belief: The Church of Worcester from c. 870 to c. 1100*. Farnham: Ashgate, 2010.

Traeger, Jörg. *Der reitende Papst: Ein Beitrag zur Ikonographie des Papsttums*. Munich: Verlag Schnell & Steiner, 1970.

Turner, Ralph V. 'Richard Lionheart and English Episcopal Elections'. *Albion* 29, no. 1 (1997): 1–13.

Twyman, Susan E. 'Papal *Adventus* at Rome in the Twelfth Century'. *Historical Research* 69, no. 170 (1996): 233–53.

——*Papal Ceremonial at Rome in the Twelfth Century*. London: Boydell Press, 2002.

Ullmann, Walter. 'The Pontificate of Adrian IV'. *The Cambridge Historical Journal* 11, no. 3 (1955): 233–52.
——*A Short History of the Papacy in the Middle Ages*. 2nd edn. London: Routledge, 1974.
Urry, William. *Canterbury under the Angevin Kings*. London: The Athlone Press, 1967.
Vaughan, Richard. *Matthew Paris*. Cambridge: Cambridge University Press, 1958.
Vaughn, Sally N. *Archbishop Anselm 1093–1109: Bec Missionary, Canterbury Primate, Patriarch of Another World*. Farnham: Ashgate, 2012.
Veach, Colin. 'Henry II and the Ideological Foundations of Angevin Rule in Ireland'. *Irish Historical Studies* 42, no. 161 (2018): 1–25.
Vincent, Nicholas. *The Holy Blood: King Henry III and the Westminster Blood Relic*. Cambridge: Cambridge University Press, 2001.
Warner, David A. 'Ritual and Memory in the Ottonian Reich: The Ceremony of Adventus'. *Speculum* 76, no. 2 (2001): 255–83.
Warren, W. L. *King John*. 3rd edn. New Haven: Yale University Press, 1996.
Wasner, Franz. 'Fifteenth-Century Texts on the Ceremonial of the Papal "Legatus a Latere"'. *Traditio* 14 (1958): 295–358.
——'"Legatus a Latere": Addenda Varia'. *Traditio* 16 (1960): 405–16.
Watt, J. A. 'The Papacy'. In *The New Cambridge Medieval History: V, c.1198–c.1300*, edited by David Abulafia, 107–63. Cambridge: Cambridge University Press, 1999.
——'The Theory of Papal Monarchy in the Thirteenth Century: The Contribution of the Canonists'. *Traditio* 20 (1964): 179–317.
Webster, Paul. 'Crown, Cathedral and Conflict: King John and Canterbury'. In *Cathedrals, Communities and Conflict in the Anglo-Norman World*, edited by Paul Dalton, Charles Insley, and Louise J. Wilkinson, 204–19. Woodbridge: Boydell Press, 2011.
Weigand, Rudolf. 'The Transmontane Decretists'. In *The History of Medieval Canon Law in the Classical Period, 1140–1234: From Gratian to the Decretals of Pope Gregory IX*, edited by Kenneth Pennington and Wilfried Hartmann, 174–210. Washington, D.C.: The Catholic University of America Press, 2008.
Weiler, Björn K. U. *Henry III of England and the Staufen Empire, 1216–1272*. Woodbridge: Boydell Press, 2006.
——'How Unusual Was Matthew Paris? The Writing of Universal History in Angevin England'. In *Universal Chronicles in the High Middle Ages*, edited by Michele Campopiano and Henry Bainton, 199–222. York: York Medieval Press, 2017.
——'Matthew Paris in Norway'. *Revue Bénédictine* 122, no. 1 (2012): 153–81.
——'Matthew Paris on the Writing of History'. *JMH* 35, no. 3 (2009): 254–78.
——'The *Rex Renitens* and the Medieval Idea of Kingship, ca. 900–ca. 1250'. *Viator* 31 (2000): 1–42.
——'William of Malmesbury on Kingship'. *History* 90, no. 297 (2005): 3–22.
Weiss, Miriam. *Die* Chronica maiora *des Matthaeus Parisiensis*. Trier: Kliomedia, 2018.

Wethered, F. T., ed. *St. Mary's, Hurley, in the Middle Ages: Based on Hurley Charters and Deeds*. London: Bedford Press, 1898.

Whelan, Fiona. *The Making of Manners and Morals in Twelfth-Century England: The Book of the Civilised Man*. London: Routledge, 2017.

White, Stephen D. *Custom, Kinship, and Gifts to Saints: The 'Laudatio Parentum' in Western France, 1050–1150*. Chapel Hill: The University of North Carolina Press, 1988.

Wiedemann, Benedict. 'The Character of Papal Finance at the Turn of the Twelfth Century'. *EHR* 133, no. 562 (2018): 503–32.

———'Doorkeepers, the Chamberlain and Petitioning at the Papal Court, c.1150–1200'. *Historical Research* 91, no. 253 (2018): 409–25.

———*Papal Overlordship and European Princes, 1000–1270*. Oxford: Oxford University Press, 2022.

Wild, Benjamin Linley. 'A Gift Inventory from the Reign of Henry III'. *EHR* 125, no. 514 (2010): 529–69.

Williamson, Dorothy M. 'The Legate Otto in Scotland and Ireland 1237–1240'. *The Scottish Historical Review* 28, no. 105 (1949): 12–30.

———'Some Aspects of the Legation of Cardinal Otto in England, 1237–41'. *EHR* 64, no. 251 (1949): 145–73.

Willis, R. *The Architectural History of Canterbury Cathedral*. London: Longman & Co, 1845.

Winroth, Anders. *The Making of Gratian's Decretum*. Cambridge: Cambridge University Press, 2000.

Withington, Robert. 'The Early "Royal-Entry"'. *Publications of the Modern Language Association* 32, no. 4 (1917): 616–23.

Woodruff, C. Eveleigh. 'The Financial Aspect of the Cult of St. Thomas of Canterbury. As Revealed by a Study of the Monastic Records'. *Archaeologia Cantiana* 44 (1932): 13–32.

Wright, Craig. 'The Palm Sunday Procession in Medieval Chartres'. In *The Divine Office in the Latin Middle Ages: Methodology and Source Studies, Regional Developments, Hagiography: Written in Honor of Professor Ruth Steiner*, edited by Margot E. Fassler and Rebecca A. Baltzer, 344–71. Oxford: Oxford University Press, 2000.

Young, Charles R. *The Royal Forests of Medieval England*. Philadelphia: University of Pennsylvania Press, 1979.

Yunck, J. A. *The Lineage of Lady Meed. The Development of Medieval Venality Satire*. Notre Dame, IN: University of Notre Dame Press, 1963.

Zey, Claudia. 'Die Augen des Papstes. Zu eigenschaften und Vollmachten päpstlicher Legaten'. In *Römisches Zentrum und Kirchliche Peripherie. Das Universale Papsttum als Bezugspunkt der Kirchen von den Reformpäpsten bis zu Innozenz III*, edited by Jochen Johrendt and Harald Müller, 99–103. Berlin: Walter de Gruyter, 2008.

———'Stand und Perspektiven der Erforschung des päpstlichen Legatenwesens im Hochmittelalter'. In *Rom und die Regionen: Studien zur Homogenisierung der lateinischen Kirche im Hochmittelalter*, edited by Jochen Johrendt and Harald Müller, 157–66. Göttingen: De Gruyter, 2012.

Zimmermann, Heinrich. *Die päpstliche Legation in der ersten Hälfte des 13. Jahrhunderts: Vom Regierungsantritt Innocenz' III. bis zum Tode Gregors IX. (1198–1241)*. Paderborn: Ferdinand Schöningh, 1913.

Zutshi, Patrick. 'Petitioners, Popes, Proctors: The Development of Curial Institutions c.1150–1250'. In *Pensiero e Sperimentazioni Istituzionali Nella 'Societas Christiana' (1046–1250): Atti della Sedicesima Settimana Internationale di Studio Mendola, 21–31 Agosto 2004*, edited by Giancarlo Andenna, 265–93. Milan: Storia Ricerche, 2007.

——'The Roman Curia and Papal Jurisdiction in the Twelfth and Thirteenth Centuries'. In *Die Ordnung der Kommunikation und die Kommunikation der Ordnungen. Band 2: Zentralität: Papsttum und Orden im Europa des 12. und 13. Jahrhunderts*, edited by Christina Andenna, Klaus Herbers, and Gert Melville, 213–27. Schriften der Villa Vigoni. Stuttgart: Franz Steiner Verlag, 2013.

Unpublished Theses

Balfour, David Bruce. 'William Longchamp: Upward Mobility and Character Assassination in Twelfth-Century England'. Unpublished PhD dissertation, University of Connecticut, Storrs, 1996.

Briggs, Brian. 'The Life and Works of Osbert of Clare'. Unpublished PhD dissertation, University of St Andrews, 2004.

Clifford, Rose Catherine. 'England as a Papal Fief: The Role of the Papal Legate in the Early Period, 1216–1241'. Unpublished PhD dissertation, University of California, Los Angeles, 1978.

Figueira, Robert Charles Joseph. 'The Canon Law of Medieval Papal Legation'. Unpublished PhD dissertation, Cornell University, Ithaca, NY, 1980.

Gress-Wright, David Richard. 'The "Gesta Innocentii III": Text, Introduction and Commentary'. Unpublished PhD dissertation, Bryn Mawr College, 1981.

Huling, Richard Wayne. 'English Historical Writing under the Early Angevin Kings, 1170–1210'. Unpublished PhD dissertation, State University of New York, Binghamton, 1981.

Kyer, Clifford Ian. 'The Papal Legate and the "Solemn" Papal Nuncio 1243–1378: The Changing Pattern of Papal Representation'. Unpublished PhD dissertation, University of Toronto, 1979.

Kynan-Wilson, William. 'Rome and Romanitas in Anglo-Norman Text and Image (c.1100–c.1250)'. Unpublished PhD dissertation, University of Cambridge, 2012.

Nwabuzo, Cletus Chidozie. 'Ambassadors of Reform: Legates and Legatine Authority in the Pontificate of Alexander III (1159–1181)'. Unpublished PhD dissertation, Saint Louis University, 2001.

Schmutz, Richard Antone. 'The Foundations of Medieval Papal Representation'. Unpublished PhD dissertation, University of Southern California, Los Angeles, 1966.

Sommar, Mary Ellen. 'The Changing Role of the Bishop in Society: Episcopal Translation in the Middle Ages'. Unpublished PhD dissertation, Syracuse University, New York, 1998.

Sprey, Ilicia Jo. 'Papal Legates in English Politics, 1100–1272'. Unpublished PhD dissertation, University of Virginia, Charlottesville, 1998.

Underhill, Frances Ann. 'Papal Legates to England in the Reign of Henry III (1216–1272)'. Unpublished PhD dissertation, Indiana University, Bloomington, 1965.

Zenker, Barbara. 'Die Mitglieder des Kardinalkollegiums von 1130 bis 1159'. Unpublished PhD dissertation, Julius-Maximilians-Universität zu Würzburg, 1964.

Index

Abbas Antiquus, *see* Bernard of Montmirat
Abingdon Abbey and *De Obedientiariis* (customary)   101
Adalbert, archbishop of Bremen   43, 44, 45
Adventus   2–3, 49–50, 67, 76, 206, 215, 216–17
  and canon law on   65, 66
  and challenges to   5, 63–65, 66, 116, 129–30
  and history of   51, 52–53, 54
  and jurisdiction   100, 101
  and participants   65, 182
  and performance   6–8, 119–120, 121, 131, 215, 216, 222, *see also* and performance *under adventus* instructions
  as a ritual   2, 6–8, 49, 51, 55, 60, 97, 118–20, 121, 178, 182
  as a template   50–51, 54, 55, 60, 82, 97, 98, 201
  as *imitatio Christi*   53–54
  as a possession-taking (*possessio*)   13, 62, 163, 181, 182, 183, 186, 210, 214, 220–21
  at inaugurations   39, 54, 65, 225 n.3
  conceptualisation of   4, 5, 14, 49–50, 49–50, 55
  parts of   50
    ingressus   50–51, 57, 82, 201
    occursus   3, 50–51, 57, 82, 122, 167, 201, 214, 216
    preparations   51, 72, 94, 121, 201
    susceptio   50–51, 82, 83, 94, 98, 201
  sources   5, 6, 55–59
  types of
    episcopal   3 n.8, 53–54
    legatine   6, 7, 12, 14, 55–58, 60, 61–62, 70, 133
      authority   14, 57, 60, 133, 216, 218–19
      consensus building   5, 63, 70, 185, 215, 217, 218, 219, 220
      liturgical   3 n.8
      papal   3–4, 4 n.8, 38–39, 55, 61–62, 65–66, 76
      royal   3 n.8, 54

Adventus instructions   9–10, 12–13, 72–73, 82, 118, 130, 160, 186, 216–17
  and performance   8–9, 72, 73, 80, 91, 97, 99, 102, 216 *see also* and performance *under adventus*
  and production   74–76, 77, 100, 101, 102
  and reception perspectives   103
  Cistercian instruction   9–10, 73, 92–97, 98, 216–17, 229–30
    and bells   93
    and bishops   92–93
    and confusions and omissions   96
    and dignitaries   92–93, 94
    and familiarisation   95–96
    and hierarchy and authority   94–95
    and Lanfranc's instruction   93, 94, 95, 96, 97, 102, 216
    and preparations   93, 94
    and production   96–97
  Gilbertine instruction   9, 73, 98, 216
    and Cistercian instruction   98–99, 228–29
    and Lanfranc's instruction   98–99
  Lanfranc's instruction   9, 73, 80–82, 90–91, 178, 216
    and arrival and meeting   80, 89, 91
    and bell-ringing   82, 91
    and church service   83, 87–88, 91
    and dignitaries   81, 82, 88–89
    and entry   81
    and familiarisation   84, 88, 90, 91
    and hierarchy and authority   85–88, 89–90, 91
    and inclusion   82–84, 91
    and kiss   84–85, 88, 90
    and prayer   84
    and preparations   80
Ælfsige, archbishop of Canterbury   151
Aelred of Rievaulx, abbot   84–85
Albert, cardinal and papal legate   56, 114, 136, 136
Albert de Suma, subdeacon and papal nuntius   115, 125
Alessandria   59–60, 61–62
Alexander II, king of Scotland   195, 211–12
Alexander II, pope   78
Alexander III, pope   46, 62, 115, 123, 217

260 INDEX

and *adventus* into Rome   61, 62, 65–66
and Becket dispute   36, 56, 113–14, 136
and cardinals   24–25, 26, 48
and papal-imperial conflict   25, 26, 36, 58–60, 113, 136
and papal legates   12, 24–25, 26, 36 113, 114
and Roger of Howden   108
and taxation   193
as *Vicarius Christi*   21 n.19, 53–54
Alexander IV, pope   12
Alexios III, Byzantine emperor   49
Alexius, Roman subdeacon and papal legate   109, 115
Amadeus of Lyon, papal legate   33
Amatus of Oléron, bishop and papal legate   17, 24, 66
Annals of Dunstable   192
Annals of George Acropolita   41
Annals of Oseney Abbey   204 n.104
Annals of St-Bertin   39
Annals of Winchester   204 n.104
Anselm of Canterbury, archbishop and saint   63, 152
Athanasius of Alexandria, church father and saint   53, 65

Babylon   20, 51
Baldwin III, King of Jerusalem   25, 46
Baldwin of Forde, archbishop of Canterbury   13, 45, 86, 153, 158, 159, 175, 220
and archiepiscopal legitimacy   141–42, 149–51, 152
and dispute with Canterbury chapter   13, 86 n.67, 115, 125–26, 127, 133, 134, 137–39, 140, 141–43, 146, 147, 148, 149, 154, 155–56, 157–58, 160–61, 175
and election   142
and house-arrest of Canterbury chapter   135
and legatine *adventus*   133, 143, 147
and legatine insignia   133, 142, 143–45, 159
and papal legation   143–44, 149, 161
and St Thomas   137, 140, 141–42, 146
Barnwell Priory and Observances (customary)   75, 76, 89, 101–2
Bartholomeus Brixiensis, canonist   31
Bec Abbey   78, 79
Becket, Thomas, *see* Thomas Becket
Benedict, abbot of Peterborough   110
Benedictine order   186, 189, 197
and General Chapter   177
and Rule of St Benedict   73, 84
and Cistercians   74, 92
and hospitality   74

and humility   85, 159
and isolation   74, 75–76
and pastoral care   184
and prayer   84
and virtues and notions   159, 184, 185, 189
attack on   153
in England   74, 132
Benencasa of Arezzo, canonist   31
Bernard of Chartres, philosopher   vi
Bernard of Clairvaux, abbot and saint   48
Bernard of Montmirat, canonist   28, 41, 46
Bernard of Parma, canonist   28
Bernard of Pavia, canonist   29
Boso, cardinal and biographer   25, 48, 58, 62, 71, 182
and biography of Pope Adrian   141
and biography of Pope Alexander III   58–59
and legatine *adventus*   59–61, 62, 63
and papal *adventus*   61, 65–66
and papal office   21 n.19, 53–54
and pope Alexander III   58–59
Bulgaria   22
Bury St Edmunds, Benedictine abbey   100–1, 102, 174–75, 177, 100–1, 199

Canterbury, see and cathedral
and archbishop-abbot   79, 132
and architectural connections to Rome   151–52
and Benedictine chapter   132
and legatine commissions   63–64, 136
and satire/humour   153–55
Canterbury dispute (archbishop vs. cathedral chapter)   78, 125–26, 137–38, 139–40, 150
and archbishop as abbot   132
Canterbury–York dispute (archbishop vs. archbishop)   121, 122, 123, 145
Cardinalate, *see* cardinals
Cardinal-legates, *see* legate *a latere* under legates
Cardinals   1, 25, *see also* legate *a latere under* legates
and their entourages   26, 68, 178–79
as embodiments of the pope   26, 37, 48, 62
insignia   42–43
Carthusians and their customary   99–100, 101
Celestine III, pope   66, 116, 136
Christ   38, 48, 54, 74, 75, 89, 160
and desolation   205
and entry into Jerusalem   52

and humility   85
and papal legates   21–22, 29, 38, 62, 69, 71, 216
and St Peter   17
and the pope   18, 22, 53–54, 61, 62
imitation of   53
Cistercian order   74, 91–92, 93, 157
  and *adventus* instruction, *see* Cistercian instruction *under adventus* instructions
  and *Ecclesiastica Officia* (customary), *see* *Ecclesiastica Officia under* monastic customaries
  and the Gilbertine order   74, 98–99, 229–30
Clement III, pope   28, 114, 125, 136, 137, 139, 230
Close Rolls   9 n.28
Cluny Abbey   79
Compromise of Avranches   56, 114, 115, 121
Council of London in 1237   42, 45, 182, 197, 209
Council of Trent   27
Council of Worcester in 1240   209
Crusades and crusading   2, 6, 36, 112–13, 169, 173–74
  Albigensian crusade   68
  Third Crusade   11, 77, 109, 112–13, 114, 127, 129, 139
Curia, *see* papal curia
Customaries, *see* monastic customaries

Daniel of Beccles, author of *Urbanus magnus*   77
Denmark   40
Dominicans   199
Dover   56, 77–78, 126, 147–48, 149, 182, 203
Durandus/Duranti/Durantis, *see* William Durand

Eadmer of Canterbury, biographer and historian   63–65, 69, 71, 151, 152
Ecclesiastica Officia, *see Ecclesiastica Officia under* monastic customaries
Edmund of Abingdon, archbishop of Canterbury and saint   200, 202, 204–5, 213, 217, 221, 222
Edward I, king of England   113
Edward the Confessor, king of England   182
Eleanor of Aquitaine, queen of England   126, 167
Eleanor of England, wife of Simon de Montfort   197
Eleanor of Provence, queen of England   188, 200, 205, 213

Electio Hugonis, *see* Nicholas of Dunstable
Election decree of 1059   4
England   3, 14, 74, 88, 90, 154, 190–91, 197, *see also* and England *under* France
  and legatine missions   12, 23, 113–16, 135–37, 168–69, 192–93, 194–96
  and relations with the papacy   3, 8, 10–12, 77, 113–14, 116, 121, 135–36, 140, 152, 162–63, 168–69, 171–72, 193–96, 197–98, 213, 220–21
  as a papal fief   10, 11–12, 13, 162–63, 170, 190–91, 193, 211, 221
Epistolæ Cantuarienses   126, 137–38
Evesham abbey   86–87, 100 n.126, 138, 157, 175–76

Florence   54–55
Fourth Lateran Council   41
  and clerical dress   42, 44, 209, 225, 226–27
  and legatine retinues   68, 179
  and the cross banner   45
France
  and England   21, 36, 109, 110, 114–15, 118–19, 125, 137, 192, 194, 197
  and papal legates   21, 23, 36, 114–15, 118–19, 126, 137, 167, 193, 194, 197
Franciscans   199
Frederick I Barbarossa, German emperor   26, 59, 60, 136, 167
Frederick II, German emperor   47, 194, 196, 211
Frithericus, cardinal and papal legate   39

Geoffrey, archbishop of York   66, 125, 145
Geoffrey, provost of Beverley   108
Geoffrey of Trani, canonist and cardinal   28, 34
Geoffrey Ridel, bishop of Ely   120, 123
Gerald of Wales   155
Germany   5, 7, 23, 47, 59 193
Gervase of Canterbury   13, 219
  and *adventus*   13, 133, 142, 143, 148, 150, 158–59, 160, 161, 162, 219, 220
  Sandwich (Kent)   143, 147–49, 220
  and architecture   151–52
  and Canterbury dispute   13, 132, 134, 137, 160
    appeal to Rome   138, 142, 143
    dream visions   141, 142, 147
    legates   133, 144, 146, 147, 155, 156, 160, 219–20
    papacy   133, 141, 150, 155, 156, 160, 220
    Sword of the blessed apostle Peter   141, 142, 148, 160
    Thomas Becket, archbishop of Canterbury and saint   134, 137,

140, 141–42, 146, 147, 148–49, 151, 155, 220
   with Baldwin, archbishop of Canterbury   13, 133, 134, 137, 142–43, 147, 149–50, 155–56, 157, 159, 160, 161
   with Hubert Walter, archbishop Canterbury   134, 135, 148, 150
   with Richard, king of England   134, 157, 159
   and dissenters among the monks   157–58, 220
      Osbert, monk at Christ Church   157
      Roger Norreys, prior of Christ Church and abbot of Evesham   157, 175
   and Herbert of Bosham, biographer of Thomas Becket   148
   and Honorius, prior of Christ Church   139, 142, 143
   and Hugh de Nonant, bishop and papal legate   146–47
   and Hugh Pierleoni, cardinal and papal legate   158
   and John of Anagni, cardinal and papal legate   125, 158, 220
   and legatine insignia   144, 161, 220
      cross   45, 144, 145, 149, 220
      mitre   43, 45, 142, 144–45, 149, 151, 160, 220
   and *memoria* and archiepiscopal lineage   150–51
   and narrative strategy   133, 138, 142–43, 144, 146, 147, 148–49, 50, 155–56, 159, 220
      humility   159, 220
      humour   155, 156–57
      teleology   147, 149, 159
   and Nigel of Whiteacre, monk at Christ Church and author   154
   and Octavian, cardinal and papal legate   146
   and reason for selection   9, 13, 133
   and reception perspectives   132, 159–60
   and relationship with Thomas Becket, archbishop of Canterbury and saint   140, 150
   and Thomas, brother of Gervase   133, 135
   and Thomas Becket dispute   134, 140–41
   authorship   113, 133, 134–35, 138, 150, 155, 159–60
   biography   133–34
Gesta Innocentii III   49, 140, 207–8
Gift-giving   88, 124, 226
Gilbertine order   74, 97–99, 229–30

   and the Gilbertine *adventus* instruction, *see* Gilbertine instruction *under adventus* instruction
   and the Gilbertine customary, *see* Gilbertine Order, rule of *under* monastic customaries
   and the Gilbertine rule   9–10, 98
Gratian's *Decretum*   23, 67
Gregory, cardinal-legate to Denmark   40
Gregory I the Great, pope   151
Gregory VII, pope   17, 18, 23–24, 33, 67, 69
Gregory VIII, pope   136, 139
Gregory IX, pope   2, 27, 28, 100, 193, 195, 196, 198, 218
Gregory X, pope   225 n. 3
Gregory Nazianzen, theologian and biographer   53, 65
Guala, cardinal and papal legate   12, 167, 170, 171, 192, 198
Guillaume Durand, *see* William Durand
Gunner, bishop of Viborg   40

Hackington (Kent)   137
Henry I, king of England   64–65, 69, 71, 134, 211
Henry II, king of England   11, 115, 116, 120–21, 122, 149, 168
   and Cardinal Vivian   43–44, 56, 58, 123–25, 226
   and Pope Alexander III   113–14, 136
   and the legatine *adventus*   117–18, 119, 121, 123, 125, 131, 149, 158, 219
   and Thomas Becket   113–14, 134, 136, 140–41
Henry III, king of England   11–12, 165, 193, 197, 213, 214
   and Edmund of Abingdon   202, 203, 204–5, 213
   and Frederick Barbarossa   196
   and Matthew Paris   14, 187, 188, 192, 194, 200, 203, 204, 205, 210, 211, 212, 213, 221
   and Otto de Tonenga   34, 68, 191, 197, 198, 202, 204, 205, 206, 207, 208, 210, 211, 214
   and papal authority   171, 191, 194–96, 197, 201, 203, 210, 211, 212, 221
   and papal privilege   47, 211, 221
   and rebellion   170–71, 190–91, 194, 195
   and St Albans   188
   and Scotland   195, 196, 197, 211
   and Westminster   182 n.113
   minority   170, 197
Henry of Blois, bishop of Winchester   20, 135
Henry of Marcy, cardinal and papal legate   36, 112

Henry of Segusio, *see* Hostiensis
Henry the Young King   122
Herbert of Bosham, biographer of Thomas Becket   147–48
Hildegard of Bingen, German abbess and preacher   75–76
Honorius, prior of Christ Church   149
   and dream visions   141–42
   and suspension   143, 147, 160
   at Rome   138–39, 143, 152, 154
Honorius II, pope   145
Honorius III, pope   11, 23, 170, 192–93
Hostiensis, cardinal and canonist   41
   and legatine insignia   41, 43, 44, 225, 226, 227
   and legatine powers   32, 34
   and letters of credence   30–31
   and papal legates   28, 48–49
Hubert de Burgh, justiciar   194
Hubert Walter, archbishop of Canterbury   145, 169
   and Canterbury dispute   134, 135, 137, 139–40, 148, 150
   and processional cross   145
   and the legatine *adventus*   158–59
   as papal legate   77, 100–1, 168
Hugh, abbot of Bury St Edmunds and Bishop of Ely   174–75
Hugh de Lacy, Lord of Meath   119
Hugh de Nonant, bishop and papal legate   45, 122, 127
   and *adventus*   116–18, 132
   and Canterbury dispute   127, 146–47
   and coronation of Prince John   115, 116
   and expulsion of his monastic chapter   146, 153
Hugh de Puiset, bishop of Durham, 63, 108, 122, 127, 128, 129
Hugh of Die, bishop of Die and papal legate   24, 33
Hugh Pierleoni, cardinal and papal legate   115, 121–22, 123, 124, 158
Huguccio, canon lawyer   31

Imre, king of Hungary   22
Ingressus, *see ingressus* under parts of *under adventus*
Innocent III, pope   114, 121, 178, 182
   and canon law   178–79
   and gift-giving   207–8
   and papal legation   18–19, 21–22, 30, 32–33, 49, 56–58, 68, 69, 100, 169, 218
   and papal letters   180–81
   and papal self-perception   22, 184–85
   and taxation   193–94
   and the bishop's marriage to his church   54–55
   and the Canterbury dispute   139–40
   and the enfeoffment of England   11, 162–63, 169, 172–73
   and the Stephen Langton affair   11, 29, 56–58, 162, 169, 172–74, 185
   as *Vicarius Christi*   18, 21
Innocent IV, pope   28, 34, 41–42, 47, 211
Insignia (cardinals), *see* insignia *under* cardinals
Insignia (legates)   12, 38, 39, 67
   baldachin   41, 46
   cross   41, 44–45, 67, 144–45, 160
   horse, white   41, 43–44, 225–26
   horse tack and accessories   44, 225, 226–27
   meaning   5, 46–49, 70, 71, 225–26
   mitre   43, 144–45, 160
   precedence   28, 45
   red clothing   41–43, 44, 209, 225, 226
   sources   40–41
Insignia (papal)   38–39, 40, 41, 42–43, 44, 67, 144
Ireland   109
   and Henry II, king of England   115, 116, 118, 119, 125
   and John, king of England   11, 115, 116, 118, 119
   and papal legates   110, 115, 118, 123, 125, 143, 195
Isabella, countess of Arundel   188
Isle of Man   124–25, 131
Italy   5, 36, 47, 60–61, 62, 78

James, master, *see* Master James
Jerusalem   25, 52, 53, 54, 61, 149
Jesus, *see* Christ
Jocelin of Brakelond, monk and chronicler   100
Johannes Faventinus, canonist   31
Johannes Teutonicus, canonist   26, 30–31, 34
John, cardinal and papal legate to Jerusalem   25, 46–47
John, king of England   120, 165, 168–69, 171, 172, 174, 178, 182
   and *adventus*   56–58, 66
   and Honorius III, pope   11–12
   and Innocent III, pope   11, 56, 162, 169, 170, 172–73, 174, 181, 184, 185
   and Ireland   11, 115, 116, 118–19
   and kingship   165–68, 177–78, 182–83, 185
   and Nicholas of Tusculum, cardinal and papal legate   29, 56–58, 181
   and peace negotiations with the English Church   172–73
   and Stephen Langton affair   11–12, 56, 162, 169, 172–73, 180, 185, 192

and the first barons' war   169–170
and William Longchamp   116
enfeoffing England   10, 11, 162, 169, 172–73, 191, 192
John Cumin, archbishop of Dublin   117, 120
John of Anagni, cardinal and papal legate   115, 219, 220
  and *adventus*   78, 125–27, 131, 158, 220
  and Canterbury dispute   78, 115, 125–27, 137, 139, 146, 158
  and Richard, king of England   77–78, 115, 126–27, 128, 131, 146, 219
John of Salerno, cardinal and papal legate   116, 128
John of Salisbury   vi, 48, 153
John of Wallingford, abbot of St Albans   176
John 'the Scot', claimant to the see of St Andrews   115
Jordan de Fossa Nova, cardinal and papal legate   116
Judges-delegate   35–36, 139, 175

Lambeth (Surrey)   137, 139, 140
Lanercost Chronicle   113
Lanfranc of Canterbury   51
  and the papal curia   78
  and William the Conqueror, duke of Normandy and King of England   78
  biography   78
  Monastic Constitutions of, *see* Lanfranc's Monastic Constitutions *under* monastic customaries
Langton, Stephen, *see* Stephen Langton
Legate *a latere*, *see* legate *a latere under* legates
Legates   69
  and authority   1, 28–29, 32–34, 68–69, 70–71, 72, 87, 100, 127–28, 218
  and canon law   19–20, 26–28, 30–32, 48–49, 217
  and romanisation   19–20
  and secular sphere   36, 37, 114
  and their entourages   67–68, 178–79, 198
  archbishop-legates   35
  attacks on   68, 198
  conceptualisation   1, 2, 18–19, 21–23, 29, 38
  dispatch and invitation   5–6, 29–30, 34, 222
  history   23–27
  legate *a latere*   12, 23, 24, 27–28, 38, 217, 218
    as cardinals   1, 24–25, 27, 48–49

  as embodiments of the pope   2, 4, 17, 18, 48–49, 57, 70, 71, 155, 160, 218
  legatus missus/nuncius apostolicus   27
  legatus natus   27
  non-papal legates   18–19, 22–23
  solemn nuncios   34–35, 36
Legatine mandate   30, 31–32, 118, 121, 162, 180
Legation, *see* legates
Leo IX, pope   43, 78
Leo Brancaleoni, cardinal and papal legate   22
Liber Extra   27–28
Liber Pontificalis   55
Lombard cities   36, 59
London   57, 118, 145, 149, 163, 182
Longchamp, William, *see* William Longchamp
Louis VIII, king of France   170
Louis IX, king of France   194
Lucian of St Werburgh's Abbey, monk and writer   21, 152–53
Lucius III, pope   136

Mandate, *see* legatine mandate
Master James, papal legate   212
Matthew Paris, chronicler   13–14
  and *adventus*   200–1, 203, 214, 218
    dating of event   203–4
    desolation and division of England   187, 205, 206, 217
    prelude part   201, 203, 204
    reception part   201, 206
    space jumps and elongation   206–7, 216
    time jumps   206
  and Alexander II, king of Scotland   211–12
  and Anglo-Papal relationship   187, 190, 194, 206, 213
  and Benedictine worldview   189
  and Edmund of Abingdon, archbishop of Canterbury and saint   202, 204–5, 213, 217, 221
    Thomas Becket imitation   205
  and Eleanor of Provence, queen of England   188, 205, 213
  and enfeoffment of England   187, 191, 221
  and gift-giving   200, 202, 205, 206, 207–9, 214, 221
  and Henry III, king of England   14, 187, 191, 213
    as papal vassal   191, 210, 211, 212, 214
    foreigners in royal service   190–91
    kingliness   204, 206, 212

privilege to deny admittance to papal
  legates   47, 211, 221
and legatine insignia   47, 211
  cross   45
  mitre   43
  red clothing   42, 209, 214
and magnates   202, 204, 205, 213, 217, 221
and Monastic Constitutions of
  Lanfranc   79, 178, 201
and Nicholas of Tusculum, cardinal and
  papal legate   176
and Otto de Tonenga, cardinal and
  papal legate   14, 190, 198, 214, 217
  authority   34, 201–2, 207, 212, 214
  departure from England   198
  gift-giving   207–9, 214, 221
  praise of   199, 208
and reason for selection   9, 13–14,
  187–88
and reception perspectives   187–88,
  213–14
and Richard of Cornwall, earl and
  prince   188, 194
and Roger of Wendover,
  chronicler   164, 165, 184, 187, 189,
  190, 213–14
and the English prelates   14, 187, 206,
  207, 209, 212, 213–14
as artist   189
as chronicler   188, 189–92, 202, 213
  narrative strategies   14, 165, 184,
  201–2, 203, 205, 211
  biography   188, 192
Mauger, bishop of Worcester   157
Maurice de Sully, Bishop of Paris   63, 130
Monastic customaries   9, 56, 57, 72–73,
  76, 102
  Barnwell priory, the Observances, *see*
    Barnwell Priory and Observances
  Bury St Edmunds customary   100–1
  Carthusian customary, *see* Carthusians
    and their customary
  De Obedientiariis, *see* Abingdon Abbey
    and *De Obedientiariis* (customary)
  Ecclesiastica Officia   9, 73, 76, 92,
    96–97, 102
  Gilbertine Order, rule of   9, 73, 98
  Lanfranc's Monastic Constitutions   9,
    51, 73, 102, 162
    and St Albans   162, 178, 201
    creation   79
    use   79–80
  Norwich Cathedral Priory customary,
    see Norwich Cathedral Priory and
    customary

Nazianzen, Gregory, *see* Gregory
  Nazianzen
Nicholas II, pope   4, 21
Nicholas of Dunstable and the *Electio
  Hugonis*   100, 174–75, 177
Nicholas of Tusculum, cardinal and papal
  legate   51, 169, 172, 192, 221
  and *adventus*   13, 56–58, 100, 163, 174–
    75, 177–78, 181–82
  and Bury St Edmunds   174–75
  and Evesham Abbey   175–76
  and legatine authority   29, 32–33, 57–58,
    71, 86–87, 175, 178, 181, 218
  and legatine mission   172–74, 178
  and Matthew Paris   176
  and own account of *adventus*   56–58
  and peace talks   173, 179–80, 183–84
  and retinue   67, 68, 178–79
  and Roger of Wendover   13, 162–63,
    176–77, 179, 180–81, 185–86, 213
  and St Albans   176–77
  and Westminster Abbey   183
  as tyrant   162–63, 185, 212
Nidarholm Abbey, Norway   188
Nigel of Longchamp, *see* Nigel of
  Whiteacre
Nigel of Whiteacre, monk at Christ
  Church and author   154, 155, 157
Normandy   66, 78, 114–15, 116, 118, 126,
  127, 137
Norwich Cathedral Priory and
  customary   101–2

Occursus, *see* occursus under parts of *under
  adventus*
Octavian, cardinal and papal legate   115,
  116–19, 122, 128, 132, 146.
Osbert, monk at Christ Church,
  Canterbury   157
Osbert of Clare, monk at Westminster
  Abbey   84
Otto de Tonenga, cardinal and papal
  legate   196–97, 217, 218
  and accusations of greed   198–99, 208
  and *adventus*   187–88, 190, 200–1, 206,
    210, 213, 214, 221
  and authority   2, 34, 191, 197, 198, 207,
    209, 211, 212, 221, 222
  and English benefices   206, 208–9, 214
  and gift-giving   207–8
  and Henry III, king of England   34, 68,
    191, 197, 198, 202, 204, 205, 206, 207,
    208, 210, 211, 214
  and legatine insignia   42, 43, 45, 209,
    214
  and legatine mission   196–97
  and Matthew Paris   14, 33, 187, 190, 191,

266   INDEX

198, 201–2, 203, 213, 221
 and Oseney Abbey   68, 198
 and relations with the English   197–99, 202–3, 205
 and Scotland   196, 211–12
 appointment   195–96
 as *nuncio*   192–93, 194
 date of arrival   203–4
Otto of Freising, bishop   48
Øystein, archbishop of Nidaros   79

Papal curia   5, 21, 38, 40, 55, 78, 195–96, 222
 and corruption   21
 and gift-giving   207
 and legates   69–70
 and Rome   4, 65
 and self-perception   21, 48, 58
 and the legatine *adventus*   4, 12, 59, 71, 215, 222
 and the papal *adventus*   4, 65–66
 as court   10, 35, 138–39, 194
Papal States, see St Peter's patrimony
Paris   63, 130, 200, 206, 207, 208, 209
Peter di Sant'Agata, papal legate   115, 125
Peter of Blois, theologian and diplomat   84
Peter of Capua, cardinal and papal legate   167
Peter of Pavia, cardinal and papal legate   112
Peter Pierleoni, cardinal and papal legate   63–65, 69, 71
Peter's pence, tax   193
Philip II Augustus, king of France   109, 118, 120, 167, 169, 174
Philip of Poitou, bishop of Durham   108
Pipe Rolls   9 n.28, 43–44, 124, 226
Primacy over the English Church   11, 122, 123
Procurations   28, 29, 30, 67, 124
Province (legatine)   6, 68, 69
 and entry   5–6, 30, 31, 38, 57, 67, 70, 71, 215, 218
 and legatine powers   27, 29, 30, 31, 32, 37, 67, 71, 216, 218
 and size   30

Radulf, archdeacon of Hereford   117
Ralph Arundel, see Willam, abbot of Westminster
Ralph de Diceto, chronicler   166
Ralph of Coggeshall, chronicler   166
Reception, see *adventus*
Reform papacy   1, 2, 4, 19, 23–24, 33, 35, 38–39, 215, 217, 222
Reginald fitz Jocelin, bishop of Bath   127

Richard, king of England   111, 131, 166–67, 169
 and Canterbury dispute   86, 126–28, 134, 157, 175
 and Henry II, king of England   119
 and Hubert Walter, archbishop of Canterbury   77, 168
 and John, king of England   116, 165, 167, 185
 and John of Anagni, cardinal and papal legate   77–78, 115–16, 126–28, 131, 146, 219
 and Peter of Capua, cardinal and papal legate   167
 and Philip II Augustus, king of France   109, 167
 and Third Crusade   109, 113
 and William Longchamp, bishop of Ely   11, 77, 116, 129, 168
Richard Marshall, 3rd Earl of Pembroke   170–71, 195
Richard of Cornwall, earl and prince   188, 191, 194, 197
Richard of Dover, archbishop of Canterbury   114, 122, 123, 142, 158–59
Richard of Ilchester, bishop of Winchester   123
Ritual   6–8, 47, 49–50, 51, 54, 55, 60, 70, 73, 90, 119–20, 217, 222 see also as a ritual *under adventus*
Robert, father of Roger of Howden   108
Robert de Beaumont, 3rd Earl of Leicester   120
Robert Grosseteste, bishop of Lincoln   188, 199, 203
Robert Magnus, master of the schools of York   118
Robert of Jumièges, archbishop of Canterbury   151
Roger de Pont L'Évêque, archbishop of York   145
Roger Norreys, prior of Christ Church and abbot of Evesham   86–87, 157, 175–76
Roger of Howden, chronicler   13, 147, 149, 159, 211
 and *adventus*   107, 117, 119, 130–31, 219
 and the English king   107, 111, 117, 118, 119, 122, 123–25, 126–28, 130–31, 219
 refusing to be received   66
 unwelcome legates   66, 123–24, 125–27, 131, 219
 welcome legates   116–17, 121–22, 131
 and attitude towards papal legates   122, 123, 128

and legatine authority   118, 121, 122,
    127–28, 219, 221
and legatine insignia
    cross   45, 117–18
    mitre   43, 117–18
    red clothing   41, 117–18
and reason for selection   9, 13, 107
and reception perspectives   107–8,
    123–24, 128, 130
and Thomas Becket, archbishop of
    Canterbury and saint   114, 116
and William Longchamp, bishop of
    Ely   63, 129–30
as chronicler   110–13, 118–19, 122–23,
    176–77
as escort to foreign dignitaries   109, 118
as eyewitness   109, 111–12, 120–21, 122,
    125, 148
biography   108–9
Roger of Wendover, chronicler   13, 195,
    212, 213–14, 220
and *adventus*   162–63, 166–67, 177,
    185–86, 220, 221
    as possession-taking   163, 181, 182,
        183, 186, 221
    narrative strategies   181–82, 183, 186
    prelude part   177, 178
    reception part   177, 178
    sarcastic mockery   178, 181, 183, 186,
        221
and enfeoffment of England   162, 163
    167–68, 170, 171, 172–73, 181, 220, 221
and Innocent III, pope   162, 178, 179–
    80, 184–85
    letters of   180–81, 184
and John, king of England   162, 165–68,
    178, 182–83
and legatine authority   162–63, 167–68,
    176, 177, 178, 180, 183, 186, 212
and legatine retinue   67, 178–79
and Matthew Paris, chronicler *see* and
    Roger of Wendover, chronicler
    under Matthew Paris
and Nicholas of Tusculum, cardinal and
    papal legate   162–63, 177, 178–80,
    185–86, 212, 221
and reason for selection   9, 13, 14
and reception perspectives   163, 186
and Richard, king of England   165–68,
    185
and the papacy and its self-
    perception   172, 184–85, 186, 211,
    221
and William of Trumpington, abbot of
    St Albans   176–77, 185–86
as chronicler   163–68, 176–77

biography   163
Roland, papal subdeacon and papal
    legate   109
Roman Church   17, 19, 38, 62, 152
Roman Empire   23, 41, 52, 153
Romanisation and Romanness   19–20,
    70, 133
Romans, *see* people of *under* Rome
Rome, *see also* papal curia
    city   3–4, 62, 65–66, 138–39
    concept and representation   19, 20–21,
        38, 62, 150, 152–53, 216
    people of   4, 52, 53, 61, 65–66

St Andrews, see of   115
St Augustine   75, 151
St John   52, 54
St Mary's Abbey and customary   101
St Paul   54, 59, 200, 203–4
St Peter   21, 152–53, 200, 203–4
    bestowing authority to govern   5, 17,
        151–52
    defending Alessandria   59–60, 62
    defending Christ Church,
        Canterbury   141, 142, 148–49, 160
    present in papal legates   17, 18, 38, 62,
        69, 71, 148, 216
    present in the pope   21, 38, 59–60, 62,
        148, 160
St Peter's Church, Rome   152
St Peter's Church, Westminster, *see*
    Westminster Abbey
St Peter's Patrimony   62
St Werburgh's Abbey   21, 152, 153
Samson of Tottington, abbot of Bury St
    Edmunds   100, 174
Sandwich (Kent)   143, 147–49, 220
Schism   24–26, 36, 46–47, 58–59, 113, 116,
    136, 217
Scotland   113, 196
    and England   113, 120, 195, 197, 211–12
    and papal legates   110, 115, 116, 118, 123,
        125, 197, 211–12
    and Roger of Howden   109, 118, 120
Sicardus of Cremona, historian and
    canonist   31
Silvan, abbot of Rievaulx   109
Simon de Montfort, rebel leader   170–71,
    197
Simon of Bisignano, canonist   31
Spain   17, 47
Stephen, king of England   135
Stephen Langton, archbishop of
    Canterbury   11
    and dispute with King John   162, 169,
        192

268   INDEX

and Nicholas, cardinal and papal legate   56, 57–58, 68, 181–82
Stephen of Vienne, archbishop   33
Stigand, archbishop of Canterbury   78, 151
Summa 'animal est substantia', anonymous canon law tract   31
Summa Bambergensis, see Summa 'animal est substantia'
Susceptio, see susceptio under parts of *under adventus*
Sylvanus, abbot of Rievaulx, *see* Silvan, abbot of Rievaulx
Synod of Ponthion   39

Tewkesbury Annals   198, 204
Thangmar of Hildesheim and *Vita Bernwardi*   39
Theodwin, cardinal and papal legate   56, 114, 136
Third Lateran Council   26, 67–68, 115, 125, 179
Thomas, brother of Gervase of Canterbury   133–34, 135
Thomas Becket, archbishop of Canterbury and saint   13, 133 n.6, 205
  and authority at Canterbury Cathedral   150, 151, 155
  and Canterbury dispute   137, 140, 141–42, 146, 147, 148, 151, 152, 155, 159, 160, 220
  and dispute with Henry II, king of England   36, 56, 113–14, 116, 123, 134, 136, 140–41, 152, 220
  and Nigel of Whiteacre   154
  and Roger, archbishop of York   114, 145
  and sainthood   114, 134, 140, 142
  and Sandwich (Kent)   147–49, 220
  and the legatine *adventus*   13, 133, 147–49, 160
  murder of   114, 134, 124
Thomas of Marlborough, monk and abbot at Evesham   86–87, 138, 157, 175–76, 177
Triumphus   52

Urban II, pope   66
Urban III, pope   136, 137
  and coronation of Prince John and later king of England   11, 115, 116–17, 118
  and Gervase of Canterbury   134, 139
Urbanus Magnus   77

Vicarius Christi   18, 21, 38
Victor IV, antipope   25, 46

Vita Bernwardi, see Thangmar of Hildesheim
Vita Gunneri   40
Vivian, cardinal and papal legate   115
  and *adventus*   124–25, 131
  and Henry II, king of England   123–24, 125, 131, 226
  and legatine insignia   43–44, 58, 124, 226
  and Roger of Howden   109, 110, 118, 128, 131
Vivian, jurisconsult   56

Walter de Cantilupe, bishop(-elect) of Worcester   195–96
Walter de Coutances, archbishop of Rouen   66
Walter of Coventry, chronicler   113
Waverly Annals   182
Westminster Abbey   87, 117, 134, 148, 177, 181–83, 213, 220
William I, duke of Normandy and king of England   78, 182
William I, king of Scotland   115, 120
William I, king of Sicily   141
William II, earl of Arundel   120
William Durand, canonist and bishop of Mende   34, 55–56
William FitzRalph, seneschal of Normandy   66
William Longchamp, bishop of Ely and papal legate
  and *adventus*   63, 129
  and legatine insignia   45
  in exile   63, 66, 116
  regent of England   11, 77, 114, 129–30, 168
William Marshal, regent of England   170
William of Malmesbury, chronicler   20
William of Newburgh, chronicler   113
William of Trumpington, abbot of St Albans   163, 176–77, 183, 185, 186
William of Tyre, archbishop and chronicler   25, 46–47
William [Ralph Arundel], abbot of Westminster   177, 182, 183

Yāqūt, Arab geographer   21
York and Yorkshire   101, 108, 128, 129, 211, 212
York–Canterbury dispute (archbishop vs. archbishop) *see* Canterbury–York dispute

**Other volumes in
Studies in the History of Medieval Religion**

Details of volumes I–XXXIV can be found on the Boydell & Brewer website.

XXXV: Monasteries and Society in the British Isles
in the Later Middle Ages
Edited by Janet Burton and Karen Stöber

XXXVI: Jocelin of Wells: Bishop, Builder, Courtier
Edited by Robert Dunning

XXXVII: War and the Making of Medieval Monastic Culture
Katherine Allen Smith

XXXVIII: Cathedrals, Communities and Conflict in the Anglo-Norman World
Edited by Paul Dalton, Charles Insley and Louise J. Wilkinson

XXXIX: English Nuns and the Law in the Middle Ages:
Cloistered Nuns and Their Lawyers, 1293–1540
Elizabeth Makowski

XL: The Nobility and Ecclesiastical Patronage in Thirteenth-Century England
Elizabeth Gemmill

XLI: Pope Gregory X and the Crusades
Philip B. Baldwin

XLII: A History of the Abbey of Bury St Edmunds, 1257–1301:
Simon of Luton and John of Northwold
Antonia Gransden

XLIII: King John and Religion
Paul Webster

XLIV: The Church and Vale of Evesham, 700–1215:
Lordship, Landscape and Prayer
David Cox

XLV: Medieval Anchorites in their Communities
Edited by Cate Gunn and Liz Herbert McAvoy

XLVI: The Friaries of Medieval London: From Foundation to Dissolution
Nick Holder

XLVII: 'The Right Ordering of Souls':
The Parish of All Saints' Bristol on the Eve of the Reformation
Clive Burgess

XLVIII: The Lateran Church in Rome and the Ark of the Covenant:
Housing the Holy Relics of Jerusalem, with an edition and translation of the
Descriptio Lateranensis Ecclesiae (BAV Reg. Lat. 712)
Eivor Andersen Oftestad

XLIX: Apostate Nuns in the Later Middle Ages
Elizabeth Makowski

L: St Stephen's College, Westminster:
A Royal Chapel and English Kingship, 1348–1548
Elizabeth Biggs

LI: The Social World of the Abbey of Cava, c. 1020–1300
G.A. Loud

LII: Medieval Women Religious, c. 800–c. 1500: New Perspectives
Edited by Kimm Curran and Janet Burton

LIII: The Papacy and Ecclesiology of Honorius II (1124–1130):
Church Governance after the Concordat of Worms
Enrico Veneziani

LIV: Women and Monastic Reform in the Medieval West, *c.* 1000–1500:
Debating Identities, Creating Communities
Edited by Julie Hotchin and Jirki Thibaut

LV: Thomas of Eccleston's *De adventu Fratrum Minorum in Angliam* "The
Arrival of the Franciscans in England", 1224–c.1257/8: Commentary and Analysis
Michael J.P. Robson

LVI: Religious Conflict at Canterbury Cathedral in the Late Twelfth Century:
The Dispute between the Monks and the Archbishops, 1184-1200
James Barnaby